THEOLOGY
of the
NEW TESTAMENT

THEOLOGY
of the
NEW TESTAMENT

by

Karl Hermann Schelkle

English Version by

William A. Jurgens

IV
THE RULE OF GOD:
CHURCH--ESCHATOLOGY

THE LITURGICAL PRESS

Collegeville,   *Minnesota*

THEOLOGY OF THE NEW TESTAMENT

Volume One: CREATION: WORLD — TIME — MAN

Volume Two: SALVATION HISTORY — REVELATION

Volume Three: MORALITY

Volume Four: THE RULE OF GOD: CHURCH —
ESCHATOLOGY

THEOLOGY OF THE NEW TESTAMENT — IV THE RULE OF GOD: CHURCH — ESCHATOL-OGY is the authorized English translation of *Theologie des Neuen Testaments* — IV/1 *Vollendung von Schöpfung und Erlösung*, and IV/2 *Jüngergemeinde und Kirche* by Karl Hermann Schelkle, copyright © 1974 and 1976 Patmos-Verlag.

Nihil obstat: Rev. Robert C. Harren, J.C.L., *Censor deputatus*. *Imprimatur*: †George H. Speltz, D.D., Bishop of St. Cloud. August 2, 1978.

Printed by North Central Publishing Company, St. Paul, Minnesota.

FOREWORD

I present herewith the final volume of my *Theology of the New Testament*.

The first of the four volumes of this work appeared in German in 1968, with the English translation following in 1971. The beginning and initial attempts at the work reach back, of course, much further. That my interpretations and judgments have been subject to some development over this lengthy period of time will easily be perceived by anyone who uses these books. This apparent development may be attributable in part to circumstances external to the work, not the least of which is the fact of the considerably changing viewpoints and conditions within the Church. The individual volumes are united, however, in their efforts for the sake of the abiding word in the human words of the Scriptures, and in the faith and doctrine of the Church.

"The Bible is an eternally effective book, because, as long as the world shall last, no one will step forward and say: 'I grasp it in its entirety and understand it in all its parts.' We can only say in all modesty: 'In its entirety it is sacred, and ever pertinent in all its parts'" (J. W. von Goethe).

— *Karl Hermann Schelkle*

PREFACE OF THE TRANSLATOR

A few words here may obviate a certain confusion otherwise likely to arise for those who may wish to compare the present English edition of Volume 4 of K. H. Schelkle's *Theology of the New Testament* with its German original.

The German edition from which this fourth volume is translated was announced already in 1968, under the title *Theologie des Neuen Testaments: Gottesherrschaft, Kirche, Vollendung*. It actually appeared only after some years, and in two separately bound half-volumes, of slightly different title. Actual production of this fourth volume of the German was beset with difficulties of various sorts, the least of which, perhaps, were several legions of printer's devils. What ought logically to have been the latter part of the volume was ready first, and was published in 1974 as a hardbound half-volume, entitled *Theologie des Neuen Testaments, IV/1: Vollendung von Schöpfung und Erlösung*. What by the same token ought to have been the earlier part of the volume appeared two years later, in 1976 — again, of course, a hardbound half-volume, under the same general title, *IV/2: Jüngergemeinde und Kirche*. In the production of this latter half-volume, moreover, the whole section of Chapter Two on the Gospel of John, with its four subsections, was inadvertently omitted from the printing; and these pages were supplied to translators by the Patmos-Verlag of Düsseldorf (and from the pen of K. H. Schelkle himself, of course) in April 1976. The reader, then, may be assured that, although he will, on comparison, find nothing in the original German edition to correspond to §2, 3, *e* through §2, 3, *e*, 4 in the present English edition, this section was in fact written by K. H. Schelkle, and constitutes both an integral and an authentic part of the work.

In preparing the present translation, I have, therefore, presented in its proper place the section of Chapter Two that is missing from the original German edition. Moreover, in presenting the two half-volumes of the German as a single English volume, I have restored the material to its proper and logical sequence. Thus, Schelkle's Volume IV/2 has become my Part 1, Chapters 1–11; and his Volume IV/1 has become my Part 2, Chapters 12–20.

— W. A. Jurgens

CONTENTS

THEOLOGY
of the
NEW TESTAMENT

I

THE RULE OF GOD--CHURCH

§ 1. SPECIAL COMMUNITIES AND THE
COMMUNITY OF DISCIPLES

Jesus' special community of disciples arose as a special community of Israel, but which separated itself from Israel. The process of its development is comparable to that of other special communities of Israel. The comparison can appeal to the Acts of the Apostles, since here, just as with the community of Sadducees (Acts 5:17) and that of the Pharisees (Acts 24:5; 28:22), the Christian community is termed a "party" (αἵρεσις).[1]

The word *haíresis*, which, in its first significance, simply means "choice," did not yet have the reprehensible connotation of sectarianism or heresy that it has already in Acts 24:14 and quite clearly also in 1 Cor. 11:19, Gal. 5:20, and 2 Peter 2:1.

In Hellenistic Greek, *haíresis* designates a school of philosophy, and accordingly, in Philo (*Contemplative Life* 29) and in Josephus (*Jewish War* 2, 8, 118 and *Autobiography* 12), it is employed in respect to the communities of Essenes, Sadducees, and Pharisees. The linguistic usage of the Acts of the Apostles is in accord with this. When, therefore, the Christian community is also called a "way" (Acts 22:14), the moral ordering of the Christian community and of its teaching is designated as its distinguishing characteristic.

Of the aforementioned special communities of Pharisees, Essenes, and Sadducees, two must be taken into account: the Pharisees and the Essenes, the latter because they are represented in the community of Qumran. The Sadducees are of no special importance in our context.

3

1. Pharisaism

a) History of Pharisaism

The name Pharisee,[2] which means "the separated ones" (from *pharos* = to separate), characterizes the Pharisees as those who constitute a community apart, a special community. Their origins belong probably to the second century B.C., when, in the defense of the Law in the face of the overpowering culture of Hellenism and the political designs of Hellenistic princes, they shaped themselves into a relatively small group, visible from that time and through the period of the New Testament, living both in Jerusalem and in the countryside. The Pharisees constituted a lay movement. They nevertheless took upon themselves the laws of purity and holiness pertaining to the priests in Jerusalem, and they adhered rigidly to the prescriptions of tithing for the Temple.

The Scribes, those learned in the Scriptures, belonged to the Pharisaic community. Under the influence of the Scribes, the Pharisees practiced and demanded above all else rigid adherence to the holy Law of God. In order to avoid any infraction, they did more than was absolutely required. Through additional prescriptions they erected a "fence around the Law" (*Sayings of the Fathers* 1, 1; 3, 13). By their radical demands, the Pharisees came into sharp conflict with the religions and political authorities of Judaism, the priests and princes.

In the first century B.C. the Pharisees obtained entry into the Sanhedrin, that is, the Jewish civil council, where they soon achieved prominent importance. After the destruction of Jerusalem and the forfeiture of political existence in 70 A.D., Israel, under the guidance of Pharisaism, rallied anew around the Law. It is to this circumstance in considerable measure that Israel will owe her survival.

b) Synoptic Gospels

The Pharisees exerted themselves with earnestness, zeal, and self-sacrifice for the sake of God's Law and for the sake of legal righteousness; and indeed, that is why Paul himself belonged to the Pharisaic party (Phil. 3:5; Acts 23:6). That the Pharisee fasted twice a week and gave tithes of his total income (Luke 18:12) is not contested in the Gospel. It would, therefore, seem to be easier to explain if Jesus had come into conflict with the amoral and irreligious Jews than with the pious and just.

The Gospels recount that Jesus accepted the invitations of Pharisees to banquets (Luke 7:36-50; 11:37-43; 14:1-5), and the Gospels show Jesus in conversation with the Pharisees and with the teachers of the Law. From this it is easily inferred (Matthew 22:15, 34f.) that they wanted to test Jesus. While in Mark 12:28-34 no such imputation is made about the question of the Scribe as to the most important command, and Jesus joyfully recognizes the insight of the teacher of the Law (Mark 12:34), Matthew 22:35 says that the Pharisees, skilled in the Law, wanted to test Jesus. Matthew no longer elicits any praise for the questioner. Likewise, in the non-Johannine text of John 8:6 the Scribes and Pharisees are trying to test Jesus. In tradition, judgment on the Pharisees becomes increasingly unfavorable.

The opposition between Jesus and the Pharisees arose in the course of Jesus' public actions. The Gospels mention as grounds for their opposition differing interpretations of the Law. The accounts correctly note that the Pharisees added the traditions of the ancients to the Law (Mark 7:5, 8); in so doing, nevertheless, they relaxed the commands of God. They increased the commandments on external purification, while forgetting internal attitudes (Mark 7:5-15). Through fictitious votive offerings for the Temple (Mark 7:9-13), they circumvented the command to honor parents and to care for them.

The Pharisees demand a rigid Sabbath observance. Jesus teaches, however, that regard for humanity allows a tempering of the Sabbath commandment (Matthew 12:1-8). Jesus therefore heals on the Sabbath (Matthew 12:9-14; Luke 14:1-5). The Pharisees are deeply scandalized at Jesus' allowing himself the companionship of sinners (Matthew 9:11; Luke 36:50). The parable of the two sons (Matthew 21:28-32) means that tax collectors and prostitutes are doing God's will ahead of the righteous. The three parables, however, of the lost sheep, the lost coin, and the prodigal son impressively vindicate Jesus' attitude (Luke 15:3-32).

All this can be explained as follows: In the judgment of the Pharisees, Jesus was endangering the arrangement of the Law and ultimately thereby the Jewish concept of God, according to which God was understood as the God of the righteous. Opposition is vocalized

in discourse. Jesus reproaches the Pharisees with practicing their kind
of righteousness in order to be seen by men (Matthew 6:1-4). The
righteousness of the Pharisees does not suffice for the impending kingdom of heaven (Matthew 5:20). Jesus denies the Pharisees a miraculous sign from heaven, because their demand for one only betokens
their disbelief and malice (Matthew 12:38f.; 16:1-4). Jesus warns about
the "leaven of the Pharisees and the leaven of Herod" (Mark 8:15).
The saying was difficult to understand; Matthew 16:12 explains it in
reference to "the teaching" of the Pharisees, Luke 12:1 in reference to
their "hypocrisy."

In accord with Jewish linguistic usage, leaven can designate the
force serving as bulwark to their teaching and which motivates it, as
also the evil inclinations and wicked intentions of men. In its context
(Mark 8:11), the leaven in Mark 8:15 might indicate the basically
perverse attitude of both the Pharisees and Herod, which attitude put
an obstacle to the coming of faith; with the Pharisees it may be their
false legalism, with Herod (the Herodians), their political intrigues.
The opposition is finally vocalized in the discourse of Jesus against
the Scribes and Pharisees (Matthew 23:2-36). In this discourse, and
perhaps in many other remarks before, the opposition between the
Jewish and Christian communities of a later time is exposed (see below, §10, 1, b, 3).

c) Acts of the Apostles

The information offered by the Gospels is supplemented by indicative hints in the Acts of the Apostles. Pharisees were joining the community of the disciples of Jesus (Acts 15:5). Contrary to the high
priests and Sadducees as the opponents of the community, the Pharisee Gamaliel cautioned forbearance and justice (Acts 5:34-39). In the
high council, or Sanhedrin, the Pharisees take sides with Paul (Acts
23:1-9).

In the Jewish Christian community of Jerusalem, the Pharisees want
to impose observance of the Law, and circumcision especially, on the
Gentile Christians (Acts 15:5). The Acts of the Apostles rightly affirms
that for the Pharisees the question of the validity of the Law is an essential point of dispute. On the other hand, it is true that the Pharisees
and the Christians are united against the other Jewish religious parties

in their belief in the resurrection of the dead, in angels, and in the spirit (Acts 23:6-8). In the Acts of the Apostles, the relationship between Pharisees and Christians is, on the whole, not disadvantageous.

Mention may be made of the account of Josephus (*Jewish Antiquities* 20. 9, 1), according to which the high priest Ananias the Younger, who belonged to the Sadducee party, made use of an interim period when no Roman governor had been appointed, to allow James, the brother of Jesus, and some others who had been accused of transgressing the Law, to be stoned, an action "which incensed the distinguished persons of the city and the most zealous guardians of the Law." These opponents of the Sadducees were probably the Pharisees, who, therefore, stood on the side of justice and of the Christian community.

d) Gospel of John

The Gospel of John (3:1) tells of the Pharisee Nicodemus, who sought out Jesus at night to converse with him. Nicodemus defended Jesus before the high council (John 7:50f.). At the burial of Jesus, he brought a lavish amount of precious aromatic spices (John 19:39). According to John 9:16, after Jesus healed the blind man, a division arose among the Pharisees. Part of their group wanted to recognize Jesus.

Nevertheless, in John's Gospel the Pharisees are overwhelmingly the enemies of Jesus. The opposition comes about, just as in the older Gospels, because Jesus breaks the Sabbath command by healings (John 9:16). A further basis for this enmity is, in the Synoptics, Jesus' companionship with sinners; here in John, similarly, it is his devoting himself "to a rabble, which does not know the Law" (John 7:49). The Pharisees, in their disbelief, are "blind" (John 9:49). They want to expel the disciples of Jesus from the synagogue (John 9:22, 34; 12:42). They try to lay hold of Jesus and to kill him (John 7:32; 11:53). If in John's Gospel it is "the Jews" who are the enemies of Jesus (see below, §10, 6), it is the Pharisees in concert with the high priests (7:32; 11:47; 18:3) who are leading and disposing the Jews.

e) Pharisaism and Church

As a special community within Judaism, Pharisaism, largely by its opposition to the community of Jesus, forced this latter to define itself, to draw its ranks together; and in this way it soon had to separate it-self from Israel. Nevertheless, Pharisaism had a voice in determining some not unessential characteristics of the future Church. In a comparison of Pharisaism and Church, high esteem of the Old Testament Law and therefore of the Bible as the word of God and "Sacred Scripture" is a prominent feature. The New Testament carried on this esteem and included its own writings therein (see the present work, Vol. 2, pp. 8-20). The New Testament also continued the interpretation of Scripture that was fostered in early Judaism and above all in the rabbinate. Especially in Paul, as also in the Acts of the Apostles, not infrequently the connection and context of passages is explained with Jewish exegesis. The obligation to law understood as divine is, for the community of Pharisees as also for the Christian community, the basis of earnest moral endeavor.

2. The Qumran Community

a) History of the Community

The monastic settlement in the desert at the Dead Sea, known as the Qumran community,[3] was founded about the year 150 B.C. by Jewish priests who refused to recognize the high priest at the Temple in Jerusalem because he was not of the family of Aaron. The spirituality and piety of the community was rooted in the later apocalyptic-messianic expectation, as attested in the Book of Daniel. It was influenced also by political zelotism. The Qumran community was probably a part of the Essenism known mostly from Josephus. Apparently the community had its more remarkable development in the first century A.D., until it met its collapse in the Jewish-Roman war of 66–70 A.D. For some decades, then, its period of existence coincided with the Church of the apostolic age. It is important, therefore, to see what relationship or mutual influences, if any, there may have been between the two communities.

b) The Teacher of the Community

For the Qumran community, as also for the Christian community, the figure of a great teacher was of decided importance. This founder and teacher is "the teacher of righteousness." "God raised up for them the teacher of righteousness, to lead them on the ways of his heart" (*Damascus Document* 1:10f.). The teacher of righteousness is one of the grand figures in the history and religion of Israel. He lived in the first century before Christ. His name is not known to us. His opponent was a high priest in Jerusalem. Neither has the latter's name been handed down to us. It seems that names meant nothing, and only the significance of their works was to be preserved. But little is known even of the life of the great teacher. He came from a priestly family (1 QpHab 2:8; QpPs 37:3, 15). Like the other priests, he probably passed as a descendant of that Zadok (*Damascus Document* 4:1-3) whom Solomon had appointed as chief priest (3 Kgs. 2:35).*

Some dates for the life of the teacher may possibly be gotten from the Qumran psalms or thanksgivings, the *Hodayôth*, which probably are, in notable part, the teacher's compositions, and accordingly treat of himself. God imparted to the petitioner of these psalms special illumination and knowledge of divine mysteries (1 QH 4:53; 7:26f.); the teacher imparted this knowledge to others (1 QH 2:8-15; 4:27). Thus the teacher became the "father" of the pious (1 QH 7:19-25). He is the "foundation of the truth and of understanding" (1 QH 2:10). As teacher, he was above all else the interpreter of the Scriptures. God has given him "to the community, to explain all the words of his servants the prophets" (1 QpHab 2:8f.; 7:4f.). The biblical commentaries found in Qumran are based on this concern for the Law.

The teacher of righteousness speaks with a high consciousness of his vocation: "Through me you have illumined the countenance of many. . . . For you have made known to me your wonderful mysteries" (1 QH 7:26f.). He is filled with the Spirit: "To me, your servant, you have graciously imparted the Spirit of knowledge" (1 QH 14:25). Nevertheless, the teacher also speaks very disparagingly of

---

*[*Translator's note*: The *Damascus Document* is known also as the *Zadokite Document* (or *Damascus Fragment, Zadokite Fragment*), the name given it at the time of its discovery, in two twelfth-century fragmentary copies, by Solomon Schechter in a Cairo genizah in 1896–1897. Only with the discovery of the Dead Sea, or Qumran, Scrolls did the true nature of the work and its relationship to the Qumran community become evident. A fragment of the work in an earlier recension was actually found along with the Qumran Scrolls].

himself: "Since I am but made from clay, who am I? A thing kneaded
with water, to whom am I of any worth?" (1 QH 3:23f.). He has the
consciousness of being a sinner: "I remember my errors and also the
infidelities of my fathers. Therefore I said: 'Because of my sins I am
excluded from your convenant.' But because I remembered the power
of your hands and the abundance of your mercies, I pulled myself
upright" (1 QH 4:34-36).

Like the whole community, so too their priestly teacher was heavily
oppressed and persecuted by the "godless priest" in Jerusalem (1 QH
4:8f.; 5:5). Even in the community he had opponents (1 QH 5:22-25).
The teacher was overwhelmed with blows and with illnesses (1 QH
8:26f.), but God strengthened him: "You have made me strong in
the face of the onslaughts of sacrilege and all its ruin" (1 QH 7:7f.).
God manifested his might in him (1 QH 4:8, 23): "Blows became
healing for me, . . . my stumbling was turned to eternal strength"
(1 QH 9:25). God willed that in this pain the teacher should establish his celebrated community (1 QH 8:11).

The teacher of Qumran made no claim of possibly being the Messiah. The judgment of his community held fast to this. After the death
of the teacher, the community waited for the arrival of the two Messiahs, from the family of Aaron and from the family of David (*Damascus Document* 19:25–20:1).[4]

The differences between the Qumran teacher and Jesus are essential.
Jesus never speaks of any guilt of his own. For the gospel, even the
events of Jesus' life are important, and for that very reason they are
immediately presented by tradition in their significance for salvation
history. They are, by virtue of the incarnation, the primordial sacraments of salvation. The New Testament confers great messianic titles
of majesty on Jesus, which are based on his words and works (see the
present work, Vol. 2, pp. 177–220).

3. The Qumran Community and the Community of Jesus' Disciples

a) The Concept of God

If the Qumran community and the community of Jesus' disciples
were to be compared, a very deep difference between them would

have to be noted at the outset. In the writings of Qumran, which are high testimonials to the faith and piety of Israel, God is called, above all else, "Lord" (1 QH 2:20, 31; 3:19). Jesus, however, teaches that God is our Father (see the present work, Vol. 1, pp. 103–106). Here there is a new gospel, and this, too, can have been of decisive importance for the ways of the mission.

b) Holy Scripture

For Qumran, the Old Testament Bible was of fundamental importance. The community wants to heed the word of the Law, and by this means achieve order and life. The teacher of righteousness knows and teaches the mysteries of the prophets (1 QpHab 7:4f.). Even the community is obligated to the study of the Law: "In a place where there are ten men, there shall not be lacking one who can research the Law continually day and night. And the members in general are to keep awake the third part of all the nights of the year, in order to read the Book and to study the Law" (1 QS 6:6f.).

The fruit of this Scripture study is the commentaries found at Qumran on the books of Habakkuk, Micah, Nehemiah, Isaiah, on Psalm 37, and smaller interpretational works. The texts are, as is especially evident in the instance of the *Commentary on Habakkuk*, referred expressly and unhesitatingly to the then present times. Selected verses are arranged in collections: thus, the messianic texts in *4 Qtest.* and eschatological texts in *4 Qflor.* Certain Old Testament texts seem to have been of special interest both to the biblical proof of the New Testament and to the exegetes of Qumran; thus, Deut. 18:18 in 4 Qtest. 5 and in Acts 3:22; Amos 9:11 in 4 Qflor. 1:12 and Acts 15:16.

The Genesis apocryphon of Qumran develops further the history of Lamech and Noah, as well as that of Abraham. The concept of a possible miraculous origin of Noah may be reminiscent of the biblical accounts of the virgin birth. In the *Discourses of Moses* (1 QDM = 1 Q 22), scattered biblical texts of the discourses and laws of Moses are gathered together. It is done with considerable freedom in regard to the precise wording of the original texts, but apparently in the conviction that the actual meaning and content will thereby be brought out more clearly. This reminds one of the way Paul brings Old Testament texts together and interprets them, for example, in Rom. 3:10-18.

As with the pious of Qumran, so too it holds good of the primitive community in Jerusalem, that they "searched the Scriptures" (Acts 17:11).

c) Brotherhood

The members of the community of Qumran, like the Christians, regarded themselves as brothers and a brotherhood (1 QS 6:22; 5:3f., 24-26; 10:25–11:2). The brotherhood was a closely knit community in which it held good that "I repay no one evil for evil, and only with goodness will I prevail over a man" (1 QS 10:17f.). Offenses against the community are severely punished and penance is prescribed (1 QS 6:24-27; 7:1-9). The membership of those accepted into the community is perpetual, and they hold their property in common (1 QS 1:11f.; 5:2f.; 6:19-23). The community takes care of all who are in need. Each month the members give two days' wages—tithes, approximately—into the hands of the overseer. "From this they are to provide for the orphans, and from this they are to support the poor and needy, and also the elderly who are near to death, the man who is homeless, and those who have been led away captive into a foreign nation, and the young girls who have no protector [who are without a dowry?] (*Damascus Document* 14:14-17).

The primitive Christian community likewise practiced an ideal of community ownership (Acts 2:44) and took care of the poor (Acts 6:1).

d) New Covenant

The Qumran community lived in the consciousness of God's covenant. The people of that community considered that the promise of the new covenant in Jeremiah 31 was realized in their midst. They wanted the "new covenant to be in the land of Damascus" (*Damascus Document* 6:19). It was a "covenant of conversion (*ibid.*, 6:19B). The covenant demanded a change of life, to conform to the Law of Moses (1 QS 1:11f.; 5:8; *Damascus Document* 1:4; 2:6). The covenant certainly did not embrace the whole people; rather, the community understood itself as the "holy remnant" (1 QH 6:8; 1 QM 13:8; 14:8f., with 3 Kings 19:18; Is. 7:3; 10:20f.; Zeph. 3:13; *Damascus Document* 1:4; 2:6). The members knew themselves as "the elect of Israel" (*Damascus Docu-*

ment 4:3f.); as "the men of holiness" (1 QS 5:13; *Damascus Document* 20:2); "the sons of righteousness" (1 QS 3:20); the "sons of his good pleasure" (1 QH 4:32f.; 11:19); "the favored poor" (1 QH 5:22); a "supremely holy house of holiness for Israel" (1 QS 8:5-9; 9:6).

The New Testament community also understood itself as the new covenant (1 Cor. 11:25). It, however, was to embrace all Israel (Matthew 10:6; Acts 2:14). Only when the greater part of Israel rejected the gospel did the Church refer the promise of the remnant to herself (Rom. 11:4). Christians too knew themselves as the saints, i.e., the holy ones, and the elect (Matthew 24:24; Rom. 1:7; 1 Cor. 1:2), as "the men of his good pleasure" (Luke 2:14), and also as the poor (Matthew 5:3; Rom. 15:26).

e) Baptisms

The Qumran community was a baptismal movement. As a priestly community, it practiced the ritual purity prescriptions almost beyond measure in many washings and re-washings (see below, §8, 2). The rule of the community prescribed this (1 QS 3:4-9; *Damascus Document* 10:10-13); and archeologcial excavations there have brought to light extensive bathing installations. But in all, one knew that external washing was useless if inner purification was lacking (1 QS 4:20).

The community of Jesus' disciples likewise lived by baptism (below, §8).

f) Righteousness

The elect and holy ones of the community in Qumran are sure of justification, which certainly is not the work of men but of God's salvation. "My justification is with God, and in his hand is the perfection of my conduct and the rectitude of my heart; and by his righteousness is my sin blotted out" (1 QS 11:2f.; see also 1 QS 11:14 and L QH 4:30f. for similar statements).

While the New Testament, with Paul as its spokesman, teaches that righteousness is bestowed on faith and must be realized in life, Qumran requires, as prerequisite to grace, new works of fulfilling the Law. This becomes evident in their differing interpretations of Hab. 2:4. Whereas the *Commentary on Habakkuk* explains that God "saves the doers of the Law," those who fulfill the rigid demands of the teacher of righteousness (1 QpHab 7:17–8:3), Paul finds expressed even in that word of Habakkuk, that "by faith will the just man live" (Rom. 1:17; see also the present work, Vol. 3, pp. 181–185).

g) Priests

The Qumran community is a priestly community. The membership calls itself the "sons of Zadok" (*Damascus Document* 4:3f.), after Zadok, who was a priest of Solomon (3 Kings 2:35). The priests determine authoritatively the order and life of the whole community. The teacher of righteousness is a priest (1 QpHab 2:8f.). Priests of Aaron's lineage have the first place and honor above all others (1 QS 5:2, 9; 9:7). In the community's council there are, with twelve laymen, also three priests (1 QS 8:1). A priest presides at the meal. He says the blessing over the bread and wine, and begins the meal (1 QS 6:4f.; 1 QSa 2:1-22). Levites are assistants to the priests (1 QS 1:21-23; 2:4, 11). Priests and levites have special rights in the annual plenary convention (1 QS 2:19f.; 1 QSa 2:1-3, 11-14).

A priest fills the important office of "overseer" (*mebaqqer*—1 QS 6:12, 14). Reports on transgressions of the Law (*Damascus Document* 9:17-22) and other kinds of reports come to him (*ibid.*, 14:11f.). Even the priests must consult with him (*ibid.*, 13:5f.). He is the teacher and shepherd of the community (*ibid.*, 13:7-10). He decides on the acceptance or rejection of prospective members (*ibid.*, 13:11f.; 15:7-11). Subject to him are the priests, and also a college of ten judges, consisting of four priests and six laymen (ibid., 10:4-10). The *mebaqqer* has the duties of teaching, of discipline, and of deciding justice. His title means the same thing as bishop (= overseer). Even his duties are comparable to those of the bishop of the Christian community (see below, §4, 7).

All fully accepted members of the community of Qumran adhere to the customs of the priests in Jerusalem. In their period of service, these latter were obligated to special prescriptions of purity, like washings and baths before Temple service and before common meals. Qumran kept all these prescriptions, and even increased them (1 QS 3:4-12). The priests in the Temple held a ritual meal every evening; the brethren in Qumran celebrated their meals in rigid and solemn ritual (1 QS 6:4f.; 1 QSa 2:1-22). Only priests without physical blemish

could perform Temple duty; cripples were excluded from the convo-
cation in Qumran (1 QSa 2:3-9; *Damascus Document* 15:15-19B = 4
QDb).

The differences between this and the New Testament are evident.
The Gospels tell that the sick, the blind, the deaf and mute are healed
(Mark 7:31-37; 8:22-26). All, and even they, are invited to the feast
(Luke 14:13, 21). In the earliest descriptions of the Eucharistic Meal
(1 Cor. 11:4f., 17, 34; 14:22-33), there is never any talk of a presiding
or celebrating priest. The whole community has the same rights and
obligations.*

h) Laity

In the Qumran community the laity too had their statutory rights.
In the annual assembly of the fully accepted members, in which the
laity were in the majority, they had their facultative rights next to the
priests and levites (1 QS 2:21-26; 1 QSa 1:25–2:2). This assembly had
to assent to the acceptance of new members and decide upon penalties
(1 QS 6:24–7:25; 8:16–9:2). At the head of the community stood a
council of twelve laymen and three priests (1 QS 8:1). The twelve
laymen represent the twelve tribes of Israel (as do the twelve Apostles
afterwards, in Matthew 19:28), and thus the three priests are probably
representative of the three orders of levites (Num. 3:17).

In contrast to the priestly community in Qumran, the New Testament may be described as essentially a lay movement. Jesus is the true
and only High Priest of his community (Heb. 4:14). His lineage, however, is not of the levitical priesthood, but from the offspring of Judah
(Heb. 7:14). In the community of Jesus' disciples, priestly descent is
of no importance. The whole Church has in fact a priestly character
(1 Peter 2:5; Apoc. 1:6; 5:10; 20:6; see below, §4, 2).

*[*Translator's note*: Possibly. Nevertheless, anyone who cares to check the
references in 1 Cor. will find that they are hardly to the point, making the final
sentence above entirely gratuitous. There is certainly a multitude of evidences of
a functional hierarchy in the New Testament. St. Clement of Rome belongs to
the apostolic age, his *Letter to the Corinthians* having been written most probably in the year 80 A.D., earlier even than several of the canonical Epistles. I
would suggest that the reader refer to that work of Clement, 40:1-5, which is no.
19 in my *The Faith of the Early Fathers, Vol. I*, hereafter referred to simply as
Jurgens, with the pertinent passage number.]

i) Legal Arrangement

The hierarchical ordering of the Qumran community bespeaks a fully developed legal system with a penal code, advocates, judges, and trials (1 QS 6:24–7:25; *Damascus Document* 9:9–10:10). The successive appeal to correction is closely regulated. "One is to correct another in truth, humility, and love. . . . No one shall allege a statement against his neighbor before the full assembly unless he is able to confront him with witnesses to what was said" (1 QS 5:25–6:1).

This is so very much the same rule that is prescribed in Matthew 18:15-18 that one must reckon with the possibility that the arrangement of the New Testament community took its pattern from Qumran (below, §5, 5, c).

j) Sinners

As a holy community, the pious men of Qumran keep themselves apart from the mass of sinners. The rule requires not only love for the brethren but also hatred against sinners: "to love all that he has chosen, and to hate all that he has cast away" (1 QS 1:3f.; similarly in 1 QS 1:9-11; 2:4f.; 8:6f.); "eternal hatred against all men of the pit" (1 QS 9:21f.). The pious men of Qumran are of the conviction that the enemy of God is their enemy.

Jesus, however, calls sinners, and his commandment is love. The Sermon on the Mount says: "You have heard that it is said, 'Thou shalt love thy neighbor and hate thy enemy.' I, however, say unto you, 'Love your enemies!'" (Matthew 5:44). Nowhere does the Old Testament demand hatred against enemies. Where, then, was the audience of the Sermon on the Mount taught such a thing? Is there a reference here to Qumran's teaching?

k) Temple in Jerusalem

As a priestly community that posed exacting and digid requirements, Qumran came into sharp opposition with the priesthood of the Temple in Jerusalem, whose life was perceived to be shockingly luxurious. "They gather riches and gain, by plundering the people." For punishment they will fall into the hands of the Kittaeans (1 QpHab 9:5-7), who probably are the Romans.

In particular, violent hands will be laid upon the unnamed high priest of the Temple. "Because he exercised rule over Israel, his heart became proud, and he abandoned God and betrayed the commandments for the sake of riches" (1 QpHab 8:8-13). He is the "lying prophet" who leads many astray, "in order to build a deceitful city by bloodshed" (1 QpHab 10:9-11). He persecuted the teacher of righteousness and oppressed the community sorely (1 QpHab 10:9-12; 12:6-10). For this, according to Qumran's conviction, he bore God's punishment. "The godless priest did God give into the hands of his enemies, because of the wickedness which that priest had practiced against the teacher of righteousness and the men of his council (1 QpHab 9:9-12). Is there a reference here to the history of Hyrcanus II, who in 40 b.c. was deposed and taken captive by the Parthians? The end of the blasphemous priest will be the fiery judgment (1 QpHab 10:9-13).

The Qumran community held itself aloof from the Temple, the only place in Israel at which sacrifice could be offered to God. "Those who have entered the covenant are not permitted to go into the sanctuary in order vainly to keep alive there the flame of the altar" (*Damascus Document* 6:11f.). Thus the community could make only a spiritual offering. The pious understood their lives as propitiatory sacrifice for the country and offered sacrifice of praise. The community knew that it was called upon "to atone for the guilt of transgression and for sinful deeds, thus bringing the divine pleasure upon the land more effectively than by the flesh of burnt offerings or by the fat of bloody sacrifices. The oblation of the lips according to precept is like a sacrificial odor of righteousness, and perfect conduct like a pleasant freewill offering" (1 QS 9:4f.; similarly in 1 QS 8:2f.; 1 QSa 1:3). The prophets had already demanded a spiritualization of the sacrifices, e.g., Hos. 6:6: "I desire mercy and not sacrifice." Prayer (Ps. 141:2) and fidelity to the Law (Sir. 35:1-4) are sacrifice. In the persecutions, Israel had discovered a theology of martyrdom, according to which the righteous atone for the guilt of the nation (*4 Macc.* 17:22). Thus too did Qumran explain the sacrificial life of the just.

Qumran's attitude to the Temple will surely be compared to the New Testament attitude to the same. Jesus, too, criticized the manner of worship, in his purification of the Temple (Mark 11:15-19) and in his threatening words against the Temple (Mark 13:2; see below, §14, 1). At first the Christian community continued to take part in divine service in the Temple (Acts 2:46; 3:1), but it was soon seen that they had to separate themselves from the Temple. Paul too designated Christian life as a "holy sacrifice, pleasing to God, . . . as spiritual service of God" (Rom. 12:1; similar in 1 Peter 2:5). The Church's sacrifice, too, is "sacrifice of praise, the fruit of lips, and dispensing of charity" (Heb. 13:15f.). The Qumran teaching about the propitiatory sacrifice of the just is ultimately comparable, when the death of Jesus is understood as vicarious sacrifice of atonement (Mark 10:45; 14:24; see the present work, Vol. 2, pp. 104–106).

m) Calendar

Out of the controversy between Qumran and the Temple there came a new calendar. The teacher of righteousness propagated a new solar calendar, while Judaism followed a lunar calendar (4 QpOs 16). According to this new calendar, no feast fell on a Sabbath, a concurrence that had always resulted in certain Sabbath transgressions. The reason for the calendar reform, therefore, was the strict sanctification of the Sabbath.

Jesus, too, demanded sanctification of the Sabbath. Nevertheless, in the Gospel the Sabbath is for the sake of men (Mark 2:27; see the present work, Vol. 3, pp. 214, 290–291).

n) God's Edifice

The Qumran community reckoned itself as God's edifice and city: "I was like one who comes into a fortified city and takes refuge behind a high wall until his deliverance. . . . You laid a foundation on rock. . . , to erect a strong wall, which is not shaken. . . . No stranger will enter through its gates. . . . An army with its engines of war will not penetrate it" (1 QH 6:25-28; similarly, 7:8f.). The community is a "firmly established house in Israel, the like of which never before existed until now" (*Damascus Document* 3:19f.). The teacher of righteousness is appointed "to build up the community of truth, which will not waver" (4 QrPs 37:16).

Such texts and images bring to mind the New Testament comparisons of the Church with a strong building (Matthew 16:16f.; 1 Cor. 3:9; Eph. 2:20; Apoc. 21:14; see also below, §5, 5, b, 1).

The community in Qumran can also be described as God's eternal planting, the roots of which reach to the primordial waters, and the trees of which spread their shade over the whole earth. There the beasts dwell and graze (1 QH 6:15-17; 8:4-11). Possibly Old Testament imagery is drawn upon for this description (Ps. 104:12; Ezek. 17:23; 31:6; Dan. 4:9, 18).

In the New Testament, the Church too is described as God's planting (Mark 4:30-32; 1 Cor. 3:6-9).

o) Imminent Expectation

Qumran and the Church alike are motivated by the imminence of their eschatological expectation. Qumran knew itself as the "Israel at the end of days" (1 QSa 1:1). The kingdom of God is present in the community (1 QM 6:6). The endtime is now, even if the precise moment of the consummation remains hidden (1 QpHab 7:1-8). The delay in the endtime is but a warning for watchfulness (1 QpHab 7:10-14). The Qumran community lives in the apocalyptic expectation of the late Old Testament (Dan. 12:2), just like the Judaism of that same period.

The New Testament too is a witness to such expectation (see below, §13, 2-3). Endtime expectation and building up of the community are not mutually exclusive. On the contrary, even in the dire straits of the endtime, the community is to be a powerful protection for the elect.

4. QUMRAN AND THE CHURCH

Finally, we may well ask why the special community of Qumran disappeared while leaving no effective mark in history; and why, from the community of Jesus' disciples, the Church came forth.

In the first place, external events were decisive. Since the reports about Qumran cease with the Jewish-Roman war (66–70 A.D.), and since no coins more recent than that are found at the site, we must accept that the settlement went to ruin at that time. It was probably destroyed by the Roman military forces. The inhabitants fled or were killed, after they had concealed their precious books in the caves nearby.

The community of Jesus' disciples, however, was not affected by the catastrophe. The Jewish Christians still abiding in Jerusalem left the city before the seige, and had fled into the land east of the Jordan (Mark 13:14). The gospel, moreover, had long since been proclaimed to the world.

The destinies of Qumran and of Christianity were also determined on internal bases. The community in Qumran was concentrated in a narrow area and severed itself utterly from the lost world outside. The Christian community of disciples was open to all. It immedaitely set in motion intensive missions in the world. The gospel was a message for all nations (see below, §11).

Deep and essential differences informed the communities to the shape and work of their founders. The teacher of righteousness was acknowledged by his community as father and lord. The community of disciples of Jesus, however, recognized in him incomparably more. They declared this in his titles of majesty, with which they confessed their faith (see the present work, Vol. 2, pp. 177–220).

§ 2. COMMUNITY OF DISCIPLES AND THE CHURCH

1. Historical and Dogmatic Formulation
of the Question

Certainly no one will contest that Christianity, and the Church[5] as the form and situation of Christianity, in the way that this Church is encountered in history now and for nearly two thousand years past, has its origins in the person, in the words, and in the works of Jesus Christ. The question, however, is whether Jesus intended this history, and whether he wanted to found and establish the Church as a stable organization for all times. This question is responded to in different ways by the research of secular history, and even by the different Churches and confessions and their theological research and teaching.

The same question can be formulated even for other established religions, such as Mosaic Judaism, Buddhism, and Islam, and similarly too in respect to other spiritual movements. Mention might be made of Plato and his teachings, which were and still are even today a powerful spiritual force in the history of the Western world.

Convinced of the truth, indeed, of the utter necessity of his philosophy for the sake of prosperity, Plato wanted it to be realized in community and state. In the ideal state or republic, which Plato described over and over again in new drafts, philosophy was to hold the form and power of government. He founded his school, which he firmly organized as a cultic union to honor the muses. It existed for more than a thousand years. Plato's community already at a very early time paid divine honors to its founder. His school endeavored, through the exegesis of his writings, to live by the spirit of Plato and to increase and develop further the heritage of his spirit. This was the situation of the "academy" until it was closed by the Emperor Justinian in 529 A.D. Plato could not have predetermined the full course of such a history. Was Platonism, then, the legitimate community of the disciples of its founder?

In reference to the origin of the Church, probably something of the following view and explanation will be defended by the historical sciences. Jesus formed around himself a community of disciples. He gathered them himself, inasmuch as he summoned them to follow him. Moreover, Jesus certainly intended that his doctrine, and the faith that takes its life therefrom, should remain valid and effective at least in Israel, and probably even outside Israel. Jesus proclaimed the kingdom of God as approaching (see below, §13, 3-4). The Son of Man was to confirm the community of disciples at his coming (Mark 8-38). Did Jesus intend to establish a stable community for the interim period until the arrival of God's kingdom? Was it to continue in a messianic kingdom until the endtime consummation?

After the death and resurrection of Jesus, after his exaltation and the sending of the Spirit, the community of disciples had to understand, order, and represent itself anew on the basis of those events. The community termed itself, in accord with the Old Testament prototype, an ἐκκλησία = Church (see below, §2, 3, a). With this designation the community of Jesus' disciples declared that it understood itself as the true and perfected Israel.

Catholic teaching wants to bring the Church into close and immediate union with Jesus. History, however, fails to recognize the representation, be it made, that in the perspective of a lengthy future, Jesus established his Church in its concrete particulars, with its hierarchical structure and government, with its teaching office and its seven sacraments, in the same way, perhaps, that the founder of a religious order sets up his establishment. On the contrary, what is to be investigated and described is how the Church emerged from the community of Jesus' disciples.

Modernism unleashed within Catholic circles a weighty discussion, with its explanation of the genesis of the Church. Alfred Loisy[6] formulated it in the often quoted statement: "Jesus proclaimed the kingdom of God; the Church arose." If, then, the Church was not founded directly by Jesus, she can, nevertheless, as she presents herself in history, appeal to Jesus. There does exist a true union between the gospel of the Church and the gospel of Jesus, and therefore also between Jesus and the Church. Insofar as the Church intends to serve the gospel, she is founded on the intentions of Jesus.

In the Gospels the community of disciples is gathered around the earthly Jesus, in following him and in leading a common life with him, trained in the message of the kingdom of God, fully empowered to bring it about in the conquest of evil (Matthew 10:8). The Church, however, is an established community with an office that is presented in teaching, worship, and organization. She becomes possible only because of and after the resurrection of Christ and the pouring out of the Spirit. For the Church exists as the community of the exalted Lord, and in the fullness of the Spirit. She awaits her consummation in the kingdom of God. The latter will no longer be a Church. What is decisive is the question of whether and how such a continuity exists between the community of disciples and the Church that both may be understood as founded by Jesus. Continuity and discontinuity alike can be defended. Between community of disciples and Church, the boundary is marked out by the resurrection and the pouring out of the Spirit.

The most recent official magisterial pronouncement on the Church and on her having been founded by Jesus is declared in the dogmatic constitution of the Second Vatican Council, *Lumen gentium*, or *Light of Nations*.[7] In chapters 1 and 3 the decree treats of the origin and establishment of the Church. The Church is included in God's eternal will to save, which is brought to realization in the mission of his Son (no. 3).

The first creational event of the Church is the work of Christ. He "inaugurated his Church, inasmuch as he proclaimed the message of the arrival of the kingdom of God." "Even the miracles of Jesus prove that the kingdom has already come on earth" (no. 5).

The second creational event of the Church is the outpouring of the Spirit on Pentecost. The Spirit is the life of the Church. "By the power of God, [the Church] grows visibly in the world" (no. 4). "The eternal Shepherd, Jesus Christ, built the holy Church, inasmuch as he sent the apostles, just as he was himself sent by the Father" (no. 18).

The choosing and the sending of the Twelve give the Church its historical beginning. With the apostles and with Peter as their head, Jesus institutes the hierarchy. The bishops are the successors of the apostles, the Bishop of Rome the successor of the Apostle Peter (nos. 19-20).[8] "The Church is a visible assembly and a spiritual community, . . . which is formed in a coalition of human and divine elements" (no. 8).

The full reality of the Church, therefore, is at one and the same time humanly visible and, as an intellectual-spiritual reality, invisible. Her visibility is her historicity, her invisibility her pneumatic reality and truth. Historicity calls for historical consideration of the genesis of the Church. The divine truth endures every question and still stands firm. It is not affected by it, much less is it destroyed; on the contrary, it shines through and is brought to efficacy.

2. CONTINUITY

The post-paschal Church knew herself as a community founded by Jesus Christ. She preached in the belief that she was the valid continuation of the community of disciples called by Jesus, indeed, that she was essentially identical to that community.

a) Christology

Of decisive importance to the Church was the continuity of Christology. The Church was of the conviction that the One whom she believed and proclaimed as the Exalted One was, as a Person, the same as the earthly Jesus. The glory yet hidden in the earthly life of Jesus was now manifested in the Church (Mark 9:9).

The Church declared her faith in Jesus Christ in titles of majesty, and she likewise found contained in these titles of majesty the founding of the Church. She proclaimed Jesus as Messiah, Son of David, Son of Man, Lord, and Son (see the present work, Vol. 2, pp. 177–220). Contained in all these titles is the implication that a community belongs to the One to whom they are applied; and that community is the Church.

The Messiah is the Prince of Israel. To him belongs the people renewed in holiness. The kingdom of the Messiah is to preceed the kingly rule of God (see below, §18, 3, h). The Church believes that she is herself the messianic kingdom, whose Lord is the exalted Christ.

As Son of David, Jesus is the new and endtime King David. Eternal rule is promised to him (2 Sam. 7:12-16). The gospel of the Church proclaims that she belongs to that kingdom of David, which will have no end (Luke 1:32f.).

"The kingdom that will never be destroyed belongs" to the Son of Man. "The kingdom will be given to the people of the saints of the Most High" (Dan. 7:13f., 27). The Church knows that she herself is in the kingdom of the Son of Man.

Jesus is the Son (Matthew 11:25-27). To the Son belong the other sons of the Father (Matthew 17:26; Rom. 8:14-19; 2 Cor. 6:18). The sons now form the community of Christ.

The Church knows that she is united with the former community of Jesus' disciples in the one salvific work of Christ. The Jesus of the Gospels desires, by the gift of life, "to redeem the many" (Mark 10:45), and to gain the one great congregation (John 10:11-16). The Church, as "the new covenant in the blood of Christ" (Mark 14:22-25), is the fruit of redemption. She is the community of the elect, the justified, and the sanctified (see the present work, Vol. 2, pp. 104–109). She lives in Christ's resurrection as with the First-born of the dead (Col. 1:18).

The Church is established as a redemptive work of the Crucified and Risen One.

The Church is the community of Jesus, which lives in following him as his disciples. Those who belonged to the earthly Jesus and those who belong to the exalted Jesus are, in one and the same way, His "disciples" (μαθηταί — Mark 8:34; Matthew 28:19; Acts 6:1-7).

b) Gospel

The Church guards the word of Jesus and lives by that word. In order to preserve the words of Jesus, the Church writes the Gospels. His word is "gospel" in the same way before and after Easter (Mark 1:1, 14; Acts 15:7; 20:24; Rom. 1:1). The word of Jesus has a most important content, which remains essential to the post-paschal Church. Thus the tidings that God is the Father (Matthew 6:9; Rom. 8:15; Gal. 4:6). The great commandment of the love of God and of neighbor determines true discipleship (Mark 12:28-31; John 13:34; Rom. 13:9). The whole moral ordering of life has its basis in the law of Jesus Christ. Also pertaining to this message is the expectation of the imminent kingdom of God. The security of the community of disciples at the time of Jesus was ordered to this expectation, and so too is that of the Church of the exalted Jesus (see below, §13, 3, a-e).

c) Salvational Work

The Church celebrates the sacraments, which Christ instituted and which bestow salvation. These sacraments are baptism (Matthew 28:19) and the Eucharist (Mark 14:22-25).

Just as Jesus healed and transferred to his disciples the full authority to do likewise (Matthew 10:8), so too has the Church received from her Lord the power of wonders and healings. These miraculous healings characterize the messianic era in the same way before and after Easter. The Gospels do not describe these wonders merely as past historical events; rather, the Lord now acts in the same way in his community.

The multiplication of the loaves is described with the words of the Eucharistic Supper (Mark 6:35-44; 14:22). The history of the calming of the storm on the sea presents the Christ who is always with his Church (Mark 4:35-41). After Easter the Church possesses miraculous power in the name of Jesus (Acts 3:1-10; 5:12-16; 9:34). Paul works signs and wonders in this power (Rom. 15:19; 2 Cor. 12:12).

The Church is endowed with the fullness of the Spirit, whom Jesus promised to send (Matthew 3:11; 10:20; John 3:5f.; 7:39). The Spirit is poured out upon the community as the Spirit of the exalted Christ, and the community lives on "in the Holy Spirit." Paul says in a special way that the Spirit of the Church is the Spirit of Jesus Christ (Rom. 8:2, 9; 2 Cor. 3:17; Gal. 4:6). The Spirit now works the multiplicity of the charisms.

d) Apostolic Office

The Church is one, before and after Easter, by virtue of the one office of the apostles. By Jesus, they were called as the Twelve (Mark 3:13-19), and confirmed by the Resurrected One as apostles and witnesses (1 Cor. 15:5). They lead the community in Jerusalem (Acts 2:37, 42; 4:33, 35f.; 6:6; 15:2, 22f.; Gal. 1:18f.). They are the abiding foundation of the Church (Eph. 2:20; Apoc. 21:14; see below, §4, 1). Before and after Easter, Peter is first among the Twelve (see below, §5). Inasmuch as in the discourse with which the Twelve were sent out there are themes drawn from later mission experience (Matthew 10:17-25), the apostolate of the Twelve is seen in unity with the later office of the Church. Even the community arrangement in Matthew 18 contains words of Jesus as later prescriptions (Matthew 18:15-20). The community of disciples and the Church are seen in each other.

The post-paschal Church has an awareness and conviction of having come forth from the former community of Jesus' disciples, and of being essentially the same. Just as historical-critical exegesis is able to posit its question on the awareness of continuity and identity, so too, nevertheless, it is able to affirm the testimony of the awareness of continuity, at least in this regard, that the Church makes explicitly audible and visible what is implicitly contained and laid out in the words and works of the earthly Jesus.

3. Concepts and Terms

a) Ekklesía

The usual designation of the New Testament Church is *ekklesía* (ἐκκλησία). In profane Greek the word signified the plenary assembly of the legally enfranchised citizens of a city. Its basic significance as "the community turned out" was soon lost, and attributing to it its Old Testament conceptual content (i.e., the Church as community convoked from out of the world) will scarcely be justified.

In the New Testament the word has its prototype in the Greek translation of the Old Testament, where it is used (about one hundred times) for *qahal*. The Hebrew term *qahal* means enrollment and assembly (Deut. 9:10; Micah 2:5; Ezra 10:8), and even cultic congregation (Ps. 21:23; Joel 2:16; 2 Chron. 6:3). Inasmuch as the New Testament employs Israel's Old Testament title, it lays claim to being the fulfillment of the Old Testament.

In the Old Testament, the people of Israel is designated as the people of the covenant mostly with the term ʿedah, a term which in the Greek Old Testament is rarely translated by ἐκκλησία, but in the overwhelming majority of instances by συναγωγή.

The Qumran scrolls employ *qahal* in some instances for the common assembly (1 QSa 2:4; 1 QM 14:5; *Damascus Document* 11:22; 12:6). The community's designation for itself is ʿedah (1 QSa 1:3f., 9; 2:21; 1 QM 2:5; 3:4).

In the New Testament, the term "synagogue" designates the house of the Jewish community; and only in James 2:2, after the Jewish prototype, does this same term designate the local Christian community. In the synagogue the Law of Moses was proclaimed and explained; hence synagogue characterizes in a peculiar way the Jewish religion. For its part, the community of Christ was determined by the gospel. For that reason the community of disciples avoided the term synagogue and called itself the *ekklesía*.

In the Gospels, the term *ekklesía* is used only in Matthew 16:18 and 18:17. Indeed, the word appears here on the lips of Christ. The saying, however, is shown to be a later construction (see below, §5, 2). The use of the future tense in Matthew 16:18, "I will build," points to the future after the death and exaltation of Jesus. The logion also shows thereby that the Church first appears after the resurrection of Jesus. In Matthew 18:17, *ekklesía* is the place of the assembled community. Since the Gospel of Matthew may be dated about the year 90 A.D., its use of the word *ekklesía* presupposes usage of the term for an already long time in the proclamation and teaching of the Church.

Luke avoids the word *ekklesía* in his Gospel, but uses it quite frequently in the Acts of the Apostles, where the term designates first of all the community in Jerusalem (Acts 5:11), as also the mission communities (Acts 8:1; 14:23). Accordingly, it designates both the individual local community (Acts 9:31) as well as the collective Church (Acts 8:3). Luke makes it abundantly clear that the Church first appears after the exaltation of the Lord.

The word *ekklesía* is of very frequent occurrence in the Pauline collection of Epistles.[9] The oldest letter of Paul is First Thessalonians, addressed in 1:1 "to the Church of the Thessalonians in God the Father and in the Lord Jesus Christ." God calls and creates the Church through the salvation bestowed in Christ. Its level of effectiveness is as the local community. The foundation of the Church in God's salvation is declared by Paul when he calls her the "Church of God" (1 Cor. 1:2; 2 Cor. 1:1; Gal. 1:13 *et passim*). Sometimes he calls her also the "Church of Christ" (Rom. 16:6) or "in Christ" (Gal. 1:22). The Apostle also uses the term Church in speaking of the visible, historical community in Corinth (1 Cor. 1:2; 2 Cor. 1:1), in Judea (Gal. 1:22), in Galatia (Gal. 1:2), in Macedonia (2 Cor. 8:1), in Asia (1 Cor. 16:29), and moreover, of the Churches, using the term in the plural (1 Cor. 7:17; 14:33f.).

The smallest unit of the Church is the household community (Rom. 16:5, 23; 1 Cor. 16:29; Philemon 2). But the term Church can also embrace the whole Church (1 Cor. 10:32; 12:28; 15:9; Gal. 1:13; Phil. 3:6). The Church is the daybreak of the expected kingdom of God and of the exalted Lord (Rom. 4:17; 1 Cor. 4:20; 1 Thess. 2:12). Under another manner of considering it, the Church is the fellowship of the saints (see the present work, Vol. 3, pp. 175–178). She is united in love (see the present work, Vol. 3, pp. 131–136).

In the Apocalypse of John (2–3; 22:16), *ekklesía* designates the individual communities.

Finally, in Heb. 12:23 we have the word *ekklesía* in the passage: "You have come to Mount Zion and the city of the living God, to the heavenly Jerusalem and the myriads of angels, to the festal gathering and to the multitude of the first-born (ἐκκλησία πρωτοτόκων) who are inscribed in the heavens, and to God, the Judge of all." The text is sometimes so understood that the Church is represented here in an eschatological setting, with the earthly Church belonging already to the perfected and eternal world of God. Nevertheless, it is apparent that in this passage the term *ekklesía* does not mean the earthly "Church," but simply a "multitude"; and the fullness of the heavenly world is described in the three sets of double-termed groupings.

b) Body of Christ

The designation of the Church as the Body of Christ (σῶμα Χριστοῦ), a terminology found in the Pauline and Deutero-Pauline Epistles, is of great importance.[10] In Paul the term Body of Christ is of multiplex significance. It designates first of all the body of Christ delivered up to the Cross, and Christ crucified. "You have died to the Law through the body of Christ" (Rom. 7:4). In the Last Supper liturgy, the Bread signifies the body delivered up to death. "This is my body, for you" (1 Cor. 11:24). The Supper brings about communion with the Body of Christ. The one Bread creates the body of the Church. "Because it is one Bread, we, the many, are one body. For we are all participants of the one Bread" (1 Cor. 10:17).

In 1 Cor 12:12-27, the Apostle draws conclusions from this reality: "Just as the body is one and has many members, and all the members of the body, many as they are, constitute one body, so also is it with Christ" (1 Cor. 12:12). The unification of the members into the one body takes place in baptism (1 Cor. 2:13). Though there are many members, each one has its one task. That is how God joined the body together. "You, however, are Christ's Body and, considered as parts, members thereof" (1 Cor. 12:27).

This imagery is taken up again in Rom. 12:4f., where it is written: "Just as in one body we have many members, so we, the many, are one body in Christ."

The concept and comparison are given further development in the Epistles to the Colossians and to the Ephesians. In Col. 1:24 it is stated that the Church is the Body of Christ. "I make up in my flesh in place of Christ what is still lacking in the sufferings of Christ, for his Body, the Church." In a hymn that probably referred originally to the cosmos and is now transferred to Christ, Christ is designated as Head of the Body. "He is the Head of the Body, the Church" (Col. 1:18). Probably it was said first of all of the cosmos: "From its Head the whole body, supported and held together by joints and sinews, achieves the growth which God gives it" (Col. 2:19).

The Epistle to the Ephesians also designates Christ as Head of the Body. "He laid everything at his feet and gave him as Head over the whole Church, which is his Body" (Eph. 1:22f.). "Holding fast to the truth in love, we want to grow in all parts into him who is the Head, Christ" (Eph. 4:15). Christ is "the Head of the Church, as Redeemer of his Body" (Eph. 5:23).

Exegesis endeavors to explain the image of the Church as the Body of Christ from its origins and in its history. An earliest source is Plato (*Timaeus* 30 B; 47 C-E; 92 B), who perceived the world as a body animated and accompanied by the divine reason. The world is conceived as God's body also in the Orphic mysteries. Thus, in an Orphic hymn (see Otto Kern, *Orphicorum fragmenta*, Berlin 1922, p. 201f., *Frag.* 168), Zeus is called "the first and the last, the head." All bodies are included in the magnitude of Zeus. He is "beaming, limitless, immovable, motionless, strong, overwhelming body." There is similar expression in Fragment 21a, p. 91.

Usage of such imagery worked an influence also on Hellenistic Judaism, where Philo describes the All as powerful body, which is led by the divine Logos as the head (*De plantatione Noë* 9; *De mundi opificio* 82). World and man are comparable to each other, since both consist of a body and a thinking soul (Philo, *Quis rerum divinarum haeres sit* 155). The Stoa understood the idea rationally and sociologically. Chrysippus (in J. von Arnim, *Stoicorum veterum fragmenta*, Vol. 2, 2nd ed., Stuttgart 1964, p. 124) designates the popular assembly (ἐκκλησία) as body: "Often a body consists of many separate bodies, like an assembly and an army and a choir. Life, thought, and learning is suited to each."

The fable of Menenius Agrippa in Livy, 2, 32, is quite well known. The Roman people is like the organism of a body. Just as the members of the body form a unity, so too with the members of a nation. The fable was afterwards developed further in manifold ways. Cicero, in his *De officiis* (3, 5, 22), applies the image of the body to human society: "Just as the whole body would necessarily be weakened and destroyed if each member were convinced that it could augment itself if it were to draw to it the power of another member, so too would human society and fellowship be destroyed if each one of us were to seize for himself the well-being of the other and take from each whatever powers he could use for himself."

Seneca addresses the Emperor: "You are the soul of your government; it is your body" (*De clementia* 1, 5, 1). "The clemency of your disposition will spread itself abroad little by little throughout the whole body of the empire. . . . Well-being proceeds from the head, entering into all parts of the body" (*ibid.*, 2, 2, 1).

This use of imagery calls to mind 1 Cor. 12:12-27, where Paul speaks of the many members of the one body of Christ. Paul applied the image Christologically. The idea of the Head of the body is added in the Deutero-Pauline Epistles. At this point some exegetes, including E. Käsemann and H. Schlier, reckon with Gnostic influences in the New Testament. The Gnosis knew the myth of the superman, who was a divine being. With the passage of time, the superman himself fell into the power of the ruler of darkness, but was afterwards able to free himself at least partially. His head succeeded in returning into the world of light, but his other members remained fettered to matter. In order to redeem these members, the redeemed head went down again into matter. The redeemer collected his dispersed members, which are the souls of men. This representation, it is supposed by some exegetes, could have been used by the Deutero-Pauline writings, wherein Christ is the Head of the Church and, with the redeemed, forms but a single body, which is himself.

Such explanations are attested, for example, in the *Odes of Solomon*; thus, in 17:14: "And the faithful received my blessing and came alive, and they came together with me and were redeemed. For they have become members and I their Head. Praise to thee, our Head, Lord, Christ! Alleluia!"

The critics of this exegesis question and examine whether the Gnostic myths of the cosmos as body had already been developed at the time of the New Testament. It can hardly be denied that the texts come from a period later than the New Testament, while, naturally, their content can be earlier. The *Odes of Solomon* belong to the second century A.D. Manichaean examples are even more recent.

Unquestionably Gnostic texts have been accepted into many biblical-Christian themes, and this is probably the case too with the images of the body and its Head.

Closer to the New Testament, no doubt, are the early Jewish and rabbinic speculations on corporate persons in whom subsequent generations are included. From one Adam come the bodies and souls of all men. The patriarchs include in themselves the whole later nation. Applications of this consideration can be found in Rom. 5:12-21 and 1 Cor. 15:21f., 45-49. Christ is the new and eschatological Adam, embracing in himself all future generations. Further texts, nevertheless, are demonstrably of later origin. In extra-biblical cultural areas one encounters the myths of the All-God as Great-Man, and the world as the body of a giant — thus in the Babylonian teaching on creation, in the Norse *Edda*, and in ancient Indian texts.

Paul and the Deutero-Pauline writings, when they represent the Church as Body of Christ and Christ as Head of the Body, were accepting ancient traditions.

In our time the conceptualization of the Church as "Mystical Body of Christ" has become especially frequent and emphatic. The theology of the Fathers designated primarily the Eucharistic Body of Christ as Mystical Body, which creates the body of the visible Church. If exegesis has been at some pains to understand and explain the New Testament concept of the Body of Christ in all its implications, then certainly and increasingly the significance of the concept of the Church as the Mystical Body of Christ is not an easy one for the congregation.[11]

c) Covenant

The Church knows herself as the "new covenant."[12] Israel understood herself as nation of the covenant on the basis of the covenants concluded by God with Noah (Gen. 9:8-18), Abraham (Gen. 15:18; 17:2-10), the patriarchs (Exod. 6:4), and again with the whole people at Sinai (Exod. 24:3-8), and with David (2 Sam. 7:14f.).[13]

The covenant is concluded with a sacrifice (Gen. 15:9f.) and a meal (Exod. 24:11). It is sealed with sacrificial blood (Exod. 24:8; Zech. 9:11). The covenant is God's arrangement and gift (Gen. 9:9-12). It requires Israel's obedience as return gift, which is summarized in the commandment of love (Deut. 6:4f.; 11:1). Israel's apostasy and sin does not annul the covenant. God's fidelity to his covenant bears it and carries it through (Deut. 7:9, 12; 3 Kings 8:23; Hos. 11 and 14). The term covenant becomes in itself a designation for the Jewish religion (Dan. 11:28, 30; Micah 3:1).

For the messianic era of salvation, a "new covenant" is promised, which will no longer be an exterior and legal arrangement, but will be constituted by a new heart and a new spirit (Jer. 31:31-34).[14] It will be an "eternal covenant of peace" (Is. 54:10; Ezek. 37; 26). An eternal covenant will embrace all nations (Is. 55:1-5).

The idea of covenant remained alive. Pentecost, or the Feast of Weeks, was begun as an annual celebration of the renewal of the covenant. The Qumran scrolls have frequent admonitions about the covenant of God with the fathers. The community knows itself as the "eternal covenant" (1 QS 3:11f.; 4:22; 5:1f.). The pious man lives in the covenant of God (1 QH 3:28; 7:49f.). The community in Damascus frequently makes mention of the covenant with the fathers (*Damascus Document* 1:4; 6:2; 8:8; 15:8f.; 16:1) and terms itself, with special emphasis, the "community of the new covenant" (*Damascus Document* 19:33).

The New Testament calls attention to the covenant that God made with the patriarchs (Luke 1:72; Acts 3:25; Rom. 9:4; Apoc. 11:19). The discoursing of Jesus at the Last Supper takes up the promise of the new covenant in Jer. 31:31 and explains it as being fulfilled (1 Cor. 11:25; Luke 22:20). This covenanting too takes place in blood, the blood of Christ (1 Cor. 11:25; Mark 14:24). If Jesus and the Gospels say comparatively little about the covenant, the reason for this may be the fact that the proclamation of God's kingdom takes its place.

In consequence of the designation "new covenant," Paul calls the former covenant the "old covenant" (2 Cor. 3:14). In consideration of the present new covenant, the old seems to be of lesser worth. The old covenant effected bondage, the new is operative unto freedom (Gal. 4:24f.). In detailed comparison, Paul contrasts the old and new covenants one to the other (2 Cor. 3:6-18). The former was a covenant of the killing letter; the present one is a covenant of the living Spirit. If the former was a covenant of passing glory, this one is a covenant of stable glory. The prophetic promises of a new convenant (Is. 59:21; Jer. 31:33f.) are now fulfilled (Rom. 14:27). Now the Gentiles have entered into "the covenants of the promise" (Eph. 2:12).

The Epistle to the Hebrews gives a further development to the theology of the covenant. The Epistle quotes twice (Heb. 8:6-13; 10:16f.) the promise of a new covenant in Jer. 31:31-34. By this promise, the former covenant was declared obsolete and near its end by God himself (Heb. 8:13). The new covenant is fulfillment of the old, which had its importance and worth as a prototype (Heb. 8:5), and was but a foreshadowing of the new (Heb. 10:1). The new covenant is better and more powerful (Heb. 7:22; 8:6). Like the old covenant, the new is established in blood (Heb. 10:29; 12:24). That is how redemption from sin took place in the old covenant (Heb. 9:15). The blood of Christ is "blood of the eternal covenant" (Heb. 13:20). The endurance of the covenant down through the ages makes it evident that one and the same Divine Will unites Israel and the Church in a single salvation history.

In profane Greek, the term διαθήκη almost always signifies testament, in the sense in which we speak in English of a "last will and testament." This same meaning finds voice in the New Testament. Thus, in Gal. 3:15-18, Abraham and his progeny are the testamentary beneficiaries of the promises. The Law of Moses, which came later, cannot annul this testament.

In Heb. 9:16-20 both meanings of διαθήκη, covenant and testament, are intertwined. The Epistle recalls that a testament becomes effective at the death of the testator. So too the Old Testament promises become effective in the death of Christ, in whom the new covenant is established.

It is from this linguistic usage of διαθήκη, meaning testament in the sense of last will and testament, that our designation of Old Testament and New Testament is derived, and thus the terms are invested with a meaning that is not immediately evident.

d) People of God

The Church of the New Testament knows herself as the "people of God" (λαὸς θεοῦ).[15] With the term λαός, less used in profane Greek literature and probably having certain overtones of solemnity, the

Greek Old Testament often designates Israel as people of God (while the Gentile nations, the pagan peoples, are ἔθνη; see below, §11, 1). God's word often calls Israel "My people," and Yahweh wants to be "her God" (Exod. 3:7; 1 Sam. 9:16; Is. 51:16; Jer. 24:7; Ezek. 11:20; Amos 7:8; Hos. 2:23; Zech. 8:8). Israel is God's "people, peculiarly his own" (Exod. 19:5; Deut. 7:6; 14:2). She is a "holy people" (Exod. 19:6; Num. 16:3; Deut. 14:2), because she has been received into the fellowship of the saints of God (see the present work, Vol. 3, pp. 171f.).

In the early Jewish and rabbinic writings it is a cornerstone of the religion that Israel is God's chosen people. Thus in the Qumran writings too, Israel is God's chosen people (1 QM 1:12; 10:10, 19; 13:7, 9).

In the New Testament, too, Israel is called "people of God" or simply "people." Jesus will "redeem his people from their sins" (Matthew 1:21). He is "the glory of God's people, Israel" (Luke 2:32). God has "shown himself friendly to his people," inasmuch as he sent them the Prophet, Jesus (Luke 7:16; 24:19). As "the people," Israel is set in opposition to the Gentiles, who are "the peoples" (Acts 4:25f.; Rom. 15:10) or, as we generally have it in English translations of Scripture, "the nations."*

Israel remains God's people (Rom. 9:6). God has not cast her off (Rom. 11:1). Certainly the Church too now bears the title of honor, of being God's people. From among the peoples (i.e., nations, Gentiles), God has, according to Amos 9:11f., called and created this people (Acts 15:24). What once was a non-people, God has, in accord with the promise in Hos. 2:25, termed people and sons (Rom. 9:24f.).

The words of Lev. 26:12 now apply to the Church: "I will be your God, and you shall be my people" (2 Cor. 6:16; 1 Peter 2:10). The Church is now, as Israel was previously, a "people peculiarly owned" (Titus 2:14; 1 Peter 2:9). Christ has, by his blood, set aright the sins of his people (Heb. 9:28); and by his blood he has sanctified those who are his own (Heb. 13:12). The Church is the wandering people of God, which is privileged to enter into the Sabbath rest (Heb. 4:9).

---

*[*Translator's note*: German applies the singular *Volk*, translated "people" or "nation" to Israel; in the plural, *Völker*, denoting "peoples" or "nations," means the "Gentiles." Another term for Gentiles is *Heiden*, meaning also "pagans." The German *Heiden*, of course, has the same linguistic origins as our English term "heathen."]

In the Apocalypse of John, the Church is the people protected by God during the eschatological distress (Apoc. 18:4). The perfected Church is "his people, and God himself will dwell with them" (Apoc. 21:3). Zech. 2:14 and Ezek. 37:27 have now been fulfilled. The title of the Church as people of God indicates her identity with the people of God of the old covenant, even if through a new creation.

Modern biblical theology has renewed for the Church the title and concept people of God. In the Second Vatican Council's dogmatic constitution on the Church, *Lumen gentium*, in the whole of the second chapter the Church is described as "people of God."[16]

e) Gospel of John

Those terms for the Church (*ekklesía*, people of God, new covenant, Body of Christ, the saints) which the rest of the New Testament employs with self-evident certainty of meaning are not found in the Gospel of John. Only the "Twelve" are mentioned (John 6:67, 70; 20:24), with Simon, of course, as Cephas-Peter (John 1:42). Certainly there is no talk of the office that puts the community in order and in which the Church would be presented as visibly and recognizably structured. The sacraments of baptism (John 3:5) and of Eucharist (John 6:52-59) are mentioned; but they are not stressed.[17] There is no narrative of the institution of the Lord's Supper.

Nevertheless, John's Gospel does attest the existence of the community. And that testimony is still able to be heard today, if the external institution of the Church is permitted to be supplemented for us by the description of its interior form.

1) Shepherd and Flock. As an image for the Church, the New Testament uses that of the flock and the shepherd.[18] This image is employed in a special way in the Gospel of John. It is not simply an image taken from everyday experience; rather, it brings with it a long and varied history, primarily, of course, from Old Testament tradition. The patriarchs of the Israelite people, Abraham, Isaac, and Jacob, were princely shepherds. David was called away from his flock to become king (1 Sam. 16:11f.). King David became prototype of the Messiah.

The image of the shepherd was, in Israel, so much a symbol of human existence that the shepherd became a figure of God, and the flock a figure of God's people. Yahweh is the Shepherd of Israel (Ps.

80:2), and Israel is the people he pastures (Ps. 95). Just as the shepherd carries the exhausted sheep, so does Yahweh carry his people (Ps. 28:9). God is the Shepherd of every pious man (Ps. 23). In Israel, God will set up the Messiah as true Shepherd (Ez. 34:23). The Prophet (Zech. 13:7-9) beholds a Shepherd of God who will be killed, whose death will nevertheless bring about a turning-point. According to the *Psalms of Solomon* (17:45), the Messiah will be Israel's Shepherd: "He guides the flock of the Lord in fidelity and justice, and allows none of them to perish in the pasture."

The imagery is continued when it represents Jesus, in accord with his own words, as Shepherd. Jesus sees Israel as "sheep without a shepherd" (Matthew 9:36). Just as he knows himself as "sent to the lost sheep of the house of Israel" (Matthew 15:24), so too does he send the Twelve first of all "to the lost sheep of Israel" (Matthew 10:6). He wants his disciples to constitute the "little flock" of the messianic people of God (Luke 12:32). In his death he fulfills the image of the shepherd delivered up, as in Zech. 13:7: "I will smite the shepherd and the sheep will be scattered" (Mark 14:27). Even as Judge, at the end he will be like the shepherd who separates the sheep (Matthew 25:32).

In the detailed figural discourse of John's Gospel, 10:1-18, 26-29, Jesus is the good Shepherd, the true Shepherd. An inner relationship unites the Shepherd to each of his sheep individually. They know the Shepherd and follow him. The Shepherd leads them to good pasture. He guards them from thieves and from wild beasts, and lays down his very life for his sheep. The flock goes beyond Israel and embraces even the Gentiles. In the appendix chapter (21) of John's Gospel, there appears at last the theme that Peter is commissioned to pasture the lambs.

The image of Christ as the Shepherd was taken up by the Church's Christology. Christ is "the great Shepherd of the sheep" (Heb. 13:20). The Christians were "like straying sheep; but now they have come back to the shepherd and guardian [i.e., the bishop] of souls" (1 Peter 2:25). Christ is seen as the "chief Shepherd" (1 Peter 5:4). He pastures the nations with an iron staff (Apoc. 2:27; 12:5; 19:15). Later testimonies may be added to these. Bishop Abercius of Hierapolis in Phrygia Salutaris reckons himself as "a disciple of the Chaste Shepherd who feeds His sheep on the mountains and in the fields, who has great

eyes surveying everywhere, who taught me the faithful writings of
life" (*Epitaph of Abercius*, written by himself, ca A.D. 180/200 [Jurg-
ens, no. 187]). From St. Clement of Alexandria (*The Instructor of
Children* 1, 53, 2f.—before A.D. 202) onwards in the East, and from
Tertullian (*Repentance* 8—A.D. 203/204; and *An Exhortation to Chas-
tity* 7, 10—A.D. 208/212) in the West, the Fathers of the Church make
reference to the biblical parables and comparisons involving the figure
of a shepherd. The figure of the Good Shepherd is represented in plastic art by the statue of a shepherd who bears the lost sheep on his
shoulders, as likewise in paintings, notably in the catacombs, as well
as on gold drinking vessels, lamps, gems, rings, on tombs and in mo-
saics, at Rome, Ravenna, Naples, Sicily, in North Africa, and as far as
Dura Europos on the Euphrates.

Moreover, in the further historical development of the Church, the
shepherd image gained significance in the designation of ecclesiastical
office as office of shepherd (John 21:15f.; Acts 20:28; Eph. 4:11).

Does the Old Testament suffice to explain the origin and thematic
elements of the New Testament imagery of the shepherd, and in particular that of John 10?

Since early Greek times, Hermes Kriophorus (= carrying a ram)
has been represented in plastic art as archetype of divine solicitude for
creatures. This image has undoubtedly been a partial influence on the
Christian image of the Good Shepherd.[19]

In all Eastern religions the gods are called shepherd. In the *stylus
curiae* of Sumerian, Babylonian, Assyrian, and Egyptian texts, the title
of shepherd is transferred to the king. In Homer, Hesiod, and Plato,
the ruler is "shepherd of the peoples." According to Philo (*De agri-
cultura* 51), God is "Shepherd and King." The Logos, his first-born
Son," exercises in God's stead "solicitude for the holy flock." The Logos
himself is "Shepherd and King" (*De mutatione nominum* 116).

Mandaean literature knows shepherd allegories drawn in broad
strokes. The bestower of revelation appears as a "good shepherd, who
guards his sheep" (*Ginza*, p. 181., ed. M. Lidzbarski, Göttingen and
Leipzig 1925). In the Mandaean *Book of John* (p. 44–54, ed. M. Lidzbarski, Giessen 1915), the Redeemer says: "I am a Shepherd who loves
his sheep. . . . On my shoulders I carry the sheep, and give them to
drink from the hollow of my hand. . . . I bring them to the good

fold and pasture them beside me. . . . No wolf leaps into our fold, and they have nothing to fear from a fierce lion. . . . No thief penetrates their fold, and they need not worry about an iron knife. . . . Each and every sheep that hears my call and listens to my voice, I protect in both my hands."

The similarities between the Gospel of John and the Mandaean writings are significant. The Shepherd is not the royal ruler (as in the Old Testament), but purely a shepherd. Between him and his sheep there is a mutual and intimate union. The sheep are threatened by thieves and wolves. The New Testament gospel is the self-surrender of the Shepherd even to death, for his sheep.

Since, nevertheless, the Mandaean writings were written down centuries after the New Testament and have undoubtedly been influenced by the New Testament, it can in no way be regarded as certain that the imaginal discourse of John 10 is dependent upon Mandaeanism. It is possible that even in this present instance the Mandaean writings have in fact been influenced by the New Testament; and ultimately it is likewise conceivable that the imaginal discourses in both instances — John's Gospel and the Mandaean writings — have fed at a common source.

Be that as it may, when the Gospel expressly designates Jesus as the good and true Shepherd, there is perhaps a polemical accent here, if, in the face of earlier and contemporary shepherd images, Christ is proclaimed as the consummational Yes of God to all hopes and expectations (2 Cor. 1:19f.).

The true community is described, in the figure of the Shepherd and his flock, in the intimate communion of faith and of love between Christ and the disciples.

2) The Vine. The nature of the Church as an organic union of disciples is presented again and in a broader way in John 15:1-8 in the parable of the vine.[20] Jesus is the true Vine, the disciples are the branches. The Father is the vinedresser. If the disciples remain in Jesus and in his words, they can bring forth abundant fruit. Branches that do not remain in him wither; they are cut off and cast into the fire. By the disciples' bringing forth fruit, the Father is glorified.

The imagery of the discourse describes the Church in her communion with Christ. The love of the disciples for each other is founded on Christ's love for them (John 15:9f.). The Father shapes the community.

The imagery of the discourse is to be explained not only from the commonplace experiences of daily life, but also from tradition. In the Old Testament, Israel is often understood under the image of the vineyard planted by God (Is. 5:1-7; 27:2-4), and of the vine (Hos. 10:1; Jer. 2:25; Ezek. 15; 19:10-14; Nahum 2:3; Ps. 80:9-20). The barren vine is threatened with judgment (Jer. 5:10f.; 48:32; 49:9). Such thematic elements coincide with those of John 15:10. God is the planter, and the bearing of fruit is required. Nevertheless, in the Old Testament the vine is a figure of Israel, while in John 15:1-8 it is an image of the Messiah. But still, in the Old Testament it is also the case that personified Wisdom is compared to the vine: "Like a vine I put forth graceful shoots, and my sprouts were full of beauty and riches" (Sir. 24:17). The transferral to the rule of the Messiah is found also in the *Syriac Apocalypse of Baruch* 39:7, where the messianic kingdom is likened to a mountain and to a vine.

Again, however, there are Gnostic Mandaean texts which are very much like John 15:1-8. The bringer of revelation says of himself in the *Ginza* (pp. 59f. in M. Lidzbarski's edition) : "We are the vine, the vine of life, a tree, on which there is no deceit, the tree of praise, whose odor gives life to all. The eyes of anyone who hears his discourse shall be filled with light. The soul of anyone who reforms shall never be cut off." The mystical vine is described in similar fashion in the Mandaean *Book of John* (pp. 204f. in M. Lidzbarski's edition) : "The vine that bears fruit mounts up, that which bears none is cut off here. Whoever does not let himself be enlightened and taught by me is cut off and falls into the great Reed Sea" (i.e., the Red Sea).

The Mandaean texts and the imaginal discourse of John 15:1-10 are very close to each other in the total picture and in their individual thematic elements. John's own is the interpretation of the relationship between vine and branches as an organic union of disciples with Jesus. Here again the two possibilities of dependency must be weighed: of the Gospel upon Mandaean literature, and vice versa.*

*[*Translator's note*: And in weighing these possibilities, it will be well to keep in mind the fact that, whatever the origins of the Mandaeans, supposed followers of John the Baptist, whose doctrines betray a deep and essential hatred

And it is also possible that both come from a common source, which certainly is no longer available to us. Perhaps it is ultimately the primordial notion of the paradisial garden planted by God, in which marvelous plants are growing, the tree of life (Gen. 2:9) as well as the vine. If this be the case, then John would have been interpreting the tradition Christologically, since he emphasizes that Christ is the true vine.

3) His Own; His Friends. As in the imaginal or metaphorical discourses, in some other sayings too the Church is described as the community of disciples. This is the case with the assertion that the disciples are Jesus' own (ἴδιοι). His "own" are certainly the companions of His household and companions in faith (John 16:32; 19:27; 1 Tim. 5:8; Acts 4:23); and in John 1:11, hardly Israel, but rather the world: "He came unto His own, but His own received Him not." World and men belong to God (and to the Logos; John 1:3), as property to its Creator. But this creation does not accept the Logos. The Shepherd calls sheep "that belong" to Him (John 10:3). They recognize His voice and follow Him. They belong to Him because the Father has given Him them (John 10:29), and because He, as Shepherd, has pledged and is pledging His life for them (John 10:11). The Redeemer loves "his own," who are in the world (John 13:1). God has given them to him, from out of the world (John 17:6f.). The contrary concept is to belong, as property, to deceit (John 8:44) or to the world (John 15:19).

Gnostic literature speaks in a comparable fashion of "His own"; thus in the *Odes of Solomon* 7, 12: "He surrendered himself to reveal himself before his own, so that they might know him, who made them"; similar expressions are found in the same work, 26, 1.

The internal union of the community of disciples and its communion with Jesus is expressed in terms of loving friendship (φιλεῖν, φιλία, φίλος).[21] The love of God, which belongs always to the Son (John 5:20), is bestowed also on the disciples, because they love the Son (John 16:27). Jesus is said to call "tax collectors and sinners his friends" (Matthew 11:19). He himself calls his disciples friends. "I tell you,

of Judaism and Christianity alike, few if any of their writing can be demonstrated to be older than the ninth or tenth century of the Christian era. It is clear, of course, that their traditions are older than their writings; but how much older has proved as yet to be an insoluble problem.]

my friends, do not be afraid of those who kill the body" (Luke 12:4). The designation is of special significance in John's Gospel. In a way that is an example to the disciples, Lazarus and his own are friends of Jesus (John 11:11). To all, he says sympathetically, "I call you friends, because all that I have heard from my Father I have made known to you."

The names "friend" and "brother" are interchangeable (Mark 3:35; Matthew 23:8; John 20:17). The terms characterize the community as God's family. The family is assembled around Jesus as its founder and focal point (Mark 3:35). Even this friendship is not like one between peers. The disciples are friends of Jesus in their belief in Jesus (John 16:27), and they do what he commands them (John 15:14). His command, however, is essentially the commandment of love, which he himself lives perfectly (John 15:17) and which his disciples are to carry out, even to the laying down of their lives (John 15:12f., 17). "Friends" probably became a term of self-designation among Christians (Acts 27:3; 3 John 15).

Christ himself is the inner form of the Church, through his efficacious word and the Spirit going forth from him. The disciples belong to the Church, inasmuch as they abide in Christ and in his word (John 8:31; 15:4-7). They are disciples who keep his and God's word (John 8:51f.; 14:23; 17:6) and the commands of Jesus (John 14:15, 21; 15:10), just as Jesus (John 17:12) and the Father (John 17:11, 15) keep the disciples. The words of Jesus are "spirit and life" (John 6:63). The Spirit abiding with the disciples reminds them of Jesus' words and makes those words ever present to them (John 14:26; 15:26; 16:13). The Spirit is the bond of the Church with the exalted Christ.

4) The Unity of the Church. The Church of John's Gospel is not just an assembly of individuals. The Gospel speaks also of the external form of the Church. The communion of friends is not entirely introverted; it has also a mission to the world (John 17:18). The work of the mission is already described, the same mission in which, in distant fields, future generations would sow and reap (John 4:35-38; 10:16).

For the Gospel, the internal and external unity of the Church [22] is a matter of deep concern. From the Epistles of the apostles (such is the case with the Second Epistle to the Corinthians, the Epistle to the

Galatians, the Epistle to the Philippians, the Pastoral Epistles, the Epistles of John, and the Epistle of Jude), we can easily see how very much this unity is endangered by factions. Against the background of prophecy (Ezek. 34:23; 37:24) which promises the endtime Davidic King as the one Shepherd of the one flock, the imaginal discourse about the Good Shepherd depicts the unity of the flock. Assembled from Israel and from the nations, the Church is to be "one flock and one Shepherd" (John 10:16).

The Father gave the disciples to the Son. No one can take them from the Father and from the Son and scatter them (John 10:28f.). Christ's own belong to him from the first as children of God. He must gather them together in one, from out of the world (John 11:52). The high-priestly prayer of Jesus implores the unity of the Church. She must be one in all times and places. She is established by the one word and the one faith (John 17:20f.).

The unity of the Church has its basis in the unity of Father and Son. As they are to each other, so also are the disciples to be to each other (John 10:30; 17:21).

Unity is the necessary consequence of the oneness of God's name (John 17:11) and of the truth of the one revelation of God (John 17:6).

Unity is ever Christ's gift to his Church. "The glory which you gave me, I have given to them, so that they might be one" (John 17:22). Also, unity is ever the divine work of the Father: "Keep them in your name, which you have given me, so that they might be one as we are one" (John 17:11).

At the same time, unity is even yet the constant duty and goal of the Church, who, by her unity, must reveal to the world the unity of God (John 17:22). Only as the one Church is she worthy of belief in the world (John 17:21). Only as the one undivided Church can she bring to perfection those works that are greater even than the works of Jesus (John 14:22).

Thus, unity has ever to be realized now, even if it is only in the eschatological consummation that "they may be made perfect in unity" (John 17:23).

The Church is one in Spirit, peace, faith, and love. Thus she is the redeemed community of God in a world sundered by irreconcilable antitheses, flesh and spirit, falsehood and truth, darkness and light, death and life (John 14:17, 19, 22, 27; 15:18f.).

§3. CHARISM AND OFFICE

1. Charis and Charisms

In the New Testament, the words *charis* (χάρις) and *charisma* (χάρισμα) appear with great frequency and with a new specific meaning.[23]

a) Charis in Hellenism and in the Old Testament

Charis (derived from χαίρω = *I rejoice*) means specifically the act of rejoicing. In classical Greek, *charis* usually designates the favor of the gods; nevertheless, it is not a centrally religious concept. In late antiquity the word mostly signified the favor of princes and potentates (as also in Acts 24:27; 25:3). Epictetus (*Diss.* 1, 16, 15) uses the word *charis* for the favor of God: "Instead of thanking God, we reproach him for having shown us less care (χάρις) than he has for the beasts."*

Lactantius (*De ira Dei* 2, 7f.; 4, 6) gives a precise account of the doctrine of the older philosophers on God's wrath and on his favor. Epicurus taught: "Just as there is no anger in God, so too there is no favor." The Stoics, however, and other philosophers as well, "had a broadly better conception of the Godhead, inasmuch as they maintained that in God, although there is no anger, undoubtedly there is favor." The truth is that "God is angered, just as he is moved to favor."

In the Old Testament, the comparable word *ḥesed* designates the salvational event in the covenant between Yahweh and Israel. In the

---

*[*Translator's note*: English readers will do well to remember that while χάρις is translated by *Gnade* in German, English is a richer language and forces us to choose between "grace" and "favor."]

Psalms, it is frequently used in reference to God's gracious kindness, translated mostly by ἔλεος. In the Greek translation of the Old Testament, χάρις is not a theological term.

b) Charis in the New Testament

In the New Testament, the content of the word χάρις can be favor and love shown by God, and the salvational power of God as effective grace.

The word *charis* appears in several places in the Lukan writings. When chosen to be the Mother of the Messiah, Mary has "found favor with God" (Luke 1:30). "The grace of God was upon the child Jesus" (Luke 2:40). Jesus "advanced in wisdom and age and grace before God and men" (Luke 2:52). The words of Jesus are "words of grace," because they herald the endtime salvation (Luke 4:22). The term is more frequently encountered in the Acts of the Apostles. God's grace was with the apostles and with the community (Acts 4:33; 11:23; 14:26; 18:27). Stephen, "full of grace and power, worked great wonders and signs" (Acts 6:8). The gospel is "God's grace" (Acts 13:43; 14:3; 20:32). Through the "grace of the Lord Jesus" the redemption takes place (Acts 15:11).

The word "grace" is of decided importance for the Apostle Paul. All Christian existence is in grace. God's grace gives justification and redemption (Rom. 3:23f.). Christians are not to receive God's grace vainly (2 Cor. 6:1). The Law, as a way to salvation, is now terminated and suspended by grace (Rom. 3:21; 6:14f.; 11:6; Gal. 2:21; 5:4). Paul points this out with the example of Abraham; for even Abraham was righteous, not through works of the Law, but "through faith unto grace" (Rom. 4:13-16). Grace is mightier than all sin (Rom. 5:20f.). The grace of God is manifested and bestowed in Jesus Christ (1 Cor. 1:4; Gal. 1:6). It can also be designated as grace of Christ (Rom. 16:20; 2 Cor. 8:9; 13:13).

The special *charis* of Paul is his apostolic office (Rom. 1:5; 15:15; 1 Cor. 3:10; Gal. 2:9). The real wish of the Apostle, endowed with grace, is the wish of grace for the community (Rom. 1:7; 1 Cor. 1:3). When Paul says that his visit should be a renewed *charis* for the community (2 Cor. 1:15), this can hardly mean only that the community is to receive anew the favor of the Apostle, but rather that the Apostle procures for the community the grace of God.[24]

The office is, for the one who holds it, God's grace (Eph. 3:7f.; 4:7); but God's grace is also operative in him for the community. "The grace of God has been dispensed to me for you" (Eph. 3:2). Statements about grace become formalized. With Paul for their precedent, the Deutero-Pauline Epistles speak further of the riches of grace (Eph. 1:7; 2:7f.; Col. 1:6), as do also the Pastoral Epistles (1 Tim. 1:2; 2 Tim. 1:9; Titus 2:11), the Epistle to the Hebrews (4:16; 12:28) and the First Epistle of Peter (1:2, 10; 3:7).

c) Charisms

Charisma is the bestowal of grace coming immediately from God, and the equipping of a member of the community for service in the Church.

The term *charisma* is not found in profane Greek, and in the Greek Old Testament Bible it is not of essential importance. It is, however, of both frequent and important occurrence in the Epistles of Paul. Here charism designates first of all the collective salvational gifts. Thus the term is found, in contrast to the single, decisive sin of Adam, as referring to the single, conclusive salvational act of the one Christ (Rom. 5:15f.). *Charisma* is described as "the superabundance of the grace and of the gift of justification" (Rom. 5:17). *Charisma* is the "power of the Spirit" (Rom. 1:11). "The *charisma* of God is eternal life in Christ Jesus" (Rom. 6:23). *Charisma* is received in the thanksgiving that is the Eu*charist* (2 Cor. 1:11).

The one all-embracing *charisma* discloses itself in the charisms. These are extraordinary, ecstatic abilities, and anything that serves to edify the community.*

As being among the charisms, a list is given in Rom. 12:6-8. Here mention is made of prophecy, administration (*diakonía*), teaching,

---

*[*Translator's note*: When the term *charism* is referred to the special and rather spectacular gifts, which Paul several times reviews — and not entirely with an unjaundiced eye — the old theological definition is still serviceable: a charism is a *gratia gratis data*; and while the literal translation of "a grace freely given" may in itself say very little, its implication is that it is given not for the sake of the one receiving it, but for the sake of others.]

admonishing, leadership, showing mercy; and afterwards in 1 Cor. 12:4-11, there is utterance of wisdom, utterance of knowledge, faith, gifts of healing, deeds of power (miracles), prophecy, distinguishing of spirits, speaking in tongues. According to 1 Cor. 12:28-31, the grace of God has constituted "first, apostles; second, prophets; third, teachers; and besides these, miracles, gifts of healing, services of help, administrations, and speaking in tongues." Paul sets apart numerically three personal charismatic vocations; the service-ordered gifts mentioned afterwards are not to be distinguished so precisely.

For a long time the notion was broadly accepted that the New Testament Church had had in the beginning a purely charismatic constitution and was directed exclusively by those who had been charismatically called and endowed.[25] According to this notion, when the charisms began to fail and finally died out, then human law was created in the Church. This might be accepted in any case only as a makeshift; but it is contradictory to the nature of the Church.

If such an exclusive changeover cannot have taken place, it is nevertheless true that the relationship between spirit and office is a problem of the early history of the Church, and perhaps of her history in all times. The charisms were a wonderful and powerful endowment of the Church. The Church must allow their validity always. "Do not extinguish the Spirit" (1 Thess. 5:19). "Do not hinder the gift of speaking in tongues" (1 Cor. 14:39).

In the older Pauline Epistles, nothing is said of the selection and institution of officials. It probably took place — usually, at any rate, and insofar as possible — through the Spirit, in that charismatics entered into the services and offices. This does not, however, exclude spiritual and legal arrangements. According to Rom. 12:7f., administration and leadership are charisms; according to 1 Cor. 12:28, "services of help, and administrations." Charisms, accordingly, are also services of ordering and governing. Spirit and service or ministration are one, since New Testament office is described as "ministration of the Spirit" (2 Cor. 3:8).

Among the charisms Paul mentions faith (1 Cor. 12:8); and as the greater charisms, love (1 Cor. 13:1) and prophecy, this last being the teaching and comforting word (1 Cor. 14:1). Charisms, therefore, are not just the extraordinary and unusual; rather, they are operative in the daily life of the Christian. Paul's community already knew not only the charismatics but also the hard-working holders of an office, for Paul exhorts: "We beseech you to acknowledge those who labor among you and who are over you in the Lord, . . . and heed them in love for the sake of their work" (1 Thess. 5:12f.; similar in Rom. 12:8). In the community in Philippi there are "bishops and deacons" (Phil. 1:1); and at Cenchreae a woman named Phoebe served as a deacon (Rom. 16:1).

The Church at Corinth experienced a superabundance of charisms. Paul acknowledges this. He himself speaks in tongues and thanks God for it. But he would "rather speak five words with understanding in the community than a thousand words in tongues" (1 Cor. 14:18f.). Paul contrasts the plethora of charisms with the ministering and governing apostolic office, which he himself exercises and which his helpers, like Timothy and Titus, attend to — helpers whom, for that very purpose, he sends again and again to Corinth (1 Cor. 4:17; 16:10; 2 Cor. 2:13; 7:6; 8:6; 12:18). The Corinthian community acknowledged the apostolic office, inasmuch as it accepted Paul's ministry. Possible individual conflicts have ceased to exist.

Development in the early Church united spirit and office. Men "full of the Spirit and wisdom" were selected from the community in Jerusalem for office in the community and were instituted therein (Acts 6:3-7). In Antioch, the Spirit selected Paul and Barnabas for the mission. They were commissioned through the laying on of hands (Acts 13:1-3). The leaders of the community at Ephesus, called "the presbyters" and "bishops," are "commissioned by the Holy Spirit" (Acts 20:17, 28). In this commissioning and appointing, the Holy Spirit operated through men. Each one has his charism, with which he is to minister to the community (1 Peter 4:10). All are charismatics. Each Christian life is a charism.

In the Pastoral Epistles, charism is the grace of office, which is imparted "sacramentally" through the laying on of hands and prayer (1 Tim. 4:14; 2 Tim. 1:6). Those who hold office are to be chosen with a careful view to their ability and virtue. Divine charism and human institution become as one. This is an arrangement achieved already in the New Testament, for which reason it ought to have validity in the Church.

2. OFFICE

Ministry and office can be distinguished by the fact that ministry designates a single instance or even a repeated performance. Ministries become office when the ministry is permanently joined to one person, who then accomplishes his ministry with the full authority of a specially qualified holder of office.

a) Terminology and Concepts

In its terminology and concepts of office and offices, the New Testament is partly determined by its milieu and is partly independent. The officialdom of Israel's worship and government was concentrated in Jerusalem. The Greco-Roman world established official classes in service of the state and of cities, and hence in a broadly extended profane and religious cooperative organization. This milieu offered the New Testament manifold designations for offices. If it is important to know which were accepted, it is just as important to know which were rejected, because apparently the latter were perceived as unsuitable for the Church.

As titles [26] known to the New Testament but used by it only in an extra-ecclesiastical way, we may adduce the following:

1) ἀρχή = *dominion, administrative authority.* An ἄρχων τῆς συναγωγῆς is mentioned in Matthew 9:18 and Luke 8:41. To the disciples it is said, "You will be led before synagogues and magistrates and authorities (πρὸς τὰς ἀρχὰς καὶ τὰς ἐξουσίας — Luke 12:11). Titus 3:1 admonishes: Remind them to be obedient to the official authorities (ἀρχαῖς ἐξουσίαις). Of the conduct of such rulers, however, Matthew 20:25f. says :"The rulers of the Gentiles lord it over them and their great ones make their authority felt. Do not let it be thus among you."

2) ἐξουσία = *authority; sphere of influence.* The centurion at Capernaum says: "I too am a man subject to authority" (Matthew 8:9). Jesus is subject to the "jurisdiction of Herod" (Luke 23:7). Paul speaks of "higher authorities" of the state (Rom. 13:1; see also Luke 12:11 and Titus 3:1). On the use of power, Luke 22:25 makes this judgment: "The kings of the Gentiles lord it over them, and their authorities have themselves called benefactors."

Paul uses the word ἐξουσία in 2 Cor. 10:8; 13:10 for his authority as an apostle; nevertheless, he curbs it. The office is given him by Christ for building up, not for destroying.

3) κύριος, κυριεύειν = *to be lord*. According to Matthew 20:25, the authorities lord it over the Gentiles. In 2 Cor. 1:24 and 1 Peter 5:3, such rule is denied in the Church.

4) βάρος = *importance, power*. Paul could indeed insist on the weight of his apostolic office. But he prefers to accomplish what he does by love (1 Thess. 2:7).

5) τιμή = *honor, dignity*. In Heb. 5:4 this term is used in reference to the office of the high priest.

In place of such designations of office, the New Testament mostly uses for office in general the title διακονία = *service* or *ministry*.[27] The term has its precedent in a saying of Jesus. In declining lordship after the fashion of the world, Jesus says: "Whoever wishes to be great among you, let him be the slave (δοῦλος) of all" (Mark 10:43f.). There is honor and greatness in the community, but it is the honor of ministering.

Jesus himself rejected other power and authority as Satanic temptation (Matthew 4:8). He himself has come to serve, and in that way he brings God's kingdom closer (Mark 10:45). In the midst of the disciples he is like one who serves (Luke 22:27). This is shown in John 13:4-16. The washing of feet by Christ is an example of ministry for the apostles and for the community. "I have given you an example, so that you too may do as I have done" (John 13:15).

Every office is service (Acts 1:25). Preaching is "ministry of the word" (Luke 1:2; Acts 6:4). Others have the "ministry of the table" (Acts 6:2). Charisms are offices of the "ministry" (Rom. 12:7; 1 Cor. 12:5). In all things, office must be "ministry in the spirit of ministering" (Rom. 12:7). The new covenant is "ministry of the spirit and of justification" (2 Cor. 3:8f.). Paul's ministry is to be without blame (2 Cor. 6:3). He wants to "bring honor to his ministry" (Rom. 11:13). It is true of every office: "We are not lords of your faith but ministers of your joy" (2 Cor. 1:24).

Minister soon becomes a title of office in the Church (see below, §4, 8). It thereby becomes a very generic term for an office. But it must not be forgotten that office is also designated as grace (χάρις — see above, §3, 1, a), and ministry, as gifts of grace (χαρίσματα — see above, §3, 1, c). If ministry designates office in horizontal planes according to social significance, then *charis* (charisms) designates the same office in vertical planes as divine vocation and authorization.

b) Office in the New Testament

If one attempts to extract and describe the content and exercise of office from the New Testament, naturally one ought to inquire first in the Synoptics. Belonging probably to the years 70–90 A.D., the Synoptic Gospels presuppose the Church and office. They are written about in the experience of the already existing office.

1) Synoptic Gospels. The Synoptic Gospels tell of the Twelve, who certainly have at first an eschatological task (Matthew 10:6f.; 19:28), and who therefore administrate no ecclesiastical office. Nevertheless, the apostles become, in the post-paschal Church, bearers of office (see below, §4, 1, a). They are represented in this role already in the Synoptics.[28] That it is a later period of the Church is made apparent already in the first mission of the Twelve in Matthew 10:12-23. Separation and, indeed, enmity is already presupposed between Church and Synagogue. The disciples are handed over to sanhedrins and scourged in synagogues. These are "their" — the Jews' — synagogues (Matthew 10:17).

The mission, therefore, has already pushed ahead to the Gentiles. The apostles have to give witness "before governors and kings" (Matthew 10:18). Martyrdom may be required of them (Matthew 10:28). Families are divided over the question of the Christian faith (Matthew 10:21, 35). The name of Jesus is in itself already grounds for persecution (Matthew 10:22).

The Twelve are already seen as one with the missionaries and the officeholders in the community. In the Synoptics, Mark (6:8-13) and Matthew (10:4-16) each have their one discourse for the sending out of the Twelve; Luke has two discourses, one for the mission of the Twelve (9:1-6), the other for the mission of the Seventy (10:1-20). If the Twelve represent Israel, and the Seventy represent the Gentiles (see below, §4, 1, b), it is a further indication that the mission and the message has long since gone beyond Israel to the Gentiles, and is understood as expanded to the whole Church.

According to the mission discourses, the task of Jesus' heralds is the proclamation of the kingdom of God (Matthew 10:7). They have the authority, through healing the sick, raising the dead, and expelling demons to summon up the kingdom of God as a restored world, just as Jesus himself does (Matthew 11:4f.; see the present work, Vol. 2, pp. 71–76). The word of proclamation is powerful far beyond the human word. It brings peace or judgment (Matthew 10:13f.; see below, §6, 3). Christ is identical with the heralds of the gospel (Matthew 10:40), and also with those who bear office in the Church (Luke 10:16; John 13:20; 1 Thess. 2:13; 2 Cor. 5:20; 13:3).

In a comparison of the parallel passages of Mark 6:8f., Matthew 10:9f., and Luke 9:3 and 10:4, it is clear that very much consideration was given to details. In Mark 6:8f. a pack, bread, coppers in their purse, and a change of tunics are forbidden, but sandals and a staff are allowed. In Matthew 10:9f. a pack, gold, silver and coppers in their purse, and a change of tunics are proscribed, but so too are sandals and a staff. In Luke 9:3 the Twelve are forbidden a staff and a pack, a change of tunics, bread, and silver coins; in Luke 10:4 the Seventy are to carry neither purse nor pack nor sandals.

The demands are quite severe, since even a beggar was obliged to carry a pack for bread on his journey and for his poor possessions, and with it, a staff to lean on and to use in fending off wild beasts. If Mark 6:8f. is the oldest of the texts, then sandals and staff were at first permitted. This is a bow to human frailty.[29] Poverty is increased in the later texts, when the heralds are permitted neither sandals nor staff. The demands become more rigid and more statutory. The meaning is clear: in one way or another the herald is made entirely dependent upon the faith, in which dependence he is protected and receives what is necessary for his daily living.

At the same time there is the question of the support of the heralds. The Twelve are obligated to perform their ministry free of charge (Matthew 10:9f.). They are, however, to receive hospitality (Mark 6:10). The communities are to see to the maintenance of the prophets (Matthew 10:41f.). The question of the support of the missionaries and of the holders of office will engage the communities further. Paul appeals in 1 Cor. 9:14 to a "saying of the Lord," according to which "those who minister to the gospel are to live from the gospel," which is in harmony with the logion of Source Q in Matthew 10:10 and

Luke 10:7. The question is opened again in 1 Peter 5:2 (see §3, 2, b, 3 below).

Just as with the drawing of later ecclesiastical office into the accounts of the first mission of the heralds, so too will one have to explain the Synoptic histories of the vocational summons. In Mark 1:16-20, it is effectively stated that office is a calling of God, which does not presuppose human preparation and virtue. The Twelve are called away from utterly worldly occupations, from the manual labor of the fisherman; indeed, even a tax collector of evil repute can be called (Mark 2:14).

Vocation is not invitation, but a curt and rigid injunction: Here, then! After me! (Matthew 4:19). The one called follows immediately. The One who calls and who issues the summons is Lord of the Church. His summoning word creates anew. Those called as fishermen are to become menfishers (Mark 1:17). Their former vocation experiences a new depth, a salvational-historical depth; perhaps the prophetic word of Jer. 16:16 figures in this: "I send out many fishers, and they are to fish them." The vocation of menfishers opposes the apostles, on God's side, to an immensely broad world. The kingdom of heaven, however, is like a dragnet which, cast into the sea, brings in much prey (Matthew 13:47f.).

It may already be the voice of a solicitude for a sufficiently abundant ministry in the community when this solicitude expresses its exhortation as a saying of the Lord: "Beseech the Harvest-master, that he may send workers into his harvest" (Matthew 9:38). The figure of speech is advanced by the rabbis: "The day is short, the work is much, the workers are slow, the reward is great, and the Householder is importuning" (H. L. Strack and P. Billerbeck, *Kommentar zum Neuen Testament*, Vol. 1 [1922], p. 527). The community has to learn by its experience that the eschatological harvest day is postponed. Jesus and his first disciples have sown; later generations are to reap (John 4:37f.).

In a community regulation the disciples are charged by a saying of Jesus to lead an erring brother back into the community (Matthew 18:15-17). In regard thereof, the power of binding and loosing is decreed and transmitted to the disciples. In one instance this is imparted to Peter (Matthew 16:18f.), and in another instance to the disciples universally (Matthew 18:18). We hardly have the right to understand these disciples (Matthew 18:1) as constituting only the twelve apostles (see below, §4, 1, b). This binding and loosing takes place in the teaching word and in the obligating word, as well as in the word that releases from demoniacal power.

In another form, this saying appears in John 20:22f., in the commission of the resurrected Jesus to his disciples: "Receive the Holy Spirit! Whose sins you shall forgive, they are forgiven them; and whose sins you shall retain, they are retained." In Christ, the Church has the authority to lift off the burden of sin and to impart new life. This authority is discharged in baptism, in adjudicating through the words that take away sin, and in the whole salvational ministry of the Church (see below, §8, 3, c, 1 and §8, 4).

In the Gospels, a paramount teaching authority, such as governed rabbinism, is denied. In Matthew 23:8-10, through a saying of the Lord, the titles rabbi, teacher, father, and master[30] are prohibited in the community. The words stand in sharp contrast to the adulation and attention given the teaching authority in Judaism. The rabbi is highly honored for his familiarity with the word of God and for his knowledge of that word. His learned decision is awaited and accepted. The "sayings of the fathers" were collected in books. It is inconceivable that disciples near to Jesus and near to his times did not have themselves called rabbi, teacher, father, and master.

The saying of the Lord prohibiting these titles presupposes the later conditions of the Judeo-Christian community. The public title "Christ" is likewise a later confession (see the present work, Vol. 2, p. 180).

Matthew 23:8-10 is a prophetic saying about the arrangement of the Christian community, probably a warning in the face of titles and offices already taking shape. The terms teacher, father, leader are beginning to obtain. A position of Christian Scribe might have been in the offing (Matthew 13:52; 23:24).

Perhaps in Matthew 23:8, God, the Father, is understood as being the immediate Teacher of the faith, just as the faith clearly stands in an immediate relationship to God and requires no human instruction (John 6:45; 1 Thess. 4:9; Heb. 8:10f.; §6, 4). It is accordingly that the disciples, as children of the one Father, are brothers among themselves (Matthew 23:8). Now, however, Christ alone is Teacher and Master (Matthew 23:10). In his following, the disciples are always brothers among brothers, never master over others. The disciples call themselves brothers primarily in accord with Jewish usage, since Israel, in virtue of her blood unity from her fathers, knows herself as a great family (so too in Acts 2:29 and Rom. 9:3).

Christian brotherhood is newly founded around Christ as its center, since Christ designates his disciples as brothers and sisters (Mark 3:35; John 20:17). As the "First-born among many brothers" (Rom. 8:29; Heb. 2:11f.), he is the center and head of the community of brothers. Therefore, in the community of disciples, the claim of being teacher is limited, if not prohibited. In the concept of father, however, the concept of begetting is contained; and in spiritual fatherhood, that of spiritual begetting. No disciple can claim to stand in a relationship of generation to another. It is simply and straightforwardly God who is the Father (Eph. 3:14f.).

2) Epistles of Paul. With some reflections we will treat comprehensively of the understanding of office in the Epistles of the New Testament, and in the first place, those of Paul.[31] For Paul the apostolate is *charis*, a calling accompanied with grace (Rom. 1:5; see above, §3, 1, b). The calling, commission, and appointment take place through God. "God has made some in the Church to be, first, apostles, second, prophets, third, teachers" (1 Cor. 12:28; similar in 12:6). Paul knows that he has himself been called and appointed by Christ and God. "Paul, an apostle not from men nor through a man, but through Jesus Christ and God the Father, who raised him from the dead" (Gal. 1:1).

Paul is able to distinguish the gifts in accord with the basically Trinitarian structure of the salvational operation: "There are varieties of gifts of grace, but only one and the same Spirit; and there are varieties of ministries, but only one and the same Lord; and there are varieties of operations of power, but only one and the same God" (1 Cor. 12:4-6).

In an image rich in content, Paul says that he himself, as an apostle, experiences something like being led in triumph in his farflung travels (2 Cor. 2:14f.). The triumphant Victor is God in Christ. By means of the apostle the odor of the knowledge of God is made manifest in every place. The apostle is the "fragrance of Christ for God, for some an odor of life unto salvation, for others an odor of death unto death."

Perhaps Paul combines the two images of triumphal procession and of odor for the reason that such a procession was enveloped in a cloud of aromatic odors which poured forth from the incense in thuribles carried in the procession or stationed along the streets. His imagery may also involve a calling to mind that a vaporous scent indicates for plants, animals, and men either a life-dispensing or a lethal fluid (see Job 14:9 and the commentaries thereon). The ministry of the apostle, however, produces a separation to salvation or condemnation.

God has established both reconciliation and the ministry of reconciliation (2 Cor. 5:18-20). God reconciled the world with himself. In this process no change took place in God, as if men had somehow appeased his anger. On the contrary, we were reconciled with God through God's action (Rom. 5:10). Further reconciliation takes place in the ministry of reconciliation, as the Apostle states in his message: "In Christ's place we are messengers, since through us God exhorts, 'Let yourselves be reconciled with God!'"

In the word of the apostles, God's word goes forth to the world. "You welcomed our preaching of God's word, not as human talk, but for what it truly is, God's word, which is now operative among you, the faithful" (1 Thess. 2:13; see below, §6, 2).

Paul knows also of apostles who are appointed by the Church. Even of these he says that they are "Christ's glory"— δόξα Χριστοῦ (2 Cor. 8:23). The remark can hardly be intended to mean that these apostles are an honor for Christ. In the New Testament, hardly ever does δόξα mean the honor that proceeds from men, but almost invariably the glory of God. Thus, in this place Paul means that the power and glory of God and Christ are made manifest by office in the Church and throughout the world.

Paul performs his ministry "in word and deed, through power of signs and wonders, through power of the Spirit" (Rom. 15:18f.). The Apostle will have understood as included therein powerful charismatic preaching, and perhaps with signs he includes cultic-sacramental action. But he is also convinced that he has the authority to accomplish visible miracles (2 Cor. 12:2; see the present work, Vol. 2, p. 70f.).

The authority of office is answerable to God and to the community. Paul is conscious of his office as an apostle. He is able to admonish and to command by the "grace" which has been given him (Rom. 12:3). He appeals to his authority, which certainly cannot be at his personal disposal. As given by the Lord, it is tied to the building up and not the tearing down of the community (2 Cor. 10:8; 13:10). Paul is steward of the mysterious revelations of God, and therefore certainly obligated even in this regard as servant of Christ (1 Cor. 4:1). The apostle is ambassador of God (2 Cor. 5:20), and at the same time he is minister of God and of Christ (Rom. 1:1; 1 Cor. 3:5). He must not, therefore, proclaim himself (2 Cor. 4:5). The divine mission of the apostle does not cover arbitrarily favored contentions. On the contrary, it precludes human pretensions and human authority.

Paul can designate himself and his co-workers as "God's co-workers" (1 Cor. 3:9; 1 Thess. 3:2). At 1 Thess. 3:2; some of the manuscripts read "God's minister." Nevertheless, the original is probably "God's co-worker." The change was probably intended to soften the statement, because "God's co-worker" seemed too pretentious. But it is said of the work common to God and men: "I planted, Apollos watered, but God gave the growth. So neither he that plants is anything, nor he that waters, but it is God, who gives the growth" (1 Cor. 3:6f.). The human work is to be done before God, and before God it must be answered for.

When bound by God's law, Paul always endeavored to base his decisions and his teaching on the Old Testament Scriptures. God's work is all that counts. The apostle, instead of commanding, beseeches and admonishes "for the sake of God's mercy" (Rom. 12:1). The authority to which Paul is subject and which he must make count is the word of Christ (1 Thess. 4:15; 1 Cor. 7:10; 9:14). Freedom is grounded in the Spirit, and it must so remain. "Where the Spirit of the Lord is, there is freedom" (2 Cor. 3:17).

When it is necessary, Paul regards his office in respect to the Church as unqualifiedly true; this is the case with the altercation with the Judaizers in Galatia (Gal. 3:5) and with the false apostles in Corinth (2 Cor. 10–13). Because his appointment is not from the community, the apostle is over it and is subject neither to its mandate (Gal. 1:1) nor to its judgment (1 Cor. 4:3). Basically, however, Paul does want to arrive at his decision in agreement with the community. "If you and my spirit be gathered together with the power of the Lord, it will be in the name of the Lord Jesus" that a guilty member is expelled from the community (1 Cor. 5:3-5).

On the exclusion and re-admission of a member of the community who has insulted Paul personally, he wants to decide along with the majority (2 Cor. 2:6, 8). The Apostle does not want "to put a halter" on the Corinthians (1 Cor. 7:35). Paul appeals to the insight of the community (Rom. 6:16; 1 Cor. 6:19; 10:15; 11:13). He admonishes for conscience' sake (Rom. 13:5). Even natural and rational ethics is valid (Phil. 4:8). A basic principle is: "Everything is to take place honorably and in proper order" (1 Cor. 14:40). For "God is not a God of disorder but of peace" (1 Cor. 14:33). In the difficult question of the orderly arrangement of marriage, Paul argues in a versatile and penetrating way (1 Cor. 7); and likewise in respect to the veiling of women (1 Cor. 11:3-16). The apostle is obligated to tradition, and this he hands on (1 Cor. 11:16; 15:1-8).

3) First Epistle of Peter. 1 Peter 5:1-5 provides a glimpse of office and the administration of office in late apostolic times.[32] The Epistle composed under the name of Peter is probably to be dated toward the end of the first century. Peter appeals to "the elders" as their "fellow-elder." These elders, i.e., presbyters, are not the members of the community more advanced in age, but the superiors or leaders of the community who obtained their office by election, in a comparable fashion to the elders of the synagogues (see below, §4, 3). The community has presiding officials. Peter stands in their ranks. He shares with them the labors and the hopes. Peter and the elders are witnesses of Christ, he as eyewitness, they as witnesses through preaching. The two kinds of testimony are of like importance. The office of an apostle and the office of an elder of the Church are conceived as being of like station. The office of elder of the Church, therefore, is one of high regard and of weighty claim in the community.

Peter exhorts the elders (often termed "presbyters" in English, the latter term being simply the comparative degree of the Greek adjective meaning "old"): "Pasture the flock of God." The office is like the ministry of a shepherd, following after and tending his sheep, even as it is described in other places (John 21:15f.; Acts 20:28; Eph. 4:1).

In 1 Peter 5:4; Christ is termed the Archshepherd, whose parousia the Church awaits (just as in Heb. 13:20, Christ is called the Great Shepherd). The holders of office are in that way made comparable to Christ, the Lord of the Church; and they perform his ministry in the community. The shepherds (or pastors, if you will) are to perform their ministry "not being constrained thereto, but eagerly in accord with God's mandate, not out of ignoble greed, but with a free giving of oneself." Office can already be perceived as a troublesome burden which one accepts reluctantly and bears unwillingly, whether because of the numerous and onerous duties it involves, or in the face of the impending persecution (1 Peter 4:12-19), which can make the office a danger to the one who holds it.

The admonition presupposes that office is transmitted firmly and permanently. Otherwise it would be possible for its possessor to give it up when he became tired of it.

Office is "God's mandate." This mandate from God takes place through election and appointment by the community. Office obligates not just before the community but before God.

The elders must conduct themselves in their office "not greedily, but with a free giving of oneself." Thus, office can already bring emoluments. The holders of office can accept donations from the community. There is already the temptation of money. The problem appears already in the discourse at the mission of the Twelve (Mark 6:8f.; above, §3, 2, b, 1), as also when Paul (1 Cor. 9:7-12; 2 Cor. 12:13-17) maintains that the community owes support to the apostle and to his wife, even though Paul and Barnabas make no use of this right. The admonition is continued when 1 Tim. 3:3; Titus 1:7, 11; and the *Didache* 15:1 (Jurgens, no. 9) demand of bishops freedom from self-interest and greed.

Peter further exhorts the holders of office not to discharge their office as if they were "lords of the inheritance, but as an example to the flock."[33] Like greed, the striving for power can likewise endanger the administration of office. The elders must not lord it over the community, as the great ones among the Gentiles do (Mark 10:42; see above, § 3, 2, a). The community is an inheritance. This will be understood in accord with Old Testament linguistic usage. Just as the land is assigned by God to the Israelites as an inheritance and a gift (Num. 33:53f.), so too the community is really the property of God (Acts 26:18; Col. 1:12). The surest means of administrating one's office properly, however, as Peter ultimately says, is by one's own good example, and not by command.

4) Pastoral Epistles. The Pastoral Epistles, written perhaps about the year 100 A.D., show that toward the end of the apostolic age, office has become quite significant. As disciples and friends of Paul, Timothy presides over the church of Ephesus (1 Tim. 1:3), and Titus over the church of Crete (Titus 1:5). Neither carries any title of office; they have their fullness of power by the directive and authority of Paul.

No longer is there any talk of Spirit-imparted charisms in the community. There is only the charism of office, which is transmitted to new officials through prayer and the imposition of hands.[34] The community's role in this is certainly one only of listening and praying (1 Tim. 2:1, 8; 4:13-16; 2 Tim. 1:6).

Such a rite for the transmission of office and installation therein is the practice already in the Old Testament. Thus Moses, in accord with God's commission, installs Joshua as his successor (Num. 27:21-23; cf. 4 Kings 13:16). It is by a laying on of hands that the rabbi is installed in his office as fully authorized teacher, a practice testified to since the first century A.D., in which ceremony the teacher, with two assistants participating, imposes hands on the subject.

New Testament office, like the rabbinate, probably carries with it also the right and duty of teaching (1 Tim. 1:3; 4:13; 5:17), and, more than this, the celebrating of the divine ministry (1 Tim. 2:1) and the leadership of the community (1 Tim. 3:15, 5:1f.). The bearer of office is to be an example in everything (1 Tim. 4:12; 6:11-14). He is a minister of Jesus Christ (1 Tim. 4:6).

The laying on of hands does take place, however, "through prophecy" (1 Tim. 4:14). In the installation, the essential pledge indicates, through externally visible action, an intellectual and spiritual continuity. The pledge must be taken in the faith that unites the generations. There is such a continuity of doctrine when the ordinand is admonished to pass on to others what he has himself heard through many witnesses (2 Tim. 2:2). Thus he is to be "in the grace of Jesus Christ" (2 Tim. 2:1). Apostolic succession is not a mechanical or magical succession of impositions of hands, but a fullness of apostolicity.

§ 4. OFFICES

With every enumeration and description of the individual offices[35] in the Church, it can be stated in advance that the essential offices are attributed also to Christ. He is Apostle (Heb. 3:1), Priest (Heb. 3:1), Prophet (Luke 7:16; 24:19; John 6:14; Acts 3:22), Teacher (Matthew 23:8; 13:13; John 10:11; Heb. 13:20; 1 Peter 2:25; 5:4), Bishop (1 Peter 2:25), and Deacon (Mark 10:45; Luke 22:27; Rom. 15:8). All the ecclesiastical offices make effective the one work of Christ.

1. THE TWELVE AND THE APOSTLES

If the individual offices in the Church are to be described, the apostolate[36] must certainly be mentioned first. And with the apostolate, the question of the Twelve must be distinguished from the question of the apostles. The two concepts were later united and equated.

a) The Twelve Apostles

The importance of the number twelve even in our own culture, both as an ordinal number and as a measure (consider that there are twelve pence to the shilling, twelve inches to the foot, twice twelve hours to the day, twelve months to the year, twelve semi-tone progressions to the octave, etc.) is of Babylonian inheritance. In Babylon, using a duodecimal rather than a decimal system, the basic unit was not ten but twelve. Precisely why that number was employed is not explicable with a clarity that is entirely convincing.

Israel was, like some other peoples of the Mediterranean world, organized as a nation of twelve tribes. The basis may be that these lived in amphictyony around a sanctuary (the holy ark?) in which each tribe was obliged to minister one month in the year. At the time of the New Testament, the twelve tribes had long since ceased to be a reality, but were more an idealized historical memory. The writing entitled *The Testaments of the Twelve Patriarchs*, to be dated in the first century B.C., is already the product only of this memory. According to the *Psalms of Solomon* 17:28, the Messiah will reign justly over the tribes of Israel. In Qumran twelve laymen and three priests formed the council of the community (1 QS 8:1). The twelve men probably represented Israel's twelve tribes, while the three priests represented the participation of Levi's sons (Num. 3:17).

Certainly it was in reference to the twelve tribes that Jesus chose the twelve disciples whom he sent out as messengers to Israel. He promised them: "In the rebirth when the Son of Man shall sit on the throne of his glory, you too shall sit on twelve thrones, to judge the twelve tribes of Israel" (Matthew 19:28; expanded in Luke 22:28-30).[37] The more original form of the saying is more likely that contained in Matthew rather than that of Luke. Whereas Matthew speaks of twelve thrones, Luke speaks only of thrones, not specifying a number, possibly because he supposes that no throne could have been promised to the traitor Judas.

The promise employs the old concept of the heavenly throne of Yahweh (Is. 6:1; 66:1; Jer. 17:12f.). In the vision of Daniel (7:9-28), the Ancient of Days sits on a heavenly throne, those judging seated on thrones around him. Apocalyptics and rabbinism developed the notion further. At the final judgment the Messiah appears on the "throne of the divine glory" (*Ethiopic Apocalypse of Henoch* 45:3). This representation is used also in the Christian apocalyptics. The throne of God is viewed in awesome mystery (Apoc. 4). Christ is enthroned with the Father (Apoc. 3:21). At the beginning of the messianic rule, the saints on their thrones sit in at the judgment (Apoc. 20:4). At the general or world judgment, God appears on a "great white throne" (Apoc. 20:11). In accord with such a tradition, the saying of the Lord in Matthew 19:28 declares that at the arrival of the kingdom of God the Twelve will judge with the Son of Man, as eschatological princes of Israel.

The Twelve were not originally princes of the Church. This probably explains also the quite remarkable fact that the Twelve, even though they were appointed by Jesus, have, as individuals, so little importance in tradition, or at least, in that of the Gospels. The commission of the Twelve was limited. Only a few of the apostles enter, as historical figures, into the history of the Church.

The calling of the Twelve is told in such a way in Mark 3:13-19 (and parallels; see also Acts 1:13) that a list of twelve names is adduced in the text. This cannot be understood as if the historical Jesus had, at that hour, called the Twelve individually and one after another. Mark (1:16) has already told previously of the calling of Simon and Andrew, as well as the sons of Zebedee, James and John (1:19) and of Levi (2:14); now he names them again among the Twelve. Moreover,

John 1:35-51 tells of the calling of several, and among them some of the apostles, in another way.

The lists of the Twelve are not handed down in an entirely uniform tradition. They are in total accord only in giving the number as twelve. Mark and Matthew mention (in the tenth position) a Thaddeus; Luke, in his Gospel and in the Acts, names (in eleventh position) a Jude, son of James. Another old tradition names in place of Thaddeus a certain Lebbeus. The later identification of Jude-Thaddeus-Lebbeus is questionable.

The list is always headed by Peter, who, in the tradition of the New Testament, is the proto-apostle; and it always closes with Judas Iscariot, the traitor. Later appraisal is mirrored in the ordering of the list. The origin of the list of the Twelve is not clear. It does not seem to be a gleaning from a proportionately broad tradition of the life and missionary work of the twelve apostles. Of the twelve in the list, the missionary operations only of Peter and of Zebedee's sons, James and John, are known. Otherwise entirely unknown are James, the son of Alpheus; Thaddeus; and Simon the Cananean, also called the Zealot, although it must remain questionable whether the Simons called Cananean and Zealot, are ready to be identified.

The oldest tradition, contained in Mark, does not, in referring to the Twelve, call them apostles. It says only that Jesus summoned the Twelve "in order to send them out" (Mark 3:14; 6:7). Upon their return, he terms them "messengers that were sent out" ($\dot{\alpha}\pi\acute{o}\sigma\tau o\lambda o\iota$). They do not bear the name regularly, but only on the occasion of their mission. In Matthew 10:2, the Evangelist attaches the title apostles to the Twelve. It is first stated in Luke 6:13 that the Twelve were called apostles by Jesus himself. Matthew and Luke both reproduce, each in a different way, the result of the development by which the Twelve had long since borne the name of apostles in the Church.

According to 1 Cor. 15:5, "the Twelve," not yet called apostles in this place, experienced the appearance of the resurrected Christ. This explains at the same time their mission as witnesses. This renewed commissioning and sending out of the (eleven) apostles is recounted also in Matthew 28:19; Luke 24:46-49; and Acts 1:4-8. At this appearance of Christ, Judas Iscariot now being dead, it is a question really, of course, of only eleven.

This, nevertheless, will not suffice for concluding that 1 Cor. 15:5 knew nothing of the selection of the Twelve by the historical Jesus and of the death of Judas Iscariot; this would tend to indicate a tradition that the Twelve were called for the first time by the resurrected Christ. The Gospel accounts of the calling of the Twelve by Jesus would be unhistorical. When 1 Cor. 15:5 mentions Twelve, it is simply a reference to the college of disciples, long since known collectively as the Twelve.

Tradition perceived it as a difficulty that the traitor Judas belonged to the Twelve, so that one tried to account for this failure and to preserve Jesus from any error. For this reason the Gospels say that Jesus knew who was to betray him (John 6:64). Jesus sends the traitor himself to his work (John 13:27). It could hardly be a satisfactory explanation that the community had invented this image of Judas in order to excuse it afterward. Thus, for the most part, the calling of Judas and therefore of the Twelve by Jesus must be regarded as historical.

In the Acts of the Apostles, the Twelve are regularly termed "apostles," the center and leaders of the community (Acts 1:2; 2:27; 4:35–5:18; 6:6; 8:1; 11:1; 15:2-30). Peter (Acts 1:15; 2:37; 3:1; 5:29; 8:14; 11:2; 12:3) and John (Acts 3:1; 8:14) are called apostles by name. The doctrine of the apostles is authoritative (Acts 2:42). They are, in the persecution now beginning, witnesses of the faith (Acts 4:13, 33). Through the laying on of hands they impart the Spirit (Acts 8:14-17).

Since by the rule educed in the Acts of the Apostles (1:21-26) in accord with the Gospels, only those were to be apostles who had had a personal companionship with Jesus, Paul and Barnabas accordingly do not belong to the (twelve) apostles. As men "sent out by the Holy Spirit" (Acts 13:4) they are called apostles in Acts 14:4, 14 only as messengers. This makes clear the great respect Luke has for the title and office of apostle, and perhaps also an intention to guard the name of apostle against abuse; for it was already being used falsely (2 Cor. 12:11; Apoc. 2:2; *Didache* 11:3-6 [Jurgens, no. 7a]).

Paul[38] too established contact with the apostles in Jerusalem. But on two visits there, the first time he met only Cephas (Gal. 1:18f.), and the second time only Cephas and John (Gal. 2:1-10); and both times he met also James, "the brother of the Lord." There is no talk of the

Twelve. Paul designates the old apostles as "the men in authority" and, drawing a figure from the structure of a church building, "the pillars,"[39] the latter, however, it would appear, with the reservation of their "being considered the pillars" (Gal. 2:2, 6, 9). In any case, the claim of the pillars is limited to the Judeo-Christian area. The apostolate of Paul to the Gentiles has equal importance and dignity (Gal. 2:9).

Paul is probably defending his apostolate against its having been impugned when he emphatically maintains that he is "an apostle, not from men, but through Jesus Christ and God the Father, who raised him from the dead" (Gal. 1:1). He is an apostle not merely as an ambassador of the community (2 Cor. 8:23). He is Apostle like the Twelve called immediately by Christ (2 Cor. 8:23); if he was not called by the earthly Jesus, he was nonetheless called by the exalted Lord, whom he saw in the apparition on the road to Damascus (1 Cor. 9:1, 15:8).

In late apostolic writings, the apostles are guarantors of right faith and doctrine (1 Tim. 2:7; 2 Tim. 1:11; Jude 17; 2 Peter 3:2). The conviction of the teaching office of the apostles is taking shape. The apostles are the foundation bearing the weight of the Church (Matthew 16:17; Eph. 2:20; Apoc. 21:14). They are also her heavenly witnesses and guardians (Apoc. 18:20).

If the apostles are, in the narrower sense of the term, those disciples whom Jesus himself called and ultimately sent out in his apparitions, and who were among the first to receive the Spirit (Acts 1:21-26; 2:1-4), then there can be for them no substitute and no successor. To be sure, the college was brought once more to its ideal number of twelve through the late election of Matthias (Acts 1:26). After the death of James (Acts 12:2), no such election took place.

Insofar, however, as the apostles left communities, as was the case in Jerusalem, others would have to undertake this ministry. To assist the apostles, the primitive community had already appointed seven men, who were to minister primarily to the social welfare of the community (Acts 6:1-6). The community of Antioch dispatched Paul and Barnabas on mission (Acts 13:1-3). Paul mentions assistants and helpers in his Epistles (1 Cor. 1:1; 2 Cor. 1:1; Gal. 1:2; Phil. 1:1; 1 Thess.

1:1; Philemon 1f.). According to the Pastoral Epistles, Paul appointed his disciples Timothy and Titus as leaders of the churches in Ephesus (1 Tim. 1:3) and Crete (Titus 1:5).

b) Other Apostles

The New Testament mentions other apostles besides the Twelve. According to Luke 10:1, after the Twelve, Jesus sent out still another seventy disciples. If the Twelve were sent to the twelve tribes of Israel, then the seventy were sent to the Gentiles (in accord with Gen. 10). As men sent out, these too were "apostles." Did they also bear the name?

According to 1 Cor. 15:7, the resurrected Christ appeared, after the Twelve, to "all the apostles." These apostles were probably other than and a larger number than the Twelve. Through the appearance of Christ these apostles too were made witnesses and were "sent out." Paul, too, knows himself as an additional apostle, called by the exalted Lord (1 Cor. 9:1; 15:8; Gal. 1:15f.). But Paul also tells that Christ appeared "to five hundred of the brethren all at one time." Certainly these were not all apostles. The apparition of Christ does not of itself make an apostle. Also required is mission.

Paul makes mention of Andronicus and Junias as "outstanding among the apostles." They were fellow-countrymen of Paul, therefore Jewish Christians; and they were Christians even before Paul (Rom. 16:7). By whom were they called to be apostles? Probably by the Spirit. The apostles mentioned in 1 Cor. 12:28 in first place as charismatic apostles were hardly the Twelve; rather, they were apostles called by the Spirit. This will hold gold also for Eph. 4:11, according to which the exalted Christ has appointed some to be apostles in the Church and others to other ministries.

In 2 Cor. 8:23 Paul mentions "apostles of the communities." They were commissioned and dispatched by the communities, possibly as having previously been charismatically endowed. The "apostle" Epaphroditus, mentioned in Phil. 2:25, is a man commissioned by the community.

In sharp altercation Paul mentions opponents who presumably styled themselves apostles, the "great apostles" of 2 Cor. 11:5 and 12:11, and the "lying apostles" of 2 Cor. 11:13. They probably regarded themselves as "ministers of Christ" called by the Spirit (2 Cor. 11:23).

There was a larger circle of apostles, who explained their being commissioned in various ways. This was probably the original perception and mode of expression. The name apostle was only later applied to the Twelve and was finally limited to them.

c) *The Term* Apostle

The word ἀπόστολος = *apostle* is not easy to explain.[40] In profane Greek the word usually signified a fleet sent out or an army of colonists; only rarely did it designate an individual person. In the Gnosis, the ambassador sent from God as the agent of divine revelation can be called an apostle.[41] In the Greek Old Testament Bible, only once is a prophet designated "apostle." Nevertheless, the word ἀποστέλλειν = *to send out* is frequently used in the Septuagint; thus, in significant texts like Exod. 3:10-15; 4:13; Jer. 7:25. Of the prophets above all it is said that they are "sent"; thus in Is. 49:1 (echoed in Gal. 1:15); Is. 61:1 (quoted in Luke 4:18 and Matthew 11:5); Mal. 3:1 (quoted in Matthew 11:10 and Mark 1:2). One may accordingly accept that the primitive community, when it employed the term ἀπόστολος, would have had a recollection of the use of the term ἀποστέλλειν in the Greek Old Testament; but if it did not wholly re-create the term, it did so very nearly, because the term as yet had but very little of the meaning that the New Testament gives it.

The New Testament borrowed almost all the titles of the officials of the Church from its Jewish and Greco-Roman surroundings. We will treat first of such titles as originate in Judaism.

2. PRIESTS

If religion goes back to the earliest days of mankind, so too does a priesthood. Priests mediate between the community to which they belong and the divinity, in such a way that they represent men before God and God before men. It is difficult for the history of religion to make a rigid distinction *ab initio* between magician, medicine man, and priest. The person and office of the priest is clarified only with the definite development of religion. In its origins, the office of priest can be united to that of other positions commanding respect in the community, and, therefore, with the head of the family or clan, or with kingship.

Heb. 5:1f. offers a description of the priestly office: "Every high priest is taken from among men and appointed on men's behalf for ministry before God, so that he may present gifts and sacrifices for sins. Himself shackled in weakness, he is able to feel compassion for the ignorant and erring." The priest's duty, therefore, involves both mediation and the care of souls.

The concept of priest in the Epistle to the Hebrews is drawn from both the past and the present of Israel. According to Exod. 28, Lev. 8, and Num. 8, Moses, with Aaron, from the tribe of Levi, established the levitical priesthood in the family of Aaron. After priesthoods in individual tribes with their holy places, an organized priesthood took shape in Jerusalem (as also in the northern kingdom) in the time of the kings. Its duty was first of all a ministry of worship and Temple, but involved also instruction in the Law.

In the post-exilic period, the priests in Israel, where religious and governmental communities were one, were a distinguished and authoritative class. This was especially the case with the priests of the Temple in Jerusalem, though not so much with the priests living throughout the rest of the country, who only came to Jerusalem for Temple service.

After the forfeiture of the kingship, the high priest was president of the governing council of the Sanhedrin, and he functioned as the superior head of state. The New Testament knows and often enough mentions this priesthood. Jesus recognizes it (Mark 1:44), but he also criticizes it (Luke 10:31f.). The high priests were mainly responsible in the death of Jesus. In the primitive Christian community, the Jewish priesthood is of no significance. Jewish priests who entered Jesus' community were simply disciples there (Acts 6:7).

The New Testament is aware also of pagan priesthood. It mentions one a priest of Zeus (Acts 14:13).

Nevertheless, the New Testament never once calls an official of the Church a "priest" ($\iota\epsilon\rho\epsilon\upsilon\varsigma$).[42] It declines absolutely the use of the term ἱερὸς = *holy* for the Church; and in designating the Church's holiness it uses the word ἅγιος (see the present work, Vol. 3, p. 171, and note 79 on p. 360). Words like ἱερεὺς and ἱερὸς were probably perceived as too charged with the Jewish and pagan religions, in regard to which those terms are frequently used in the New Testament. For Christians, the terms indicated all too much of arbitrary and magical human dealings in religion.[43]

For the New Testament, as for all religions, an essential duty of the priesthood is mediational ministry between God and the world; and according to the Epistle to the Hebrews (2:17; 4:14–5:10; 7:15–8:6), the one, eternal High Priest of the new covenant is Jesus Christ.[44] As our brother (2:11f.), he is the Priest who can sympathize with us and help us (2:17f.; 4:15). "Through the eternal Spirit he has offered himself as an unblemished sacrifice to God" (Heb. 9:14). He entered into the heavenly sanctuary "to intercede for us before the face of God" (Heb. 9:24). "Through Christ we now offer God always a sacrifice of praise" (Heb. 13:15). Jesus comes, nevertheless, not from the priestly stock of Aaron, but from the stock of Judah (Heb. 7:14). He thereby abolishes the priesthood "of the fathers and according to the flesh" and established a new priesthood before "the Father of the spirits" (Heb. 12:9).

The priesthood of Christ founds and effects the universal priesthood of the Church. "By his blood Christ has made us into a kingdom, made us into priests for God, his Father" (Apoc. 1:6). If there is an echoing here and in 1 Peter 2:9 of Exod. 19:6, the New Testament, nevertheless, goes far beyond the Old. In the Old Testament, while the members of the tribe of Levi were each one a priest personally, there is, as in 1 Peter 2:9, a priestly character attributed only to the nation of Israel as a whole. In Apoc. 1:6 and 5:10, however, each individual of the redeemed is termed a priest.

The constituting of a priest is grounded in the sacrifice of the Lamb, who has made those who are to be purchased at the price of his blood "into a kingdom and into priests for God" (Apoc. 5:9f.). Thus is fulfilled the grand vision that Yahweh will take priests and levites even from among the Gentiles (Is. 66:21). Those who arise in the first resurrection are to rule (on earth) as priests, along with the Messiah (Apoc. 20:6).

As already intimated in Apoc. 1:6, the priesthood of the Church is described in detail in 1 Peter 2:9 in terms of Exod. 19:6: "You are a chosen race, a royal priesthood, a holy nation, a people acquired for possession."[45] This passage from 1 Peter 2:9 echoes also Is. 43:20. By means of these Old Testament citings, the New Testament priesthood is described as a fulfillment of the divine order and of the messianic hope, of being someday God's priestly and royal free people (Is. 61:1; 62:3).

Kingship is freedom and self-determination of life. Priesthood is the honor of ministry in the Temple itself, while the people until now were allowed to come only to the threshold of the Temple. Now the whole Church has freedom of entry to God. (Rom. 5:2; Eph. 2:18). The priesthood of the Church is made known in the proclamation of God's wonderful deeds (1 Peter 2:9), through the word (1 Peter 2:15; 3:15), and also in the very testimony of the manner of one's life (1 Peter 2:12; 3:1).

This proclamation is mandated to all (see below, § 6, 2). Even the administration of the sacraments is entrusted to the whole Church. If this, according to common understanding, holds good for baptism (Matthew 28:19), it must also hold good for the celebration of the Eucharist (1 Cor. 11:24f.; see below, § 9, 3, a) and the forgiveness of sins (Matthew 18:18 [below, § 8, 4]).*

The Church is a "holy priesthood, for the sake of presenting, through Jesus Christ, spiritual sacrifices pleasing to God" (1 Peter 2:5). The sacrifice is not a material one, but a spiritualized offering, as an enlightened religious sentiment had long since recognized (Hos. 6:6; Micah 6:6-8; Pss. 50:19; 140:2). The sacrifice is not pleasing to God through human worship, but only through Jesus Christ, who is himself the Sacrifice pleasing to God (Eph. 5:2), as well as a "spiritual Sacrifice." These are not unreal sacrifices; on the contrary, they are starkest realities, because they are celebrated in the power of the Spirit filling the Church.

---

*[*Translator's note*: It would be well also to bear in mind that what is committed to the whole Church is not necessarily committed to each of her members individually. And what is committed to each of her members individually is not necessarily committed to each in the same way.]

In spite of its emphasis on the universal priestly office, it can never-theless be said that the New Testament knows the beginnings of the individual priestly office, in which the universal office presents itself. This is evident in a saying of the Apostle Paul: "The grace is given me by God, of being, for the Gentiles, Jesus Christ's litiurgical min-ister (λειτουργός), who carries out the gospel of God in a holy ministry (ἱερουργοῦντα), so that the Gentiles, sanctified in the Holy Spirit, might be made acceptable as a sacrificial gift. . . . Through me, by word and deed, Christ has made the Gentiles obedient to the faith" (Rom. 15:15-19).[46] The phrases of Paul's statement are full of the intense language of worship. The meaning of worship finds its fulfillment in the escha-tological era of salvation. It takes place, not in accord with the former visible rite, but in a new way in the Spirit.

As in Rom. 1:5 and 12:3 (§ 3, 1, b), "grace" can be understood as meaning office. The Apostle is a "leitourge." Even if in Rom. 13:6 the term used is a purely profane word meaning a tax officer, it is still made use of here in reference to the service of worship (as occasion-ally in biblical Greek, and in Heb. 8:2). The ministry of the Apostle is to prepare the Gentiles for becoming a sanctified offering. In a holy ministry Paul carries out the gospel, which is essentially more than mere instruction. He performs his ministry "in word and in deed." Deed so joined to word certainly refers to the efforts of his missionary labors; but perhaps it refers also to the working of "signs and won-ders" (Rom. 15:19; 2 Cor. 12:12). Paul accomplishes all of this not by his own power; it is alone the Spirit of God who is able to do all of this. It calls to mind other sayings of Paul, such as Rom. 1:9f., wherein Paul says of the ministry of the gospel and of prayer that he performs therein "a holy ministry before God."[47]

Paul is joined with his community in their divine ministry. Both perform a priestly ministry. The Apostle is "poured out as a libation in the community's sacrifice of the liturgy of faith" (Phil. 2:17). In its liturgy the community presents the sacrifice of its faith and of its faith-ful living, along with the sacrifice of prayer. The Apostle's becoming a sacrificial co-victim probably refers to his approaching martyrdom.

St. Clement, bishop of Rome (*Letter to the Corinthians* 40:1-5 [Jurgens, no. 19]), compared the liturgical ministers of the community to the priests and levites of the old covenant, though it is not to be supposed that those presiding in the Church were already called priests. [*Translator's addition*: And he carefully distinguishes their role from that of the laity when he says: "To the high priest, indeed, proper ministrations are allotted, to the priests a proper place is appointed, and upon the levites their proper services are imposed. The layman is bound by the ordinances for the laity."]

In the *Didache* 13:3; the "prophets" of the community (see below, § 4, 4) are called "your high priests." If the prophets are not accorded this title, it is indicative of a distinction between community and officials in respect to the ministry of worship. Since *Didache* 15:1 says, ". . . bishops and deacons . . . also serve you in the ministry of the prophets and teachers," it probably indicates that the ministry of bishops and deacons is of equal honor to that of the prophets and teachers; in fact, 15:2 continues, ". . . bishops and deacons are your honorable men, together with the prophets and teachers."

St. Ignatius of Antioch, in his *Letter to the Philadelphians* 4 (Jurgens, no. 56), exhorts to ecclesiastical unity, which is exhibited in the one Eucharist, one altar, and one bishop together with the presbytery and the deacons. The bearers of these offices have a special connection with the Eucharist, which cannot be celebrated without the superiors of the community.

According to Tertullian, in *Baptism* 17 (Jurgens, no. 310), in the conferring of baptism, "the primary right is had by the high priest, that is, the bishop; and, after him, the presbyters and the deacons, though not without authority from the bishop."

For St. Cyprian, the bishops are, and probably exclusively, "the priests" (*sacerdotes*).

In St. Hippolytus of Rome (*Refutation of All Heresies*, 1, Preface), himself a bishop, bishops are designated as "successors of the apostles, participating with them in the same grace, doctrine, and high-priestly dignity."

Eusebius (*History of the Church* 10, 4, 2) addresses the assembled clergy as "friends of God, and priests."

The awareness of the priestly office of the whole Church, attested to so penetratingly in the New Testament, was gradually diminished.

This was conditioned above all by the counter-reformational doctrine of the Church, which had to protect the special priestly office against the attacks made upon it by the Protestant reformers. The Second Vatican Council has brought again into prominence the idea of the universal priestly office, especially in its decree on the lay apostolate.

3. ELDERS

In the Old Testament, "elders"[48] are encountered early on as heads of families, and already even as representatives of the people in general. During and in the period following upon the Babylonian Exile, they are representatives of the people's self-government and the representatives of prominent families. The "Council of Elders" ($\pi\rho\epsilon\sigma\beta\upsilon\tau\acute{\eta}\rho\iota\upsilon\nu$) becomes the Jewish superior administrative authority in Jerusalem. In the later Sanhedrin, the elders were representative of the laity along with the priests and scribes. In the local communities, seven elders formed the council of the synagogue. In the community assemblies in Qumran, the elders were seated behind the priests and in front of the people (1 QS 6:8-10). If elder was originally a designation of age, it had long since become a title of honor.

In the New Testament, the elders were specified as members of the Sanhedrin (Mark 8:31; 11:27), this being especially the case in the account of the Passion of Jesus (Matthew 26:3, 47, 57; 27: 1, 20, 41). As the leaders of a synagogue congregation, it was the elders who were sent to Jesus by the Gentile centurion (Luke 7:3). In the formula "tradition of the elders" (Mark 7:3, 5), they would seem to be scribes.

In Jewish Christian communities the elders, clearly with the practice of the synagogue as model, were elected to their post of special authority as representatives of the communities. They took the gifts of the Gentile Christian communities to Jerusalem (Acts 11:30). Together with the apostles, they formed the final court of doctrinal authority (Acts 15:2-29). They formed the council around James, the leader of the primitive community (Acts 21:18). In James 5:14, after the fashion of a synagogal board, the elders appear in the Christian community in their concern for the ill. In 1 Peter 5:1-4 the elders are the shepherds of the community.

In the original Epistles of Paul and afterwards in the Pauline communities, elders were not named. If they appear in the Acts of the Apostles, in the Pastoral Epistles, and in Gentile Christian communities, it is only because of the later supposition that there would have been elders as officials in all the communities. Accordingly, Paul and Barnabas would, after prayer and fasting, have appointed elders in Lystra, Iconium, and Antioch (Acts 14:21-23). Elders ruled in Ephesus. Appointed by the Holy Spirit, they are the "bishops and shepherds" of the community. Paul, while active in Ephesus, instructed them in the faith (Acts 20:17-38).

According to the Pastoral Epistles, the elders are the overseers of the community. Titus appointed them city by city (Titus 1:5). The elders form a college which cooperated in the installation of Timothy through the laying on of hands (1 Tim. 4:14). Tested elders are worthy of special honor (1 Tim. 5:17). Timothy is to hear complaints against elders only on the declaration of two or three witnesses (1 Tim. 5:19). They have, therefore, special legal protection. In the Church of the Pastoral Epistles, the elders are probably the same as bishops (§ 4, 7 below).

After further canonical legal developments, the present-day situation is achieved already in the second century, in the *Apostolic Tradition* of St. Hippolytus (Jurgens, nos. 394a-c). As "high priests," bishops have the fullness of authority of office, and therefore of the transmission of office. Presbyters are their councillors and participants in the priestly office. They cooperate in the celebration of the Eucharist and impose hands at ordinations. The decons are the helpers of the bishops.

The English term "priest" derives from the Greek word *presbyteros*, through the ecclesiastical Latin term *presbyter*. The term, initially designating an office of full authority, gradually took on the cultic and sacramental element that originally was foreign to it. The Old High German language borrowed the foreign Latin term and reshaped it as *priester* (our English word *priest*), which term was to dislodge the Old High German *êwart* (combined from *êwa* = "duration," "eternity" [cf. English "ever"] and *wart* = "watchman," "guardian" [cf. English "warder"]) and such Gothic terms as *gudja* = "one whose dealings are concerned with God," or *weiha* = "one who is consecrated."[49]

4. PROPHETS

The word προφήτης[50] (from πρόφημι = to speak out) means initially a speaker or proclaimer. In this meaning the term is found even in profane Greek. In Delphi, Pythia was the prophetess of the god Apollo. Generally the prefix προ carries also something of the connotation of "beforehand." Accordingly, the prophet is one who tells in advance or forecasts. Since the promising of messianic and eschatological salvation also belongs to the proclamations of the biblical prophets, prophecy can on that account also signify foretelling and predicting.

In the Old Testament, prophets are of immense importance both as ecstatic prophets (1 Sam. 10:9-13; 19:18-24; 3 Kings 18; 19; 22), and as writing prophets (Hos. 9:7f.; Jer. 1:5; Ezek. 2:5; Hab. 1:1; Haggai 1:1; Zech. 1:1). Intertestamental Judaism was convinced that the gift of prophecy was extinguished. Thus it is recounted in 1 Macc. 4:46 that the stones of the desecrated altar of the Temple were set aside "until a prophet should arise who could give a decision as to their disposition." There were no longer trustworthy prophets in Israel (1 Macc. 9:27; 14:41).

The *Syriac Apocalypse of Baruch* 85:3 laments: "The pious are gone away, and the prophets have fallen asleep." According to the words of the rabbis, the spirit of prophecy speaks no more, but only the teaching of wisdom. Prophets gifted with the spirit are expected again for the messianic era (see H. L. Strack and P. Billerbeck, *Kommentar zum Neuen Testament*, Vol. 2 (1924), pp. 127–134).

In the New Testament, the Old Testament prophets are frequently mentioned, quoted, and acknowledged. Jesus himself is called a Prophet (Matthew 21:11, 46; Luke 7:16; 24:19; John 4:9; 7:40; 9:17; see the present work, Vol. 2, pp. 62–67).

In accord with the Old Testament model, in the New Testament prophets in the community are designated as extremely important charismatic heralds. In the Acts of the Apostles (11:27; 13:1; 15:32; 21:10f.) they are prominent and authoritative members of the community. Paul values prophecy as one of the greatest charisms (1 Cor. 12:10, 28f.; 14:1). The prophets are ranked immediately after the apostles (1 Cor. 12:28f.; Eph. 3:5; 4:11; Apoc. 18:20). The prophets have

a vital role in the divine ministry. The prophet speaks "words of edification, admonition, and consolation" (1 Cor. 14:3).

In the community assembly, women too have the right of prayer and
prophecy, and therefore of liturgical fulfillment and of proclamation
(1 Cor. 11:5; § 10, 4 below). Nevertheless, Paul abhors unbridled
prophecy. Two or three prophets are allowed to speak; this is enough
(1 Cor. 14:29-32). Paul knows that he had command even of the
prophets (1 Cor. 14:37). The Church is "built on the foundation of
the apostles and prophets" (Eph. 2:20).

In the Apocalypse of John, the prophets are the teachers of the
Church (10:7; 19:10; 22:9), and they are her martyrs (16:6; 18:24).
Their consummation is with the saints (18:20).

The Gospels presuppose that there are already prophets in the communities. Christian prophets are mentioned in Matthew 10:41: "Whoever receives a prophet in the name of a prophet will receive a prophet's
reward." Since the saying is a promise for the future, it is certainly
not said of Old Testament prophets. And inasmuch as the immediately
prior discourse in Matthew 10:40 is about the apostles, the ranking of
prophets directly after apostles is seen here too, as also in 1 Cor. 12:28f.
and elsewhere.

It is Christian prophets who are meant also in Luke 11:49: "For this
reason also the Wisdom of God has said, 'I will send them apostles
and prophets, and some of them they will kill and others they will
persecute.'" It appears that Christ, who is speaking here, is quoting
himself, following a representation according to which he is the Wisdom of God. The prophets, then, can only be New Testament prophets.

Even more telling is the reference to the present in the saying in
Matthew 23:34: "I am sending you prophets and wise men and scribes;
some of them you will kill and crucify, and some of them you will
scourge in your synagogues and persecute from one town to another."
The one sent is Jesus himself. What is described is the destiny of the
martyrs of the community. Stephen (Acts 7:59f.) and James (Acts
12:1) will be killed. Others will be scourged and persecuted from city
to city (Acts 8:1; 12:17; 2 Cor. 11:24).

A certain criticism of prophecy is also voiced. On Judgment Day, an
appeal to prophesying will be of no avail: "Did we not prophesy in
your name . . .?" (Matthew 7:22; see also below, § 18, 3, b). In the

distress of the endtime, there will be false messiahs and false prophets (Mark 13:22; below, § 14, 2, a).

The prophets are highly valued in the *Didache*. There the prophets may celebrate the Eucharist howsoever they desire; for the Spirit prompts them to speak (*Didache* 10:7; Jurgens, no. 7). Speaking in the Spirit is not to be made subject to the criticism of the community (*Didache* 11:7; Jurgens, no. 7a). Certainly there are also false prophets. They unmask themselves by their greed (*Didache* 11:6, 8; Jurgens, no. 7a). The prophets are the "high priests" (*Didache* 13:3). Prophets are not elected at the discretion of the communities, the way bishops and deacons are. But the bishops and deacons "also serve you in the ministry of the prophets and teachers" (*Didache* 15:1; Jurgens, no. 9). The office of prophet is granted by the Spirit, who governs as he will.

Where is there prophecy in the Church today?[51] Insofar as the word is entrusted to the Church, so too is prophecy, as proclamation of the word, committed to her. The Church must remain charismatically prophetic. Prophecy is spoken of, and achieves reality in, the history of the Church's great saints of creative genius. Alongside the charism of office (§ 3, 1, c above), the non-institutionalized charisms must also have their rights in the Church. Office in the Church must not be exclusive and totalitarian. Not everything in the Church can be controlled. There must also be a freshness and a freedom of the Spirit. Christ, who is the Spirit (2 Cor. 3:17), is always immediately and himself the Lord of the Church, who can raise up children to Abraham from the very stones (Matthew 3:9). The Church is to be "one body and one Spirit" (Eph. 4:4).

5. Teachers and Evangelists

Along with the title prophet, the names teacher and evangelist[52] likewise designate the teaching ministry in the Church. Jesus himself is very often accorded the title Teacher, the term translating the very respected title Rabbi. There is a good basis for likening Jesus to a rabbi, since he gathered his disciples about him, even if there are other respects in which he is sharply different from a rabbi (see the present work, Vol. 2, pp. 59f.).

Jesus mandated teaching of his disciples and his community. The earthly Jesus had already sent his disciples out for that purpose (Mark 6:30). The resurrected Christ promised his disciples the power of the Spirit for their witness until the end of time (Acts 1:8). The exalted Christ mandated to his Church the instruction of all nations (Matthew 28:20). The saying presupposes the worldwide mission. Obstacles, such as Paul had overcome in his proclaiming of the gospel among the Gentiles, have already long since been experienced.

The Acts of the Apostles recounts that the apostles (4:18f.; 5:42), Paul (28:31), and other members of the community taught and proclaimed. Paul enumerates teaching among the charisms (Rom. 12:7). The richer testimony of the Deutero-Pauline Epistles discloses something of the development of teaching. In teaching, Christ is proclaimed (Col. 1:28; 2:7; 3:16). In instruction and teaching, Christ himself enters into the discussion in a deeper way, and it is he that is heard (Eph. 4:21). Doctrine is already of firm tradition (2 Thess. 2:15; 1 Tim. 4:11; 6:2). It is "dependable word, worthy of all acceptance" (1 Tim. 4:9). The form-critical method of treating even the Pauline Epistles and then later texts shows that in the New Testament there is already contained a firm body of teaching.

And just as there are false prophets (§ 4, 4 above) and false apostles (§4, 1, b above), so too there are false teachers (1 Tim. 4:1f.; Titus 1:1).

In the community of disciples, the teachers probably constituted, even if not in a way sharply defined, a specific group under their own title. Thus they are named along with the apostles and prophets (Acts 13:1; 1 Cor. 12:28; Eph. 4:11).

In Gal. 6:6. the κατηχῶν, who imparts instruction in Christian doctrine, is contrasted with the κατηχούμενος, who receives that instruction. The latter is to "share all good things" with the former, which probably means that the catechumen is to recompense the catechist. Thus the status and rights of an independent and authoritative teaching vocation are established in the community (as appears also from 1 Cor. 9:11). The catechists of Gal. 6:6 are to be equated with the teachers of 1 Cor. 12:28 and Eph. 4:11. In Gal. 6:6, Paul uses a very rare word and creates thereby a term in regard to Christian instruction which characterizes the special status of Christian teaching.

Through sayings like that of Matthew 23:8f., all teaching in the Church is defined (above, § 3, 2, b, 1).

The Epistle of James (3:1) warns: "Let not so many of you be teachers, knowing that as teachers we shall undergo a more exacting judgment." What is the probable reason for such a warning? Perhaps the esteem for the teacher in the community and the prospect of such an undertaking could mislead some into becoming teachers without considering the responsibility that was joined to the function (1 Peter 5:2). Perhaps, too, there is an echo here of the community's unhappy experiences with erring teachers and with teachers who led others into error (1 Tim. 4:1f.).

The most important content of Christian teaching was the gospel. That is why the Christian teacher is sometimes called an evangelist (εὐαγγελιστής — Acts 21:8; Eph. 4:11; 2 Tim. 4:5). The term is certainly indicative more of a function than of an office or position. All of the apostles, the Twelve and the wider circle of apostles as well, were undoubtedly also evangelists.

6. Shepherds

In the Old Testament, God is the Shepherd[53] of Israel (Yahweh in Gen. 49:24; Ps. 23; Elohim in Gen. 48:15). In God's place, the Messiah is the true Shepherd of Israel (Jer. 3:15; 23:4; Ezek. 34:23f.; Zech. 13:7). According to the *Psalms of Solomon* 17:40, the Messiah will "pasture the flock of the Lord in faith and justice." In the Gospel, Jesus is the messianic Shepherd (Matthew 15:24; Mark 14:27; John 10:1-18). In the Epistles, Jesus is represented "as Shepherd and Guardian of souls" (1 Peter 2:25), the "chief Shepherd" (1 Peter 5:4), the "great Shepherd of the sheep" (Heb. 13:20).

The linguistic imagery by which men can be called shepherds is manifold. In the ancient East, the ruler is called a shepherd. In Homer, kings are "shepherds of nations." In the Qumran community, the *mebaqqer* is to be "merciful, as a father is merciful to his sons, and all the scattered he is to bring back, like a shepherd tending his flock" (*Damascus Document* 13:9).

In the Christian community, officials are termed shepherds. "He appointed some to be apostles, others to be prophets, others to be evangelists, others to be shepherds and teachers" (Eph. 4:11). Peter is to be shepherd for the whole Church (John 21:15f.). Bishops are admonished: "Take heed to yourselves and to the whole flock, in which the Holy Spirit has placed you as bishops, to shepherd the community of the Lord" (Acts 20:28). To the elders it is said: "Pasture the flock of God which is with you" (1 Peter 5:2).

St. Ignatius employs the image further. Thus he says in his *Letter to the Romans* (9:1 (Jurgens, no. 55): "Remember in your prayers the Church in Syria which now, in place of me, has God for its shepherd. Jesus Christ, along with your love, shall be its only bishop." The bishop is the shepherd: "Where the shepherd is, there the sheep will follow" (Ignatius, *Letter to the Philadelphians* 2:1). In ecclesiastical language, the terms and titles shepherd and chief shepherd have found further rich application.

7. BISHOPS

There are still several titles to be discussed which passed over into the New Testament from its Greek milieu. Ἐπίσκοπος (overseer)[54] is found in literature and inscriptions from the fifth and fourth centuries before Christ and on into the Christian era; and in Egyptian papyri beginning with the third century before Christ, it is found as the title of civil, communitarian, and federational officials. On the island of Rhodes in the second century before Christ, a list of officials enumerates: chiefs, commanderds-in-chief of the army, treasurers, secretaries, and overseers (πρυτάνεις, στρατηγοί, ταμίαι, γραμματεῖς, and ἐπίσκοποι). It is worthy of special note that among the federations in Greece, on Rhodes, as also in Syria, there were brotherhoods of worship. The bishops or overseers seem to have been primarily in charge of finances, commissioned to look after maintenance and supplies, or, in general, they seem to have functioned as business managers.

In the Greek Old Testament, the term bishop is applied to stewards (Judg. 9:28; 1 Macc. 1:51), Temple overseers (Num. 4:16; 4 Kings 11:18; 2 Chron. 34:12), leaders of the priests (Neh. 11:9), and also to the leaders of military forces (Num. 31:14; 4 Kings 11:15).

It is significant, however, that in the writings of Qumran a new term, *mebaqqer*, appears (above § 1, 3, g). Like "bishop," the name means "overseer." He is leader of the common assembly as "mebaqqer over the many" (1 QS 6:12, 14, 20). The duty of the mebaqqer is described in detail in the *Damascus Document* 13:6-9: "He is to instruct the many in the works of God. . . . And he is to show them mercy like a father with his sons, and is to lead back all their strayed ones, like a shepherd his flock. And he is to loose all their fetters, so that in his community there be no one oppressed or shattered."

The mebaqqer is to test all who want to gain admittance to the community. He watches over all purchases and sales. The mebaqqer has, therefore, the duties of teaching, of the care of souls, of discipline, and of property administration. The question poses itself, of whether or not the mebaqqer was in any way the prototype of the Christian bishop. In the New Testament, the term *episkopos* is used only once of Christ: "You have returned to the Shepherd and Guardian (ἐπίσκοπον) of your souls" (1 Peter 2:25). The concepts of shepherd and guardian, referred to Christ, can easily go together, just as in the Old Testament Yahweh can be designated as both Shepherd and Guardian (Job 20:29 in Septuagint; Wis. 1:6; Ezek. 34:11f.). Both terms characterize shepherdly care also in Acts 20:28 and 1 Peter 5:2. With both terms Christ is designated as the one who in the most personal and deepest way knows, guards, and protects the community and each individual (John 10:14). Moreover, at the time of the First Epistle of Peter, bishop was already a title of office in the Church. It is also said, therefore, that Christ himself is present and operative in the officialdom of the Church.

In various writings of the New Testament, the holder of ecclesiastical offices is accorded the title of *episkopos* = bishop. Its earliest appearance is in the address of the Epistle to the Philippians (1:1): "To all the saints in Philippi, with the bishops and deacons." The title appears here and in the other places in the area of the Gentile Christian communities. First the community is greeted, then the officials. Bishops are mentioned in the plural; they therefore form a college. The Epistle to the Philippians is presumably one of Paul's later Epistles. In this later period, therefore, this office has taken shape, an office which was not mentioned in the earlier Epistles, apparently for the obvious reason that it did not yet exist. Why are there bishops in Philippi? No

certain reason is to be perceived. A most uncertain probability might
be drawn from the fact that, according to Phil. 4:16, gifts were brought
to the Apostle in prison. Are the bishops, like the secular bishops of
the pagan world and like those of the Qumran community, entrusted
with financial and commercial cares?

According to the narrative in Acts 20:17, Paul called the elders (presbyters) of the community of Ephesus to come to him in Miletus. He
admonishes them: "Take heed to yourselves and to the whole flock
in which the Holy Spirit has placed you as bishops, to shepherd the
community of the Lord" (Acts 20:28). Presbyters and bishops, then,
are the same. The bishops form a group by themselves. They are appointed through the Holy Spirit, which probably means through men
in whose resolves and actions the Spirit operated. In the Pastoral
Epistles, the office of bishop is a stable office, such that one can strive
for it. "If anyone is eager for the office of bishop, he desires a good
work" (1 Tim. 3:1).

The moral prerequisites of ecclesiastical office are described in "mir-
rors" of bishops (1 Tim. 3:2-7; Titus 1:5-9) and in a "mirror" of deacons (1 Tim. 3:8-13). They are for the most part soberly traditional
catalogs of virtues and vices (see the present work, Vol. 3, pp. 207–212,
261–262). According to 1 Tim. 3:2, it is necessary that a bishop be
"hospitable, equipped to teach." Not infrequently there were traveling
missionaries and brethren who needed shelter. The duty of teaching
is mentioned again and again (see below). The bishop is not to be
one of the recently baptized, but is to have stood the test (1 Tim. 3:6)
and, for the sake of the community, is to be one who enjoys a good
reputation (1 Tim. 3:7). In another list of requirements (Titus 1:5-9),
the description is rather of a basically Christian posture: the bishop's
children are to be of the faith; he is to be blameless, as God's steward;
a friend of goodness, being just, God-fearing, continent, and holding
firmly to doctrine.

It can hardly be doubted that the term *episkopos* as designation of
ecclesiastical office was borrowed from the terms of the profane offices
in the Hellenistic milieu of the Scriptures. Perhaps the term was deliberately chosen because it was not charged with any overtones of
meanings in respect to religion and worship. From the very beginning,

however, it was invested with new content and meaning. To the office of bishop belong solicitude for the community, doctrine, order, and the liturgical ministry.

8. DEACONS

The terms "minister" and "ministry" are quite universal. The term "deacon" (διάκονος)[55] is frequently used in the special sense of the servant at table. In inscriptions of the third to first centuries before Christ, deacons appear as community officials and in organizations of worship. Two dedicatory inscriptions mention, along with the priest as leader, a college of deacons. In Epictetus (*Diss.* 3, 22, 69), the philosopher is the servant of God (διάκονος θεοῦ). He rightly knows his fellow-man "as a father, as a brother; he is the servant of God, of the Father of us all." Eastern thought esteemed service of a great lord as an honor. Thus too the pious man can understand himself as servant of God, a notion impossible in Greek religion (see the present work, Vol. 1, pp. 101–103).

Jesus reckoned himself as the servant of the many and of his disciples (Mark 10:45; Luke 22:27). Ministry (service) is a term for office in the Church (see above, § 3, 2, a). Accordingly, deacon, servant, or minister becomes a title of officials in the community. In Phil. 1:1, deacons are mentioned along with bishops. In the Church of the Pastoral Epistles, the deacons constitute a station in the community. That station is described in 1 Tim. 3:8-13 in accord with human requirements and ecclesiastical ministries. The deacons are to be worthy men. They are to bear "the mystery of the faith with a pure conscience." Those who carry out their ministry well will gain the respect of the community and "all confidence in the faith, in Christ Jesus." The spiritual aspect of the diaconate is emphasized. There is no mention of any teaching duty. Probably their most important function is in the area of social service in the community.

Even women could discharge the diaconate. The deaconess Phoebe is mentioned in Rom. 16:1. In Tim. 3:11, it is probably not the wives of deacons who are spoken of, but women who are deacons: "The women are to be honorable, not slanderers but reserved, dependable in all things."

In the synagogue, there was the office of the leader and of the minister (ἀρχισυνάγωγος and ὑπερέτης). This minister was, however, confined to worship, and he was never called *diakonos*. Thus, the office and name of deacon are probably the creation of the Christian community, but probably with a connection to profane usage. The office increased in importance as the charismatic offices decreased.

In the Pastoral Epistles, bishops (and presbyters) are mentioned with much greater frequency and with a considerably broader range of duties than the deacons. The position of the deacons is well behind that of the bishops. Since in Tim. 3:8-13 the deacons are mentioned immediately after the bishops (1 Tim. 3:1-7), they are probably the servants of the bishops. There is no talk of a sacramental laying on of hands for the deacons as there is with the bishops. They were, therefore, inducted in a simpler way.

9. Superiors and Leaders

a) Superiors

The New Testament speaks repeatedly of those who "stand before" or "preside" (προΐστασθαι).[56] The earliest and most ample text reads: "We beseech you, brothers, to be considerate of those who work among you and are over you in the Lord and who admonish you, and to have a loving respect for them above all for the sake of their work" (1 Thess. 5:12-13). The "superiors" or "presidents" are members of the community who fulfill a special ministry. The nature of this ministry is clarified by the terms of its context. Paul asks that there be consideration of the superiors' endeavors. "To endeavor" or "to spend oneself" often betokens apostolic and missionary activity (John 4:38; Rom. 16:12; 1 Cor. 15:10; 1 Tim. 5:17). "To admonish" or "to exhort" signifies the ministry of solicitudinal, spiritual instruction (1 Thess. 5:14; 1 Cor. 4:14; 2 Thess. 3:15; Acts 20:31). The admonitions in 1 Thess. 5:14 to take in hand the idlers, the fainthearted, and the weak may be addressed particularly to the superiors. The other members of the community ought to be considerate of this ministry. Respect and love are due the superiors because of their labors.

The text provides a view of a community of members ordered according to duties and ministries. A charism as a particular community ministry is indicated in Rom. 12:8: "Whoever presides, let him do it zealously." Presiding is important as an office in the Pastoral Epistles. "The presbyter who fulfills well the office of president is to be held in double honor, especially those who labor in the word and in teaching" (1 Tim. 5:17). The office of superior or president is assigned to a part of the presbyters. One who discharges two offices deserves double reward. 1 Tim. 5:12 quotes: "Thou shalt not muzzle the ox that threshes the grain" and "The laborer is worthy of his wage," suggesting also that there is some thought of recognition through payment.

The president or superior in the community is compared to the father of a family (1 Tim. 3:4-6, 12) in the sense that the former involves a task similar to the latter, but of even greater importance and difficulty.

In other places "to preside" emphasizes excelling in good works; thus in Titus 3:8, 14, "to distinguish oneself in good works.

In profane Greek, προΐστασθαι means to place oneself at the head, to lead, to rule ("to rule Greece," in Herodotus 1, 69; "to rule the city," in Thucydides 2, 65, 5); and thus in 1 Macc. 5:19, "Take charge of this people!" To take charge, to preside over, to be the superior of, to rule with solicitude, was probably not at first an office and title. It is a part of the term's content, however, by the time of the Pastoral Epistles.

b) Leaders

In some places of the New Testament, "leading men" are raised up from the community.[57]

According to the saying of the Lord, in the community "the one who leads is to be like one who serves" (Luke 22:26). In Acts 15:22, Judas and Silas are "leading men among the brethren." Heb. 13:7 admonishes: "Remember your leaders (τῶν ἡγουμένων ὑμῶν), who have told you the word of God! Consider how their lives ended, and imitated their conduct!" The Epistle recalls first of all the leaders of the past generations of the Church. Their authority depended upon their proclamation of the word (comparable in 1 Tim. 5:17), but also in their faithful life and death.

The Epistle to the Hebrews then speaks of the present leaders: "Obey your leaders and follow them. For they watch over your souls as men who must render an accounting for them. They are to perform their ministry with joy, not with sighing (Heb. 13:17)." Paying heed to the leaders is demanded here because of the care which those leaders exercise in behalf of the community and its each individual member. One may be reminded of the prophets' office of watchman (Ezek. 3:17-21; 33:2-9).

The Epistle concludes with the greeting: "Greet all your leaders and all the saints" (Heb. 13:24). The saints are those called to the holy community of God (Heb. 3:1; 6:10). The leaders are greeted before the saints, which is indicative of their superior rank. Leaders are always mentioned in the plural; they form, therefore, a college without a monarchical head. Their ministry is described as proclamation of the word and care of souls. There is not talk of any special cultic function. With the community, they will "offer a sacrifice of praise to God through Christ" (Heb. 13:15).

If "leading," when first mentioned (Luke 22:26; Acts 15:22), was described as ministry, in the Epistle to the Hebrews the "leaders" are an important and governing body in the community. Perhaps notice of this is taken also in Matthew 23:10: "Let none of you be called leader"; this, then, would certainly have been pointing to the development of a possible abuse (see above, § 3, 2, b).

If one wishes to consider, as with other titles of office in the New Testament, comparable arrangements of the same period, one may think of the Jewish milieu, in which the community heads are called leaders or superiors. Their authority rested in their knowledge and teaching of the Law (as perhaps the authority of the leader in Heb. 13:7, in proclaiming the word).

Hellenistic papyri mention ἡγούμενοι ἱερέων as leaders of pagan priesthoods. Papyri designate prefects of princes as ἡγούμενοι. In the Greek Bible, army leaders are so designated (1 Macc. 9:30; 2 Macc. 14:16), as also persons of power (Sir. 17:17; 41:17; Acts 7:10). In Sir. 30:27 (33:19) "the great one of the people" are the "leaders of the assemblies" (μεγιστᾶνες λαοῦ — ἡγούμενοι ἐκκλησίας).

In Matthew 2:6, the ἡγεμόνες 'Ιούδα and the Messiah as ἡγούμενος are mentioned side by side. In the Roman ordering of offices, ἡγεμών is the title of a governor (also in Acts 23:24 and 26:30). The *First Letter of Clement to the Corinthians* (5:7; 32:2; 51:5; 55:1) readily refers to secular authorities as ἡγούμενοι.

The title of the leaders of the community, therefore, in the Epistle to the Hebrews, is to be understood as Hellenistic nomenclature, easily drawn afterward, from Jewish tradition, into the Christian community, where it was invested with a new content.

10. Women and Ecclesiastical Offices

Since the question of the office of women in the Church of the New Testament is also and primarily a question of social order, it must be understood in the total context of the then current Jewish circumstances.[58] In the Temple in Jerusalem, women were restricted to its forecourt. In the synagogues they had special places, generally in the gallery. In divine service, women had to be silent. They were permitted neither to read aloud nor speak, neither to expound nor teach. Women, slaves, and children were not obligated to recite the *Sh^ema'*, the profession of faith. Neither were they allowed, when men were present, to recite the meal prayer. The voice of a woman in public was "something shameful." Women were not to learn the Law. "Anyone who teaches his daughter the Law, teaches her foolishness." A husband was not to speak with a wife. "That is intended of his own wife; how much more does it hold true, then, of the wife of another." It is true: "Many women, much sorcery; many girls, much unchastity."

In spite of such sayings, the Jewish teacher of the Law certainly was not forgetful of the fact that the original account of creation says something about women that is quite extraordinary for that time and in view of surrounding cultures when it says that woman is given to man as of equal right, and to be a companion and helpmate at his side. The man knows the woman and accepts her in enraptured joy as his only counterpart. Created separately one from the other, man and woman strive together to achieve again the most intimate unity (Gen. 2:18-23). The Canticle of Canticles is a love song of the greatest artistry. The

Book of Proverbs (31:10-31) celebrates the wife and mother. In marriage a woman in Israel was respected far beyond anything that is found elsewhere in antiquity (see the present work, Vol. 3, pp. 241–242).

In the face of the circumstances of its time, here too the New Testament is "new creation," whereby Jesus expressly appeals to the divine order of creation which he wants to restore (Mark 10:6f.).[59]

It needs to be expounded that in the Gospel it is a woman, Mary, who is the prototype of the Church endowed with grace (Luke 1:30), of the hearing and believing Church (Luke 2:19; 11:28), and of the grieving and caring Church (John 2:3; 19:26).

Jesus himself in his associations with women did not hold to custom and its constraint; rather, he broke through it. He called no woman to the band of the twelve apostles. In view of the circumstances of the time, to have done so would have been simply an impossibility. Yet this is surely not to be fixed upon alone.

When Jesus was proclaiming the gospel of the kingdom of God, he was followed, along with the twelve apostles and the seventy disciples, by "some women whom he had healed of evil spirits and illnesses: Mary of Magdala, . . .; Janna, the wife of Herod's steward Chuza; Susanna, and several others who served him with their resources" (Luke 8:2f.).

Women were disciples of Jesus. He ignored the tenet of public opinion, according to which women were unworthy of religious instruction. Those women disciples were apparently aristocratic and wealthy women who placed their resources at the service of the gospel. Since Jesus kept these women in his company and accepted their help as thanks for their having been healed, he gave them full honor before God and men. Mark 15:40, 47 also knows about the women who were about Jesus in Galilee. If tradition has retained the names of some of them, this too testifies to their high repute in the community.

Luke 10:38-42 and John 11:1; 12:1-3 tell of the house of Mary and Martha, where Jesus stayed. The two sisters sat at the feet of Jesus, who wants to be their teacher; and they care for him as their guest. The teachers of Israel, however, thought it a useless thing, to teach a woman.

John 4 narrates in detail the story of Jesus and the Samaritan woman.

The disciples had gone into the city to buy food. "When they came back, they were surprised that Jesus was speaking with a woman" (John 4:27). The disciples are surprised, because the teachers of Israel have absolutely nothing to say to a woman. Christ, however, confronts man and woman with his word and call, as he wills. The Samaritan woman has hastened into the city and said to the people: "Come and see whether the man is the Messiah" (John 4:29). Many believed in him, first because of what the woman said, and afterwards because of the word of Jesus himself, who stayed there for two days. The woman became the intermediary who, for those who wanted to hear, established contact with Jesus.

The Easter narratives recount that on Easter morning it was women who first found the tomb empty, met the resurrected Lord, and brought the disciples news of the resurrection. Those women were the first witnesses of the paschal faith, and so long as the Easter Gospel is repeated, they are the Church's witnesses to the paschal faith. They proclaimed the gospel even to the dispirited apostles. To them, therefore, belongs the title of honor, "Apostles of the Apostles" (Bernard of Clairvaux, *Sermons on the Canticle of Canticles* 758 = Migne, *PL* 183:1148).

That the new covenant has begun also for women is stated not only by the Gospels but also by the writings of the apostolic age following upon the Gospels, and also, therefore, by the Acts of the Apostles and the Epistles of Paul.

The Acts of the Apostles depicts the primitive community that was awaiting the pouring out of the Spirit: "The apostles continued of one mind in prayer, together with the women, with Mary, the Mother of Jesus, and with his brothers" (Acts 1:14). Mary is the center of the praying Church. The women, however, are equally enfranchised in it (otherwise than in the synagogue!).

The Apostle Peter depicts the Pentecost event with the words of the prophet Joel: "I will pour out my Spirit on the whole of mankind. Your sons and your daughters will proclaim in prophecy. . . . In those days I will pour out my Spirit upon my servants and my handmaids" (Acts 2:17f.). Men and women will be filled in the same way with the Spirit. Both will be called in the same way for prophetic proclamation in the Church. Such was the prophet Joel's vision (3:1-5) of the ideal Israel of the messianic era of salvation. This is otherwise than the

Israel of the old covenant, as it actually was in the time of the prophet himself. There the women had to take a place behind. It pertains to the new, messianic covenant that men and women have a like vocation in the Church. The Acts of the Apostles (21:8f.) mentions that four daughters of the deacon Philip taught prophetically.

The Acts of the Apostles (18:1-19) makes further mention, and with the greatest respect, of the Jewish Christian married couple Aquila and Prisca already mentioned by Paul. Aquila was a wealthy Jew, a tentmaker by trade. The New Testament mentions his presence in Rome, Corinth, and Ephesus. He was an international merchant. Paul came to know the married couple Aquila and Prisca during his sojourn in Corinth. It was in their house that the Corinthian congregation assembled (1 Cor. 16:19). Paul, also a tentmaker, entered into Aquila's employment; he regarded it as necessary to his freedom that he provide for his own support. Afterwards Paul journeyed with Aquila and Prisca to Ephesus, where, on this occasion, he remained only a short time.

After Paul had gone away — he went to Jerusalem — a man named Apollos came to Ephesus. He was a learned Jewish theologian of the Bible, now become a Christian. He preached in the synagogue, where Prisca and Aquila heard him. "They took an interest in Apollos and explained to him more fully the way of God" (Acts 18:24-26). Prisca is often mentioned before her husband. She was a woman experienced and wise, even theologically qualified. They instructed the scholarly theologian and convinced him of their view of the gospel and of the faith.

Even the Epistles of Paul show how highly the ministry of woman was prized in the Church of the New Testament. Foremost among all the texts of Paul proclaiming this is the list of greetings in the final chapter of the Epistle to the Romans. Paul commends first of all "our sister [i.e., a Christian] Phoebe" (Rom. 16:1f.), who was "a deacon of the church at Cenchreae." "She was a support for many, and also for myself [Paul]." The community in Rome is to welcome her in a way of the saints, and support her every need.

Just as Phoebe served the church at Cenchreae (near Corinth, where Paul wrote the Epistle to the Romans) in an eminent way, so too it seems that she had a special commission in Rome. Phoebe was not only an important and respected woman in the primitive community; she had ministry and office in the Church. She was a deacon. Such deacons are mentioned along with the bishops in Phil. 1:1. In subsequent writings of Christian antiquity, deaconesses are mentioned not infrequently. Like the deacons, they were probably installed through prayer and the imposition of hands.*

Among the Christians in Rome, it is Prisca and Aquila as "co-workers in Christ" (Rom. 16:3) that Paul greets first. For Paul they had "presented their necks," that is, they put their lives on the line for him. Paul thanks them, and "all the churches among the Gentiles owe them thanks" (Rom. 16:4).

Furthermore, the names of many other women are found in the list of greetings, and they are singled out for words of praise. Mary has labored much for the community. Tryphaena, Tryphosa, and the dear Persis have expended themselves much in the Lord. Julia and the sister of Nereus are greeted. Rufus's mother has become like a mother to

---

*[*Translator's note*: Scripture does not use the term "deaconess." Phoebe, though clearly a woman, is called a "deacon," with the masculine form of the term. Deaconess as a term first occurs in the patristic age. When Schelkle says that the deaconesses were probably installed through prayer and imposition of hands, this is, of course, an entirely gratuitous statement. It is possible, of course; but even if it were demonstrated that a ceremony attached to a woman's becoming a deaconess, it would still be invalid to conclude, as some have, that the deaconesses therefore received a sacrament.

Furthermore, the statement rests somewhat upon the implied assumption that the female deacon of the Scriptures and the deaconesses of the patristic age are to be equated as to their functions; and this too is gratutitous. The deaconesses of the patristic age seem to have acquired their title simply from the fact that their names were kept on the same lists or rolls on which the names of the local clergy of a community were enrolled, while in fact they were simply the elderly women and widows who had no income or support, and were dependent upon the alms of the community. For this they may have rendered some social or domestic service to the community. This, at any rate, seems a likely enough description of the status of the deaconesses in view of a number of patristic passages in which deaconesses are mentioned. It would seem likely enough also that the wife of a deacon was, with no implication of ministerial function or office of any kind, termed a deaconess, just as the wife of a priest was sometimes called a priestess.]

Paul himself (Rom. 16:6-13). Even Paul, the restless wanderer, can treasure the solicitude of a woman. Praising them in some way, Paul mentions in the community of Philippi, Evodia and Syntyche, who have, with him, "struggled in the service of the gospel" (Phil. 4:2f.).

In the Epistle to Philemon (1), Paul sends greetings to Philemon in Colossae; to Philemon's wife, the "sister," that is, the Christian woman, Apphia; and to the congregation that meets in their house. So we hear again of a married couple whose house accommodates the community. According to 1 Cor. 9:5, the apostles and the brothers of the Lord are, as missionaries, accompanied by their wives. The missionaries and their wives accompanying them receive their support from the community.

When, in the First Epistle to the Corinthians, Paul depicts the divine service of the community, he mentions also the function of woman.[60] He says of man and of woman in an equal way that in the assembly "they pray and speak prophetically" (1 Cor. 11:4f.). They both have the same calling and the same right of liturgical prayer in the community and of the Spirit-filled proclamation of God's word. Man and woman share in a universal priesthood.

It is immaterial if Paul wishes that the woman (corresponding to Jewish custom) should, in the openness of the community, wear a veil (1 Cor. 11:5-16; above, § 4, 4). A little further on in the same Epistle, however, in regard to the ordering of divine service, it says: "As in all the communities of the saints, women are to remain silent at assemblies. If they want to know something, let them ask their husbands at home" (1 Cor. 14:33-35). But one must not quote this last saying, that a woman is to be silent in church, in an isolated way, as is often done. 1 Cor. 11:4f. must also be considered. Then it will be seen that 1 Cor. 14:34f. does not forbid women to speak absolutely, but demands only that they do not participate in the vocal instruction in the community assembly. Even with this, it remains rather difficult to reconcile the two declarations of the Epistle.

The verses 14:33-35 (or 14:32b-34), however, interrupt the context, which treats of the prophets. The text seems to betray linguistic usage that is stylistically un-Pauline. Moreover, in some important manuscripts, old translations, and in the Ambrosiaster, the passage (1 Cor. 14:33-35) follows 1 Cor. 14:40. From such indications, exegesis is arriving increasingly at the conclusion that 1 Cor. 14:33-35 is a later insertion. If this is the case, perhaps these verses were fashioned with 1 Tim. 2:11-15 in mind.

With the Pastoral Epistles, it may be considered that 1 Tim. 2:9-15 was written about the year 100 A.D. In these rather late texts women were admonished to simplicity, efficiency, cheerfulness, and good works. Fanaticism, it would appear, is swaying the Church from within. Perhaps women themselves are accessory to this fanaticism. Marriage, as will soon afterwards happen in Gnosticism, is disparaged and depreciated by erroneous teachers as a work of the flesh, and indeed, as work of the devil. Therefore the Epistle now orders the following in regard to community life and the divine service: In divine service, woman has basically the same right of prayer as man. Like the men, women too "are to pray in suitable attire." But then it is said, "Woman is to learn in silence, keeping herself submissive. I do not allow a woman to teach, nor to raise herself above her husband." The Epistle protects the right and the holiness of marriage in the Church when it says: "Woman will achieve holiness through motherhood if she lives a modest life and is constant in faith, love, and holiness." The Pastoral Epistles bear witness that in the late apostolic age the ministry of woman in the Church must have declined. Perhaps this took place in a self-defense against abuses that developed in some sects, in which, according to the accounts of Church History, women stepped in as prophetesses.

On the other hand, however, the Pastoral Epistles are still important authorities for the ministry of woman in the Church. In 1 Tim. 3:5-13 the office of the deacon in the community is described in detail. In this passage it is stated (3:11), "The women are to be honorable, not slanderers, but reserved, faithful in everything." Since the time of the Church Fathers, it has been argued whether the passage is to be referred to deaconesses or to the wives of deacons. If the latter are intended, then it must nevertheless be said that the wives of the deacons participated in the latter's ministry.

The Pastoral Epistles, nevertheless, are sure witness to the establishment of an office and position of widows in the Church. "She is to be accepted as a widow who is not less than sixty years of age, and the wife of one man, and has a reputation for good works, having raised her children, practiced hospitality and washed the feet of the saints, supported the oppressed, and having practiced in general every good work" (1 Tim. 5:3-16). There was in the community a special position for widows, with its own rights and duties. The ecclesiastical writers of the second century and later also speak of this position. According to the Pastoral Epistles, the widows have a duty also in prayer (1 Tim. 5:5). This will mean not just personal prayer, but also liturgical prayer in the community. Above all, however, the widows had duties of a social and charitable kind. Specially mentioned are house visitations (1 Tim. 5:13).* Their support was no doubt borne by the community (1 Tim. 5:16).

No where in antiquity, in the house and especially in the public places of government and of worship, did a woman have the same freedom and possibilities of activity that were available to a man. Here as elsewhere (for example, in the question of slavery — see the present work, Vol. 3, pp. 295-297) the New Testament mainly allows the social relationships and circumstances to remain. But these relationships are prevailed over from ground up in the new creation of grace: "There is neither Jew nor Greek, there is neither slave nor free, there is neither man nor woman. You are all one in Christ" (Gal. 3:28).

In the Church of the present day the question of the priestly office of the woman is being argued. For two thousand years the priestly office in the Church has been practiced only by men. Its form, structure, and content has been shaped thereby. Women probably could not enter suddenly into a priesthood so conditioned and determined. Church and office would first have to find another structure if women were to participate in the priestly office, supposing even that this be possible. What would be needed first is a lengthy and arduous effort in the communion of the faith, of doctrine, and of love.

---

*[*Translator's note*: Only in a certain backhanded way can the passage imply that house visitations are a duty of the widows. What the passage actually states is that young women should not be enrolled as widows because "young widows . . . learn how to be idle and go round from house to house; and then, not merely idle, they learn to be gossips and meddlers in other people's affairs, and to chatter when they would be better keeping quiet."]

§ 5. PETER

1. Common Tradition of the Gospels

Simon Peter[61] belonged to the first disciples of Jesus. The accounts of his calling (Mark 1:16-20; Matthew 4:18-22; Luke 5:1-11; John 1:41f.) differ so much among themselves that they cannot be mutually reconciled. The narratives are probably ideal representations of the vocation to discipleship. Another tradition told of vocation to the circle of the Twelve (Mark 3:16 and parallels).

According to common tradition, Jesus gave Simon the surname Kepha (Cephas) or Peter. Mark 3:16 mentions this in its account of Peter's being called to the circle of the Twelve. According to Matthew 16:18, Jesus gave Simon this name after Simon's acknowledging him as the Messiah at Caesarea Philippi. According to John 1:42, Jesus promised Simon the surname already at his calling him. Paul, too, knows the surname, both as Kepha (Gal. 1:18) and as Peter (Gal. 2:1, 7). When Simon obtained the surname cannot be decided, either as to place or time. Modern exegesis connects the conferral of the surname even with the first appearance of the resurrected Jesus (1 Cor. 15:5).

In the Gospels, Peter has a preeminence above the other disciples of the circle of the Twelve. With James and John, the sons of Zebedee, Peter is among the elect confidants of Jesus in the house of Jairus (Mark 5:37), at the transfiguration (Mark 9:2), and on the Mount of Olives (Mark 14:33). Along with John, Peter is given the commission of preparing the Passover (Luke 22:8). The women are to announce the tidings of the resurrection "to the disciples and Peter" (Mark 16:7).

Peter is spokesman for the disciples at the marvelous catch of fish (Luke 5:3-10), in confessing the Messiah (Mark 8:29-33), and in the question of how often one is to forgive (Matthew 18:21). The tax collector addresses himself to Peter (Matthew 17:24). The disciples are designated as "Peter and his companions" (Mark 1:36; Luke 9:32). Even in John's Gospel, Peter stands forth among the disciples as spokesman after the multiplication of the loaves (John 6:68f.), at the washing of feet in the supper room (John 13:6-10), and at the betokening of the betrayer (John 13:24). Peter and the beloved disciple hasten to the grave of Jesus (John 20:2-10). At the appearance of the resurrected Jesus on the Lake of Gennesaret, Peter is treated with distinction in the circle of disciples (John 21:2-23).

All four Gospels tell of the fall of Peter (Mark 14:26-31, 54, 66-72). The strikingly detailed narrative shows the interest that tradition had in it. This interest is made even clearer in the deliberate changing of individual features. The calling down of curses on himself and vehement denial in Mark 14:71 is softened in Luke 22:60. The constancy and fidelity of Jesus toward the disciple is apparent in the look that Jesus casts in Peter's direction (Luke 22:61). In Matthew 26:75 and Luke 22:62, the intensity of Peter's contrition is heightened. In John (18:17, 25f.), the denial is a denial of disciplehood. All this interest is indicative, too, of the period during which Peter comes to be acknowledged as Prince of the Apostles.

2. Special Tradition of Luke and John

The short history of Peter's call in Mark 1:16-20 is replaced in Luke 5:1-11 by the history of the bounteous catch of fish, which the Evangelist took from his special tradition.[62] Jesus sits teaching in Peter's boat, and goes out with him onto the lake (5:3f.). The core of the narrative in 5:4-7 is very similar to the narration of the marvelous catch of fish, with the resurrected Jesus, in John 21:3-11 (see directly below).

Both narratives must surely be derived from one original tradition. The marvelous manner of the history points toward an account of a paschal appearance. But Luke has understood his history, not as a paschal narrative, but as a marvelous event from the life of Jesus. Luke 5:1-7 especially is a thoroughly realistic portrayal. The theme of the fisher of men (Mark 1:17) appears at the end (Luke 5:10). But Peter calls Jesus, whom he, in spite of 4:38, hardly knows, "Master" (5:5), in a passably reverential way. As soon as Peter recognizes and experiences the revelation of God in Christ, he falls terrified to his knees and calls him "Lord" (5:8). In the presence of the Holy One, Peter knows himself as a sinful man. But even as a sinner Peter is called (5:10). This fits well in the Gospel of Luke, in which Jesus is the Savior of sinners (7:36-50; 15:1-32; 18:9-14; 19:1-10). Jesus accepts the sinner Peter anew (Luke 22:61). From the beginning onward, Peter is over-powered by the divine mystery of Jesus. Thus he is destined to be the "rock" of the Church. In Luke 5:8 he is already called Simon Peter.

In Luke 22:31-34, at the Last Supper, there are words of the Lord addressed particularly to Peter. In Luke 22:31-32 there is the address, Simon; and the verses are peculiar to Luke. They promise Peter a special mission to his brother disciples. In 22:33-34 the Apostle is ad-dressed as Peter; and the verses, a prediction of his denial, correspond to Mark 14:30-31. Luke has garnered his passage in 22:31-34 from two different sources. The part in which the address "Peter" is used will be later, since Peter is indicative here of his official position as leader. In 22:31-32 it is said that Satan wants to put the disciples to the test, similar to what is recounted in the history of Job (1:6-12; 2:1-7). Jesus prays for one of them, Simon, that his faith may not fail (Luke 22:32).[63] Simon is one day to strengthen the faith of all. Luke makes reference to the first apparition, of which he too is aware (Luke 24:34). Dogmatic exegesis finds herein a mission to Peter and to his successors. But the conversation does not concern such.

As first among the apostles, Peter was recipient of the apparition of the risen Lord (Luke 24:34; 1 Cor. 15:5; see the present work, Vol. 2, pp. 113–115). This was a distinction which was highly significant for the position of Peter in the college of apostles and in the community. His preeminence, already visible, was thereby ratified. Peter is to gather together again the community of disciples after their dispersal; and he will do it. If the apparitions mean the sending forth of the apostles into their missions, Peter is again the first.

Exegesis occasionally surmises that only after and in consequence of the first apparition did Peter become head of the circle of Twelve and of the community, and thereby obtain the surname Kepha or Cephas. In view of the Gospels as source material, this is just as questionable as the conclusion that the circle of Twelve first came to be after the resurrection, and was called and created through the appearance of the resurrected Jesus (above, § 4, 1, a).

In the narration of Jesus' being taken prisoner, John 18:30 mentions Peter by name. Peter stands out among the disciples for his act of human fidelity, even if Jesus cannot accept it.

In the two pericopes which, as chapter 21, form the appendix to
John's Gospel, Peter is the central figure in the events. In the narration
of the catch of fish in John 21:1-14, Peter throws himself into the sea,
in order to be the first to reach the resurrected Jesus. Peter pulls ashore
the wonderfully filled net, which does not break. The apostles are
fishers of men (Mark 1:17). The overflowing net signifies the great
numbers of the faithful who will be won through the missions. That
the net does not break is symbolic of the Church's unity. Peter, however, is head of the missions and of the universal Church (John 21:1-
14 is a doublet to Luke 5:1-11; see above).

In the second pericope in John 21:15-23, the commissioning of Peter
to the leadership of the community is depicted. Certainly Peter can
give no simple response to the question of whether he loves Jesus more
than the others do. Nevertheless, the narration contains the answer.
Jesus commissions Peter to pasture his lambs, that is, to guide the community (21:15-17).

The relationship of Matthew 16:17f. to John 21:15f. can hardly be
determined as historical sequence of promise of an office of leadership
and its definitive bestowal; rather, the two texts are to be understood
as variants in the transmission of one and the same historical tradition.
If in John's Gospel it is dated as post-paschal, the promise in Matthew
16:18f. also points to the future, that is, to the time after Easter. Jesus
announces Peter's violent death (John 21:18f.). The beloved disciple,
however, will "remain," by which it was understood that he would
remain until the parousia of the Lord (John 21:20-23). Was he, therefore, to take up the leadership of the community after the death of
Peter? The community certainly had to experience the fact that this
other disciple too died before the parousia. There is nothing indicated
as to how the succession is to be regulated.

3. PETER IN THE COMMUNITY AT JERUSALEM

In the Acts of the Apostles, Peter is the leader of the community of
disciples in Jerusalem. He orders the election of Matthias (Acts 1:15-
26). He championed the community of disciples on Pentecost (Acts

2:14-41). Peter and other apostles bear witness before the high council, the Sanhedrin (Acts 4:8; 9; 5:29). Peter goes with John to Samaria (Acts 8:14-25). Peter works wonders (Acts 9:32-43). He receives the first Gentiles into the Church (Acts 10:1–11:18). He is miraculously freed from prison (Acts 12:3-17). At the Council of Jerusalem, Peter has the first word (Acts 15:7:11).

Paul visits Peter twice in Jerusalem (Gal. 1:18; 2:1-10). He accounts Peter among the "leaders" and the "pillars" (Gal. 2:6, 9; above, § 4, 1, a). The second visit took place probably on the occasion of the Council of Jerusalem, depicted in Acts 15:1-35. Even in the vehement altercations of Paul with Peter in Antioch (Gal. 2:11-21), and even by means of it, the distinctive importance of Peter is acknowledged.[64]

James the brother of the Lord stands forth beside Peter in the community of Jerusalem. It is probably to this James that the resurrected Jesus gave distinction with an apparition (1 Cor. 15:7). He is the second speaker in the assembly of the community (Acts 15:13-21). He expects a reckoning from Paul on the occasion of the latter's visit to Jerusalem (Acts 21:18). At his visit to Jerusalem, Paul meets with James (Gal. 1:19; 2:9). In Gal. 2:9, Paul mentions James before Peter. Did James have a preeminence ahead of Peter? In the New Testament canon there are Epistles under the names of James and of his "brother" Jude (v. 1). If both letters are pseudepigraphal, even that very fact would mean that James and Jude were authorities whose Epistles one would have wanted to read in the canon.

4. Epistles of Peter

In the canon of the New Testament there appear also two Epistles of Peter. If, as seems apparent, the Epistles are pseudepigraphal, they still betoken the importance of Peter, since the letters were written under his name. In the First Epistle of Peter, Peter addresses himself with authority to the churches in the whole of Asia Minor (1:1). The Epistle comes from "Babylon" (5:13), which probably means that it was written in Rome, or its author means to represent it as written in Rome, which qualifies as the new Babylon (Apoc. 14:8; 16–18).

The Second Epistle of Peter (3:1) is, like the first, addressed from Rome to the whole Church (1:1f.). Finally (3:15f.), Peter and Paul stand side by side as the two apostles of the Roman Church. In a similarly impressive way they are named together as the Roman apostles by St. Clement of Rome in his *First Letter to the Corinthians* 5, 3-7 (Jurgens, no. 11; about the year 80 A.D.); by St. Ignatius of Antioch in his *Letter to the Romans* 4, 3 (Jurgens, no. 54; about the year 110 A.D.); and by St. Irenaeus of Lyons in his *Against Heresies* 3, 1, 1 (Jurgens, no. 208; between the years 180 and 199 A.D.). This is the beginning of the Roman Catholic Church in the New Testament.

5. Special Tradition of the Gospel of Matthew

a) In General

Matthew supplements the common synoptic tradition with special material on the history of Peter. The lists of the twelve apostles always begin with Peter (Mark 3:16 and parallels). Matthew 10:2, however, says expressly: "*first*, Simon, called Peter." Is this a reference in advance to Matthew 16:17-18? Peter is first in his confession of faith; is he first also as leader of the community?

Matthew 14:28-33 tells of Jesus' walking on the water. Peter gets out of the boat, and Jesus saves him from sinking. The narrative is probably a lesson on faith, illustrated with the example of the experience of Peter. The story is transferred to the area of earthly-historical conditions. Perhaps it is a paschal event predated into the life of Jesus, elaborated with Old Testament (Pss. 77:20; 18:17; 69:2-3, 15; 144:7) and early Jewish themes (*Odes of Solomon* 39:8-13). Is the ship the ship of the Church (Matthew 14:24)? The Lord makes peace for his community (Matthew 14:32). The community, like Peter (Matthew 16:15), confesses its faith in the Son of God (Matthew 14:33 — see the present work, Vol. 2, pp. 82–83; Vol. 3, pp. 86–87).

In Matthew 17:24–27, a tax collector demands of Jesus and his disciples the Temple tax; and in seeking payment, he turns to Peter. Although Jesus maintains that the sons are free, he nevertheless directs Peter to catch a fish, in the mouth of which a drachma piece will be found. Perhaps the story presupposes debates of the Jewish Christian community over its obligation in respect to the Temple. Since the collection of the Temple tax ceased with the destruction of the Temple in the year 70 A.D., it no doubt predates this latter event. Ultimately, it employs the old folk-theme of the fish which contains a treasure (see the present work, Vol. 2, p. 84).

The special tradition that is most important by reason of its content and later history is that of the promise of the primacy (Matthew 16:17f.), in connection with Peter's confession of the Messiah (Matthew 16:16). Matthew supplements Mark in the instance of this text. He reshapes the confession of the Messiah. While it says in Mark 8:29, "You are the Messiah", in Matthew 16:16 we hear, "You are the Messiah, the Son of the living God." Is God called "the Living" in accord with the Old Testament formula (4 Kings 19:4, 16; Is. 37:4, 17; Hos. 2:1; Dan. 6:21), or is there already a calling to mind here of the message of the resurrection? The full title of majesty, "Son of the living God," presumes an already long dogmatic development (see the present work, Vol. 2, pp. 193f.).

The text of Matthew 16:17f. will be explained in greater detail immediately below, § 5, 5, b, 1-2.

In the special tradition, the historical character of pericopes like Matthew 14:28-33 and 17:24-27 is not easily determined. Even Matthew 16:17-19 is shown further on to be a post-paschal account (§ 5, 5, b). Thus one must come to the conclusion that the generality of the special Petrine content of Matthew displays an advanced stage of the development of tradition.

b) Matthew 16:17-19

1) Exposition. At Peter's confession of the Messiah, Jesus answers with the glorification (Matthew 16:17): "Blessed are you, Simon bar Jonah, for flesh and blood has not revealed this to you, but my Father, who is in heaven." In the parallel account in Mark 8:30, Jesus does not decline Peter's confession of him as Messiah, but he does immediately attach to it an announcement of suffering. The glorification is shaped in the contrasting of flesh and blood as the human world with heaven as the divine sphere. Man cannot of himself come to know the mystery of God. It must be disclosed to him, just as is stated also in the saying about revelation: "No one knows the Son except the Father, and no one knows the Father except the Son, and him to whom the Son chooses to give revelation" (Matthew 11:27; see the present work, Vol. 2, pp. 46–47).

Since God has chosen Peter, Jesus wants to distinguish him (Matthew 16:18): "I say to you that you are Peter, and on this rock I will build my Church, and the gates of the underworld will not overcome it."[65] He singles him out with the name Peter, which is immediately clarified in a play on words. "Peter" means "rock," and Simon is given this surname, because he is the rock on which Jesus will build his Church. A rock juts out, and a rock is unshakable. For that reason it serves as the supporting foundation.

The image is found also in the Old Testament. God is "the rock of salvation" (Deut. 32:4, 15, 18). "The Lord is my rock and my fortress and my Savior" (Ps. 18:3; again in Ps. 31:4). "God lays a stone in Zion, a select stone, a precious cornerstone, a firm foundation stone" (Is. 28:16 = 1 Peter 2:6). Abraham can be called a rock: "Consider the rock from which you were hewn, the quarry from which you were cut. Consider Abraham, your father" (Is. 51:1f.).

Even the image of the construction of God's house is common biblical property. God can build, plant, erect Israel (Jer. 1:10; 24:6). "Wisdom builds herself a house" (Prov. 9:1). The Messiah will build the house of the community. "The Just and Chosen One will cause the house of his community to appear again" (*Ethiopic Henoch* 53:6).

In the writings of Qumran, the image is employed repeatedly. The community is "firmly grounded in the truth, for the eternal planting, a holy house for Israel, a circle of the Most Holy One. . . . This is the tested wall, the precious cornerstone. Its foundations will not fail, nor weaken in their place" (1 QS 8:5-9). "You have erected my building on the rock, and eternal foundations are its groundwork" (1 QH 7:8f). "The soul is delivered to the gates of the underworld." Yet the petitioner is saved "in the fortified city, which is built on rock by God" (1 QH 6:22-27).

The figure of the building appears with increasing frequency in the New Testament. Israel is God's house (Matthew 10:6; 15:24). The Messiah will build a new temple (Mark 14:58). The Epistles employ the image further. The community is God's building (1 Cor. 3:9f.).

It is built on the foundation of the apostles and prophets (Eph. 2:20).
The Church is the spiritual house, built on Christ, the living and
precious keystone chosen by God (1 Peter 2:4-7).

According to Matthew 16:18, the Church is at a future time to be
built on the rock which is Peter. This futurity is manifestly the messianic-eschatological time; in the understanding of the New Testament
community, however, it is the time after the exaltation of Jesus. The
house is designated as community (*ekklesía*), with which term the
Greek Old Testament designates the *qahal Yahweh* (assembly of
God). The New Testament community is the fulfillment of the Old
Testament hope. Perhaps the house was first to be afforded protection
in the eschatological time of misery (see above, § 1, 3, m). Then, however, it would still be understood as an enduring home. The word
ekklesía is found in the Gospels only in Matthew 16:18 and in the
materially related passage in Matthew 18:17. Jesus is speaking in this
latter place, however, not of the community of God (as in the Old
Testament, as also in 1 QM 4:10 and in the *Damascus Document*
7:17), but of his own community. He speaks as the Exalted One, the
Lord of the Church, who is in the companionship of God.

The "gates of Hades" is the terminology used in the Greek. The
gates of Hades will not conquer the community.[66] Hades means the
world of death (Is. 38:10; Ps. 9:14; Sir. 51:5f., 9; Wis. 16:13; *Psalms
of Solomon* 16:2; 1 QH 6:24). The gates of Hades close behind anyone who once passes through them. The power of death is not to overcome the rock or the community. The word has an apocalyptic-escha-
tological sense, but it is not easily explained. It can scarcely be stating
that Peter, the rock, will not die because he will experience the intervention of the parousia. The community, then, will not be forfeit to
death, perhaps because it will remain until the soon to be expected
parousia. Or the faithful are not to fall victim to death because they
are to be granted entry into eternal life (see below, § 15, 4).

Jesus announces further: "I will give to you the keys of the kingdom
of heaven" (Matthew 16:19). This kingdom of heaven or of God is
the endtime kingdom of God. It has already begun or is still drawing
near (see below, § 13, 3, b). The kingdom is described with the image
of a palace having doors. The notion is reminiscent of Is. 22:20-25,

where Eliakim is invested as steward of the royal house: "I am placing the key of the House of David on his shoulder; should he open, no one shall close; should he close, no one shall open."

According to Matthew 23:13, the scribes close the kingdom of heaven to men and do not themselves enter in. The scribes exercise their power through their teaching. Accordingly, the saying in Matthew 16:19 will signify the full authority of teaching and determining, which is given to Peter. "What you will bind on earth shall be bound in heaven, and what you will loose on earth shall be loosed in heaven" (Matthew 16:19).[67] The saying is to be understood according to Jewish rabbinic linguistic usage. Accordingly it means: by doctrinal decision, to pronounce either as forbidden or permissible; to impose or take away an obligation; to receive into a community, or to exclude therefrom.

The saying, then, is indicative of full authority in teaching and in regulating, which is conveyed to Peter. The content of Matthew 16:19 is similar to that of Matthew 18:18, where the full authority of binding and loosing is conveyed to all the disciples (§ 5, 5, c, below), as also in John 20:23 (§ 8, 4, below). In Matthew 16:19, Church and kingdom of heaven are coordinated one to the other, probably because the former precedes the latter, and because the former looks to entry into the latter. This too is a rabbinic viewpoint, that along with the Law, God has turned over to Israel even its interpretation and application. God recognizes the decisions of the earthly court in particular in the instance of the pronouncement of excommunication (H. L. Strack and P. Billerbeck, *op. cit.*, Vol. 1 [1922], pp. 741–747).

2) Place and Time. Matthew inserted his passage 16:17-19 into the Markan model that he had already before him. He took the words from a special tradition on Peter that he had available. There will hardly be any consideration here, then, of time or place. Matthew inserts the passage at this point because it seems well-suited to Peter's confession of the Messiah.[68]

In general, the logia of Matthew 16:18f. convey the impression of being post-paschal. After this interpretation was increasingly defended by, among others, J. Weiss, A. Loisy, and R. Bultmann, and is now advanced even in the newer commentaries (by W. Grundmann, E. Schweizer), it is presently accepted even by Catholic exegesis.[69] An express saying about the building of the Church and its abiding structure seems possible only after the consummation of the work of salvation in the death and resurrection of Jesus. The account of imparting the office of shepherd to Peter in John 21:15f. and the granting of full authority over the forgiveness of sins in John 20:23 must, no doubt, be regarded as essentially related or even essentially identical. These histories in John, however, belong to the time after the exaltation of Jesus. That being the case, it calls to mind the accounts of the first apparitions to Peter, in Luke 24:34 and 1 Cor. 15:5. Do these apparitions result in the commissioning and authorizing of Peter that is recounted in Matthew 16:18f.? Even Catholic exegesis questions whether it is conceivable that the resurrected Jesus spoke in structured language. If this is not to be accepted, perhaps in Matthew 16:17-19 it is Christian prophets (above, § 4, 4) who are speaking, and who give witness in the Spirit to the self-awareness of the Church (below, § 8, 3, b).

Nevertheless, the language of Matthew 16:17-19 does bear clear evidence of Aramaisms.[70] In Matthew 16:17 the pronouncement of blessedness, the not yet certainly explained surname bar Jonah, and the expression "flesh and blood" reveal Semitic conventionalities of language. The play on words with Kepha as a surname and as foundation of the Church fits perfectly only in Aramaic, in which language Kepha can be the term used in both places, while in Greek this perfect agreement is disturbed by having to use Πέτρος and πέτρα. ἐκκλησία is a translation of *qahal* (see above, § 5, 5, b, 1). The metaphorical terms of a building on a bedrock foundation, the gates of Hades, the keys of the kingdom of heaven, and the binding and loosing are Old Testament Jewish terms and concepts (§ 5, 5, b, 1). The terms in Matthew 16:17-19 point back to the Aramaic-speaking primitive community. Can one seek further for a possible *Sitz im Leben*?

Some conjectures are expressed under the presupposition that the Gospel of Matthew originated about the year 90 in the Syro-Palestinian locale. If this Gospel discloses a special interest in Petrine tradition, this interest is not merely a purely historical one. Does this Church see herself as joined to Peter in a special way? Is Peter the special guarantor of the true faith for her? In opposition, perhaps, to a Jewish Christian community, which appeals vigorously to James, the brother of the Lord, the "first bishop of Jerusalem"? Or are we to reckon with a possibility that the Church has now to appeal to her interpretation of the Law, stemming from Peter, against a Judaism which, after the destruction of Jerusalem in 70 A.D., is forming herself anew around the Law and its rigid interpretation? Or was the Jewish Christian interpretation of the Law tracing itself back to Petrine tradition in opposition to Pauline Gentile Christian teaching? [71]

c) Matthew 18:18

In content and in actual manner of expression, there is further general agreement between Matthew 16:19b and Matthew 18:18, "Whatever you bind on earth shall be bound in heaven, and whatever you loose on earth shall be loosed in heaven." The full authority of binding and loosing, granted in Matthew 16:19b to Peter personally, is conveyed in Matthew 18:18 to the disciples as a group. Matthew 16:18, however, includes doctrinal and administrational authority, so the full authority seems, by reason of its abridgement and above all by reason of its contextual relationship to Matthew 18:17, to be restricted to administration.

The saying in Matthew 18:18 is in one of the conversations of Matthew's Gospel which are indisputably proper to Matthew. The original source of the words is no longer to be determined. The whole conversation in Matthew 18 is, according to 18:1, addressed to "the disciples." These are not the twelve apostles, but the whole community of disciples. Since in 18:17 the talk is directly of the Church, and the Church is mentioned again in 18:20, in 18:18 the full authority is granted to the whole community of disciples. Dogmatic exegesis might have had an interest in this if the full authority of binding and loosing had been granted to the twelve apostles, and potentially therewith to their successors, the bishops. The evidence of the text will not allow such a restricting interpretation.

According to the context, Matthew 18:18 seems to have a close connection with 18:15f. If that is the case, a rule is given here on correction and on expulsion from the community. Correction is to be first of all between two, and then subsequently in the presence of a pair of witnesses; then the case can be brought before the community. The succession of instances has its close parallel in the administrational rule of Qumran (1 QS 5:25–26:1; above, § 1, 3, i). The decision, according to which the one expelled is to be regarded as if he were a "pagan and a tax collector," is hardly reconcilable with the conduct of Jesus, since he did indeed call even pagans and tax collectors. The saying, then, will be a secondary and probably Jewish Christian construction. The whole context, however, surely showed that after the hard saying in Matthew 18:17 about the expulsion, in 18:18 there could still be talk of the possibility of the loosing of the excommunication, while in 18:19f. there is a requirement that the whole matter be attended to under the guidance of the community's mutual prayer and, according to 18:21f., of unlimited fraternal forgiveness.

The relationship that Matthew 16:19b and Matthew 18:18 have to each other is an important question. Matthew 16:18f. and 18:18 have certainly developed in tradition from a single original saying. Which is the earlier and which the later form? How do Gospel and community understand the relationship of the two passages? Are both concerned with full authority, so that it can be made use of at the same time by the one Peter and by the whole community? Or was the full authority, given first to the one Peter, imparted afterwards to all the disciples? Or was the universal and full authority of the community afterwards narrowed down to Peter alone? To these questions exegesis supplies mutually opposed answers.

Some exegetes regard Matthew 18:18 as earlier than Matthew 16:19b. If this is the case, then the universal full authority was drawn only later to Peter and restricted to him.[72]

Other exegetes regard Matthew 18:18 as later than Matthew 16:19b. If this is the case, they will then explain the relationship between the two passages thus: After the death of Peter, the whole community laid claim for itself to the fullness of power which had at first been invested in Peter. Accordingly, the whole Church would be the successor of the first apostle.[73]

The problem of the relationship between Matthew 16:19b and Matthew 18:18 probably cannot be settled with certitude.

d) Matthew 16:18f. in the Early Church

The Bishops of Rome certainly did not from the beginning onwards adduce Matthew 16:18f. as a basis for their transcendent position

among the bishops. In the beginning they show nothing of the consciousness that they, as successors of the Apostle Peter, would have to
bring Matthew 16:18f. to validity in the Church. Tertullian, in his
work entitled *The Demurrer against the Heretics* (*De praescriptione
haereticorum*) 22, is the first among the early Christian writers to cite
Matthew 16:18f. To the Gnostics who appeal to Paul and maintain
that there were many things of which Peter, who was rebuked by
Paul (Gal. 2:11), was unaware, Tertullian replies by asking whether
anything could have been hidden from Peter, "who was designated
the rock for the foundation of the Church, and who held the keys of
the kingdom of heaven, and who had therewith the power to bind
and to loose in heaven and on earth." The Apostle John was likewise
initiated in everything.

Nevertheless, Tertullian does not say in this place that Peter has his
successors in the Bishops of Rome. In his later work *Modesty* 21, 9-10
(Jurgens, no. 387), a work in which he is extremely embittered and,
in his Pentecostalism, has turned utterly against the Catholic Church,
he says that the promise in Matthew 16:18f. was verified only in Peter
personally and not in his successors. Can it be concluded from Tertullian's emphatic denial that others were advocating the broader interpretation?

According to Cyprian (*Letter to the Lapsed* 33 [27], 1; Jurgens, no.
571) the promise made to Peter is verified in all bishops. Pope St.
Stephen I (244-257 A.D.) was the first Roman Bishop to appeal to
Matthew 16:18f. in the sense in which we understand it, when he
claimed to be the possessor of succession from Peter, from which succession he derived his supreme authority over the Churches. This is
apparent in the letter of Bishop Firmilian of Caesarea in Cappadocia
to Bishop Cyprian of Carthage, preserved as letter no. 75 in the corpus
of Cyprian's letters. Here, after referring to Matthew 16:18f. (Jurgens,
no. 602), Firmilian says that Stephen "glories so much in the place of
his bishopric and contends that he holds the succession of Peter"
(Jurgens, no. 602a). Firmilian reproaches Stephen severely because the
latter recognizes the validity of baptism conferred by heretics.

Afterwards, the Roman interpretation of Matthew 16:18f. first appears clearly again in the *Decree of Damasus* (366-384 A.D.), belonging to the Acts of the Roman Synod of 382 and repeated in the Gelasi-

an Decree.[74] This *Decree of Damasus* (Jurgens, no. 910u) explains that the Roman Church received the primacy through the word of the Lord: "You are Peter, and upon this rock I will build my Church . . . ." Further development belongs to the subject matter of the history of dogma.

§ 6. WORD

There is nothing that seems more ephemeral and powerless than speech.[75] Scarcely is a word uttered, and it exists no more. Nevertheless, an extraordinary human word can sometimes have the power of effecting either good or evil in society and in government. Hence it is understandable that the Bible, like other religious documents, attributes speech to God and speaks of the power of God's word.[76]

1. POWER OF THE DIVINE WORD

a) Ancient East

We esteem speech as a means of understanding and instructing. In the estimate of the ancient East,[77] the word is first and foremost a power effective in blessing and cursing. The divine word is creative. According to Egyptian mythology, the creator-god Ptah created with "heart and tongue." A saying about the word of Thoth is reminiscent of Old Testament sayings of the prophets: "What comes forth from his mouth happens; what he says, that will be." The power of God's word is lauded in Babylonian hymns. "His word, which goes forth like a storm, which rends the heavens above, which convulses the earth below, his word is like a gale."

b) Greco-Roman Antiquity

In Greco-Roman antiquity, the logos signifies the creating and ordering rationality in the world. Logos becomes an essential term and concept of Greek intellectuality. From the time of Heraclitus, philosophy begins to develop its theory of the word. For Heraclitus, logos is certainly speech and learning, but it is also the law and the truth of the world (H. Diels and W. Kranz, *Die Fragmente der Vorsokratiker*, Vol. 1, 6th ed., Berlin-Grunewald 1951, pp. 150f., Frag. 1 and 2).

For the Stoa, the logos is the eternal law of the divine All, indeed, of God himself. In the *Hymn of Cleanthes*, "the one eternal logos of all things" is equated with Zeus (J. von Arnim, *Stoicorum veterum fragmenta*, Vol. 1, Stuttgart 1964, pp. 121f., Frag. 537, v. 8f.). "The human logos has come from the divine. . . . The divine logos teaches men what one must do that is beneficial" (Pseudo-Epicharmus, in Diels and Kranz, *op. cit.*, Vol. 1, p. 208, Frag. 57). The universal logos achieves its existence in man: "Where a work can be perfected in accord with the universal logos of the gods and of men, there is nothing evil" (Marcus Aurelius, *Communings with Himself* or *Meditations*, 7, 53).

c) Bible

1) Old Testament. In the Old Testament, the word of God is spoken as word of creation, of prophecy, and of law. The word of creation calls the world and man into existence (Gen. 1:3–2:4a). Of this word, Isaiah (55:11) says: "My word, which comes forth from my mouth, does not return to me empty, but achieves what I have resolved and carries out that for which I sent it forth." The work of the word is abiding. "He speaks, and it takes place. He commands, and there it is" (Ps. 32:9). The ordination of law has its source and center in the ten words, i.e., the ten commandments, of Yahweh on Sinai (Exod. 20:1-17; 34:28; Deut. 5:6-21). The primordial law became more developed and was focused on new relationships, as in the Book of the Covenant (Ex. 21–23) and in the whole of Deuteronomy.

In many instances in which the Old Testament recounts a word of God, it is a word of God to the prophets and through them. The prophet is under the superior power of the word. "The lion roars, and is anyone not afraid? The Lord Yahweh speaks, and does anyone not prophesy?" (Amos 3:8). The word of God proves itself in its authenticity and truthfulness, inasmuch as it is fulfilled in judgment and salvation in regard to Israel and the nations. "I have said it, and I bring it to pass; I have planned it, and I carry it out" (Is. 46:10f.).

The primordial word of God has made itself incarnate in the Scriptures. Yahweh himself writes the "ten words" on two stone tablets (Exod. 24:12; 31:18; 32:15). Moses writes down the words (Exod. 24:4; 34:27f.), and Joshua the "Book of the Law of God" (Josh. 24:26). Prophets set down in their books the word of God that came to them (Hos. 1:1; Joel 1:1; Micah 1:1; Zeph. 1:1).

2) New Testament. The New Testament recognizes in the words of Jesus and in the preaching of the apostles the word of God, which went forth like those in ancient times (see the present work, Vol. 2, pp. 20–46). Neither the historicity nor the human character of the word of God is thereby denied when men like Moses, David, and Isaiah are at the same time designated as the spokesmen of God's word. The judgment of Jesus on the bill of divorce (Mark 10:1-12 and parallels) is significant. The law of the bill of divorce is proclaimed in Deut. 24:1 as law of God. Jesus, however, designates the bill of divorce as a law of Moses, which contradicts the primordial law of God in Gen. 1:27 and 2:24. The word of Scripture, maintained as divine, can therefore very well be humanly circumscribed.

The New Testament never says that Jesus imparted a word of God as the prophets did, because the New Testament has for its message that Jesus is himself the Word of God (John 1:1; 1 John 1:1; Apoc. 19:13; see the present work, Vol. 2, pp. 59–67).

What the Bible calls the word of God is always spoken by men in human language, concretely, in the Hebrew or Greek language. God has neither mouth nor speech. If he were to speak, how could men endure it? The term and concept "word of God" is apparently not to be understood in a literal sense. Declarations, then, that God has spoken and speaks are, if not a mythology,[78] manners of expression which make use of analogy.[79]

If Sacred Scripture is sometimes designated simply as "word of God," this can be done, nevertheless, only with certain reservations. The Bible is, in its totality, certainly not the resounding word of God, but rather the account of God's word once issued forth; and for the most part, it is the account of events which are in no way a literally spoken word.

From the account, therefore, a challenge or summons must first be deduced. The preparatory draft of the declaration of the First Vatican

Council on revelation originally contained the statement that Sacred Scripture is "truly and properly the word of God — *vere et proprie verbum Dei.*" G. R. Meignan, Bishop of Tours, achieved, nevertheless, by his intervention, the setting aside of this formulation. He was able to make it accepted that one must distinguish on the one hand between the immediate word of God to the prophets and the word of Christ to his apostles, and on the other hand, the accounts of the Sacred Writings, (which were not written down precisely as revelation of God, even though written under divine influence (*Sacrorum conciliorum nova et amplissima collectio*, ed. J. D. Mansi, Vol. 50, 1924, pp. 291f.).

The Second Vatican Council went further on this point with its statement: "The Sacred Writings contain the word of God, and, because they are inspired, they are truly God's word" (Constitution *Dei verbum* 6, 24).

God's word is necessarily perfect — true. Dogmatic teaching, equating the word of God and Sacred Scripture, has deduced the perfect inerrancy of the Bible. Since the biblical evidence and the condition of the Bible itself had not been considered, dogmatics was forced to a fruitless apologetics of its composition. Modern Catholic exegesis, and probably dogmatics as well, has stopped insisting upon the inerrancy of the Bible (see the present work, Vol. 2, p. 12, for a hint to a better understanding of this no-doubt-true but much oversimplified remark — *Translator*).

2. Word and Scripture

Antiquity and the New Testament as well know and declare that the living spoken word far surpasses the written word. Teachers of early times, whom the memory of mankind accounts as the greatest, left no written word behind. It was their students who first recorded their discourses. True of Buddha and Socrates, this is equally true of Jesus. Plato (*Phaedrus* 275 A–278 C) says, however, that in a written discourse, much is by-play that has and confers only the semblance of wisdom. He is certain (7th Letter 341 C; 2nd Letter 314 C) that on the ultimate truths of his teaching there could be no scholastic writings.

"Only in ongoing mutual discourse about a subject as well as from intimate meeting together is an idea suddenly enkindled in the soul, just as a light is ignited from a spark of fire, which, after it has begun, increases of itself."

Even a Paul speaks with some reservation of the written word. "The written word kills, but the spirit makes alive" (see 2 Cor. 3:6; Rom. 2:29 and 7:6). In these passages Paul is contrasting the old and new covenants. The former is written in a book, the latter is a free spirit. Paul is drawing on Jer. 31:33, where it is said of the new covenant: "I will place my law within you and write it in your hearts." Paul could not have so written if a written "New Testament" had already existed in his time. To that extent, what Paul says is a thoroughly critical word about the written New Testament, soon to arise.

3. WORD OF GOD IN THE CHURCH

If the living word is surpassingly more powerful than writing, it must also be understood that that which is written wants to come alive again in speech. The Old Testament certifies this tendency of the written to become word again, by its internal development, in which older texts are taken up and reiterated in later ones, being made real and hearable again and again in the present. Often enough older declarations, when brought to speech, are treated and presented critically in the newer proclamation.

The Church of the New Testament believes that salvation is approaching in the word of God. Thus a remark of Jesus in the Gospel says: "If you enter a house, offer the greeting of peace. If that house is worthy, your peace will come upon it. But if it is not worthy, your peace will return to you" (Matthew 10:12f.). The word of greeting becomes judgment between salvation and loss, such as God alone can distinguish. Paul[80] is convinced that in preaching, it is God's word that falls upon the ear. "You welcomed from us the preached word of God not as human speech but as what it truly is, God's word, which is now operative among you, the faithful" (1 Thess. 2:13). The powerfully concise formulation of the statement is expressive of its unusual circumstances. The word comes incontestably from the Apostle, so that it might well be heard simply as human speech. Nevertheless, it is in the word of the Apostle that the word of God comes to the Church and to the world — indeed, the word of the Apostle is God's word.

In a similar fashion, it is said in 2 Cor. 5:18f.: "Everything is from God, who has reconciled us with himself through Christ. He gave us likewise the ministry of reconciliation, since God was indeed in Christ, who reconciled the world with himself . . . and raised up among us the message of reconciliation." God's action in Christ embraces both, not reconciliation only, but also the establishment of the word or message of reconciliation, in which reconciliation now continues to take place through God. The divine message of reconciliation is now spoken in the word of the Apostle. "In Christ's stead we exercise the office, since God does indeed exhort through us. In Christ's stead we bid you: 'Let yourselves be reconciled with God'" (2 Cor. 5:20). Rom. 10:14, 17 is also to be understood thus: "How should you believe in that which you had not heard? . . . Belief, therefore, comes from hearing, and hearing from the word of Christ."

Since the mission of the apostles comes from Christ (Rom. 10:15), the word of him who commissions is in the word of the one commissioned. In the word of the Apostle, the word of Christ is heard. Titus 1:2f. also knows the quality of being in each other that is found in the word of God and in the word of the Apostle: "Before the eternal ages God promised everlasting life; but at its proper time he has manifested his word in the preaching which was entrusted to me through the command of God our Savior." In the preaching of the Apostle, God's word is made manifest, and this is effective of everlasting life.

The word of God is not merely the recounting of that which once took place; rather, what that word declares is taking place now. When, therefore, the word is called "word of life" (Phil. 2:16), "word of salvation" (Acts 13:26), "word of reconciliation" (2 Cor. 5:18f.), "word of God's grace" (Acts 14:3; 20:32), it does not mean simply that the word tells of the earlier salvational event, but much more, that it actually effects that of which it speaks: reconciliation, salvation, grace, and life.

The word is called "word of truth" (Eph. 1:13; 2 Tim. 2:15) as the word which, in the biblical sense, creates truth. It discloses man's situation; as word of judgment, condemns his guilt; and as word of salvation, makes him just. The word once gone forth and now going forth is ever effective: "For the word of God is living and effective, and it cuts better than a double-edged sword, and it penetrates to the parting of soul and spirit, of joints and marrow, and it is able to judge the thoughts and intentions of the heart" (Heb. 4:12). It is said first of all of God that he lives and effects. This can be said of the word, because the word contains God's power and life (Acts 7:38; John 6:68; Phil. 2:16). God's word reaches into the innermost recesses of the spirit and the soul, as also of corporeal life. "The concepts and terms of Heb. 4:12f. are in part, nevertheless, quite singular in the New Testament; and they betray a special tradition that was Hellenistic."[81]

The manner of the word's effectivity can be compared to that of a sacrament. Just as in baptism the signal act of washing in water is effective beyond anything that is visible, so too the sanctifying word is effective beyond all audibility and natural power. Just as the sacrament is received only in faith, so too the word, where its hearing encounters belief (1 Thess. 2:13; Heb. 4:2). The word achieves a dignity and reality similar to that of a sacrament. Employing and continuing Augustine's formulations, one designates a sacrament as *verbum visibile* (Migne, *PL* 35:1840; and *PL* 42:356f.), and the word as *sacramentum audibile* (Migne, *PL* 27:969). Theology speaks, there, of the sacramentality (or at least of the quasi-sacramentality) of the word.*

The constitution of the Second Vatican Council on the liturgy teaches of the presence of Christ in the worship of God (Art. 7): "Christ is present in the sacrifice of the Mass . . . in the sacraments . . . in his word . . . , which he himself speaks when the Sacred Scriptures are read in the Church." Some Fathers of the Council raised objections that the presence of Christ was declared in the same

---

*[*Translator's note*: There is a very pertinent passage and some food for thought also in Origen's *Homilies on Exodus* 13, 3 (Jurgens, no. 490), wherein that monumental author writes: ". . . when you have received the Body of the Lord, you reverently exercise every care lest a particle of it fall, and lest anything of the consecrated gift perish. You account yourselves guilty if any of it be lost through negligence. But if you observe such caution in keeping his body, and properly so, how is it that you think neglecting the word of God a lesser crime than neglecting his Body?"]

way in reference to the word as in reference to the Sacrament. But the Council held firm to its formulation. To criticism of the expression that Christ himself speaks in the words of Scripture, the commission replied: "In the liturgical traditions it is said of Christ that he is speaking when the Scriptures are read. The presence of Christ in the Gospel is celebrated especially in the liturgies of the East." [82]

The power invested in the word is manifested in the sacrament, in the performance of which the word explains the content and perfects it with the symbol.[83] Word and sign are a unity. In the commission to baptize in Matthew 28:19f., the performance of baptism is bound up with the perfecting and teaching word. Eph. 5:26 says of baptism that Christ "sanctifies the Church, in that he cleanses her by the bath of the water in the word." According to 1 Peter 3:21, "that baptism saves, which is not a washing of the filth of the flesh, but prayer to God for a good conscience by virtue of the resurrection of Christ." The word here is the prayer, which entreats for a good conscience, and therefore for the interior fulfillment of the exterior action of baptism.

The laying on of hands imparts the Spirit and the gift of office, but, according to 1 Tim. 4:14, with "prophecy"—therefore, with a signifying and entreating word.

In the Lord's Supper, the Bread and the Chalice, by means of the word, are referred to the death of Christ, which is thus applied to the participants of the Meal. By sign and word the sacrament is "proclamation of the death of the Lord" (1 Cor. 11:26; see below, § 9, 3, c, 3). Paul can designate word and sacrament as proclamation. The sacrament has verbal character, while the word has sacramental character. In the broadest and deepest manner, however, the word becomes effective of salvation in the incarnation of God's Logos in time and world. All the sacraments are extensions of Christ's incarnation. Since, however, Christ is ever the Word, all the sacraments are also word.

If preaching is indeed to be heard as God's word, the preacher can nevertheless change that word. There were and are false prophets (Matthew 24:11), erring deceivers (2 John 7), and false teachers (2 Peter 2:1). On the other hand, preaching may yet remain intact in spite of a preacher's motives of self-interest. "Many proclaim Christ out of envy and contentiousness, others, however, from good will. But what difference does it make, so long as in every way, in pretense or in truth, Christ is proclaimed?" (Phil. 1:15f.). Still, a preacher can also falsify the word (2 Cor. 4:2). A preacher can "conduct a base traffic with the word, which many do" (2 Cor. 2:17). Preaching can "deceive the hearts of the simple with flattery and smooth words" (Rom. 16:18).

Paul mentions criteria for the authenticity of the word. The preacher must himself have experienced the mercy of God (1 Cor. 7:25). The word must be adduced in love. "We wanted to let you participate not only in the gospel of God, but also in our heart" (1 Thess. 2:7f.). The Apostle demands clarity and truth of proclamation in frankness toward God and men (1 Thess. 2:3f.; Gal. 2:14; 2 Cor. 2:17; 4.2; 5:11; 13:8). Required as a necessary characteristic of preaching is "the candor to tell all" (Acts 4:29; 2 Cor. 3:12; Eph. 3:12; Phil. 1:20; Heb. 4:16). Preaching must take place in the Spirit and from the Spirit. "Since we have the same spirit of faith as shown in that which is written, 'I believe, therefore do I speak,' so too we believe, and therefore do we speak" (2 Cor. 4:13). The listening Church will be certain of the authenticity of the word when the mind of Christ bestowed on her (1 Cor. 2:16) and her common endowment with the Spirit (1 Cor. 2:13-15) perceive in the proclamation the Spirit of Christ (1 Cor. 14:29). Every Christian shares in this ability to distinguish. "If someone is spiritual, he will recognize that that which I write to you is the word of the Lord" (1 Cor. 14:37).

4. DIRECT WORD OF GOD

The direct word of God is not just a thing of the past. According to the Old and New Testaments, it belongs to God's sovereignty to be silent and to speak, however he will. Again and again the New Testament declares its certainty that the direct word of God never ceases, but always goes forth as it did originally. Thus in 1 Thess. 4:9; "You have no need of my writing you about fraternal love; you are indeed taught by God himself to love one another." Then in John 6:45; "It is written in the prophets, 'You will all be taught by God.'" Heb. 8:11f. quotes Jer. 31:31-34, "I will place my law in your minds. No one will have to teach his neighbor, no one will have to instruct his brother and say to him, 'Know the Lord.' For they will all know me."

These three texts are widely separated from each other in the New Testament and have no textual interdependence. What is declared here is a common consciousness in the New Testament. The passage in John 6:45 appeals to "the prophets." The evangelist did not have in mind a particular place; rather, he means that this is the universal conviction of the prophets. As a particular example, Is. 54:13 in the Septuagint might be mentioned, a passage cited by the rabbis as proof that in the messianic and eschatological age Israel will be the recipient of Yahweh's direct instruction; likewise Jer. 31:33, and therefore passages from the celebrated, and in subsequent times, often-quoted messianic promise; and finally, Joel 3:1f., which is repeated in the Pentecost preaching of the Apostle Peter (Acts 2:16-21).

The Qumran writings (*Damascus Document* 20:4; 1 QH 2:39; 7:10, 14; 8:36) also speak of "God's students." Additional sayings in the New Testament belong to the same general mode of thinking. In all ages and everywhere, God's light shines forth. "God illuminated our hearts to make bright the knowledge of God's majesty in the face of Christ" (2 Cor. 4:6). Everywhere that God is, there is light; and wherever there is light, God is there. All receive God's revelation (Phil. 3:15). All have received the anointing to know the truth, and have no need of being taught (1 John 2:21, 27). The whole Church enjoys prophetic endowment (Acts 2:17; Rom. 12:6; 1 Cor. 12:10; 14:1; Eph. 4:11; 1 Thess. 5:20). From this follows the vocation and obligation of all to declare and to proclaim the word of God (1 Cor. 14:24; 1 Peter 2:9; Jude 3). This holds good also for women (Rom. 16:1-13; 1 Cor. 11:5).

§ 7. SACRAMENTS

1. Jesus and Practice of Worship

Jesus found Israel's worship already arranged in the old covenant.[84] Even this part of the Law he was not to abolish but to perfect (Matthew 5:17). According to the accounts of the Evangelists, Jesus heeds the arrangement of feasts in their yearly course (Mark 14:12; Luke 2:42; John 2:23; 5:1; 7:10). He celebrates the meal in accord with the formalities of worship (Mark 6:41; 8:6; 14:22). Since he accepts the baptism of John, he participates in the baptismal movement (Mark 1:9). The purification of the Temple from its secularization bespeaks the zeal of Jesus for God's house (Mark 11:15-17).

Jesus presses, nevertheless, for the true sense of cultic celebration, which is to be a blessing for men. Therefore the hungry disciples must be permitted to pluck ears of grain on the Sabbath [85] (Mark 2:23-28).[86] For the sake of such a fulfillment, Jesus appears to have transgressed the Sabbath law in a challenging manner. Even so, Jesus demands the true sense of sacrifice. The God to whom man sacrifices is the merciful God who wants mercy (Matthew 9:13). A sacrifice in worship of God, therefore, is possible only if brotherly love is practiced. Only after this — "*Then* come and offer your gifts" (Matthew 5:23f.). It is not possible to offer sacrifice and under false pretexts ignore the obligation of loving one's neighbor (Mark 7:10-13).

In his threatening address against Pharisaism, in every condemnation of perverse behavior, Jesus speaks with deepest reverence for the Temple and for worship. Temple and altar sanctify the offering. The Temple is God's house (Matthew 23:16-22). At his trial the mysterious saying of Jesus is quoted, according to which he, after the end of the earthly Temple, will erect a new eschatological temple (Mark 14:58; below, § 14, 1). He claims that he himself is "more than the Temple" (Matthew 12:6). Jesus describes the eschatological consummation with images drawn from worship. Jesus recognizes the arrangement of the priesthood. He tells the leper who was healed: "Show yourself to the priest," and he requires him to make the prescribed sacrificial offering (Mark 1:44). And is it in fact a criticism of priesthood and the order of worship when, in the parable of the Good Samaritan, Jesus says only of the priest and of the levite that in their calling and in their concern for ritual purity they hastened by their neighbor in need (Luke 10:31f.)?

Jesus did react, however, in a negative manner to the notions and prescriptions in reference to ritual purity. The zealous striving for ritual purity, which in this degree was not a prescription of the Old

Testament Law but a determination of the rabbis, is idle. No external
things, but wicked thoughts and actions make men impure (Mark
7:14-23). Jesus throws it up to the "blind Pharisees" that they purify
the outside, while the inside is full of corruption (Matthew 23:25f.).
Jesus puts himself above the requirements of ritual purity by his companionship with sinners (Matthew 9:10; 11:19; Luke 7:37; 15:2; 19:7).
In this a total opposition between Jesus and Qumran is to be seen.
Jesus calls sinners, while the pious of Qumran keep apart from them
(see the present work, Vol. 2, pp. 101–106).

It bespeaks the conduct of Jesus, and follows therefrom, that the
primitive community continued in the beginning to participate in the
divine worship in the Temple (Luke 24:52f.; Acts 2:46; 3:1). It did,
however, abandon the commandments of ritual purity (Acts 10:14f.).

2. New Testament Sacraments

Following the concept in the Church's teaching, a sacrament is an
action in sign, signified through the spoken word, which, by reason
of its institution by Christ, dispenses God's salvation. The developed
doctrine enumerates seven such sacraments. The New Testament describes no concept and has no term for sacrament. The Latin translation of the New Testament, however, employs the word *sacramentum*
for μυστήριον. With the New Testament as its lead, Greek theology
calls sacramental doctrines and processes, especially baptism and Eucharist, "mysteries."

Outside the New Testament, the term *mysterium* (μυστήριον) designates the ritual celebrations of the mystery religions; in philosophy,
divine secrets; and finally, anything that is secret. In the Bible, Old
Testament and New, *mysterium* designates the secret or mysterious
revelation of God, which takes place in word and in sign (Matthew
13:11; 1 Cor. 4:1; Rom. 16:25) and presses forward to the eschatological consummation (Apoc. 10:7). Christ is the *"mysterium* of God"
(Col. 2:2; Eph. 3:4). Since the Latin Bible frequently translated the
term μυστήριον with the word *sacramentum*, the concept of sacrament
took something from that Greek word. In Odo Casel's theology of

mysteries, the concept of *mysterium* is brought again to validity (below, § 8, 3, c, 9).

The word *sacramentum* was introduced into the theological language of the Church by Tertullian. In the profane language, the word signified something of the notion of an oath of initiation. With *sacramentum* Tertullian designated God's whole salvific arrangement, but in particular, as ritual salvific event, baptism and Eucharist.[87] The enumeration of the sacraments as seven was a calculation of the High Middle Ages, after an unequivocal concept of sacrament had been established.[88]

New Testament theology does not hesitate to speak of New Testament sacraments. It designates baptism and Eucharist as original sacraments. The later and modern Catholic concept of sacrament is fashioned in accord with their New Testament status, since for these two sacraments the essential notes of the concept are evident, which are the action in sign, word, and establishment by Christ. Baptism and Eucharist appear already in the New Testament as closely interconnected, in texts like 1 Cor. 10:1-4; and also in 1 John 5:6-8 and John 19:34, if blood and water here designate Eucharist and baptism (see below, § 9, 3, c, 7).

In later parts of the New Testament there is mention of further ritual performances which were eventually accounted as sacraments: laying on of hands for conferral of the Holy Spirit (Acts 8:17; 18:6; see below, § 8, 3, c, 3); installation in office by prayer and imposition of hands (Acts 14:23; 1 Tim. 4:14; 2 Tim. 1:6; above, § 3, 2, b, 4); forgiveness of sins (Mark 2:5; John 20:22f.; below, § 8, 4); anointing of the sick (Mark 6:13; James 5:14f.; below, § 8, 4).

By concept, sacraments are something essentially different from memorial recollection or purely symbolic application of signs, such as might be practiced by the prophets (Jer. 19; Ezek. 4; 5; 24). Baptism and Eucharist impart to the cooperating recipient a manifold endowment of grace. On the other hand, the sacraments are absolutely distinct from magic. In magic and conjuration the marvelous result can take place even without and, indeed, against the will of him toward whom the magic is worked. In the New Testament, the faith of the recipient is a requisite for the effective reception of the sacrament.

Baptism and Eucharist do not of their nature guarantee security, but make such possible, while they do also require moral perfection (Rom. 6:6; 11; 1 Cor. 10:5). Moreover, the gift of the sacrament is not physical increment of life but a spiritual or pneumatic gift (John 6:63; 1 Cor. 10:3f.).

§ 8. BAPTISM

In numerous texts the New Testament speaks of baptism[89] as the beginning and foundation of being a Christian and as initiation into the Church. Between the years 200 and 206, Tertullian wrote the first book on baptism in the Church, a work which even so early embodied a rich development of the celebration of conferring baptism and shows a doctrine drawing upon and deliberately employing the Bible, Old Testament and New.

For Christianity of the earliest times, baptism was an experience of the utmost significance. It was in a Church that was yet a distinct minority, and especially in the times of the persecution it was a radical decision in one's life. Baptism was the fulfillment of what the Christian had been preparing for in a lengthy catechumenate. Celebrated on the night of Easter or on the vigil of Pentecost in the public worship of God, baptism was the assumption of an obligation before the entire community.

In the modern Church, baptism is no longer such a significant experience by far. The reasons for this may be consequent upon the circumstances of infant baptism. With the universal practice of infant baptism, we no longer have a conscious acceptance of baptism and a baptismal experience. We have no personal memory of our own baptism, and hardly even of the celebration of baptism, since almost without exception baptism does not take place publicly in the Church but before only a few participants. A further reason may be that we are hardly able to think in terms of symbolism, so that in baptism the symbolism of the ritual bath in the terse ceremony of the pouring of water over the head of the child can scarcely anymore be perceived.

1. RITUAL BATHS (HISTORICAL RELIGIOUS ENVIRONS)

To begin with, we might call to mind the manifold human experience and long history of the ritual bath.[90] Water is the prerequisite of all life in the plant and animal world. All life begins and grows in water. Pure water cleanses, especially flowing water, carrying away with itself all uncleanness. In the primordial religious viewpoint, the superhuman creative power of water is divine. Water is regarded itself as a divinity, or is animated by the divinity. Gods, spirits, and demons dwell in the water and rule it. It receives ritual consecration, or again it serves as a medium of worship, inasmuch as it is involved in the sacred purification or in the mysterious furtherance of life. In rites water is drunk or poured out over a man, or the man is immersed in a bath of water.

It was perfectly natural that for ancient man and even today in many religions (like Islam, for example), cleansing and purification was required before engaging in the procedures of worship. "With unwashed and bloodstained hands one dare not pray to Zeus" (*Iliad* 6, 266f.). In front of temples notices were posted, requiring a cleansing. At the gates of the temple stood basins of purifying water, with which one washed or sprinkled himself. Before initiation into the Eleusinian mysteries, one had to take a bath in the sea. Baths pertained also to initiation into the cults of Isis and Mithras.

2. OLD TESTAMENT AND JUDAISM

Israel knew and practiced many kinds of washings and baths. When the high priest entered the Holy of Holies on the Day of Atonement, he first had to wash his body in water and put on the sacred vestments (Lev. 16:4). Before the Temple service, the priests took ritual baths (Exod. 29:4), as well as the whole people (Deut. 23:12, 15). Further prescriptions required ritual washings after any contamination (Lev. 13:6; 15:18-27; Num. 5:23; 19:7-22). The prophets promise the purifying eschatological judgment in the imagery of the bath (Is. 4:4; Mal. 3.2f.), and similarly the messianic sanctification in the endtime (Ezek.

36:25; Zech. 13:1). The forgiveness of guilt is like a purifying washing (Ps. 51:4, 9).

The excavations at Qumran[91] brought to light an extensive network of bathing installations. The Qumran writings demand numerous baths (1 QS 5:13; *Damascus Document* 9:21-23; 10:5-13). The immersional baths prescribed for the priests of the Temple in Jerusalem were taken by all the pious at Qumran. They all aspired to priestly holiness. But they knew that in spite of all external washings, he remains impure "who contemns the statutes of God and does not discipline himself in the communion of God's counsel." True purification takes place through the fulfillment of the law of God (1 QS 3:4-9).

These baths at Qumran, nevertheless, in distinction to the singular Christian baptism, were iterable. Acceptance into the novitiate may have been done with a bath which, in this peculiar circumstance, was not repeatable.

Only from the first century after Christ is a baptism of proselytes attested, which may, however, have been the practice even earlier. Gentiles who desired incorporation into a full membership with God's people Israel had to submit to circumcision, to a ritual immersion for the purpose of purification, and they had to bring forward a victim for immolation, the blood of which was shed for the absolution of the Gentile. The bath made the newly won Jew qualified to perform the sacrifice. The baptism of proselytes was, like Christian baptism, a ritual bath that could not be repeated; but unlike Christian baptism, it was a bath by immersion in which the proselyte immersed himself.

Paul finds baptism already in the Old Testament. The fathers, all of whom were under the cloud (Exod. 13:21; Ps. 104:3f. in the Septuagint) and passed through the sea (Exod. 14:21), were baptized in the cloud and in the sea (1 Cor. 10:2). Here Paul is giving a midrash in the scholarly manner, in which he may be employing themes from rabbinic interpretation. For 1 Peter 3:20f., the salvation of Noah and of his family through the water by means of the ark is a prototype of baptism, in which, however, the point of comparison, the water, is differently employed. In the deluge, the water was a punishing and destroying element, whereas in baptism it has saving power. Many examples of a typological explanation of an Old Testament text about water, in reference to New Testament baptism, are assembled in the eleventh chapter of the so-called *Letter of Barnabas* (for one such example, in *Barnabas* 11:10-11, see Jurgens, no. 34). Such exegesis of the Old Testament is continued in the ancient Church.[92]

3. NEW TESTAMENT

a) John the Baptist

Within the Jewish baptismal movements there appeared also John the Baptist. He dispensed "a baptism of repentance unto the forgiveness of sins" (Mark 1:4). The Gospels tell that even Jesus let himself be baptized by John. No serious doubt can be raised against the historicity of this event, especially since the New Testament tradition already had to justify the fact of Jesus' having submitted to John's baptism (Matthew 3:13f.). The Gospel of John seems of set purpose to avoid speaking of the baptism of Jesus by John, which can only be deduced from John 1:33f. The narration of the baptism of Jesus was shaped to a Trinitarian revelation (see the present work, Vol. 2, pp. 197f, 225, 306f.).

b) Origin of Christian Baptism

The whole of the New Testament, Gospels, Acts and Epistles, attests the fact that the Church administered baptism from the very beginning. To the question of why the Church baptized from the very beginning with such assured confidence, the New Testament answers that Jesus instituted baptism and submitted himself to baptism. John (3:5) tells that Jesus, in conversation with Nicodemus, promised the Church the sacrament of baptism: "If anyone is not born again of water and the Spirit, he cannot enter the kingdom of God."[93] What is true of all the conversation of Jesus in the Gospel of John is true of this remark also: it exemplifies the theology of the Church in that time (*ca.* 100 A.D.) and environment. John, then, in 3:5, repeats the teaching of the Church about baptism. Baptism is designated as a "rebirth."

ἄνωθεν γεννηθῆναι (John 3:3, 7) is not to be understood as "to be born from above" but as "to be born again," since in the later New Testament this designation of baptism seems already to be current (1 Peter 1:3; 23; Titus 3:5; and besides these, there is Justin, in his *First Apol-*

ogy 61, 3 [Jurgens, no. 126]. The majority of the old translations (Latin, Coptic, Syriac), as well as the Fathers of the Church, understand John 3:3 as rebirth. Even the misunderstanding of Nicodemus in John 3:4 seems to presuppose this is the correct understanding. For a man as flesh, redemption by his own power is not impossible. Baptism imparts the Spirit, which means new creation (see next below, *c*).

According to John 3:22, Jesus was baptizing along with his disciples, of whom some had previously been disciples of John the Baptist, in the countryside of Judea, all of which is clarified (in a redactional addition?) in John 4:2, to the effect that it was not Jesus personally who was baptizing, but his disciples. In any case, Jesus did accordingly associate himself primarily with the baptismal movement introduced by John the Baptist.

In the Gospel of Matthew (28:19), the risen Christ departs from his disciples, the while he commissions them: "Go forth and make disciples of all nations, by baptizing them in the name of the Father and of the Son and of the Holy Spirit."[94] The saying cannot, in this form, stand at the very beginning of the Church and of her mission. Baptism was practiced at first, no doubt, in the theology of Jesus (below, § 8, 3, c, 1). The confession in Trinitarian structure presupposes a long theological development (see the present work, Vol. 2, pp. 306f.). If the Church had known from the very beginning of her task of a world mission, it would be hardly understandable that Paul could succeed only after long and difficult struggles in establishing his right to conduct his free mission to the Gentiles.

The Gospel of Matthew is likely to have been written down about the year 80 or a little later. The command about baptizing and conducting a mission reflects the baptismal practice achieved in the Church about this time, as also the mission experience of the Church. The commission to baptize is stated in the saying of the exalted Christ. Exegesis even questions whether the risen Christ spoke in structured language.[95] The consciousness of the Church of having to receive baptism from the Lord is attested in the saying of the resurrected Lord in Mark 16:16, "Whoever believes and is baptized will be saved." This saying certainly belongs to the appendix of Mark's Gospel, which appendix is likely to have been written down about the year 150 A.D. Since it condenses the resurrection accounts of the other Gospels already existing, it presupposes Matthew 28:19. It is striking how very much this late text emphasizes faith as prerequisite to baptism. The sacrament, therefore, can in no way be administered as a magical procedure.[96]

According to the accounts in the Acts of the Apostles (2:38; 8:12, 16; 9:18; 10:47; 16:15, 33; 19:5; 22:16), baptism was administered in the Church from the very beginning.[97] In his Pentecost sermon, Peter demands: "Repent, and let each of you be baptized in the name of Jesus Christ" (Acts 2:38). If occasionally the Acts of the Apostles depends upon the community practice of its later time to predate something to an earlier time, it is nonetheless clear that with these accounts the conviction of the Church is expressed that baptism was the practice of the Church from the very beginning. This, however, is certainly completely historical.

c) Theology of Baptism

If the Church of the apostles practiced baptism from the very beginning, it thereby entered into a widespread baptismal movement. It is especially possible that the baptism of John may be continuing, particularly if earlier disciples of John became disciples of Jesus (John 1:35f.). If, as according to Acts 18:24f. and 19:1-7, at a comparatively late time there were Christian communities of disciples who "knew only of the baptism of John," it does certainly at least make it clear that the Church continued the baptism of John. A neat reason for the practice of baptism in the Church will have been the fact that Jesus himself had accepted for himself the baptism of John.

The connection between the baptism of Jesus by John and Christian baptism may be indicated if the account about the baptism of Jesus discloses a relationship to the Church's later baptism, since that account may contain themes from the Christian practice of baptism. The narrative can be understood as a catechesis on baptism, when Jesus is revealed as the Son (Mark 1:11) and the Spirit comes upon him (Mark 1:10f.), just as always the one being baptized is accepted by God as his child and is endowed with the Spirit of sonship (Rom. 8:15f., Gal. 4:6f.).

The Fathers of the Church knew this relationship between the baptism of Jesus and Christian baptism when they said that Jesus instituted the sacrament of baptism when he let himself be baptized by John. He thereby imparted to the water a sacramental power. According to St. Ignatius of Antioch (*Letter to the Ephesians* 18, 2; [Jurgens, no. 42]), Jesus, by his baptism in the Jordan and afterwards by his suffering, consecrated the (baptismal) water for the use of Christians. The same thought appears in St. Clement of Alexandria (*Eclogae propheticae* 7:1: "The Redeemer was baptized for this reason, that he might sanctify the water all at once for the reborn"); similarly in the same author's *Instructor of Children* 1, 6, 25; in Tertullian's *Baptism*, chs. 4, 8, and 9; St. Ambrose, *Commentary on the Gospel of Luke* 2, 83; St. Cyril of Jerusalem, *Cathechetical Lectures* 3, 11: "Christ made baptism holy, since he was himself baptized."

Baptism in the Church was administered by a baptizer (like John's baptism, but otherwise than the Jewish baptism of proselytes, which was a self-baptism). Paul himself says that he has baptized (1 Cor. 1:14, 16). Other texts say in harmonious agreement, "You were baptized." Even the commission to baptize in Matthew 28:19 presupposes baptism by someone else. According to universal or predominant usage, Christian baptism was performed by immersion. This is indicated in Acts 8:36; Heb. 10:22; *Didache* 7, 1-3 (Jurgens, no. 4); and the *Letter of Barnabas* 11, 11 (Jurgens, no. 34).

1) *"In the Name of Jesus."* Baptism in the Church was something different and new, by reason of a new and fuller understanding. Baptism was administered "in the name of Jesus Christ" (Acts 2:38); "in the name of the Lord Jesus" (Acts 8:16; 10:48); "in Jesus Christ" (Rom. 6:3); "in Christ" (Gal. 3:27).[98] This took place either by the name of Jesus being spoken over the one being baptized, or by the one's being baptized invoking Jesus (Acts 22:16). It was by this name that baptism in the Church was distinguished from the several non-Christian baptisms. The name signifies the presence of the salvational power of Jesus under which the one being baptized was placed. Exorcismal power may also be intended, as the disciples drive out demons in the name of Jesus (Mark 9:38f.; Luke 10:17; Mark 16:17). The salvational power invoked contains and effects the gifts of baptism.

2) *Purification from Sins.* Baptism signifies cleansing from sins. In each baptism the eternal rite is thereby a sign of the internal effect and is made fruitful. Even John's baptism was "a baptism of repentance

unto the forgiveness of sins" (Mark 1:4). The prophets of the Old Testament were calling to repentance when they proclaimed the eschatological judgment and its purification in the image of the bath (Is. 4:4; Mal. 3:2f.). John the Baptist took up such prophecy. If repentance is human effort, the consequent forgiveness of sin is action and gift of God. Guilt or its remission is a determination of God's judgment. John's baptism, then, is eschatologically directed. These factors are brought together in the *Prayer of Manasses* 7 (to be dated, perhaps, in the first century before Christ): "You promise forgiveness to those who have sinned, forgiveness through repentance; and in the fullness of your mercy, you bring the sinner to repentance unto salvation."

The eschatological character of John's baptism is made clear in Source Q, upon which Matthew 3:11f. and Luke 3:16f. depend. John accordingly proclaims the imminent baptism by the Messiah which is to take place "in the Holy Spirit and fire." If fire signifies the impending judgment, the Spirit is an eschatological gift for the sanctification of sinners for the judgment. In Mark 1:8 it is said only that the Messiah is baptizing in the Holy Spirit, and the impending eschatological factor is lacking; this baptism of the Spirit, then, can be understood of the Church's sacrament of baptism.

In general, nevertheless, the portrayal of the action of John's baptism is in accord with the understanding of Christian baptism. For the Church's baptism likewise effects forgiveness of sins. Accordingly, the sermon of Peter says: "Repent, be baptized for the forgiveness of sins, and you will receive the gift of the Holy Spirit" (Acts 2:38).

Saul-Paul receives the command, "Be baptized and have your sins washed away" (Acts 22:16). Of baptism and its effects, Paul will issue the reminder, "You are washed, you are sanctified, you are justified through the name of our Lord Jesus Christ and through the Spirit of God" (1 Cor. 6:11). The solemn triplex formula represents the whole grace of baptism. It is negatively enriched as a cleansing of sins, and positively it works sanctification (Eph. 5:26) and justification. Sanctification is, in its original sense, acceptance into the kingdom of God, who is the primordial Holy One (see the present work, Vol. 2, pp. 268–272).

In Qumran, too, purification and sanctification are conceived as effect of ritual bathing (1 QS 3:4; 1 QH 11:10-12).

In baptism the salvation of Christ is at work: the salvation, ultimately, of God's creating Spirit. "Christ has loved the Church and has delivered himself up for her, in order to sanctify her, after he has purified her by the bath of the water in the word" (Eph. 5:25f). Baptism, which is administered to each individual, seems here to be a work over the whole Church. It remains uncertain whether the Epistle may be thinking of the custom of the bathing of a bride, which, in Jewish (Ezek. 16:9f.) as well as in Greek usage, was done ceremonially.[99]

The death of Christ and baptism are associated (Rom. 6:3; below, § 8, 3, c, 9). While in Paul the union between death and baptism takes place in the baptismal action, in Eph. 5:25f., it is by Christ's will that his death is related to baptism. The effect of baptism is described negatively as purification, positively as sanctification (comparably in 1 Cor. 6:11). Heb. 10:22 likewise alludes to baptism: "Let us go in to sanctification with sincere hearts and in the fullness of the faith, our hearts sprinkled and cleansed of any bad conscience and our bodies washed in pure water." The Epistle employs Old Testament cultic language and proceeds probably from the prescriptions which, in Exod. 29:4, 21 and Lev. 8:6, 30, require a sprinkling and washing for the priest before he performs his ministry.

Christian baptism, however, is much more than the Old Testament washing. Christian baptism sprinkles the heart and cleanses entirely of guilt, while the Old Testament washings remain only external, a bodily cleansing (Heb. 9:10). The water of baptism is ritually predicted as "pure water" (Ezek. 36:25).

3) Imparting of the Spirit. In baptism the Holy Spirit is imparted. Israel expects the messianic-eschatological gift of the Spirit (Is. 32:15-17; 44:3; Ezek. 36:25-27; 37:1-14; Joel 3:1-5; Haggai 2:5; Zech. 4:6). This expectation was a living one in the time of the New Testament. The *Book of Jubilees* 1:23 says: "I will create for them a holy spirit and will make them pure, so that from this day on until eternity they will no more turn away from me." In the time of the Messiah, the nation will be full of spirit-achieved wisdom, justice and power (*Psalms of Solomon* 18:8). The pious men of Qumran knew that "the conduct of men can be steadfast only in the spirit, which God created" (1 QG 4:31). They give thanks for the proffered "spirit of holiness" (1 QH 7:6f.).

The promise is now fulfilled by baptism's gift of the Spirit. To that end Jesus promised baptism (John 3:5f.). Immediately after the great outpouring of the Holy Spirit, Peter preaches: "Be baptized . . . and you will receive the gift of the Spirit" (Acts 2:38). Even the conferring of the Spirit distinguishes baptism in the Church from John's baptism (Acts 19:1-6). The conferring of the Spirit was made ritually visible quite early through the imposition of hands (Acts 8:17; 19:6). Their union is evidenced when, for Heb. 6:2, the doctrine "of baptism and laying on of hands" is already traditional.[100] Endowment with the Spirit may have been understood at first as the bestowing of extraordinary charismatic gifts (Acts 10:46). For Paul this is the effect of baptism: "We are all baptized in one Spirit, into one body, Jews and Greeks, slaves and free, and one Spirit was given us all to drink" (1 Cor. 12:13).

The Spirit operating in baptism creates the one body of the Church. In it there takes place the lifting of every human distinction (Gal. 3:28). The Epistle to the Ephesians probably designates baptism as sealing by the Holy Spirit. "When you became believers, you were sealed with the Holy Spirit of the promise" (Eph. 1:13). "Do not offend the Holy Spirit of God, with whom you were sealed on the day of your redemption" (Eph. 4:30). Comparable are Old Testament representations of protective signs which guard and rescue (Is. 44:5; Ezek. 9:4; *Psalms of Solomon* 15:6-9). Baptism is a sealing with the Holy Spirit. He is a gift for the sake of eschatological consummation.[101]

4) Reception into the Church. By baptism one is received into the Church. "Those who accepted the preaching of Peter were baptized and there were three thousand souls received into the Church" (Acts 2:41). According to the *Didache* 9:5 (Jurgens, no. 6), no one is to be permitted to eat or drink of the Eucharist except those who have been baptized in the name of the Lord. Baptism accepts its recipient into the Church, which is the Body of Christ. "We were baptized in one Spirit into one body" (1 Cor. 12:13). "All of you who have been baptized into Christ have put on Christ. You are all one in Christ" (Gal. 3:27).[102] The figure of putting on Christ describes baptism as constituting an entirely new relationship to Christ in one's very being, a relationship which, in the one Church, belongs to each individual.

The Old Testament already used the figure of a garment. God clothes the nation in the cloak of salvation (Is. 61:10). Virtue clothes with power and glory (Prov. 31:36).

The New Testament Epistles frequently use this imagery, sometimes in the indicative, as in Gal. 3:27; and sometimes in the imperative, as in Rom. 13:14, "Put on Jesus Christ!"; likewise in Eph. 4:22-24, "Put on the new man!" If the indicative points to the sacramental event, the imperative refers to the subsequent moral perfection made possible and necessarily demanded by the sacramental event.

In the mystery religions, the mystes puts on the garment of divinity (thus in Apuleius, *Metamorphoses* 11, 24, 1-4; below, § 8, 3, c, 9). It does not seem impossible that such a representation and terminology have had an effect on the New Testament.

5) Eschatological Salvation. Baptism achieves salvation. As once the ark, floating over the waters, saved, so "now baptism saves you, baptism which is not a washing off of physical dirt, but a prayer to God for a good conscience, by virtue of the resurrection of Jesus Christ" (1 Peter 3:21). The import of this lies with the future eschatology. Baptism saves in the future judgment. In a way reminiscent of Qumran texts (1 QS 3:4-9; above, § 8, 2), it is emphasized that baptism is not an external washing. The internal action is the prayer to God that he might create a good conscience, which has its foundation in the internal purification bestowed by God for the sake of Christ's salvation. Perhaps the Epistle is calling to mind the liturgical conferring of baptism, at which the prayer for the forgiveness of sins was spoken over the one being baptized. Titus 3:5 also speaks of salvation through baptism: "He has saved us." Salvation is spoken of as present. The eschatological postponement is suspended.

6) Rebirth. Baptism is rebirth.[103] "He has saved us . . . by the bath of rebirth and renewal in the Holy Spirit" (Titus 3:5). If in John 3:5 baptism is designated as new birth (above, § 8, 3, b), this same evaluation of baptism is here expressly declared. Like birth, it is new beginning and "new creation" (2 Cor. 5:17).

The First Epistle of Peter also speaks of rebirth. It is sometimes regarded as a baptismal sermon, properly speaking. In any case, the

Epistle is someway related to the oldest baptismal preaching; and that is how it makes use of the concept and term rebirth. God "has, in his great mercy, given us rebirth unto living hope through the resurrection of Jesus Christ from the dead" (1 Peter 1:3). God works the grace of baptism. He alone can give man in his creation the new beginning of a birth. The new life is hope, not yet possession (thus also in Rom. 6:4f.). This hope, nevertheless, is not empty and dead, but the promise of life, which is anticipated and assured through the resurrection of Jesus into life. Of rebirth, 1 Peter 1:23 states further: "Reborn not of corruptible seed but of incorruptible, through the living and abiding word of God." Just as every birth takes place from seed, this rebirth takes place from the incorruptible seed that is the word of God, already designated as "abiding" in Is. 40:8. The word of God has creative power, as in Gen. 1; Ps. 33:9; Rom. 4:17; James 1:18; (see above, § 6, 1).

Whence comes the Old Testament usage of the concept of rebirth is a question for exegesis. Certainly rabbinism was able to say: "A proselyte who has converted to Judaism is like a newborn child." The comparison, however, declares only that the proselyte can begin a new life unencumbered, like a newborn child. It is not said that conversion to Judaism and proselytic baptism constitute a rebirth. Judaism speaks, in accord with its doctrine of creation, more easily of a new creation (like 2 Cor. 5:17) than of a new birth.

Terms comparable to those of the New Testament are encountered, however, in extrabiblical religious contexts. The mystes of Isis find themselves "as if reborn" (Apuleius, *Metamorphoses* 11, 21, 6; below, § 8, 3, c, 9). The initiant into the mysteries of Mithras (O. Weinreich, *Eine Mithrasliturgie, erläutert von A. Dietrich*, Leipzig 1923 and 3rd ed., Darmstadt 1966, pp. 11f) says: "I was born of a mortal body of a mother and the life-giving dew of the seed; and afterwards this is today begotten anew of you, which in this hour is called to immortality from out of many thousands, according to the decree of the infinitely good god." Further gnostic texts are probably written down only later, and have perhaps been influenced by the New Testament. Nevertheless, the possibility must be reckoned with that in Romans 6 (below, § 8, 3, c, 9), images and terms from its religious milieu are employed in explaining baptism, and perhaps also, then, the concept of baptism as rebirth. This rebirth, nevertheless, is no naturalistic deification of man; rather, the baptized abides in faith (1 Peter 1:5) and in hope (1 Peter 1:3; 3:15).

7) *Administered in Faith.* Baptism is administered in faith. The sacrament is no magical rite that can be effective even without and against the will of its recipient. The administration of the sacrament, therefore, presupposes the word of proclamation. This is already contained in the command to baptize: "Make disciples of all nations and baptize them" (Matthew 28:19). "Whoever accepted the word was baptized" (Acts 2:41). In Eph. 5:26, baptism is described as a "bath of water in the word." In the administration of the sacrament, sign and word are united. The word means that which at baptism is spoken over the one being baptized, perhaps the name of Jesus in the formula of baptism (see above, § 8, 3, c, 1). It is said again and again that those who had come to the faith were baptized (Acts 8:12; 18:8). If baptism is done in the name of Jesus (Acts 2:38; Rom. 6:3), this requires the express or implied prior confession of Jesus as the Christ. Perhaps Rom. 10:9 alludes to this when it says: "If you confess the Lord Jesus with your mouth." Ecclesiastical arrangement is described in Mark 16:16: "Whoever believes and is baptized will be saved."

If baptism is administered in faith and obliges before the exalted Lord and the Church, moral requirement follows from it. This is explained in exemplary fashion in Rom. 6, where Paul defends himself against the conclusion probably imputed to him, that if baptism blots out sin, it would be correct to say the greater the sin, all the greater the grace. To this Paul replies: "In baptism we died to sin; how then should we continue to live in it?" (Rom. 6:2).

Just as Paul can say, "You that were baptized in Christ have put on Christ" (Gal. 3:27), so too can he say, "Put on the Lord Jesus Christ" (Rom. 13:14). Paul admonishes with the recollection of the history of Israel in the wilderness. Although that generation had received prototypes of baptism and Eucharist in its passage through the sea and by its being fed in the desert, "yet God was not pleased with the majority of them. They were laid low in the desert" (1 Cor. 10:1-5).

For Christians, who have received the sacraments, it is a valid warning: "Whoever thinks to stand, take care, lest he fall" (1 Cor. 10:12). So too the penetrating admonitions about baptism in other Epistles

(Col. 3:1-17; Eph. 4:17–5:21; Heb. 10:19-31). The First Epistle of Peter seems to be in its entirety a hortatory admonition on baptism. The commission to baptize already states: "Baptize all nations, and teach them to observe all that I have commanded you" (Matthew 28:19f.; see the present work, Vol. 3, pp. 50–52).

8) Baptism for the Dead. A passage much discussed and difficult to explain is 1 Cor. 15:29: "What are they doing, who have themselves baptized on behalf of the dead? If the dead are never to rise, why do they have themselves baptized for them?"[104] This probably indicates that in Corinth the living were baptized on behalf of the dead, in order to bestow upon them salvation. Paul takes note of this custom to remind the Corinthians that if they disavow the resurrection of the dead, they are being inconsistent (1 Cor. 15:12-19). The commentaries refer to 2 Macc. 12:42f., and even to the testimony of the mystery religions, according to which the living were initiated vicariously for the uninitiate dead. Perhaps it may be accepted that the Corinthians knew about this and conducted themselves in like fashion. Paul seems to be alluding to some such custom without approving or disavowing it; and hence, the form of his open rhetorical question. We might well ask whether Paul ought not have expressed himself in a critical manner. Does he not seem in this instance to be at least tolerant of a magical understanding of a sacrament?*

9) Baptism as Death and Resurrection. In Rom. 6:1-11, baptism is related to the death and resurrection of Christ, inasmuch as baptism is signified as dying and rising again with Christ. (The proclamation of the death and of the resurrection of Christ is always a unit, as in Rom. 8:34, "He not only died, he has risen.") "We who were baptized in Christ were baptized in his death. By baptism we were buried with him in his death, so that just as Christ was raised from the dead by the glory of the Father, we too might walk in the newness of life" (Rom. 6:3f.).

The explanation of Rom. 6:5 is not unanimously agreed upon. A literal translation is possibly: "If we have grown together with the likeness of his death, we too will belong to the resurrection." The word

[*Translator's note*: On the other hand, it might seem presumptuous to judge what Paul ought or ought not to have done, when admittedly we are not certain of what he is writing about in the first place.]

ὁμοίωμα (likeness) occurs elsewhere only four times in Paul: Rom. 1:23; 5:14; 8:3; Phil. 2:7. He employs this term when he wants to make a declaration of perfect likeness. We have not grown together with the death of Jesus, in respect to the historical event. Nevertheless, the death of Jesus is not merely a once-only historical event; rather, it concerns all times and all men. In baptism it is operative in the Spirit (1 Cor. 10:3f.; 2 Cor. 3:17; see above, § 8, 3, c, 3). Thus we have grown together with him and have in him our portion (as death and resurrection is one). It does not seem necessary to amplify that passage, as is so often done: If we have grown together with him (Christ) by baptism, which is the likeness of his death (his sacramental-mystical presence), so also will we coalesce with the likeness of his resurrection. Whence does Paul come by this explanation of baptism?

Jesus himself speaks of his death under the figure of baptism. "I must be baptized with a baptism, and how it does press upon me until it be completed!" (Luke 12:50; similar in Mark 10:38). The original import of βαπτίζειν = baptize, is "to immerse." Accordingly, in the saying of Jesus, his being engulfed in his Passion can be understood as a baptism.[105] Thus far, an image is employed here which appears also in Rom. 6:1-11. But Paul continues the comparison and explains the baptism of a Christian as baptism in the death of Christ.[106] Is this explanation of baptism developed in any way with the help of notions taken from the mystery religions?[107]

In the famous mystery religions, the death and the resurrection of the divinity were celebrated, as death and new life were exemplified in the course of the seasons of the year — thus in the mysteries of Demeter and Persephone in Eleusis, of Osiris and of Isis in Egypt, and in the cult of Mithras which had spread abroad from Asia Minor. While the traditional religions of Greece and Rome had long since become a purely literary mythology, with the cultured classes turning to religious philosophy, in the mystery cults a genuine sense of religion was nurtured.[108] These latter posited ethical requirements and promised the initiates redemption and salvation.

Source materials on the mysteries are few, since the mystes were obligated to silence about the mysteries. An important text is found in Apuleius, *Metamorphoses* 11, chs. 21-25, wherein the initiation of a certain Lucius into the mysteries of Isis is described. Before the initiation a priest leads him to the bath. The priest prays over him, sprinkles him with water, and thus purifies him. For a period of ten days, Lucius must abstain from the use of meat and wine and from sexual commerce. At the solemn initiation the "bands of saints" flock together. Dressed in a linen garment, Lucius is led into the inmost part of the temple by the priest. The mystes beholds the gods of death and of life, and does himself experience death and new life. He says: "I came to the borders of death, trod on the threshold of Proserpina. After I had traversed all the elements, I came back again. At midnight I saw the sun in blinding light. . . . The gods from below and from above I saw personally and I prayed to them." After his initiation, Lucius came out, clothed with twelve robes and the "olympic stole." In the beaming crown of the sun-god, he looked like this god himself. The initiation is celebrated as a "voluntary death" and as a "salvation granted by prayer" (*ad instar voluntariae mortis et precariae salutis celebrari*). The mystes knows that he is "as if reborn" (*quodam modo renatus*). The "birthday of the sacred initiation" (*natalis sacrorum*) concludes with a festive meal. The initiating priest is "father" to the mystes.

Not a little of this is reminiscent of the New Testament (or of a baptismal liturgy soon to take shape). Thus the ascetical fasting, the purifying bath, the linen garment, and the new robes. Gal. 3:27 says of baptism: "You were baptized in Christ. You have put on Christ." For a whole week the newly baptized wore white garments. Paul too knows himself as father of the community (1 Cor. 4:15; 1 Thess. 2:11). Christians too are the "saints." The history of the god of the mysteries is celebrated in the holy drama; the mystes participates in the death and life of the divinity, much in the way that Paul describes baptism in Rom. 6:3.

The Fathers of the Church likewise have some knowledge of the mystery religions. Firmicus Maternus, *The Error of the Pagan Religions* 22, 1, supplies the words of initiation: "You mystes, be comforted! Salvation belongs to god! You too, for your efforts, shall share in salvation!" Here again it is said that the mystes, since he experiences the destiny of the god, attains to salvation for his portion. The mystes is designated as "consecrated to death" (*homo moriturus*).

If concepts from the mystery religions are employed in describing baptism, there is, nevertheless, an essential difference between the former and the Christian sacrament. In the former the mystery of nature in the passage of the seasons is celebrated; in the latter, however, the history of the death and resurrection of the Man, Jesus Christ. Paul emphasizes this reality of the Cross and draws therefrom the moral stance of obedience, of ministry, of carrying the cross in this life. "The old man has been crucified, so that the body of sin may be extirpated, so that we may no longer be alive for sin" (Rom. 6:6). The new life, however, is not a natural event, but promise and hope, and has first to be won. "As Christ was raised from the dead, we too are to walk in a new life" (Rom. 6:4).

If baptism is described in Rom. 6 through the employment of concepts from the mysteries, the question must finally be posed, who first ventured to do this? Certainly Paul asks: "Do you not know?" (Rom. 6:3). But this, of course, is only a rhetorical device. One could hardly conclude from this that in the Roman community even before Paul this application of baptism to the death of Christ was already known.

Some exegetes accept, between Jewish Christianity and Paul, a Hellenistic-Christian community, in which Old Testament Jewish doctrine was newly declared in terms of the religious sensibilities of a Christian-Hellenistic culture. Such a community might already have accepted this new interpretation of baptism. To others, however, this Hellenistic community seems much too uncertain and doubtful. In any case, however, it still remains possible that already before Paul, baptism was understood as participation in the death and resurrection of Christ.

Odo Casel and a school starting with him developed in a "doctrine of mysteries" the acceptance of the notion that concepts belonging to the mystery religions had determined in a considerable degree the theology of the New Testament sacraments, baptism and Eucharist.[109] The New Testament would have employed that high religious sensibility as a vessel for its own treasure. According to the doctrine of mysteries of the Apostle Paul and afterwards of the Fathers of the Church, the salvation history of Christ, his incarnation, death, resurrection, ascension, and return are made present in mystical-real fashion in baptism and Eucharist. The Christian mystes is participant in the sacrament of the salvation event. Nevertheless, Paul is a Jew. His thought is not channeled to the sacramental nor tied to mysteries;

rather, it is in part historical, in part juridical, like Haggadah and Halakhah, which are both forms of rabbinic theology.

The doctrine of baptism is developed also in Col. 2:11f.; "In Christ you were circumcised with a circumcision not done by (human) hands, in the complete stripping of your body of flesh, in the circumcision of Christ, buried with him in baptism, in which also you were raised up through your faith in the power of God, who raised him from the dead."[110] Baptism is compared to circumcision, which is understood spiritually (as in Jer. 4:4 and Rom. 2:28f.). Such a comparison is all the more apt because circumcision and baptism are both sacred admittance rites. Circumcision is depreciated as something done with (human) hands. What God himself does is not done with hands (2 Cor. 5:1). The Epistle's use of the passive points to God's activity in the Christian sacrament. For Paul, the body of flesh designates, in an analogical manner of expression, human existence subjected to sin and death. The figure of the stripping of the body is reminiscent of the initiation to the mysteries, in which the mystes was clothed with new garments that signify new birth (Apuleius, *Metamorphoses* 11, 23f.; see above, § 8, 3, c, 4).

If baptism, then, is described as death and resurrection with Christ, notions such as are found also in Romans 6 are being appropriated. Since the Deutero-Pauline Epistle to the Colossians incontestably employs Pauline thought, what we have here may be a direct dependency upon Paul. A new emphasis in it, however, must not be ignored. While for Paul the resurrection is yet to be realized and is the subject of hope (Rom. 6:4f.; 8:11), here it is said that the resurrection has already taken place (Col. 2:12f.; 3:1-3). To be sure, it is to be grasped in faith in God's power (Col. 2:12) and is not some kind of physical metamorphosis. Indeed, the absence of the eschatological postponement, a reservation clear in Paul, characterizes the Deutero-Pauline writings (see below, § 13, 1 and § 15, 4).

In Ephesians 5:14 a hymn is quoted: "That is why it is said,

> 'You that are sleeping,
> rise up from the dead,
> and Christ will shine on you.' "[111]

If, as seems to be the case, the baptismal liturgy is speaking here, then here too, as in Rom. 6, baptism is understood as resurrection from the dead (the death that is sin) and entry into the spiritual power of Christ.

10) John 19:34. As in Rom. 6:2-11, even if in some aspects otherwise than there, in John 19:34 sacramental baptism is grounded in the death of Jesus. The passage in John says: "One of the soldiers opened his side with a lance, and immediately blood and water flowed out."[112] In John 19:36f., the mysterious meaning of the stroke with the lance is explained as the fulfillment of two prophecies. The further substantiation of 19:34 is possibly a later addition, the product of deepening theological reflection.

In their commentaries on John's Gospel, the Fathers of the Church already see in the blood and water of John 19:34 a mysterious reference to the sacraments. According to St. Cyril of Alexandria (Migne, *PG* 74:677B), that mystery is the "image and beginning of the mystical oblation and of holy baptism." According to Apollinaris of Laodicea (J. Reuss, *Johannes-Kommentare aus der griechischen Kirche*, Berlin 1966, p. 59), the blood from the side of Jesus signifies "purification, and the water, baptism unto sanctification." Ammonius (*ibid.*, p. 345) explains: "By water is the Church reborn, and by water and flesh she is nourished." According to Theodore of Heraclea (*ibid.*, p. 167), the blood effects redemption, and the water, sanctification. Theodore of Mopsuestia (R. Devreesse, *Essai sur Théodore de Mopsueste*, Vatican City 1948, p. 413), nevertheless, explains it otherwise. For him the blood is a symbol of increated being, the water, of mystical sharing therein. Augustine (Migne, *PL* 35:1953) explains in detail: "The Evangelist chooses well his words, for he does not say, 'He pierced his side,' or 'He wounded him,' but, 'He opened,' so as to indicate all the more certainly the opening of the gate of life, whence the sacraments of the Church flowed out. . . . That blood has been poured out for the forgiveness of sin; that water is mixed in the salvational chalice; it serves both for bathing and for drinking." This is also the modern interpretation. "There can hardly be any other meaning than that in the death of Jesus on the Cross the sacrament of baptism and of the Lord's Supper have their foundation" (R. Bultmann).

For an exegesis in which in John 3:5 the mention of the water of baptism and in John 6:51c-58 the reference to the Eucharist, and in which, therefore, the significant mention of the sacraments in John's Gospel is regarded as the later addition of an ecclesial redaction, John 19:34b will also belong to this secondary state of the text (see above, § 8, 3, b; and below, § 9, 3, c, 7).

According to 1 John 5:6-8, Jesus "has come through water and blood." "There are three who bear witness: the Spirit, the water, and the blood." If water and blood, through which Jesus has come, are primarily his baptism and his death as the beginning and end of his activity, then the Spirit, the water, and the blood no doubt mean the sacraments of baptism and Eucharist, in which the salvational power of the events of Jesus' life are, through the Spirit, effective in the Church.[113] It may be significant that even Paul says of baptism that it takes place in the spirit (1 Cor. 12:13), and he designates the eating and drinking of the sacrament of the Eucharist as operation of the Spirit (1 Cor. 10:4).

If Jesus did not found the Church in such a way that already in his earthly life he set forth its arrangements in detail (see above, 2, 2), it is unlikely that he prescribed baptism as a sacramental rite of initiation. But since all the gifts of baptism, especially the forgiveness of sin, salvation, the mission of the Spirit, are according to New Testament doctrine, fruits of Christ's salvational work, the apostolic Church's regarding of baptism as instituted by Christ is essentially confirmed.

4. Forgiveness of Sins after Baptism

Baptism effects forgiveness of sin (above, § 8, 3, c, 2). This raises the question of the authority in general to forgive sins in the Church, and especially the question of forgiveness of sins committed after baptism.[114]

According to the teaching and belief of the Church, Jesus took guilt and sin upon himself. He entered into a companionship with sinners, absolved sinners, justified this in his comments, and spoke expressly of his all-redeeming ministry (Mark 10:45; 14:24; see the present work, Vol. 2, pp. 100–106).

The community of disciples and the Church continued and do yet continue, from the fullness of Christ's work of salvation, the ministry of the forgiveness of sins. The claim of authority to forgive requires proof, and this so much more, when, according to biblical belief, the forgiveness of sin belongs to the sovereign right of God alone (Mark 2:7). The high priest implores God's forgiveness; God grants it according to the prescribed ritual (Lev. 16). The Messiah will abolish sin and sinners and remove them from the world; but he is not able to forgive them (*Psalms of Solomon* 17:26-41).

Ministry to the community is indicated in the narrative of the cure of the paralyzed man in Mark 2:12 (Matthew 9:1-8 and Luke 5:17-26).[115] The narrative unites two actions of Jesus as two themes: the marvelous cure of the cripple and the forgiveness of sins. The authority to heal, which manifest, is proof of the authority to forgive sin. A considerable portion of exegesis agrees that the emphatic uniting of the themes discloses theological application. This meaning of the narration comes from the framing of the account itself, when it says in Mark 2:10, " 'So that *you* may see that the Son of Man has the authority to forgive sins on earth,' — he said to the paralytic, 'I say to you, stand up!' " Those addressed with the word *you* are the disciples and the Church, and also their opponents. For this was a dispute between Jesus and the Pharisees, and furthermore, a dispute between the Church and the synagogue, whether a man could, as Jesus did, encroach on God's sovereign right to forgive sins. There is even more significant reference to the authority of the Church to forgive sins in the concluding line of the narrative in Matthew 9:8: "The glorified God, who has given such power to men."

The authority to forgive sins is promised the Church in Jesus' express words. This is the case with the words of binding and loosing (Matthew 16:19; 18:18), insofar as these sayings refer to excluding from the community and accepting into it again (see above, § 5, 5, b-c).

The risen Lord commissions the Church to proclaim repentance unto the forgiveness of sins "in the name of Jesus" (Luke 24:47). Forgiveness is promised in the name of Jesus; therefore, by reason of his salvific work. It is realized through the word of the Church.[116]

A similar narration is offered in John 20:19-23. Jesus appeared to the disciples. After the greeting, "Peace be with you!" he commands them, "Receive the Holy Spirit. If you forgive anyone's sins, they are forgiven. If you retain anyone's sins, they are retained."

This account in John 20:19-23 discloses references to the foregoing parts of John's Gospel. Jesus came to his disciples (John 20:19). This is the fulfillment of his promise, "I will come to you again" (John 14:18). Jesus grants peace to his disciples. Of this he had assured them in the hour of his departure: "My peace I give you" (John 14:27). "The disciples rejoiced, because they were seeing the Lord" (John 20:20). From the sorrow of their parting, joy has now come, in accord with what was once said to them, "You are sorrowful, but your sorrow shall be turned to joy" (John 16:20). Their commissioning — "As the Father sent me, so am I sending you" (John 20:20) — is shaped after the high priestly prayer, "As you have sent me into the world, so do I send them into the world" (John 17:18). The resurrected Lord imparts the Spirit to his disciples by breathing on them (John 20:22). This fulfills the promise of the "streams of living water" (John 7:37). The gift of the Spirit had been promised again in the sayings about the Paraclete (John 16:7f., 13). The gift of the Spirit entails for the disciples the authority to forgive sins and to retain them.

The disciples, that is, the community (as in Matthew 28:19; 1 Cor. 11:25; see above, § 8, 2, b, 2; below, § 9, 3, c, 6), are to carry out further the judgment that came to pass in the coming of Jesus into the world (John 3:19; 5:27; 9:39). The breathing of the Spirit, since Gen. 2:7, is a creative event (thus too in Ezek. 37:5-10). Even the breath of the risen Lord is creative. The erasing of sins is new creation. The resurrection is new life. In the forgiving of sins the disciples duplicate the Easter gift.

Dogmatics is able to understand the saying in John 20:22 as the insitution of the sacrament of penance. Originally it was certainly not so closely confined. It proves and attests in general the authority of the Church to forgive sins and to impart new life. The Church carries out her commission to proclaim the absolving word in the sacramental word, and this in a special way in baptism, but in a general way in her whole salvific ministry.

2 Cor. 5:18-21 says of the apostolic ministry of forgiveness and reconciliation: "Everything is from God, who has reconciled us to him-

self through Christ, and has given us the ministry of reconciliation. For God was in Christ and reconciled the world to himself, inasmuch as he does not impute to men their sins, and instituted among us the word of reconciliation. In Christ's stead we are ambassadors, inasmuch as God admonishes through us. We implore you in Christ's stead: Be reconciled to God."

Reconciliation is an important word and an important ministry of the Old Testament (Lev. 16). Since Paul uses this word, he is explaining the long history of the Old Testament as fulfilled. He says that in reconciliation it is essentially God and not man who is acting. God creates the new relationship of grace and of peace between himself and the world. He is not an angry God who must be turned about, but always a gracious God. The change that takes place is only on the part of man, who renounces his sinful stance and accepts God's salvation.

"When we were God's enemies, we were reconciled to him by the death of his Son" (Rom. 5:10). God, who bestowed this reconciliation, also instituted the ministry of reconciliation. The "word of reconciliation" (2 Cor. 5:19) does not bespeak only the past event of reconciliation, but contains and effects what it declares, as a word of sacramental power (see above, § 6, 2). Paul performs the ministry of reconciliation and presents that reconciliation to men in preaching, in the sacrament of baptism (1 Cor. 6:11), in the Eucharist (1 Cor. 11:24f.), as also in the personal care of souls (2 Cor. 11:29). Above all, in such conduct Paul is not so far removed from the practice of the sacrament of penance as we have it today.

In the order and manner of an ecclesiastical ministry the forgiveness of sins is described in James 5:14f.: "Let the sick man call in the elders (presbyters) of the community. They are to pray over him and anoint him with oil in the name of the Lord. The Lord will raise him erect; and if that man has sins, they will be forgiven him." The community knows the institution of the elders as bearers of office (see above, § 4, 3). In the milieu of the New Testament, oil is a natural and sacred remedy. The apostles too, upon being sent out, "anointed many of the sick with oil and healed them" (Mark 6:13).[117] The rite of anointing is, in the Epistle of James, in no way a magical rite, because it is effective where it is practiced and accepted in faith and in the common possession of Jesus. To its effects belongs also the forgiveness of sins, if the sick person has committed any. Certainly there is a connection between sin and illness. Illness is due to sin.

For the Epistle to the Hebrews, to effect conversion and forgiveness of sin is an essential task of the care of souls. The Epistle concerns itself very much with a community whose zeal is already waning (Heb. 12:12f.). It is from this basic posture of the Epistle that one will understand those texts (Heb. 6:4-8; 10:26f.; 12:16f.) which are penetrating in their admonition to renewal. A new repentance by baptism is not possible. An enormous endeavor of exegetical and dogmatic interpretation has been expended on those texts. The Epistle, however, does not aim to formulate dogmatically a doctrine of penance, nor to establish an ecclesiastical ordering of penance. Rather, with great earnestness, it wants to remind and admonish that those who "were once enlightened, who have tasted the heavenly Gift and were made sharers of the Holy Spirit, and have afterwards fallen away," will perhaps never again "find opportunity for repentance" (Heb. 6:4f.).

§ 9. EUCHARIST

1. Ritual Meals (Historical Religious Environs)

Primitive man discovered that nothing so unites men as a common meal.[118] Those participating communally in a meal receive all power and life from a common food. From the very beginning the meal took on a religious aspect. For the foods were received as gift of God, with thanks to God as the giver of the meal. The divinity is also believed to be present at the meal as a guest. If the elements of the meal are taken into possession from the divine powers and energies, a man can incorporate them in himself with the food.

Among the papyri, invitations to banquets with divinities have been found. (These papyri belong probably to the second century A.D.). Thus *Papyrus Oxyrhynchus* 1, 110: "Chairemon invites you to dinner at the table (properly, at the divan) of the Lord Serapis tomorrow, that is, on the 15th, in the Serapeum, beginning at 9 o'clock." Similarly, in *Papyrus Oxyrhynchus* 3, 523: "Antonios, son of Ptolemaios, invites you to dinner as his guest at the table (properly, at the divan) of the Lord Serapis in the apartments of Claudios Serapion on the 23rd, beginning at 9 o'clock." The rhetor Aelius Aristides (*Discourse* 8) says in a discourse on Serapis that men "covet the companionship of the sacrifice with this god, so that they invite him to dinner and place themselves under his protection as a companion at table and a host." A dedicatory inscription reads: "To Serapis and to Isis, a table." In sacred meals of the cult of Mithras, the flesh and blood of a sacrificed bull were eaten, and probably also bread and wine. The Roman religion also conducted ritual banquets. One of the most famous of the Roman festivals was the *Epulum Iovis* (Banquet of Jupiter) on the Capitoline, at which Jupiter and Juno were represented by their solemnly decorated images.[119]

Even the New Testament is aware of these banquets with the gods. Paul warns: "I do not want you to be in the company of the demons. You cannot drink the chalice of the Lord and the chalice of demons. You cannot participate at the table of the Lord and at the table of the demons" (1 Cor. 10:20f.). Paul is speaking of the pagan ritual banquets which one celebrated in company with the divinity. For Paul, the pagan gods are certainly demons, just as they are for late Judaism (Deut. 32:17; Pss. 96:5; 106:37; *Book of Jubilees* 1:11; 22:17).

2. Old Testament and Judaism

It is self-evident that the Old Testament had ritual meals. The sacrificial meal is described thus: "To eat and rejoice before God the Lord" (Deut. 12:7-12; 16:10-17). Community meals unite their participants with God and before God. Moses, Aaron, and the elders of Israel hold the sacrificial meal in the presence of Yahweh (Exod. 18:12). After concluding the covenant at Sinai, Moses and the elders of Israel go up the mountain. "They beheld God, and they ate and drank" (Exod. 24:11). A meal seals agreements (Gen. 26:30; 31:46; Exod. 18:12). The installation of Saul as king is celebrated with a meal (1 Sam. 11:15). The priests hold daily sacrificial meals in the Temple (Lev. 2:2f.; 3;

6:14-29; 7:9f., 29-36; 10:12-15). An annual festal meal is the Passover meal, which Israel celebrates since its nomadic period. This meal is not only commemoration, but through its rites the participant of the meal comes into the communion of salvation which God effected for the fathers in Egypt and which he gives always and ever.

The eschatological-messianic consummation is represented as a meal of God with the redeemed (Is. 25:6; Zeph. 1:7; *Ethiopic Henoch* 62:14; *Slavonic Henoch* 42:5).

In Qumran,[120] the principal daily meal is celebrated as a ritual meal. Its participants first immerse themselves in the bath. They clothe themselves in white linen. A priest presides and pronounces the blessing over bread and wine. New members have to complete a two-year noviitate before they are permitted to participate (1 QS 6:2-5, 20f.; Josephus, *Jewish War* 2, 8, 129-133, 139).

Qumran also describes the future endtime as a banquet. It is to take place under the presidency of the priestly and royal Messiah. The ritual meal is understood as a preview of the eschatological banquet in the kingdom of God (1 QSa 2:17-22). Does participation in this present meal impart or guarantee participation in the endtime meal? Does this present meal, therefore, have a sacramental force? We are reminded of the eschatological viewpoint at the Last Supper of Jesus with his disciples (Mark 14:25; 1 Cor. 11:26). The Eucharistic meal is a symbol of the eschatological meal. The detailed prescriptions for the conduct of the meal in Qumran remind us of Paul's prescriptions (1 Cor. 11:17-34). It cannot be accepted that the meals in Qumran had a direct influence on the New Testament celebration of meals. The difference is evident: The New Testament Lord's Supper is a memorial of the death of the Lord, referred thereto in significant terms. But the banquets of Qumran proclaim the great significance of the meal for the foundation and life of a community.

3. New Testament: The Lord's Supper

a) The Last Supper

The New Testament contains four accounts of the Last Supper of Jesus with his disciples: Mark 14:22-25; Matthew 26:26-29; Luke 22:15-

20; 1 Cor. 11:23-25. These accounts are not simply narratives from the life of Jesus. The proximate source of all the accounts is the celebration of the Lord's Supper in the community, at which the accounts were recited. The pericopes were handed down separately, therefore, and apart from the account of the Passion. This is apparent in the instance of 1 Cor. 11:23-25. It is still discernible even in Mark 14:22 and Matthew 26:26, since both Gospels, although they already depict the meal taking place in Mark 14:17 and Matthew 26:20, now introduce the meal anew with the clause "as they were eating. . . ." All the accounts disclose a solemn and ever more solemn liturgical stylization.

According to the presently customary dating of the New Testament writings, the earliest of the accounts to be written down is that of Paul in the First Epistle to the Corinthians, which was written about the year 55 A.D., Paul says, however, that he gave the account of the Last Supper to the Corinthians during his sojourn there. He was in Corinth in the year 49. He turned over to the Corinthians what he had himself received from tradition (1 Cor. 11:23). The tradition, therefore, was already shaped in the years 40–50 A.D.[121] Paul is convinced that the tradition goes back to the actual history of Jesus. He has "received it from the Lord" (1 Cor. 11:23).

The account of Mark, in contrast to Paul's, may have been written down about the year 70 A.D., with the account of Matthew and Luke being still later. The account of Paul does in fact bear traces of its age, even if in many respects the newer accounts of the Gospels have preserved what is older. It is original when, in 1 Cor. 11:25, the eating of the Bread and the drinking of the Wine are separated by the meal: Jesus took "the cup after the meal." In the Gospels, the unity of the meal celebrated with Bread and Wine is understood, and they are joined. Moreover, the words over the Bread and Wine are stylized in an unequal fashion in Paul, where they read: "This is my Body for you" and "This cup is the new covenant in my Blood" (1 Cor. 11:24f.). In the Gospels a similarity is established: "This is my Body" and "This is my Blood."

On the other hand, later development is recognizable in Paul when the statement of Mark 14:22, "This is my Body," appears in a lengthened form in 1 Cor. 11:24, "This is my Body, for you." Here the theological meaning is advanced. The formula of surrender is given in

Mark 14:24 and Matthew 26:28 as "for many" (= for the many; for all); but in 1 Cor. 11:24, however, "for you." The former is an original Semitism, not understandable to the Greek mind; the latter, a universally understandable and later formulation. It is likewise an indication of advanced reflection when in 1 Cor. 11:25 the covenant is designated as "the new covenant." Here the old and new covenants are already distinguished. In contrast to Mark and Matthew, Luke 22:19 advances the command of institution once, and 1 Cor. 11:24f., twice. It makes explicit what in Mark and Matthew is presumed, if their accounts stem from the liturgy. The liturgical celebration certainly presumes and is convinced that Jesus commanded repetition. The task belongs to the Church, not just to the twelve apostles. The whole priestly Church has the authority to celebrate the Eucharistic Meal, and not just a narrow circle of priests.

Between Mark and Matthew an advance in parallel stylization is to be noted. In Mark 14:22f. it says, " 'Take it! This is my Body.' And he gave them the cup . . . and they all drank from it." Matthew 26:26f. writes the equivalent, "Take and eat! . . . All of you drink it!" In Matthew 26:28 the appended phrase "for the forgiveness of sins" is essentially a quite different but advanced theological interpretation.

Luke tells in 22:15-20 of the cup being passed around twice. Jesus passes the first cup at the beginning of the meal (Luke 22:17). If the Last Supper is a Passover meal, this is perhaps the third cup of the Passover, drunk between the meal and the shared cup. Luke's second cup is passed as the chalice of the Blood (Luke 22:20; which, then, is probably the fourth cup of the Passover meal).

A short text of Luke 22:15-19a mentions only one cup. The short text was long regarded as the original and valuable tradition, which would have been filled out later from 1 Cor. 11, since Luke 22:19b/20 and 1 Cor. 11:25 are in almost perfect verbal accord. Nevertheless, today it is almost universally accepted that the whole text of Luke 22:15-20 is original. It carries great weight that Papyrus 75, as much the oldest text preserved (from the 2nd-3rd century) offers the long text. The short text is in the Western text tradition (D), which contains not a few secondary abridgements. The longer text was shortened probably for the reason that someone wanted to avoid the double mention of a cup.[122]

b) Passover Meal

Exegesis interests itself in the question of whether or not the Last Supper of Jesus was a Passover meal.[123] At the time of the New Testament, the Passover meal took place on the 14th of Nisan, the Preparation Day for the Passover celebration, which began on the 15th of Nisan. According to the Synoptic Gospels, the Last Supper of Jesus was a Passover meal (Mark 14:12-16; Matthew 26:17f.; Luke 22:7-15). Accordingly, Jesus celebrated the Last Supper with his disciples on the 14th of Nisan, and he died on the 15th of Nisan. According to John's Gospel, however, Jesus was taken prisoner on the day before the Preparation Day (i.e., the 13th of Nisan), was condemned by Pilate on the next day, the 14th of Nisan, on which day the Jews held the Passover meal in the evening (John 18:28), and was crucified on that very Preparation Day (John 19:14).

Since the Synoptics, in contrast to John, are in general reckoned as the more historically reliable, one may here be inclined to follow their chronology. In their portrayal of the Last Supper of Jesus, the Synoptics mention nothing of the special ceremonies of the Passover meal. The blessing over the bread and wine belongs to the customs of every Jewish meal. In the explanatory words pronounced over the bread and wine, one could easily find a reference to the explanation given of the paschal lamb and other ceremonies of the Passover meal. Nevertheless, the Synoptics do not mention the eating of the paschal lamb. This is explained by saying that the particulars of the Passover meal were of no significance for the Lord's Supper (Eucharist) celebrated in the Church's liturgy. Thus the purely historical approach declined and was finally abandoned. According to the chronology of John's Gospel, Jesus died on the Cross at the very moment when the paschal lamb was slaughtered in the forecourt of the Temple. This symbolism determines, or so it is often accepted, the Johannine dating. Paul too knows this symbolism, and to him it seems to be already traditional, as one may conclude from the short formula: "Christ our Passover is sacrificed" (1 Cor. 5:7).

Attempts have been made to reconcile the different datings. It has been suggested that by virtue of divine authority Jesus advanced the celebration of the Passover meal by a day and held it on the 13th of

Nisan, as John tells it. More recently the view has been defended[124] that there were in use among the Jews at that time two calendars in reference to the Passover feast. According to the solar calendar (in use also in Qumran), this feast would have begun two days before its celebration according to the official lunar calendar observed in Jerusalem. Following the solar reckoning, Jesus would have kept the Passover meal with his disciples already on a Tuesday evening. According to the official calendar, Jesus would have died on a Friday, the 14th of Nisan. Thus both datings, that of the Synoptics and that of John, were possible. Here we can let the matter rest.

c) Terms and Concepts

Individual terms and concepts of the New Testament need to be explained.

1) Significant Terms: Body and Blood. The explanation may begin with the essential terms "body" and "blood." In the Bible's language and view of man, an individual man lives and exists as flesh and blood (Matthew 16:17; 1 Cor. 15:50); flesh and blood are not two parts of a man, separable one from the other. Body ($\sigma\tilde{\omega}\mu\alpha$) assumes the meaning of the Hebrew *basar*, which is otherwise translated by flesh ($\sigma\acute{\alpha}\rho\xi$). *Basar* means the whole man, in his life before God; thus, in Luke 3:6, "All flesh will see the salvation of God"; Gal. 2:16, "No flesh will be justified by works of the Law." The body ($\sigma\tilde{\omega}\mu\alpha$), therefore, can designate the man, inasmuch as he undergoes death. The term has this import in Mark 14:8; 15:43; John 2:21. This is expressly declared in Heb. 10:10: "We are sanctified once and for all by the sacrificial gift of the Body of Jesus Christ"; and in 1 Peter 2:24: "He has borne our sins in his body on the wood."

The Last Supper texts employ in place of the usually paired terms, flesh and blood ($\sigma\tilde{\omega}\mu\alpha$ and $\alpha\tilde{\iota}\mu\alpha$), the term body ($\sigma\tilde{\omega}\mu\alpha$), possibly because it thereby suggests life already surrendered to death. In the Last Supper texts, the term body is intended to describe the person, the "I" of Jesus, as surrendered in sacrifice. Moreover, in Hebrew-Aramaic linguistic usage, blood means life, because the blood is regarded as the seat of life (Lev. 17:11, 14). "The blood is the life" (Deut. 12:23). In the language of sacrifice, blood is the life that is surrendered (Exod.

29:16; 21). The blood of sacrifice has atoning (Lev. 16:6-17), purifying (Lev. 14:14), and sanctifying power (Exod. 29:20f.).

In the Last Supper texts, the terms "body" and "blood" designate the Lord, submitting himself and sacrificed. These two essential terms represent the event of the sacrifice of Jesus as atonement and sanctification for men. This significance is further elucidated by the appended statements: "This is my Body, for you" (1 Cor. 11:24; Luke 22:19); "This is my Blood of the covenant, which is poured out for the many" (Mark 14:24); which "is poured out for the forgiveness of sins" (Matthew 26:28); "which is poured out for you" (Luke 22:20). "This cup is the new covenant in my Blood" (1 Cor. 11:25).

These significant terms obtain their depth from the Old Testament language of sacrifice. At the consecration of the Sinai covenant, Moses sprinkled the blood of the sacrifice, half on the altar and half on the people, with the words: "Behold the blood of the covenant which God has made with you" (Exod. 24:8). A new and messianic covenant is promised in Jer. 31:31-33: "Days will come, when I will conclude with the House of Israel and the House of Judah a new covenant." (The rabbinic interpretation of this saying was important in the New Testament era; see above, § 2, 3, c). Of the Servant of God, the Prophet says: "He gave up his life in death . . . since he bore the sins of the many and interceded for the guilty" (Is. 53:12).

By means of these Old Testament references, Jesus' surrender to death is interpreted as substitution, vicarious atonement, and sacrifice. Such a mentality in regard to the words of the Last Supper would be understandable to Israel in the New Testament era, inasmuch as, ever since the martyrdoms of the Maccabean times, the attempt had to be made to understand the deaths of the saints, even as the pious of Qumran understood in their own situation, as "atonement for the nation" (1 QS 8:6-10; 9:4; see the present work, Vol. 2, pp. 104f.).

2) Symbolic Action. The symbolic meaning [125] of bread and wine, body and blood, can be understood as elucidated by the accompanying action. Bread baked as a flat disk is not cut but broken. Does this, then, at the Last Supper, point to the body and life of Jesus, about to be broken? If variants (later, of course) to 1 Cor. 11:24, add: (the body) "broken for you," that meaning is certainly brought to the fore. The wine flows in the cup. So too the blood of Jesus flowed on the Cross.

All the texts emphasize this with the term "poured out." If Jesus' Last Supper was a Passover supper, the symbolism would be even stronger, since, for the Passover supper, red wine was prescribed. "Cup," moreover, is a traditional expression for the destined suffering (Mark 10:38; 14:36; Apoc. 14:10; 16:19).

There is a significance, if the Last Supper action of Jesus is to be designated as parabolic action, to the way in which the prophets illustrated their words in actions. Jeremiah had to smash a jug; that is how Yahweh smashed the people and city of Israel (Jer. 19). Ezekiel has to shave his head and beard; that is how Yahweh wants to represent the undoing of Jerusalem (Ezek. 5). If a cooking pot represents Jerusalem, the rust on it is her guilt, and the fire under it the agony of her being laid under siege (Ezek. 24).

The Last Supper words emphasize the presentation: "He gave them" the Bread and the Cup (Mark 14:22f.). This presentation includes the gift of salvation. The invitation to take, to drink (Mark 14:22f.; Matthew 26:26f.) is the invitation to take hold of salvation. Its acquisition takes place in the form of a ritual meal.

3) Meals of Jesus and Last Supper. The earthly Jesus often held a supper with his followers. Since he traveled with his disciples, he ate his meals with them too. He ate with respected Pharisees (Luke 7:36; 11:37) and with sinners as well (Mark 2:16; Matthew 9:10f.; Luke 19:7). He took a meal with his disciples on the evening before his death, and again with them, as the Resurrected One (Luke 24:13-43; John 21:12f.; Mark 16:14). The remembrance of all this communion is included in the liturgical celebration of the Eucharistic Lord's Supper. It is a new communion with the now sacrificed and exalted Lord.

There was considerable repercussion to the thesis propounded by H. Lietzmann, accepted and further developed by E. Lohmeyer and R. Bultmann,[126] to the effect that in the time of the apostles there were two types of the Eucharistic meal: The primitive community in Jerusalem continued in its Meal, which was conducted as a "breaking of bread" and, in any case, without wine, the community table with the earthly Jesus (Acts 2:42), just as also the "Eucharist" of the *Didache* (9:1–10:6; Jurgens, nos. 6 and 7) did not mention the Flesh and Blood, the sacrifice and death of Jesus. The *Didache* in 10:6, in any event, may hint at the conversion of the death-meal to the Eucharist. Paul and the Hellenistic community, under the influence of the ritual meal in the Hellenistic mystery religions, conducted the memorial of the Last Supper of Jesus with bread and wine as symbols of the Body and Blood of Christ, and as a representation of his death.

Nevertheless, the Last Supper texts, in view of language and content, point back to the Palestinian community (see note 121), while the mystery religion meals are not shown historically to be of any influence there, and in general the supposed sharp separation between the Palestinian and Hellenistic communities seems, in view of recent findings, to be indemonstrable and questionable.

One can, with F. Hahn, summarize as the results of the discussion: We can distinguish several and certainly three roots of the Eucharistic Lord's Supper: (a) the community meals of the earthly Jesus with sinners and disciples, (b) the celebration of the Last Supper, (c) and the meals with the resurrected Jesus. Also of influence here is the tradition of the miraculous food and the parables of the eschatological meal. The Lord's Supper is gift and legacy of the whole history of Jesus. The liturgy and theology of the Lord's Supper will not have been everywhere and from the beginning of like emphasis and of like intensity; rather, they will have been subject to development and to final standardization.

With Paul (1 Cor. 11:26), the memorial of the death of Jesus is explicitated in the recollection: "You are proclaiming ($\kappa\alpha\tau\alpha\gamma\gamma\epsilon\lambda\lambda\epsilon\tau\epsilon$) the death of the Lord."[127] This proclamation shares in the power of word and of proclamation in the whole biblical evaluation thereof. With the word, that which is stated does actually take place (see above, § 6, 1). Such proclaiming is, in ancient liturgical linguistic usage, not only the publication of an event that has previously taken place, but the solemn declaration and announcement of something that is made real by the very proclamation. In the cult of the emperor, $\kappa\alpha\tau\alpha\gamma\gamma\epsilon\lambda\lambda\epsilon\iota\nu$ can substitute for $\epsilon\dot{\nu}\alpha\gamma\gamma\epsilon\lambda\dot{\iota}\zeta\epsilon\iota\nu$. The proclamation of the "gospel" makes salvation take place. Proclaiming is, at the same time, acknowledgment of the exalted Lord made present in his epiphany.

4) Eschatological Expectation. All the accounts of the Last Supper of Jesus emphasize eschatological expectation. In parables Jesus, accepting the rabbinic manner of discourse, had depicted the consummation under the image of a supper (see below, § 13, 3, b). At the Last

Supper, Jesus looks forward to that meal: "I shall no more drink of the fruit of the vine until that day when I shall drink it anew (with you) in the kingdom of God" (Mark 14:25 = Matthew 26:29).

In Luke's Gospel, the eschatological outlook is seen twice (Luke 22:16, 18). The word of promise in Matthew and Mark stands at the end of the meal; in Luke, between the Passover meal recounted by him and the Eucharistic meal. Luke 22:15-18 is hardly an old tradition, but is the creation of Luke, who, in 22:14-20, historicizes in separating the Passover meal and the new Lord's Supper. He places the eschatological promise with both of the actions of the Passover meal, since he can say of the Passover that Jesus will not celebrate it again until its consummation in the kingdom of God. Luke avoids joining the promise to the Lord's Supper, since that is being celebrated ever anew in the Church. If the promise appears at the end of the meal in Matthew and Mark, it does in any case correspond to the celebration of the (Eucharistic) Meal in the community.

Paul does not record the saying; but surely he lets it be known that the liturgy of the Lord's Supper was full of eschatological expectation, when, in 1 Cor. 11:26, he says: "As often as you eat this Bread and drink this Cup, you proclaim the death of the Lord, until he returns." The conclusion of the First Epistle to the Corinthians will form a transition after the reading of Paul's Epistle at the Eucharistic celebration. Here the eschatological tension breaks forth in the Aramaic cry: "Marana tha!" ("Come, O Lord!" — 1 Cor. 16:22).

The expectation is imminent in the Eucharistic prayer of the *Didache* 9:4 (Jurgens, no. 6): "As this broken bread was scattered on the mountains, but brought together was made one, so gather your Church from the ends of the earth into your kingdom"; so too in the *Didache* 10:5-6 (Jurgens, no. 7): "Remember, O Lord, your Church. Deliver it from every evil and perfect it in your love. Gather it from the four winds, sanctified for your kingdom, which you have prepared for it. For yours is the power and glory forever. Let grace come, and let this world pass away. Osanna to the God of David. If anyone is holy, let him come; if anyone is not, let him repent. Marana tha! Amen."

The saying about an imminent expectation of the kingdom of God will belong to the essential and ancient conduct of Jesus' Last Supper. The expectation of a new Supper in an imminent consummation with the arrival of the kingdom of God is in discord with the repetition again and again of the Supper in an ever-lengthening history of the Church. The one seems to exclude the other. And we to recognize thereby two different conceptions and traditions? In any case, the New Testament endured this discordant note. The basically eschatological posture has certainly been lost from the Church's liturgy.

5) *Hunger-satisfying Meals and Lord's Supper.* The Eucharistic Lord's Supper took place to begin with in the context of a regular hunger-satisfying meal. Judaism fostered the custom of profane and sacred banquets in groups large and small. In Greco-Roman antiquity, religious brotherhoods celebrated their banquets. The Christians too held common meals. In Acts 2:42-46 such meals are mentioned: "In companionship in their homes they broke bread; they took their food in joy and simplicity of heart." By the term "breaking of bread," as the initial ceremony, the whole meal is understood.

In Corinth, the Eucharistic Lord's Supper was celebrated in the course of a regular meal, so that the one could seem to be as important as the other, and Paul was obliged to restore order (1 Cor. 11:20f.). The Epistle of Jude (12) blames erroneous teachers severely: "There are those who eat with you at your Love Feasts and sully them by shamelessly looking after themselves alone." Here the community meals, which are both Sacrament and banquet, bear the name "Love Feasts" or "Agapes," a name known also to St. Ignatius of Antioch, in his *Letter to the Smyrnaeans* 8:2 (Jurgens, no. 65: "Wherever the Bishop appears, let the people be there: just as wherever Jesus Christ is, there is the Catholic Church. Nor is it permitted without the bishop either to baptize or the celebrate the agape").

In the second century, the Eucharistic Lord's Supper and the ordinary hunger-satisfying banquet were separated, the first witness to this separation being St. Justin the Martyr, in his *First Apology* 67 (*Translator's addition*: which passage is also the first witness to the Sunday collection — Jurgens, no. 129).

6) *Epistles of Paul.* In the First Epistle to the Corinthians, Paul[128] treats twice of the Eucharistic Lord's Supper, in 1 Cor. 10:1-5 and in 11:17-24.

In 1 Cor. 10:1-5 he finds prototypes of baptism and of the Eucharist in the history of Israel. (As to baptism, see above, § 8, 2). Of the

Eucharist, Paul says: "All ate the same spiritual food and drank the same spiritual drink. They drank, namely, from the spiritual rock, which followed them. The rock, however, was Christ." Paul finds both parts of the Lord's Supper, the eating and the drinking, already in the marvelous food, the manna (Exod. 14:4-36), and in Israel's being given to drink in the desert. In Exod. 17:6, as also in Num. 20:2-11, it is recounted that Israel in the desert was given to drink of water from the rock. Here our exegesis accepts literary doublets. Rabbinical theology, however, was of a mind that the rock traveled about with the people: "The well, which was with Israel in the desert, went up the mountains with them and descended with them into the valleys" (H. L. Strack and P. Billerbeck, *op. cit.*, Vol. 3 [1926], pp. 406–408).

According to Jewish theology, however, that well was created before time. According to Philo (*Allegory of the Laws* 2, 86), "the jagged rock is the wisdom of God."

Paul combines rabbinic exegesis with the theology of the pre-temporal, eternal being of Christ (see the present work, Vol. 2, pp. 172f.). But when Paul speaks of spiritual food and spiritual drink for Israel, then he is proceeding from the Eucharist. For him, this is primarily spiritual food and spiritual drink. Of baptism, Paul says, in 1 Cor. 12:13; that it takes place "in the Spirit." An already broadened understanding is clear when the *Didache* in 10:3 (Jurgens, no. 7) calls the Eucharist "spiritual food and spiritual drink." Even John 6:53 speaks of the necessary spiritual understanding of the Eucharist. "The Spirit and the water and the blood bear witness" (1 John 5:8). This takes place in the life of Jesus, and in the sacraments of baptism and Eucharist (see above, § 8, 3, c, 10). "The Lord is the Spirit" (2 Cor. 3:17). The Exalted is present and real in the Church, in the manner and power of the Spirit. In later language one might say: The Real Presence is presence in and through the Spirit.

The Fathers[129] acknowledged henceforth the power of the Spirit in the Eucharist. According to Fathers like St. Ephraim the Syrian, St. Gregory of Nyssa, St. Cyril of Alexandria, St. John Chrysostom, and Theodore of Mopsuestia, the Logos unites himself through the Pneuma with the offered gifts, bread and wine, so that these lose their natural identity and are changed into the Body and Blood of Christ. In the Greek liturgy, it is the Holy Spirit, called down upon the sacrificial gifts, who sanctifies and changes the gifts. This "epiklesis" is accorded great importance by the Fathers. According to St. Augustine (*Sermon* 57, 7 in Migne, *PL* 38:589), it is by the Eucharist that the faithful ever anew become participants in the communion of life with the Spirit of Christ.

In Corinth, Paul is obliged to correct abuses connected with the Lord's Supper and bring about order (1 Cor. 11:17-34). The Corinthians have profaned the Meal. Paul does not address himself to an individual official, and command him to spend himself for the sake of order; rather, he speaks to the whole community. From this one may conclude that there were not as yet any such officials as priests to conduct the Meal. Prophets, both men and women, spoke proclamation and liturgy (1 Cor. 11:4f.; 14:24.; see above, § 4, 4). In the *Didache* (10:7; Jurgens, no. 7), the prophets still celebrate the Eucharist as "high priests" (13, 3). The "we" of the Church conducts the Meal. "We bless the Cup. . . . We break the Bread" (1 Cor. 10:16). This is the fulfillment of the instituting will of Christ, who has entrusted the celebration of the Meal to the whole Church (1 Cor. 11:24f.; see above, § 9, 3, a).

The whole community celebrates the spiritual ministry of sacrifice (Rom. 12:1f.) in the universal priesthood (1 Peter 2:5, 9; Apoc. 1:6; see above, § 4, 2). Certainly the Acts of the Apostles (14:23) and the Pastoral Epistles (2 Tim. 1:6) say that Paul installed priests and bishops through a laying on of hands. But it may be that with such assertions later arrangements are being transferred back to the time of Paul (see above, § 3, 2, b, 4). Ultimately, however, it is to be conceded that, in any case, even when an ordained priest concelebrates the Eucharist, it is not he nor his human abilities that represents the Lord's Supper, but always the exalted Christ, operative in the Spirit, who conducts and fulfills the Meal. Thus it is Christ who is the High Priest who carries out his own sacrifice of himself (Heb. 7:27f.; 9:14) and who is now Priest forever in the heavenly sanctuary (Heb. 7:3; 24), in order to entreat as Mediator for the Church (Heb. 7:25; 9:24; 12:24). The Fathers say again and again that, in the Meal, Christ himself is acting and is giving to eat.

Paul warns that severe punishment is consequent upon the unworthy reception of the Eucharist: "Whoever eats and drinks unworthily eats and drinks judgment upon himself, because he does not recognize the Body. That is why many among you are sick and weak, and why many have fallen asleep" (1 Cor. 11:29f.). In spite of this strong language, one must not ascribe a largely magical way of thinking to Paul, as if the gifts of the Meal were transformed into a poison which caused one to become ill and to die. Unworthy reception calls down the judgment of God. It is he, therefore, who punishes. One may compare Apoc. 2:22f., "I am consigning her to a sickbed, and her partners in adultry to great tribulation, if they do not repent of their works. And I will let her children die." In both places the punishment is described very realistically as sickness and death. God, the Creator, is the dispenser of all life. The destruction of life in sickness and death cannot be the will and work of God. They can only be understood as punishments permitted by him. Thus the gospel (Luke 13:6) says that through healings, Satan is conquered in the sickness.

It is not sin in general that makes one unworthy of the Meal, so that only the sinless might participate in the Meal. On the contrary, the Meal is even to take away sin (Matthew 26:28). The guilt is offense against the Body of Christ. But it is not stated which Body is meant, and we cannot distinguish. What is meant is, no doubt, either the Eucharistic Body or the Body which is the Church. The Corinthians no longer distinguish the Eucharistic Body from ordinary food; or they sin against the Body which is the Church. Reception is unworthy if the meaning of the Meal is lost and perverted through selfishness at the Meal. Then the Meal, which is communion with and in the Body of Christ, is destroyed.

Paul's warning of the severe consequences of unworthy reception makes clear his conviction of the Real Presence of the Lord in the Eucharist. Although Paul does not speak of previous sins as making one's participation in the Meal unworthy, there is here, nevertheless, a beginning of the requirement of penance before the Meal. Thus the *Didache* 14:1 (Jurgens, no. 8) enjoins: "On the Lord's Day of the Lord* gather together, break bread and give thanks, after confessing

* [*Translator's note*: A redundancy making it clear that the term "Lord's Day" is already a common usage for Sunday, so much so that it is now used as a distinct term apart from its root meaning]

your transgressions so that your sacrifice may be pure." The purity of the sacrifice requires the purity of its participant.

Paul teaches the importance of the Lord's Supper for the Church. Communion with the Lord of the Supper is not only a personal event of the sojourning of the Lord in the soul, even if this experience of the Meal has engendered a high mysticism, which one certainly cannot frivolously ignore. The relationship of the Lord's Supper to the Church is conveyed in the Last Supper words emphasizing the sacrifice "for the many" and in the institution of the covenant (Mark 14:24).

Paul establishes the importance of the Meal for the communion of the Church (1 Cor. 10:15f.; 11:23-30). The Meal is, in a threefold sense, representation of the Body of Christ. In the Meal the Body of the historical Christ is surrendered to death: "This is my Body for you" (1 Cor. 11:24). In the Meal, Bread and Wine are the Body and the Blood of Christ: "The Cup which we bless, is it not the communion of Christ's Blood? The Bread which we break, is it not the communion of Christ's Body?" (1 Cor. 10:16). The one Bread effects the unity of the Body of Christ, which is the Church. "Because there is one Bread, we, the many, are one Body" (1 Cor. 10:17; on the Church as Body of Christ, see above, § 2, 3, b).

Faith experiences communion with Christ (1 Cor. 1:9). This communion is communion in suffering with Christ (Phil. 3:10). It exists as "communion of the Holy Spirit" (2 Cor. 13:13). The communion of the Blood and Body of Christ is a new and sacramentally established reality (1 Cor. 10:16). Paul explains and clarifies it with references to the religious context of the times. Israel celebrates the sacrificial banquet and banquet of sacrifice around the altar of the Temple. The people becomes thereby a great communion around the altar as its focal point (1 Cor. 10:18). Even paganism is a communion around its altars of sacrifice. Certainly its focal point is not the true God; for there is only one God (1 Cor. 8:4-6). Active in the pagan sacrificial worship are the demons. Paganism, therefore, is a fearsome reality. Communion through the Sacrament of Christ is radically different from paganism. The Body of Christ offered in death shapes and creates the Church. For the self-surrender of Jesus produces redemption, justification, sanctification, salvation, whereby the Church herself exists.

Therefore the Meal cannot be celebrated if communion is damaged or destroyed.

Paul complains, even in reference to the Meal, that factions exist in the community (1 Cor. 1:10-12). He finds it blameworthy that in Corinth each one "is in a hurry to start his own supper" (1 Cor. 11:21f.).

Among the Fathers, it was Augustine especially who emphasized the ecclesiological significance of the Eucharist. It is "the sacrament of unity." It is the sign and the means of unity between Christ and the Church, and therefore of the Church herself. The sacramental Body of Christ has spiritual significance, as Paul says: "You are the Body of Christ and his members." Augustine: "If you are the Body of Christ and his members, you yourselves are like the Mystery on the table of the Lord; you receive yourselves in the Mystery. We, the many, are the one Bread, the one Body" (*Sermon* 227, Migne, *PL* 38:1246–1248).[130]

7) *Gospel of John.* In John's Gospel, an account of the institution of the Lord's Supper during the Last Supper of Jesus with his disciples is lacking.[131] Nevertheless, references thereto echo through his farewell discourses (John 13:34f.; 15:1-8, 12; 17:17-19). And the sixth chapter of John is written against the background of the celebration of the Eucharist in the Church. The Gospel tells directly of the marvelous feeding of the thousands by Christ, which is depicted as an anticipation of the Eucharist (John 6:5-23). The miracle of the manna is a prototype of the Eucharistic Food, and of that Food which is Christ himself (John 6:31-35, 49-51, 58). Christ is the true Bread from heaven, which one must receive in faith (John 6:32-63). He gives the abiding Bread of Life, which is his "Flesh for the life of the world." The eating of the Flesh and the drinking of the Blood of the Son of Man promises the resurrection on the last day and gives eternal life (John 6:51-58).

The sacramental gifts are dispensed by the exalted Christ (John 6:62). In ultimate truth, it is the divine Spirit who effects all (John 6:63; 7:38f.). The visible sacrament is described in words of utmost realism as "chewing" and "drinking" the Elements (John 6:56). The Eucharist of the Church, however, is described in greater depth in its connections with Christology, especially with the salvific death of Jesus, with the doctrine of the Spirit, and with eschatology. Word, sacrament, and Spirit become a unity.

Like other discourses of John's Gospel, the Eucharistic discourse in John 6 has its origins in the theological altercation of the end of the first century.[132] The spirituality of the Sacrament is defended against a rudely materialistic misunderstanding (John 6:63). And on the other hand, a docetist contesting of the true humanity and historical reality of Christ, as also of the Sacrament, is refuted (John 6:53).

4. DOGMATIC EXPLANATION

The dogmatic theology of the High Middle Ages, in explaining the real presence of Christ in the Eucharist, employed the Aristotelian-Scholastic conceptuality of substance as the non-material, non-experiential essence of things, and of species as the sum total of the accidents, which are the visible and perceptible properties of things. Dogmatics formed the technical term "transubstantiation" (meaning "changing of essence"). The word was first officially used in the Church at the Fourth Council of the Lateran in 1215, and was afterwards repeated by the Council of Trent in 1551: "The Catholic Church very aptly terms this change *transubstantiation*."[133] By virtue of the consecration of the bread and wine, the substance of bread and wine is changed into the substance of the Body and Blood of Christ. The accidents remain. But if the substance is not an empirical presence but a spiritual presence, then the meaning may perhaps be comparable to declarations like those in 1 Cor. 10:4 and John 6:63, according to which the presence of Christ in the Eucharist is an intellectually-spiritual (*geistig-geistliche*) one.

Duns Scotus (and certainly dogmatics rather broadly) teaches that transubstantiation is not provable from Scripture, but only from the Tradition of the Church. It is a relief to exegesis that it does not have to produce a Scriptural proof for the doctrine of transubstantiation! If it is provable only from Tradition, certainly this indicates that transubstantiation is an explanation of the real presence that it temporally and culturally conditioned, even if of vast importance to the history of dogma. If the Council of Trent says that the concept of transubstantiation is "very apt," then it is surely not saying that it is absolutely necessary and the sole possibility.

The problematic is apparently one that is not in a negligible way of a hermeneutical kind: whether one can transpose biblical terms, concepts, and data directly into concepts of Greek metaphysics, and thereby contain them. And the problematic is only heightened for us by the fact that today we no longer designate bread or wine as substance. According to the modern conception, they are a multitude of substances, as a multitude of elementary particles.

Modern dogmatics,[134] therefore, attempts a partially new formulation. For the Eucharist it ponders the term "transignification." Bread and wine become signs, *signa*, of another and deeper reality. They are signs of the reality of the submission of Christ in his death, but also in the Meal of communion with men.[135]

Or dogmatics employs the concept of "transfinalization." Bread and wine obtain a new purpose and goal, a new end, a new *finis*. They obtain the disposition of representing the surrender of Christ and of furnishing the spiritual Meal. (As a comparison, it might be noted that if a red cloth is used as a red flag, it has essentially another and new disposition). The sign and shape of bread and wine go beyond all natural content and estimate, to transcend what is commonplace, in that they represent, promise, and guarantee eschatologically final salvation.

§ 10. ISRAEL AND CHURCH

The description of the community of disciples and of the Church in the New Testament will be concluded in this chapter and in the following, with a survey of the milieu of the Church, of her relationship to Israel and to the Gentiles, and of her mission to both.

The relationship between Church and synagogue, so important and rich in content, is founded for all time and history in the New Testament.[136]

1. Jesus and Israel

The life of Jesus, his teaching and his deeds, were all accomplished within Israel.[137] He devoted himself to all of Israel, with all her religious and social levels. He gathered his disciples from the whole nation. The calling of the Twelve took place in view of the whole Israel as a nation idealized in twelve tribes (see above, § 4, 1, a). Israel has first claim to the tidings of the approaching kingdom, as well as to the salvation visibly effected through the cures worked by Jesus. That is why Jesus sends out his messengers with the directive: "Do not go on the roads to the Gentiles, and enter no Samaritan town. Go rather to the lost sheep of the house of Israel" (Matthew 10:5). To the Canaanite woman he explains: "I have been sent only to the lost sheep of the house of Israel" (Matthew 10:5). And, "It is not right to take the children's bread and throw it to the dogs" (Matthew 15:24f.).

Israel is the community called "sons of the kingdom of God" (Matthew 8:12). Jesus recognizes Israel as children of Abraham (Luke 13:16; 19:9). Israel is, as in ancient times (Ezek. 34), God's flock (Matthew 10:6; 15:24), and, as formerly (Is. 5:1), God's vineyard (Mark 12:1). The old covenant is given a broader dimension in the new (Mark 14:24). That Israel, given the first call, does not accept the powerful deeds of Jesus, calls forth a lamentation from him (Matthew 11:20-24). In Israel and in its chief city, Jerusalem, the destiny of Jesus is to be completed even to his death (Matthew 23:37f.).

a) Association

With Jesus as its focal point, the Church remains always in a deep union with Israel. Israel bequeathed to the world her rigid monotheism (see the present work, Vol. 2, pp. 240–246). The God of Abraham, Isaac, and Jacob is also the Father of Jesus Christ. With the name Jesus, the Greek form of *Yehoshua* (= Yahweh is salvation), it is stated forever that the God of the old covenant is God also of the new (see the present work, Vol. 2, pp. 250f.).

The biblical God is the Creator and Perfecter of the world. Creation, however, is not an event of mere beginning; rather, God is indeed the Creator and Father of each individual. All creation develops in a line from beginning to consummation. The eschatological extension is the

Bible's hope, while the Greek *Weltanschauung* accepted a course of history that lay in endless and repetitious circular waves (see the present work, Vol. 1, pp. 53–61). In New Testament times, Jewish apocalyptics, which was productive of a rich literature, expected the end of the world as drawing imminently near. This is also, in a broad way, the position of the New Testament Church.

God is the One who, in the moral order, rules and sets requirements; and also, however, He is the One who is near and who is gracious. The Christian ethos, therefore, is something essentially different from a natural ethic. And this is true without prejudice to the fact that the Epistles of the apostles draw upon certain points of philosophical, ethical acceptances.

The New Testament acknowledged the Old Testament Bible as revelation and word of God, even if Jesus readily interpreted the Scriptures anew (Matthew 5:21-48; 19:3-9; 22:29). The community read the Bible in the Greek language. Every translation is by its very nature an interpretation. Thus, from the very beginning a Greek spirit was penetrating tradition. And the Church is determined essentially in language and spirit by the Old Testament and, therefore, by Israel (see the present work, Vol. 2, pp. 20–46).[138]

b) Altercation

The Gospels, nevertheless, tell in a broad way of the opposition between Jesus and his people.

While Jesus finds faith existing among the Gentiles (Matthew 8:10; 15:28), he calls the Israel who is oppressing him, and although she recites always her confession of faith, God is one . . . (Deut. 6:4f.; Mark 12:32), "an unfaithful and perverse generation" (Matthew 17:17). Because Jesus entered into the companionship of sinners, he was, in the judgment of the teachers and the pious, subverting the order of the Law (Matthew 11:19). The messianic claim of Jesus, be it now a secret or an open claim, becomes an insurmountable obstacle.

The Gospels bear witness to the opposition and altercation between Jesus and Israel. The narrative of the cursing of the unfruitful fig tree (Mark 11:12-14, 20f.), which encloses the story of the purifying of the Temple (Mark 11:15-19), surely indicates symbolically the rejection of Israel, who brings forth no fruit, while the purifying of the Temple announces her guilty finish. In a new temple all nations will worship (Mark 11:17).

1) Parable of the Wicked Vinedressers (Mark 12:1-12). The parable of the wicked vinedressers (Mark 12:1-12) depicts the passage of Israel's calling and salvation to the Gentiles. In the Old Testament, Israel is described as God's precious vineyard (Is. 5:1-7, echoed in Mark 12:1; also Jer. 2:21; Ezek. 17:5-10; and Hos. 10:1). God, the master of the vineyard, sends servants to collect the rent. They are abused and even killed. Finally the lord sends his son. The vinedressers murder him. They are punished by their destruction and the vineyard is let to others. The narrative is not difficult to interpret. The messengers are the prophets of the old covenant; the son is Jesus Christ; the punishment is the rejection of Israel and the calling of others.

While all the other parables of the Synoptic Gospels are similitudes, in which the image moiety and the subject moiety correspond in *one* point (in the *tertium comparationis*), the narrative of the wicked vine-dressers is an allegory, in which *each* element of the image has a meaning in the indicated subject. For this reason some exegetes find it questionable whether the parable goes back to Jesus. And this question is sharpened by a consideration of the parable's Christological content. Christ is "the only and beloved son" (Mark 12:5f.), a term of especially rich content in Mark, in view of 1:11 and 9:7. The son is "sent," which is the terminology also of Gal. 4:4; Rom. 8:3; John 3:17 and 1 John 4:9. Is it the confession of the Christian community that is speaking here? (See the present work, Vol. 2, pp. 177, 193–203). The death and exaltation of the Son are announced in a thinly veiled way (Mark 12:8-11). As with all the predictions of the Passion, here too one can question whether or not it may have been shaped after the event (see the present work, Vol. 2, p. 92). In any case, the prediction of the exaltation (Mark 12:10f.) gets its present form of an appendix, no doubt, as a result of the community's search of the Scriptures for proofs.

At the same time, some exegetes are more of a mind that an original and simple parabolic similitude of Jesus has been deepened and interpreted allegorically.[139] In its final historico-traditional form, the parable contains the Christological confession of the community, and it is a witness to the vehement opposition between Christian community and synagogue.

The allegorical elements are explained in the later Synoptics. Mark 12:8 said: "They killed him and cast him out," which is easily understood in accord with the details of the story. The vinedressers killed the son in the vineyard, and then threw his body out into the field for scavenging animals. In Matthew 21:39 and Luke 20:15, however, it is stated: "They cast him out and killed him." This is the sequence of events in the Passion of Jesus. He dies outside the city, beyond any human companionship. This is, no doubt, emphasized in John 19:17: "He went outside to the place of the skull." The idea is strengthened in Heb. 13:12f.: "Jesus suffered outside the gate. Let us go to him outside the camp and share with him his humiliation."

According to Mark 11:27 (as also Matthew 21:45), the parable is addressed to the "high priests, scribes, and elders." If it is these who are the primary object of the threat that the vineyard will be given to others (Matthew 22:9f. and Luke 14:21f.), these others might be the poor of Israel. But if the parable refers to the whole of Israel, then the threat signifies the passage of salvation to the Gentiles. Matthew speaks without parabolic imagery when he designates the inheritance as the "kingdom of God." Twice (Matthew 21:41, 43) he stresses that in their time those called second will produce the fruits of the kingdom. This is an open admonition and hope in respect to the Gentiles (see Matthew 3:8, 10; 7:16-20; 12:33; 13:8, 26).

Proof from prophecy is adduced in Mark 12:10 with a quotation from Ps. 118:22.[140] A messianic significance of the psalm verse is, if not precisely unknown, certainly very rare among the rabbis; for Jewish exegesis gave expression only to the exaltation of the Messiah, and not to his prior rejection.[141] The verse was important to the New Testament proof from prophecy. From Ps. 118:22, the key word "to be rejected" (ἀποδοκιμάζεσθαι) passed over into the prophecy of the Passion (Mark 8:31). Ps. 118:22 is also quoted in Acts 4:11 in a sermon of Peter, and afterwards, in a collection of citations about Christ as a sacred stone, in 1 Peter 2:4, 7, and in the so-called *Letter of Barnabas* 6:2. In Mark 12:10, therefore, it is common New Tesament scriptural proof that is speaking. In Luke 20:18 the verse is extended, uniting it to Dan. 2:44f. and Is. 8:14f. The latter is found again in the collections in Rom. 9:32f. and 1 Peter 2:8. Luke 20:18 is taken later into the Gospel of

Matthew, at Matthew 21:44. All this demonstrates the interest of the
community in the development of the proof from prophecy.

2) Parable of the Banquet (Matthew 22:1-14). The parable of the feast
(in Matthew 22:1-14, a wedding banquet; in Luke 14:15-24, a great
banquet) likewise treats of the initial call of Israel, and the later call to
the Gentiles. In the parable of Matthew, the king repeatedly sends his
servants out, who are to extend invitations to the wedding banquet.
Those invited abuse the servants; indeed, they seize them and kill
them. Angered, the king sends out his army to destroy those murderers and to burn their city. Instead of the invited, the servants call
others from the crossroads to the wedding dinner, summoning all
whom they find, good and evil alike, until the hall is full.

The meaning of the narrative in Matthew is clear. To represent the
eschatological kingdom in the guise of a feast is an ancient device (Is.
25:6; Ps. 22:27), known also to Judaism (*Ethiopic Henoch* 62:13-15;
1 QSa 2:11-21; rabbinic instances in Strack and Billerbeck, *op. cit.*,
Vol. 1 [1922], pp. 878f.), and made further use of in the New Testament (Apoc. 3:20; 19:9).

The era of salvation is a wedding feast (Hos. 2:20f.; Mark 2:19).
That the wedding feast is prepared for the son signifies, no doubt, the
era of salvation inaugurated by Jesus, the only Son (Matthew 22:2).
Those first invited represent Israel, who declines the invitation. Messengers are sent out twice. With the first, certainly the prophets are
meant (as in Matthew 21:34-36). The messengers are sent a second
time, because everything is already prepared. Is Matthew thinking now
of the apostles, sent out by Jesus? The punishment is the destruction
of Jerusalem in the year 70 A.D. Those called include both the good and
the wicked; after the destruction of Jerusalem, certainly, the Gentiles.
It is they who come from the crossroads, that is, from strange and
distant places.

In Luke's narrative, the same servant is sent out twice. The story
takes place within the course of present time. In place of the Jews first
invited, summons is next issued to "the poor and the crippled, the
blind and the lame, in the streets and alleys of the city." This corresponds to the concern of Luke's Gospel, which is in a special way
the Gospel of the poor and the sick (Luke 7:22; 12:16-21; 16:19-31;
18:22). The poor are not enough to fill the house. Further guests are

to be brought in "from the highways and byways." Here it is probably the Gentiles who are meant, those who are indeed outside. This second invitation, then, indicates the mission of the Church in its turning to the Gentiles. Luke concludes with the condemnation of Israel: "Not one of those invited first shall taste my supper."

3) Pharisaism (Matthew 23). The Gospels tell of the altercation of Jesus with the Pharisees, as with one of the leading spiritual movements of Israel (§ 1, 1).

In the parable of the Pharisee and the tax collector (Luke 18:9-14), the Pharisee cannot be perceived directly as a caricature. In Israel, he is truly a righteous man. In the judgment of Jesus, the Pharisee of the parable is lacking in righteousness because he believes that his virtue is perfect and is no longer in need of God's gift. The tax collector, however, who is in truth a sinner, is righteous, because he knows that he needs everything. This is the basis of the opposition between Jesus and the Pharisees, and ultimately, between Jesus and Israel. The pious can fancy that the foundations of Jewish legal piety are being assailed, and ultimately the very notion of God, if he is understood as the God of righteousness (see the present work, Vol. 3, pp. 178–183).

Jesus criticizes the righteousness of the Pharisees. "If your righteousness does not surpass that of the scribes and Pharisees, you will not enter the kingdom of heaven" (Matthew 5:20). The new righteousness required of the disciples is not an increased and perfected righteousness of the Pharisees; it is above and utterly beyond theirs. It is essentially quite otherwise than theirs. It is never a mere increased and more rigid legalism, but an inner responsibility in the relationship of children to the Father. Jesus rejects this and every system of morality, in favor of deciding in the freedom of love. The greater part of true righteousness is beyond human endeavor; it is, as the righteousness of the kingdom of God, hope in its eschatological gift and perfecting (see the present work, Vol. 2, pp. 30–31; and Vol. 3, pp. 183f.).

Another altercation with Pharisaism is presented in the lengthy discourse against the scribes and Pharisees, in Matthew 23:1-7, 13-33. The discourse is, like all the lengthy discourses of Matthew's Gospel, the composition of the Evangelist. This will be apparent already from the fact that sayings therefrom are found also in Luke 11:37-54 and 20:45f., but here in a different context and in a different place. The lengthy discourse of Matthew is a highly effective creation of the Evangelist, especially through the series of seven mounting cries of woe. In Matthew, the discourse is Jesus' last public address to the people. As a final and decisive parting from the leaders of Israel, the discourse is located in the concourse of the Temple in Jerusalem, that is, in the all-decisive center of Israel. After this rejection of Israel on the whole, Jesus concerned himself only with his narrower circle of disciples (Matthew 24:1).

The discourse of Jesus acknowledges directly (Matthew 23:2f.) and in an astounding manner the teaching authority of the scribes and Pharisees. They occupy the magisterial chair of Moses. Their theoretical doctrine is valid. "Do all that they tell you." Certainly, however, "They do not practice what they preach." Here it would seem to be Judeo-Christianity that is speaking, which recognizes the teaching office in Israel (comparably in Matthew 5:17f.). The adversaries are indeed reproached with a lack of harmony between their words and their deeds. In Matthew 23:13-22, however, the scribes and Pharisees are blamed for false teaching. By their rigid interpretation of the Law and by the constant attaching to it of new explanations and additions, the teachers of the Law bind up increasingly heavy burdens, which they themselves "will not lift a finger to move" (Matthew 23:4). This can hardly be intended to mean that they themselves do not assume these burdens and carry them, for that would be a contradiction of Matthew 23:23, 26; rather, they will not assist others who are so burdened. Furthermore, a conflict between appearance and reality is indicated (Matthew 23:5f.). Their piety is practiced for show.

In Matthew 23:13-32, a definite order to the cries of woe is observable. First of all, in Matthew 23:13-22, the Pharisees debase God's word and law; then, in Matthew 23:23-32, they attend to externals while what is internal remains wicked. A further cry of woe is enunciated in Mark 12:40 and Luke 20:47. It can be found as an interpolation inserted secondarily into the cries of woe in Matthew's Gospel at 23:14. The charge leveled here, that the Pharisees appropriate and consume the goods of the poor, corresponds to the charge made against the "godless" in the *Ascension of Moses* 7:6.

In the seven cries of woe, the scribes and Pharisees are charged with being ὑποκριταί.[142] Originally ὑποκρίνομαι probably means "to answer, to explain." A ὑποκριτής is a stage performer (as an interpreter of poetic work), whence the term comes to be used in a pejorative sense for one conducting himself dishonestly. In the Greek Bible, the godless man, living in falsehood and wickedness, is termed a ὑποκριτής (Job 34:30; 36:13; Sir. 1:28f.; 32:15). In the New Testament too, the word is used only with a pejorative meaning. Jesus calls those persons ὑποκριταί who can judge rightly the course of the seasons but do not recognize the signs of the present eschatological times (Luke 12:56), and those who do not hesitate on the Sabbath to lead a beast to water but protest against the curing of a sick woman (Luke 13:15).

Charged as hypocrisy, therefore, are impious and contradictory judgments and attitudes; such is the case with the saying about the splinter and the beam (Matthew 7:5), and in the opposition of lip-service and service from the heart (Matthew 15:7f.). In Matthew 6:2-5, 16, they are called hypocrites who do good works before men but not before God. In Matthew 23:23-29, the hypocrisy consists in a pious appearance and the contradiction between external works and interior thoughts. It cannot be said that this hypocrisy is always known and willed as dishonesty. It can also consist in the contradiction between ideal and real.

The first cry of woe (Matthew 23:13) says that the scribes and Pharisees close the kingdom of God to men. This is probably aimed at their false teaching (Luke 11:52), by which they prohibited entry into the community of disciples and hinder the mission. If it refers to the mission of the Church, the speaker is no longer the historical Jesus.

The adversaries themselves conduct a mission with great zeal and make every effort to win but a single proselyte (Matthew 23:15). And they turn him into a "son of hell, twice as bad as themselves." In point of fact, it was the Pharisees who conducted a world-wide mission in order to bring converts to the Jewish religion. The Sadducees were opposed to mission, because they understood Judaism as race and not as religion. Accordingly, one could only be born a Jew; one could not be converted to Judaism.

The charge against the Jewish mission is very hard. The Christian mission very often followed the ways of the Jewish mission; and Paul, for example, in foreign cities preached primarily in (Hellenistic) synagogues and won the first Christians among Jewish proselytes and among the broader assemblage of the "God-fearing" who belonged to the synagogue. This is the case in Salamis on Cyprus (Acts 13:5); in Antioch in Pisidia (Acts 13:14); in Iconium (Acts 14:1); in Thessalonica (Acts 17:1); in Berea (Acts 17:10); in Athens (Acts 17:17), in Corinth (Acts 18:4) and in Ephesus (Acts 18:19). (This uniformity may be schematic, and the statement of particular places may not in each instance be absolutely historical. Is the charge against the Jewish mission justified? Or is it so severe because the range of Jewish and Christian missions have met in an inimical fashion? If a history of the Christian missions is already presupposed, Matthew 23:15 cannot be an original saying of Jesus.

Matthew 23:16-22 is concerned with the particularized casuistry by which the scribes and Pharisees, with their distinctions, validate and depreciate oaths. If correspondences to such practice can be found in rabbinic teaching,[143] such evasions were, nevertheless, quite blasphemous in the eyes of the pious Jew. For him it was certainly true that "from any binding oath that a man has taken to perform any precept of the Law, he is not to free himself even at the cost of death" (*Damascus Document* 16:7f.; see the present work, Vol. 3, p. 282).

Far beyond the tithing prescribed in the Law (Lev. 27:30f.; Num. 18:12; Deut. 14:23), the Pharisees tithed every trifling thing (Matthew 23:23f.). The saying of Jesus recognizes their zeal in this immediately. One must not, however, neglect what is essential to the Law: justice, mercy, and fidelity (faith?). This is required by the prophets of old (Micah 6:8; Zech. 7:9; Ps. 32:5). Luke 11:42 inserts here, probably as a later interpolation, the requirement of loving God.

The lack of accord between external action and interior thought is charged in the face of the zeal of the scribes in cleansing the exterior of the dish (in accord with Lev. 11:32-38), while it troubles them not at all that the contents may have been gotten through plunder (Matthew 23:25f.). When Matthew adds that if the inside be clean, the outside will likewise be purified, a principle is thereby asserted which annuls all Jewish prescriptions of legal purity. Luke 11:41, in a radical fashion, conceives the content of the vessel as alms to be distributed, which corresponds to the high esteem this Gospel has for poverty and benefaction (see the present work, Vol. 3, pp. 309f.).

The Pharisees are compared to neatly whitewashed tombs, full, nevertheless, of foulness (Matthew 23:27f.). The adversaries are again being charged with contradiction between appearance and reality.

The Pharisees are accused of erecting monuments to the prophets and the just (Matthew 23:29-32).[144] They expect thereby to be pronounced innocent of the murder of the prophets, but they only show that they are the sons of the murderers of the prophets. Does the charge not proceed from too sharp a dialectic? In many times and among many nations monuments have been set up by descendants as an atoning remembrance for earlier misdeeds. Can one throw it up to these later persons that they only make it apparent thereby that they are the sons of the authors of those deeds?

The cries of woe end with the threat: "You serpents and brood of vipers, how will you escape the judgment of hell!" (Matthew 23:23). This recalls the preaching of John the Baptist (Matthew 3:7). What the Pharisees are reproached with is probably not the cunning of serpents, but the deadly danger they pose.

Many of the words and themes of the address against the scribes and Pharisees probably point back to the time before the destruction of Jerusalem. In Matthew 23:2-4, the rabbinate is acknowledged by the Jewish Christians. In Matthew 23:5f., the ordered relationships within a religious community in Jerusalem are depicted. The Jewish mission, which ceased when, after the catastrophe, Israel had to concentrate all her energies toward assuring her existence as a people, is in full flower (Matthew 23:13, 15). The casuistry on oaths presupposes the existence of the Temple and its arrangement (Matthew 23:16-21). Tombs are still being whitewashed as in peacefully ordered times (Matthew 23:27f.), and the monuments of the saints are still standing (Matthew 23:29).

Nevertheless, exegesis finds it a question whether the discourse can be referred back to Jesus or whether it is for the most part a later construction, without prejudice to the possibility that individuals sayings of Jesus may have been introduced into the discourse. Does the discourse not contradict justice and love, and, therefore, the spirit of Jesus?[145] The admonitions to the community of disciples (Matthew 23:8-12) probably give voice already to improper later developments in this community. The Christian mission seems already to be in formative stage (Matthew 23:13, 15; and 23:34). According to this discourse, Pharisaic righteousness is mere hypocrisy. In the parable of the Pharisee and the tax collector (Luke 18:9-14), Pharisaism is defeated in an entirely different and much more profound way. The piety and righteousness of the Pharisee is acknowledged; but it is nevertheless insufficient for the present time of expectation of the kingdom of God. This will have been the true attitude of Jesus to Pharisaism.

The woe-crying in Matthew 23:13-33 shares in a contemporaneous criticism of Pharisaism, such as is found also in the *Ascension of Moses* 7:3-10. Here those teachers are accused and condemned who regard themselves as justified and pretend to adhere super-precisely to the prescriptions for ritual piety, while they are in fact greedy and blasphemous imposters. That is how Pharisees are depicted.

The Qumran community found itself in opposition to the Temple and to the priesthood in Jerusalem. Blasphemers and false teachers are attacked with great severity in the writings of Qumran. They are "prophets of lies" (1 QH 4:16). They "subvert the Law" (1 QH 4:10); and to those who thirst, they refuse the drink of knowledge, giving them vinegar instead (1 QH 4:11); they deal in false interpretation of Scripture (1 QpHab 10:9f.; *Damascus Document* 4:3; 8:3). Here it appears that false teachers of the Law are condemned. For the pious of Qumran, the Pharisees were failing in the rigid observance of the Law![146] Not a few criticisms were leveled against the Pharisees on account of their self-righteousness and dissimulation (H. L. Strack and P. Billerbeck, *op. cit.*, Vol. 4 [1928] pp. 334-352). The judgment of Pharisaism in Matthew 23 is inseparable from its times. Moreover, it must be remembered that Matthew 23, and especially the series of woe-betide-thee's, belongs to the literary genre of invective.

Joined to the woe-betide-thee's is Matthew 23:34f. = Luke 11:49f., words of threat against the murder of God's messengers (see 10, 2, next below). The sayings come from source Q, the original form of which, at least in part, Luke will have kept. In Luke 11:49, the speaker is "the Wisdom of God." Perhaps what is meant is not just a personification of God's wisdom, but Jesus himself as Wisdom of God. When in Matthew 23:34 the saying begins, "This is why I am sending to you . . . ," probably it is the Christ who exists before time who is speaking here.[147]

According to Matthew 23:34, those sent are "prophets, wise men, and scribes"; according to Luke 11:49, "prophets and apostles." These prophets are not the Old Testament messengers of God but the New

Testament prophets (see above, § 4, 4). Also, the apostles mentioned by Luke are certainly bearers of ecclesiastical office, just as Matthew (13:52) likewise knows Christian scribes. The destiny of the Christian missionaries is depicted in Matthew 23:34: "Many of them you will kill and crucify, and scourge in your synagogues and hunt from city to city."

The murders of the righteous are summarized, "from Abel the just to Zechariah the son of Barachiah" (Matthew 23:35). The death of Abel is recounted in Gen. 4:8, while the stoning of the Prophet Zechariah is told in 2 Chron. 24:21. In the Jewish canon, Genesis is the first book of the Bible and Chronicles the last. Thus all is summarized from the beginning to the end of the Sacred Scriptures.[148]

Finally, a prophecy about Jerusalem is appended in Matthew 23:37f. = Luke 13:34. Jesus had desired to gather the children of Israel, as a hen gathers her chicks. In the Old Testament (Deut. 32:10f.; Is. 31:5; Ps. 35:8), God's protection of the pious is described in a similar fashion. Jesus is God's revelation and presence, and his solicitude for his people. But now it must be announced: "Your house will be left desolate for you." The house is probably not the Temple, which would surely have been designated the house of God, but the city of Jerusalem.[149] Such a saying, like that in Matthew 24:2, contains the prophetic threat of disaster (see below, § 14, 1).

The sayings end with the enigmatic statement: "I tell you, you will see me no more, until you cry, 'Blessed is he who comes in the name of the Lord'" (Matthew 23:39). The Gospel anticipates the parousia. It is not, however, that Israel will experience the parousia as a judgment. Rather, Israel too will greet him who returns as the bringer of blessings.[150] The long and difficult discourse of Matthew, therefore, concludes with a promise of blessing. It announces as a final conclusion, not disaster and judgment, but blessing and salvation. It is, after-all, a Gospel. (Rom. 11:25f. is comparable; see below, § 10, 5, d).

In many of its sayings Matthew 23 reveals a later time. In its entirety the discourse, which may have been composed and written down about the year 80 A.D., is to be understood, not as a discourse of Jesus himself, but as a witness to the opposition between Church and synagogue of a later time.

2. MURDERS OF PROPHETS

In Matthew 23:29-31, 37 and in Mark 12:15, Israel is blamed for the murder of the prophets.[151] The charge is found already in the Old Testament. Queen Jezabel had the prophets of Yahweh exterminated, at which Elijah laments: "Your altars they have broken down, your prophets they have killed" (3 Kings 19:10). At the command of King Joas, the Prophet Zechariah was stoned in the forecourt of the Temple (2 Chron. 24:21). King Jehoiakim had the Prophet Uriah put to the sword (Jer. 26:23). These murders took place without and even against the will of the people. One cannot, therefore, charge them with such. Brought back from the exile, however, Israel accuses herself: "They killed your prophets who admonished them" (Neh. 9:26). The charge is repeated: "They mocked God's messengers, disdained his words, and treated the prophets with contempt" (2 Chron. 36:16); but in this the murdering of prophets is not mentioned. In post-canonical tradition, martyrdoms of prophets are recounted. Micah was thrown into an abyss (*Lives of the Prophets* 3); at the command of King Manasseh, Isaiah was sawed in half (*Ascension of Isaiah* 5; *Lives of the Prophets* 13); Jeremiah was stoned in Egypt by his own people (*Lives of the Prophets* 14); Ezekiel was killed by the Prince of Israel (*Lives of the Prophets* 15).

The accusation that Israel killed her prophets, made thus generally as an accusation against the whole people, is not to be sustained in view of her history. In this self-accusation Israel pronounces too severe a judgment on herself. The assertion, however, is accepted by the New Testament. In the parable of the wicked vinedressers, it is said that those vinedressers abused and killed the many servants who were sent to collect the rent (Mark 12:5), which is again an accusation against Israel of murdering the prophets. In the woe-betide-thee's, the charge is laid baldly to the scribes and Pharisees (Matthew 23:30-32, 35, 37). Stephen accuses the Jews of old and of his own time of having persecuted and killed the prophets, even as they have now killed the Messiah (Acts 7:52). The accusation harks back to the hard statement of the Apostle Paul that the Jews killed the prophets and Jesus (1 Thess.

2:15; see below, § 10, 5, a). It is the echo of a long tradition when Heb. 11:36f. says of the righteous that they "suffered contempt and blows, were stoned, (burned), sawed in half, and put to the sword."[152]

3. Guilt in the Death of Jesus

The question of Israel's guilt in the death of Jesus is a difficult one even to the present day. History must no doubt affirm, even if the particulars of legal circumstances as well as the contest for power be unclear, that in Jerusalem in the New Testament era, it was Rome alone that had the right to pronounce sentence of death in a court proceeding, that, according to the Gospels, it was the Roman Governor Pontius Pilate who condemned Jesus to death. Crucifixion was not a Jewish but a Roman manner of carrying out a death sentence. And it was the Roman soldiers who carried out that sentence on Jesus.

The New Testament accounts do, of course, mention Pilate and the Romans, but their responsibility and guilt are minimized. In Matthew 27:24, Pilate maintains by word and gesture that he is innocent of the Just One's blood. In Luke 23:4-22, Pilate declares Jesus innocent and wants to set him free. Even in John 18:38 and 19:6, 12, the Roman indicates his conviction of Jesus' innocence. A statement of Jesus pronounces Pilate the less guilty and the Jews as the more guilty (John 19:11).

New Testament tradition forcefully emphasizes the guilt of the Jewish nation and of her leadership. In the prophecies of the Passion, it is "the elders, high priests, and scribes" who kill Jesus (Mark 8:31; 10:33; see the present work, Vol. 2, p. 92). Already in Mark 3:6; the Pharisees and Herodians resolve "to destroy Jesus." In the trial, the high priests and scribes achieve their preconceived determination of killing Jesus (Mark 14:1). Their own court is not looking for justice but for the destruction of the accused (Mark 14:55). They accuse him also before the Roman judge (Mark 15:3). In John's Gospel the Jews persecute Jesus from the very beginning, inasmuch as they are "seeking to kill him" (John 5:16, 18; see below, § 10, 6).

The preaching of the Church advances the charge. Peter says once

that the Jews acted in ignorance (Acts 3:17). The cooperation of the
Romans is mentioned (Acts 2:23; 3:13). But without mentioning the
Romans, the accusation is also made: "You crucified Jesus" (Acts 2:36;
4:10). Stephen charges: "You have become the betrayers and murderers
of the Messiah" (Acts 7:52). Paul summarizes, "They killed the Lord
Jesus and the prophets" (1 Thess. 2:15; see below, § 10, 5, a).

The New Testament wants to explain the reasons for what happened. Sin owns the deepest guilt for the Cross of Jesus. "The Messiah
was delivered into the hands of sinners" (Mark 14:41; Luke 24:7;
Heb. 12:3). Sin crucifies the Son of God again and again (Heb. 6:6).
More penetrating analysis recognizes in the surrender of Jesus the will
of God (Luke 2:34f.; Rom. 9:33; 1 Peter 2:8), indeed, God's love (John
3:16; Rom. 5:8; 1 John 4:10). Faith and preaching find an explanation
in the death of Jesus in the prophecy of the Old Testament. God's plan
of salvation, determined before time began, must be carried out. The
theology of the Cross recognizes and proclaims atonement and redemption, peace and salvation, as the fruit and work of the self-surrender of
Jesus (see the present work, Vol. 2, pp. 86–100). All human guilt, that
of the Jews and of the whole world, is finally taken away therein.[153]

4. Primitive Community at Jerusalem

After the exaltation of Jesus and the pouring out of the Spirit, a
community of disciples assembled itself again in Jerusalem. At first
they considered themselves a part of the Jewish community and appeared to be Jews like the others. If the Christians were separated from
Israel by their confession of Jesus, rejected by the leaders of the people,
as the Messiah sent by God, they hoped at first to win the whole people to this belief. It was soon seen that in general this was impossible;
and when Israel confirmed her rejection and sharpened her inimical attitude, it gave rise to the separation between Church and synagogue.

The Jewish priesthood and the Sanhedrin took action against the
apostles (Acts 4:1-22; 5:17-40). Stephen (Acts 6:8–7:60) and James, the
brother of the Lord (Acts 12:1f.), died, pouring out their blood in witness. A portion of the community, deriving probably from the Hellen-

istic-Jewish diaspora, had to leave Jerusalem (Acts 8:1-3). Further persecutions are mirrored by statements placed in the mouth of Jesus
about persecutions by the synagogue (Matthew 10:17-23; 23:34; John
16:2). The disciples were pushed to the paths of the Gentile mission.
First of all they proclaimed the faith in Samaria (Acts 8:4-13). It was
probably Antioch that produced the first Gentile Christian community
(Acts 11:19-21).*

The first Gentile Christian communities were by no means as free
of the Law as the Pauline communities would be. A synod of apostles
and elders in Jerusalem recognized in principle the freedom of the
Gentile Christian Church from the "burden" of the Law (Acts 15:1-
31).[154] As minimal requirements enabling association between Jewish
and Gentile Christians (Acts 15:19f.), the latter were to abstain from
anything sacrificed to idols, from fornication, from the meat of stran-
gled animals and from blood (i.e., from the meat of animals not ritually slaughtered; Lev. 17:10-14). The importance of the decree was
probably limited. Paul seems not to have known about it. Was it perhaps agreed upon on some other occasion, and, unhistorically, inserted
into Acts 15?

If, as seems apparent, Gal. 2:1-10 and Acts 15 recount one and the
same assembly in Jerusalem, a collection among the Gentile Christians
for "the poor and the saints in Jerusalem" was decided (Gal. 2:10).
Paul earnestly endeavored to carry out this obligation (Rom. 15:25f.;
1 Cor. 16:1-4; 2 Cor. 8-9; Acts 11:29f.; 12:25; 24:17). He thought it
only proper that the Gentiles, who had now received a share in the
spiritual goods of Israel, should serve the poor of Israel with earthly
things (Rom. 15:27). The collection betokened the bond between the
world-wide mission and the mother community in Jerusalem.[155]

If, in accord with the decree of the Synod of Jerusalem, Gentile
Christians were free of the Old Testament laws of worship, the question remained whether or not Jewish Christians might dispense themselves therefrom. Paul, "for the sake of the Jews," had Timothy cir-

---

*(*Translator's addition*: Acts 11:26 notes that the name "Christian" was first
used at Antioch. Interestingly, the first usage likewise of the term "Catholic
Church" is found in a letter of a bishop of Antioch, dating from *ca.* A.D. 110:
St. Ignatius, *Letter to the Smyrnaeans* 8, 2 [Jurgens, no. 65]).

cumcised (Acts 16:1f.), the latter being the son of a Gentile father and a Jewish mother and therefore subject to the Jewish law of circumcision.[156]

How difficult their relationships remained is indicated by the episode in Antioch, where the question of the eating together of Jewish and Gentile Christians brought to the fore a sharp disagreement between Peter and Paul, when Peter "again kept himself apart from any association at table, for fear of those who insisted on circumcision" (Gal. 2:11-21).

In actual fact, the questions were not easy. In the midst of a pagan world and its abomination, Israel owed her pure monotheism and her moral ordering of life to the Law. The Law was the constitution of the commonwealth. Israel conceived the Law, not as bondage and burden, but as a distinction and a gift of God. Could and should a man set himself apart from the Law? If the Old Testament was a sacred book to Christians, were they to regard it as valid only in part? In lengthy and intense struggles, Paul won for the Church the freedom from the Law as an obligating ritual worship (see the present work, Vol. 1. pp. 128–133).

5. Epistles of Paul

The Letters of the Apostle Paul are the most important documentation for the altercation and separation between Church and synagogue. Paul was proud of his being a Jew (2 Cor. 11:22; Phil. 3:6). He is not a "sinner from among the pagans" (Gal. 2:15). That his people now declined to accept salvation and lost it was for him "great sorrow and endless grief." If it could have benefited his brothers, he would himself have wished to be far from Christ (Rom. 9:2f.). In all his indescribable efforts in the Gentile mission, he has Israel in mind. He wants it to be a consequence of his mission that Israel will become jealous of the salvation afforded the Gentiles and will herself be converted (Rom. 11:13f.).[157]

a) 1 Thess. 2:14-16

Paul blames the Jews severely in 1 Thess. 2:14-16. The Gentile Christians of Thessalonica experienced persecutions on the part of their fel-

low countrymen, just as the Jewish Christian communities were persecuted by "the Jews" in Judea. Paul laments and complains: "They have
indeed killed the Lord Jesus, and the prophets; they have persecuted
us; they are not pleasing to God and they are inimical to all men, inasmuch as they hinder us from speaking to the Gentiles, that they
might be saved; and thereby they constantly fill up the measure of their
sins. But the wrath (of God) has overtaken them to the end."

This insertion in the letter goes far afield from the message that the
letter was intended to contain. It appears that when the Apostle was
reminded of the Jews, his anger broke forth in an unbridled way. First
the Jews are accused of the murder of the prophets (see above, § 10,
2). They reached the summit in this with the killing of Jesus, which,
with no mention of the part of the Romans, is laid unsparingly at the
doors of the Jews (see above, § 10, 3). Then Paul remembers the persecution that he himself has suffered from the Jews. He thinks of the
condemnations that he has received in Jewish courts (2 Cor. 11:23)
and of the persecutions by the Jews, recounted in the Acts of the Apostles (up to the date of the First Epistle to the Thessalonians, in Acts
9:23; 13:8; 45; 14:2, 19; 17:13; 18:6). Thus do the Jews hinder Paul in
his proclaiming of the gospel among the Gentiles. Paul accuses the
Jews of not being pleasing to God and of being inimical to all mankind.

Similar accusations were raised against the Jews by the profane anti-
Semitism of antiquity. Esther 3:8-13 already accuses the Jew-baiter
Haman of agitating against the Jews as enemies of mankind. In Egyptian papyri the Jews are called "godless." Josephus, in his work *Against
Apion* (2, 10f., 121, 125), defends Jews against their having been designated as godless and enemies of mankind. Tacitus (*Histories* 5, 4f.)
says of the Jews: "All that is holy to us is profane to them; contrariwise, they permit everything that is abomination to us. . . . Among
themselves they are very closely united; but to other men they show
themselves inimical and full of hate. . . . They hold the goods in contempt." Juvenal (*Satires* 14:96-106) ridicules the Jews: "They pray to
the clouds and to the heavens as their divinity. Every seventh day they
turn lazy. They are trained to hold the Roman laws in contempt.
Moses teaches them to point out the way and lead to their wells only
their own religious and national compatriots."

The Law forbade Jews to participate in pagan worship, while they themselves were obligated to a rigidly imageless worship of God. The Law made Jewish marriage, business, and commerce with Gentiles difficult or impossible. That is how they came to be characterized as godless and misanthropic.

Is Paul drawing upon the charges made by ancient anti-Semitism?[158] Does he not remember the reasons for the Jewish attitude? What is meant by the mysterious statement that the wrath of God (Rom. 1:18) has come upon them "up to the end"? Does it mean that the endtime has already begun, and with it the consummation of Israel's destiny? Or does the end mean the degree, so that it would mean that wrath has fallen upon them in full measure? The statement looks like a prophecy of Israel's destruction. There seems to be a re-echoing here of apocalyptic formulas of threat, like Gen. 15:16: "The guilt of the Amorites is not yet full"; and the *Testaments of the Twelve Patriarchs: Levi* 6:11: "thus the wrath fell upon them (the Gentiles) to annihilation"; or 1 QS 4:12f., on sin comes "the visitation of pestilence of the worst kind at the hands of every angel of pestilence, to everlasting destruction by God's raging anger, to unending trembling and eternal humiliation."

How does 1 Thess. 2:14-16 relate to Rom. 9-11, and especially to the promise of salvation in Rom. 11:26, "all Israel will be saved"? First Thessalonians was written probably in the year 50 A.D., Romans probably in 57/58 A.D., Has Paul's attitude changed? Has his anger abated? And if so, is it in view of the "secret" which was imparted to him and which gave him a new insight (Rom. 11:25)?

Occasionally it is suggested that 1 Thess. 2:14-16 is a foreign addition to the Epistle of Paul. In this hypothesis, parts coming originally from Paul were combined with later texts (namely, 1:2–2:16; 3:12–4:8; 5:23-27) by a post-apostolic redactor. Mentioned as bases for this theory are: stylistic differences; two apparent conclusions in the Epistle, 3:11–4:1 and 5:23-28; a looking back in 2:16 to the destruction of Jerusalem. Do these considerations suffice to exonerate Paul of 1 Thess. 2:14-16?[159]

b) Epistles to the Galatians and Philippians

While temperate Jewish Christians desired that they should themselves continue to be obligated by the whole Law, Gentile Christians to be free of the ritual cultic Law, there were also radical Jewish Christians, called Judaizers in accord with Gal. 1:13 f. and 2:14, who were demanding that even the Gentile Christians be obligated by the whole Law. Because such Judaizers had penetrated the communities of the Apostle Paul, especially in Galatia and Philippi, Paul had to involve himself directly in an altercation with them. In the difficult struggles, fundamental understandings on the relationship of Judaism and Christianity were achieved and formulated.

The majority of the Galatian Christians[160] were Gentile Christians (Gal. 4:8f.). The Judaizers demanded even for them that they be circumcized (Gal. 5:3, 12; 6:12, 15), and that they keep the Jewish feastdays, and especially the Sabbath observance (Gal. 4:10). Only thus could the Gentile Christians belong to God's chosen people and obtain his promises (3:6-16, 29; 6:16). Only with these additional obligations could the faith be made perfect (Gal. 3:2-5). Only with this could the gospel be complete (Gal. 1:7). Moreover, the Judaizers maintained that Paul's apostolate was not independent and perfect; he had received the proclamation from the original apostles, and that incompletely (Gal. 1:11f., 18f.).

Paul discovers with astonishment and exasperation that the Gentile Christians are actually willing to follow those demands. In sharp sarcasm he calls the Jewish Christians "false brethren," who enslave Christian freedom (Gal. 2:4). He makes a rude joke, saying in effect that, as to those who preach circumcision, he hopes they will practice on themselves and cut it all off (Gal. 5:12, with the ironic play on words as in Phil. 3:2, below).[161]

The Cross of Christ, the Apostle teaches, is the perfect breach with Judaism and with the world. The Christian is, with Christ, crucified to the world and to Jewish Law (Gal. 2:19f.; 6:14), and, for that reason, free of it (Gal. 3:13). Justification takes place, not through works of the Law, but only through faith, which accepts the salvation prepared by Christ (Gal. 2:21). The Law is not able to impart life (Gal. 3:21); all it can do is make sin evident (Gal. 3:22). Faith, however, gives the Spirit and the powers thereof (Gal. 3:2). Anyone who wants additionally to accept and fulfill the old Law achieves nothing, but, on the contrary, loses everything, the truth of the gospel (Gal. 4:9; 17) and Christ as well (Gal. 5:7). Paul maintains that the Law, like paganism, practices a worship of the elements of the world (Gal. 4:9f.). Our history of religions agrees with this, when it recognizes that pagan mythology personifies the powers of nature, just as the cultic observance of special days (Gal. 4:10) is an acknowledgment of the taboos enacted by cosmic forces.

According to Jewish legends, Paul notes, the Law was decreed and imparted by angels (Gal. 3:19, as also Acts 7:53). It is, therefore, of lesser worth. God's work requires no agent (Gal. 3:19f.). In an allegorical passage not easily understood, Paul explains the history of the slave woman, Hagar, and the free woman, Sarah. Israel is clearly the earthly Jerusalem, which lives in slavery. "Our mother is the heavenly Jerusalem, which is free" (Gal. 4:21-28). Scripture says, however: "Cast out the slave woman and her son. For the son of the slave woman shall never inherit along with the son of the free woman" (Gal. 4:30). An Israel enslaved cannot share in the inheritance which belongs to the Church. The Church and Israel are to separate and have nothing to do with each other.

Paul concludes with the remarks (Gal. 6:15f.): "Neither circumcision nor its lack mean anything; what counts is becoming a new creation. And to as many who are in harmony with this rule: Peace and mercy on them and on the Israel of God!"

Which is the Israel of God? Exegesis ponders three possibilities of interpretation. Perhaps the Israel of God is the Church, to which Israel's election has passed. But Paul never says straight out that the Church is the true Israel. The Church is, indeed, a "new creation." The Israel of God, therefore, must mean something else. Or perhaps the Israel of God embraces the Jewish Christian community, which is the true Israel of God, just as the faithful Jews represent the true offspring of Abraham (Rom. 4:12). "Not all who are of Israel are Israel" (Rom. 9:6). And still it is possible that the Israel of God, in spite of all disbelief, is the old people of Israel, the "whole Israel" (Rom. 11:26). This Israel is and remains the blessed people of God.

Judaizing missionaries, who are propagating circumcision, claim Paul's attention also in the Epistle to the Philippians. Thus in Phil. 3:2: "Watch out for the dogs! Watch out for the workers of evil! Watch out for the choppers!" That is how Paul characterizes those preachers who rely on physical evidence: on birth from Israel and on circumcision (Phil. 3:4f.). The opponents, therefore, are Judaizers, who have penetrated the community. In bitter irony, Paul changes "circumcision," or "cutting around" (περιτομή) to "gashing" or "chopping" (κατατομή), just as, with a similar paronomasia, in Gal. 5:12 he speaks not of περιτομή but of ἀποτομή, indicative of cutting off or amputation. In Phil. 3:2, Paul's punning refers circumcision to the pagan ritual tatooing which was such an abomination to Jews (Lev. 19:28; 21:5; 1 Kings 18:28; Hos. 7:14). Paul derides the opponents as dogs, which, for the Jews designated ignorant, godless, pagan, and generally despicable men. Although Paul could, if he wished, likewise boast of Jewish blood and circumcision, this is essentially different (Phil. 3:5). Just as the Old Testament itself had already spiritualized circumcision (Jer. 4:4), so too Paul, who, for the Church, lays claim to the true spiritual circumcision (Rom. 2:25-29; see § 10, 5, c, next below).[162]

Paul has to contend further with opponents in 2 Cor. 10-13 and Rom. 16:18-20. Whether these are Judaizers is questionable. In any case, these texts do not clearly reveal any altercation with Judaism.

c) Epistle to the Colossians

The special doctrines which were widespread in Colossae contained Jewish elements. (The Epistle to the Colossians can hardly have been written by Paul himself; it may be dated about the year 90 A.D.) Those doctrines probably represent a mixture of Judaism, the mystery religions, and Gnosticism.

The Epistle designates the doctrines as "philosophy," which is "an empty deception based on the traditions of men, on the elements of the world, and not on Christ" (Col. 2:8). They prescribed the observance of rules "in regard to eating and drinking, or of a feast of the new moon, or of the Sabbath" (Col. 2:16); and they prohibited contaminating contacts (Col. 2:21). Whether or not circumcision was required is not certain (Col. 2:11). Powers and angels were to be worshipped (Col. 2:18).

The Epistle finds its answer to these emerging questions in its advanced Christology. Christ is the Head of creation, of beings visible and invisible, and now of the Church and of redeemed mankind. He is exalted above all powers and is independent of them. He is also the fulfillment and end of the Old Testament Law, which disappears in his presence like the shadows before the light. By him the Church is redeemed from Law and legalism, and from all worry and threat (Col. 2:16-23).[163]

d) Epistle to the Romans

In the comprehensive theological doctrine which is given in the Epistle to the Romans,[164] Paul concerns himself with the history of the disaster and of the salvation history of the parts into which mankind, in this consideration, is divided — the Jews and the Gentiles. Paul recognizes as a principle of salvation history: "First the Jew, then the Greek" (Rom. 1:16; 2:9f.). Israel is chosen above all the Gentiles. Therefore the gospel must first be announced and proclaimed to her (Acts 13:46). Paul the missionary acts accordingly when in every city he always preaches first in the synagogue, and, rejected there, to the Gentiles afterwards (Acts 9:20; 13:5, 14; 14:1; 17:1, 10, 17; 18:4, 19; 28:17).

In Romans 2, and especially in verses 17-24, Paul reminds the Jews of their guilt. The Jew prides himself in his honorable name, in the Law, and in God (Rom. 2:17). He claims, instructed by the Law, to be a guide for the blind (also contested in Matthew 15:14; 23:16, 24), a light in darkness (Is. 42:6f.; 42:16), and a teacher for the ignorant. He supposes that he possesses the great benefits of knowledge and truth (Rom. 2:20f.). Yet he does not enlighten himself and is lacking in what is most elementary and basic. Paul reproaches the Jews with theft, adultery, and for plundering pagan temples (Rom. 2:21f.). "It is your fault that the name of God is blasphemed among the Gentiles" (Rom. 2:24 with Is. 52:5). Like Matthew 23:1-32 (above, § 10, 1, a, 3), Paul is speaking here of the contrast between the ideal and the real in the life of Israel.[165]

The Jew trusts in circumcision as sign of the covenant and as a guarantee of eventual salvation.[166] Hellenistic Judaism tried to explain circumcision, at which many of the Gentiles took offense. Philo (*De specialibus legibus* 1, 1-11) advances hygienic, ethical, and symbolic reasons for it. Even Paul seems to be drawn repeatedly into this discussion, and in some detail in Rom. 2:25-29. He takes up prophetic tradition, which already required circumcision not of the flesh but of the heart;

thus in Jer. 4:4: "Circumcise yourselves for God; off with the foreskin of your hearts!" (similarly in Deut. 10:16; 30:6).

For the community of Qumran, the requirement is stated in 1 QS 5:5: "In the community they are to circumcise the uncircumcised of wicked shoots and obstinacy, so as to lay for Israel a foundation of truth." In the *Book of Jubilees* 1:23 it is written: "I will circumcise their uncircumcised hearts; I will create for them a holy spirit and make them pure." With any spiritual interpretation, however, the acceptance of physical circumcision remained always a presupposition. Even the Jewish Christians in Jerusalem remain under this requirement (Acts 15:1, 5), while the Jews accuse them of having abandoned circumcision (Acts 21:21). Paul admits circumcision for the Jews (Rom. 3:1), even if really only as a direction toward obedience (Rom. 2:25). If one, though uncircumcised, obeys the requirements of the Law, it becomes circumcision (Rom. 2:26). The consequence, that the Gentile is then the true Jew and will judge the Jews (Rom. 2:27f.), must have been highly irritating to the Jews.

True circumcision takes place, not according to the letter of the Law, but in the Holy Spirit (Rom. 2:29). Phil. 3:3 says in similar fashion: "We are the circumcision, we who worship God in the Spirit." Abraham was not justified by circumcision, but by faith when he was not yet circumcised (Rom. 4:10-13). "In Christ Jesus neither circumcision nor foreskin means anything, but only faith, which is operative in love" (Gal. 5:6).

Baptism is Christ's circumcision in the faith (Col. 2:11f.). "Neither circumcision nor uncircumcision means anything; what is important is being a new creation" (Gal. 6:15). Statutory circumcision is abolished in the present eschatological realization.

In chapters 9–11 of Romans, Paul wrestles with the difficult questions that are proposed to him by Israel's history and by her present situation. For many generations Israel had to achieve righteousness and salvation, making every effort and enduring all manner of afflictions and persecutions. And now is Israel to miss out on salvation? Has God rejected his people (Rom. 11:1)? The disbelief and the calamity of the Jews put an encumbrance on the trustworthiness of the word and on the efficacy of the gospel.

Now, because Israel's glow threatens to be dimmed, Paul spreads out once more her whole incomparable riches (Rom. 9:4f.). "They are Israelites." They bear the name by which God called Jacob (Gen. 32:29) and all his progeny (Is. 43:1). The Israelites possess "the sonship." Israel is God's "firstborn son" (Exod. 4:22)! To Israel belongs "the glory of God" that was resplendent over the tabernacle (Exod. 40:34f.) and in the Temple (Is. 6:1-4). To Israel "belong the covenants" with Noah, Abraham, and Moses. Hers is "the bestowal of the Law and the ritual." The Law is Israel's distinction among all nations. She has the true divine worship. To her belong the messianic promises, and the fathers with whom God spoke and dealt, and whose rewards belong still to the people; and finally, hers too is "the Christ, according to the flesh."

For the exegete it is an old question, how the doxology in Rom. 9:5b is to be referred and understood: "Who is over all, God blessed forever. Amen." Is this still a declaration about Christ, or is it a free-standing praising of God, who held sway in the history of Israel? Purely on the basis of grammatical relationships, either is possible. If the doxology is to be referred to Christ, it is a dogmatically important testimony to the divinity of Christ. The declaration of lowliness in the incarnation of Christ (Rom. 9:5a) seems to demand, in accord with Pauline linguistic usage and thought process, a declaration also of his majesty (as in Rom. 1:3f.; Phil. 2:7f.).

Nevertheless, the doxology in Rom. 9:5b is probably to be taken structurally as a unit; and it will, therefore, be hardly possible to section it thus: "Christ, who, according to the flesh, comes from Israel, is now exalted over all. God be blessed forever." Since Paul says of Christ that he is "a Son of God" (Rom. 8:32); that he was "from eternity henceforth in God's image" and "like God" (Phil. 2:6); that he is "the image of God" (2 Cor. 4:4; Rom. 8:29), i.e., God's revelation and epiphany; and that "God was in Christ" (2 Cor. 5:19), it would not have been impossible for Paul to have offered Rom. 9:5b as a declaration of the divine estate and power of Jesus. Yet, elsewhere in Paul, the name God seems to be reserved to God the eternal Father. Thus it is more likely that the whole doxology in Rom. 9:5b is to be separated from 9:5a and is to be understood as a praising of God in the contemplation of Israel's election, just as in Rom. 11:33f., Paul concludes the description of God's salvific action with a lauding of God's glory.

In the ancient Church, Arianism, which denied the eternal Godhead of Christ, had an interest in seeing that Rom. 9:5a and 9:5b were separated. This was done even by those Fathers who were closest in time to Arianism. The Catholic Fathers had no thought of referring the doxology of Rom. 9:5b to Christ. Catholic expositions of the Bible and Catholic interpretations are inclined even to the present day to that same perception. Protestant exegesis is divided, but more recently seems probably to prefer the interpretation that the doxology in 9:5b is to be understood of God.[167]

In the face of Israel's present disbelief, Paul answers questions rising therefrom in Rom. 9:6-33. First of all, he answers the question of whether God's word does yet stand fast (Rom. 9:6). God's word remains forever. But it is spiritual like himself. Therefore it can never mean anything corporeal, though it clothe itself in the flesh and come to its goal therein. And God is always the Creator and Lord, who freely rules; and thus does his word lead on to its end. God's election is never, for men, secure possession. To belong to the national and therefore merely corporeal communion of Israel is no ultimate redemption. Paul illustrates this from Israel's history with the example of Isaac and Ishmael, Jacob and Esau, Moses and Pharaoh, Israel and the Gentile nations. The electing love of God has its reasons and its depths (Rom. 9:13). The reasons for God's manner of acting are God's secret.

In Rom. 10 Paul describes, in the example of Israel, the responsibility for election by God. What from God's vantage point is seen as election and rejection appears in time and in history as the obedience and disobedience of man. It is the fault of the Jews that they do not believe the gospel and do not accept God's righteousness. Yet it is an exceptional fault. Israel was not failing in moral duty. The Jews have "zeal for God" which, "though misguided," is nonetheless real (Rom. 10:2). With her earnest endeavor and by her own efforts, Israel wanted to discover a way to God, who alone can grant salvation. Christ is the end of the way of the Law (Rom. 10:4). Israel has renounced the mystery of her election, which is grace. She tried to reinterpret her being endowed with grace as her own worthiness and grandeur. With many Old Testament texts Paul shows that the Old Testament already refers to the way of salvation, of justification through faith (Rom. 10:1-13). Moreover, he finds the disbelief of Israel already prophesied (Rom. 10:14-21).[168]

In Rom. 11, faith permits a surmise as to how God's plan of salvation operates. A "remnant of Israel," which is the Jewish Christian community (Rom. 11:5), and Paul himself (Rom. 11:1) are proof of the fact that God's mercy extends even now to Israel, even if Israel in her present condition is shaking violently. She neither sees nor hears; her back is deeply bent (Rom. 11:8f.). "God does not repent of his gifts of grace and of his call" (Rom. 11:29). God's election and love abide over Israel. Paul says again and again that it is not a matter of having been once and formerly God's chosen people; rather, Israel remains always his chosen.

Finally the mystery has been revealed to Paul, that after the whole of the Gentiles has entered, "all Israel will be saved" (Rom. 11:25f). Since Paul believes that the end of time is near, he will hardly understand this whole of the Gentiles and of Israel as the totality of all the living in general, but only as the totality of all the called. This also is the apocalyptic expectation. According to *4 Esdras* 2 (4):35f. and the *Syriac Apocalypse of Baruch* 23:5, the number of the just must be complete before the resurrection. As happened so often to the prophets, so too the fact of the achievement of the final goal can be revealed to Paul without a revelation of the manner in which that goal will be achieved. "God has imprisoned all in disobedience in order to show mercy to all" (Rom. 11:32).[169]

6. Gospel of John

In John's Gospel and in contrast to the Synoptics, the treatment of Judaism as partner of Jesus is much reduced.[170] Prominence is given "the high priests and the Pharisees" (John 7:32, 45; 11:47, 57; 18:3), or "the rulers and the Pharisees" (John 7:48), or the high priests alone (John 18:24; 19:6, 21), or even the Pharisees alone (John 1:24; 4:1; 7:47; 8:13; 9:13; 12:19, 42). The Pharisees appear as members of the Sanhedrin or as spokesmen in disputes. The questions of the "righteousness" of the Pharisees and of their special religious observances are no longer of any interest. In practice, the fellowmen of Jesus are conceived and designated only as "the Jews." The word can be used neutrally in historical narrative (John 4:22; 11:19; 18:20; 19:20), and especially in the mouths of non-Jews (John 4:9; 18:33; 19:3).

A peculiar sense of distance is achieved when there is discussion of the "customs of the Jews" (John 2:6; 19:40); of the Passover, the "feast of the Jews" (John 2:13; 5:1; 6:4; 11:55); of the "Feast of Tabernacles of the Jews" (John 7:2); of the "Preparation Day of the Jews" (John 19:42); or of the Law as "your Law" (John 8:17; 10:34).

Jesus, his disciples (and the Evangelist?) are, of course, Jews themselves. Yet Israel seems to be a foreign nation to them. Notable is the remark that so many dared not acknowledge Jesus "for fear of the Jews" (John 7:13; 20:19). The opponents of Jesus and his friends, nevertheless, were all Jews, the one as much as the other. Yet for the most part the Jews, plainly and simply, are the disbelieving opponents of Jesus. From the very beginning they are hostile, disbelieving (John 1:19; 2:18, 20), and determined to kill Jesus (John 5:16, 18; 7:1; 10:31f.).

Certainly it is much more historically accurate when the older Gospels recount that separation between the disciples and the opponents of Jesus became visible only gradually and after some period of time. In the altercations with Jesus, the Jews come off like a chorus (John 5:10-18; 8:48-57; 10:24-31). If occasionally individuals like "the Pharisees" appear as spokesmen, they are not separate from the people but are identified with them, as representing them. Even in the trial of Jesus, "the Jews" are a collective body (John 18–20).[171]

In the Gospel of John, discussions and disputes with the Jews no longer center around the imminent kingdom of God or the moral conduct of the group of disciples, as they do in the older Gospels; nor are they concerned with the validity of the Old Testament Jewish Law, as is the case with conflicts in which Paul engages. Apparently these problems are no longer current. The dispute now is a dogmatic dispute over the person of Jesus Christ. The Gospel testifies to him as the Son who was and is in union with the Father. The Jews have to deny this contention. For them, this doctrine is blasphemy against God (John 10:31-33).

The dispute is in a broad sense a dispute over the correct understanding of the Old Testament Scriptures (John 6:31; 7:42, 51; 10:34-36). The Scriptures testify to Jesus (John 5:37). Abraham saw in advance the day of Jesus and rejoiced (John 8:56). Moses wrote about Jesus. If the Jews really believed Moses, they would believe Jesus (John 5:45f.). The Jews understand neither their Sacred Scripture nor their fathers. They misunderstand the Law so completely that they finally demand, as consequence of the Law, the death of Jesus (John 19:7). This analysis is a distillation of the dogmatic discussion between Jews and Christians about the correct understanding of Scripture. The Church wants to wrest the Scriptures from the synagogue.

The dispute between Jews and Christians continues always in misunderstandings (John 2:20; 3:3f.; 4:10-15, 32f.; 6:33f.; 7:34f.; 8:21f., 32f.; 14:4f., 7f.; 16:16f.). This is not historical account but a literary-theological manner of exposition. The world does not understand God's word, and it does not accept the Son, the Word of God, God's Revelation and Truth.[172]

A high point of the altercation between Jesus and the Jews is presented in the disputation in John 8:30-59. The conversation takes place in the Temple on the Feast of Tabernacles. The time and place are pregnant with symbolism for the decisive importance of the event. Jesus speaks of achieving freedom through truth (John 8:31f.). The Jews maintain that they are, as sons of Abraham, free, no one's servants (John 8:33), and indeed, children of God (John 8:41). Jesus counters that if they were true sons of Abraham, they would, like Abraham, believe in God's word and in the Messiah. Truly, it is not Abraham but the devil who is their father (John 8:44).[173]

This does not mean a physical begetting by the devil, but a satanic manner of acting and a spiritual adherence to the devil. There are formulas comparable to this: the uncircumcised are "the sons of Beliar" (*Book of Jubilees* 15:33); the opponents of the Qumran community are "sons of Belial, damned in the darkness of eternal fire" (1 QS 2:4-8); they go about with "Belial's lies" (1 QH 5:26).

In John's Gospel, the Jews thus characterized are no longer the one time historical and national communion of people; rather, they represent the unfaithful and wicked world which knows neither the Father nor the Son (John 17:25), and which hates Christ (John 15:18f.) and his disciples (John 7:7, 17). Satan is the father of the Jews (John 8:44) and the prince of this world (John 14:30). The Apocalypse of John knows in Smyrna (Apoc. 3:9) and in Philadelphia (Apoc. 3:9) those "who call themselves Jews and are nevertheless the synagogue of Satan."[174] The *Martyrdom of Polycarp* (12:1f.; 13:1; 17:2) recounts that the Jews even severally were participants in this martyrdom in Smyrna. They hastened to gather wood for the burning of the martyr bishop of Smyrna.

All this notwithstanding, the former and abiding worth and significance of Israel is recognized. "We (Jews) worship what we know; for salvation comes from the Jews" (John 4:22).[175] Here Jesus includes himself among the Jews. The history of Israel is the history of the true and revealing conversation and dealing of God with the world. From Israel, moreover, come faithful disciples. Many Jews believe in Jesus (John 2:23; 3:2; 8:31; 10:19, 21; 11:31-45; 12:9f.). To the one flock, which is the Church, belong Jews and Gentiles (John 10:16). "Jesus had to die for the nation, and not for the nation alone, but so that he might gather together in unity the children of God who are scattered (among the Gentiles)" (John 11:51f.). The Jews, then, do not baldly represent disbelief; they can also signify belief and a believing world.

The Gospel of John was written toward the end of the first century, probably in Asia Minor (or Syria). At that time and in that region, the Church and the synagogue face each other as two separate and mutually inimical religious communities. It is no longer a history of Jesus that is presented, but an era in the history of the Church (much as in Matthew 23; see above, § 10, 1, b, 3).

The Church stands opposed to the synagogue. The Jews, however, have also separated themselves from the Christians, and vex and oppress them with spiritual and physical force. What has already happened and is happening is placed in the mouth of Jesus as prophetic declaration. "They will expel you from the synagogues. Indeed, the hour is coming when anyone who kills you will believe that he is performing a sacred ministry to God" (John 16:2). "The Jews had agreed among themselves that anyone who would acknowledge Jesus as the Christ should be expelled from the synagogue (John 9:22; see also 12:42). About the year 90 A.D., an anathema of apostates and Christians was added, as the twelfth petition, to the *Prayer of the Eighteen Petitions* or the *Eighteen Benedictions*: "May the Nazoreans (the Chris-

tians) and the other heretics pass away in an instant. May they be
blotted out of the book of life, and may they not be written down
among the pious. Blessed be thou, O Lord, who humblest the insolent."
After that Jewish Christians could no longer participate in divine service in the synagogue.

The history of the relations between Church and synagogue is loaded
with difficult questions. Do they begin already in the New Testament?

§ 11. CHURCH AND GENTILES

1. ISRAEL AND THE GENTILES

After the annexation of the land, Israel, a small nation in the midst
of her conquered territory,[176] was obliged to live with the long settled
and more highly developed tribes of Canaan.[177] Israel therefore had to
maintain herself in the face of surrounding nations that were politi-
cally and culturally her superior, and that practiced highly impressive
religions and cults. Israel found that she was in the midst of "pagan
abominations" (1 Kings 14:24; 2 Kings 16:3). It was as a holy nation
(Deut. 7:6) that she distinguished herself from the unclean Gentiles
(Ez. 4:13). The prophets struggled against the Baals and against the
temptation offered by the fertility cults (Num. 25; 1 Kings 18). Pagan
usages and influences were warded off by reforms (2 Kings 18:4; Amos
8:14).

Investigations into the history of religions likewise arrive at the
knowledge that Israel, in the course of her history, was influenced in
her culture and in her religion by other nations, the Canaanites, the
Egyptians, the Babylonians, the Persians, by Hellenism, and by the
Romans. By promise and hope, Israel is unlocked to the Gentiles.

From early onward, the calling of Abraham embraces all the peoples
of the earth (Gen. 12:2f.; 22:18; 26:4). Jacob's blessing promises to
Judah a rule to which all the nations will be obedient (Gen. 48:10).
Yahweh is King of the Gentiles (Jer. 10:7). The servant of Yahweh
(originally understood, no doubt, as the nation of Israel) will be a light

for all the nations (Is. 42:6). God's name must be proclaimed to all the nations (Ps. 18:49f.; 96:3). To the son of man, before the throne of the Ancient of Days, "power and glory and kingdom will be given so that the peoples of all nations and tongues will serve him" (Dan. 7:13f.). From the rising of the sun to its setting, God's name will be great among the Gentiles (Mal. 1:11).

The Book of Jonah, post-exilic no doubt, is able to say in 4:3 that Yahweh's mercy is not limited to Israel but extends even to a foreign empire inimical to Israel; that his mercy extends in fact even to the beasts. The promise and expectation is many times attested that at the end of time all nations will join together in a wonderful pilgrimage to Mount Zion (Is. 2:2-4; Micah 4:1-3; Is. 18:7; 25:6-8; 60:2f.; Zech. 8:20f.; Tob. 16:4f.; *Ethiopic Henoch* 90:30-38; *4 Esdras* 13:13; 1 QM 12:13f.; Apoc. 21:24, 26). According to this expectation, the nations will not have to be won through the preaching of the mission but will of their own accord stream to Zion (Is. 66:18f.).

Israel passes severe judgment on the Gentiles. The Jews are inclined to say that the pagans are godless and are rejected by God, that they are addicted to all vices, that they oppress Israel, and that they have nothing to look forward to but judgment and hell. Yet even in Israel the grandeur and wealth of the pagan culture was acknowledged. This is especially the case in regard to architecture. In Galilee, beginning with the first century of the Christian era, synagogues were constructed after the model of the Greek assembly hall (probably the case with Luke 7:5). The private homes of wealthy Jews were constructed in the Greco-Roman architectural style. King Herod the Great, after the fashion of the Hellenistic princes, fostered a considerable architectural activity in Judea and beyond. The Temple adorned by him with broad vistas claimed the admiration even of the Jews (Josephus, *Jewish Antiquities* 15, 11, 391-402; see also Luke 21:5). Certainly the theater, circus, and stadium which Herod ordered built were rejected as being pagan (1 Macc. 1:14f.; 2 Macc. 4:9-17). The prohibition of images forbade the construction and exhibition of images of gods and of men (Exod. 20:4f., 23) and permitted at most figurative representations. Yet Rabbi Yehunda (*ca.* 150 A.D.) can say: "How beautiful are the works of this Roman people! They build roads and bridges and baths!"

Judaism acknowledges also Greek literature and learning. Books written in Greek were accepted into the canon. The Hebrew Bible was translated into the Greek language. And at the same time, the ancient traditions were to no small degree interpreted in accord with Greek cultural developments.

2. Jesus and the Gentiles According to Synoptic Gospels

a) Altercation

Judaism at the time of the New Testament knew the Gentiles [178] from its own daily experience and familiarity with them. In the cities and on the streets of Judea one encountered Roman soldiers and officials, Hellenistic philosophers and teachers, as well as industrious and avaricious international merchants. Above the highway of Shechem, on which certainly Jesus and his disciples often traveled, there loomed the ancient city of Samaria, now Sebaste, so named to honor the emperor (ὁ σεβαστός; see also Acts 25:21, 25). The layout of the city is even today most impressive, with the ruins of its theater and, above all, of its rich temple dedicated to Augustus and to Roma. Herod's magnificent religious and profane structures brought architects, artists, and engineers into the country.

It is on this level that the words of Jesus about the pagans must be understood. The Oriental especially would see their strange ways as restless activity. Thus they are dedicated to worldly cares and greed. And hence the admonition in Matthew 6:31f.: "Do not worry, do not say, 'What are we to eat?' or 'What are we to drink?' or 'What are we to wear?' The pagans (τὰ ἔθνη) worry about all this! Your heavenly Father knows you need all these things." In Luke's version (12:30) of the saying, it reads that "the nations of the world" (τὰ ἔθνη τοῦ κόσμου) [179] make these things their devout concern.

To the Jew, pagan worship could, in comparison to his own imageless worship of God and to the pure service of God's word in the synagogue, appear to be noisy pomp. [180] Jesus admonishes his disciples in Matthew 6:7: "When you pray, do not babble like the pagans! They think, by increasing their words, to make themselves heard!" The pagans reserve their practice of humaneness to their fellow-countrymen

(Matthew 5:47): "If you greet only your brothers, are you doing anything special? Do not even the pagans do likewise?"

The rulers of the pagans are tyrants (Mark 10:42): "Those who pass for rulers among the Gentiles lord it over them, and their great ones exercise authority over them." When Luke 22:35 adds that these lords "have themselves called benefactors" (which was a surname among princes), this is apparently mentioned in bitter irony. Even where the Gentiles are instruments of God, they destroy. In the distress of the endtime, the inhabitants of Jerusalem will be "led captive to every Gentile nation, and Jerusalem will be trampled down by the Gentiles" (Luke 21:24). The Evangelist describes and explains in this way what had already taken place when he was writing: that God's city would be destroyed by God's enemies. Even the Son of Man will finally surrender to the Gentiles (Mark 10:33).

b) Acceptance of Pagans

The Gospels recount that the works of Jesus already reached out far beyond Israel proper. According to Mark 3:7; Jesus is followed by a great crowd "from Judea and from Jerusalem and from Idumea and beyond the Jordan and from the region of Tyre and Sidon." If this is but a collective report prepared by Mark, it attests nevertheless to the conviction of the Evangelist that from the very beginning the Gospel was aimed at the regions of the Gentiles. Perhaps what is written down here is the program of an early mission to the pagans of northern Galilee. The Gospels tell repeatedly of sojournings of Jesus beyond Galilee (Mark 5:1; 7:24, 31).

There is a recognizable opposition between Jesus' words of criticism about the Gentiles and what he has to say in direct encounters with pagans.[181] Jesus heals the sick servant of the pagan centurion of Capernaum (Matthew 8:5-13).[182] The story appears also in Luke 7:1-10, and stems therefore from Source Q; it is recounted in another form in John 4:46-54. In Matthew the narrative is in a series of miracle narratives and declares that Jesus did not deny his assistance even to pagans. The pagan centurion knows that Jesus, as a Jew, dare not set foot in a pagan household. He is convinced that Jesus' healing power can be effective even at a distance. Jesus never disappoints faith (so too in

Matthew 15:28). He effects the cure, acknowledging the while that the faith of this pagan is greater than the faith of Israel. Jesus promises the kingdom of heaven to the pagan, while Israel is cast out into darkness (Matthew 8:11f.). The statement of Jesus combines two imaginally descriptive apocalyptic declarations: the one, of a pilgrimage of the Gentiles (see above, § 11, 1) and the other, of the darkness of hell. The formula "weeping and gnashing of teeth" is probably a redactional addition of the Evangelist (see below, § 19, 2, b). Are the logia statements of Jesus or a structure of the scriptural theology placing these themes in order? This is a difficult question to decide.[183]

The encounter with the Canaanite woman from the region of Tyre (Mark 7:24-30; Matthew 15:21-28) also displays Jesus as Savior of the Gentiles in word and in deed. Matthew 15:22-24 is lacking in Mark and may therefore be regarded probably as having been handed down as isolated logia. In the narrative Jesus himself is on the road to the pagans, which, in Matthew 10:5, is forbidden the disciples. According to Mark 7:26, the woman is Greek, therefore pagan. When Matthew 15:22 designates the woman as Canaanite, is the old and rigid opposition between Israel and Canaan coming to the fore? To the pagan woman's plea Jesus explains first that he is "sent only to the lost sheep of the House of Israel" (Matthew 15:24).[184]

In the Old Testament imagery, the people Israel is designated as a flock (Is. 40:11; Ezek. 34:1-16; Jer. 50:6; Ps. 77:21). Jesus, however, can refuse nothing to faith (as in Matthew 8:10; 13). While according to Matthew the ministry of Jesus is directed only and entirely to Israel, in Mark 7:27 this is softened: "The children should be fed first"; and indeed, by the time the Gospels were written down, the mission had long since gone beyond Israel and to the pagans. Luke waives all claim to the pericope because it no longer corresponds to his Gospel, addressed as it is to the Greek world.

Jesus exceeds the boundaries of Israel also in his conduct toward Samaria. After the conquest of the northern kingdom of Israel in 722 B.C., a contingent remained behind in Samaria, and foreign peoples with it (2 Kings 17:24-33). The Jews remaining there lost the purity of their blood and of their faith. The Samaritans had their own temple on Mount Gerizim, which was destroyed by Jewish troops in 128 B.C.

A deep-seated enmity separated Jerusalem and Samaria. Samaritans were accounted pagans by the Jews. Jews and Samaritans had no commerce with each other (John 4:9). "Samaritan" was a term of opprobrium (John 8:48). When a Samaritan village refused admittance to Jesus and his disciples, the village being on the road to Jerusalem, and the disciples wanted, because of this refusal, to call down fire from heaven, Jesus rebuked them for it (Luke 9:51-56). In the parable of the good Samaritan, Jesus places before the Jews a Samaritan as an example of merciful conduct (Luke 10:25-37). Of the ten who were cured of leprosy, the one who returns to give thanks is a Samaritan (Luke 17:11-19).

Sent out on the mission, the Twelve are forbidden to go to Samaritan towns (Matthew 10:5). The Gospel of John, nevertheless, tells in detail of the encounter of Jesus with a woman of Samaria. She believes in him as Messiah. At the woman's telling of it, many of the Samaritans believe in Jesus; and at their request, Jesus remains with them for two days.

Other sayings of Jesus declare that the Gentiles will fare better than Israel at God's judgment (Matthew 11:20-24 = Luke 10:12-15). Tyre and Sidon would have been converted had they witnessed the powerful deeds of Jesus that were done in Chorazin and Bethsaida. (Actually, the Gospels say nothing of any wonders of Jesus worked in Chorazin and Bethsaida; the saying, therefore, is not a schematic summary, and this will attest its authenticity as an original saying of Jesus). Tyre and Sidon are regarded (according to Is. 23, Ezek. 26–28 and Joel 4:4) as particularly horrible examples of godless cities. But they are better than the cities of Israel.

If wonders like the wonders of Jesus had been worked in Sodom, that city would be standing today. In biblical and extrabiblical tradition, Sodom and Gomorrah are examples of immorality and of its punishment (Is. 1:9; Jer. 23:14; Ezek. 16:48-50; *3 Macc.* 2:5; *Testaments of the Twelve Patriarchs: Nephtali* 3:4; 4:1; also Rom. 9:29; Jude 7; 2 Peter 2:6). In the same tenor, Matthew 10:15 says that on the day of judgment it will be more bearable for Sodom and Gomorrah than it will be for those cities which refuse admittance to the messengers of the approaching kingdom.

The queen of Sheba, who came from far away to hear Solomon,

will, in the judgment, condemn this generation (Matthew 12:42 = Luke 11:31). The people of Nineveh, who repented after the preaching of Jonah, will condemn this generation at the last judgment (Matthew 12:41 = Luke 11:32). Is it possible that in these predicates, "There is something more than Solomon here! there is something more than Jonah here!," there is a Christological confession? The words of praise which the nations far from Israel raise will for that very reason be proved authentically original.

The Gospels (Matthew 12:38f.; Luke 11:29f.) join to the saying about Nineveh a saying about "the sign of Jonah." It was already obscure in its ancient tradition. If Jesus, in the face of that disbelief which demanded a sign, proclaimed the sign of Jonah as a futurity, possibly it referred originally to the parousia. It is a divinely achieved return of the Son of Man from the dead, like the return of Jonah from the belly of the monster. The sign attendant upon Jesus would accordingly be the present denial of a miracle, and in its place the announcement of judgment on the disbelieving. Luke 11:30 refers the sign to the preaching of Jonah and to that of Jesus; Matthew 12:40, to the resurrection of Jesus. In either case the sign of Jonah had already been given at the time the Gospel was written down, and Israel already stands under judgment. For the Gentiles, however, the hope of salvation is opened. At the final judgment "all nations will be assembled" (Matthew 25:31-46) before the Son of Man and Judge. He will judge Jews and pagans alike, according to works of mercy (see below, § 18, 3, b).

c) Preaching and Experience of the Mission

Sayings pregnant with meaning treat of the mission of the Church, belonging to the future but already beginning (see above, § 3, 2, b, 1). In the first commissioning discourse Jesus forbids the Twelve to proclaim the gospels to the Gentiles. "Go not on the roads to the nations; and to the cities of the Samaritans go not. Go rather to the lost sheep of the House of Israel" (Matthew 10:5f.; on the designation of Israel as God's flock, see above, § 11, 2, b, on Matthew 15:24). Since the Gospel of Matthew in other passages pertinent to this matter says that the messengers will go out to the nations (thus already in Matthew 10:17f.), and the same Gospel closes with the great missionary com-

mand, certainly the Evangelist himself perceived the opposition between the statements of such passages and that of Matthew 10:5f. If at
the beginning he recounts that saying which declines a mission to the
Gentiles, it is simply that the limiting of the mission to Israel alone
has its rationale in the lateness of the eschatological hour of the commissioning discourse. The kingdom of God is pressing forward so
urgently that the short time available will not suffice even for a single
preaching in all areas of Israel (Matthew 10:23; see below, § 13, 3, b).
The Gospel of Matthew recognizes on the whole the preeminence of
Israel as the chosen people. It is to her that the Gospel must first be
announced. Rejected in that quarter, it can then be taken to the pagans.
The saying in Matthew 5:10f. is lacking in Mark and in Luke. Since
the Church had long since been conducting her mission among the
Gentiles, the statement seemed to be archaically dated.

In not a few passages of Matthew's Gospel, the mission is announced
or already described. In each such instance exegesis will have the right
to ask whether the statement presupposes that the mission is already
historically existing in the Church. From the very beginning the disciples are told that they are to be "the salt of the earth and the light
of the world" (Matthew 5:13f.). These imaginal terms appear in another form in Mark 9:50 and 4:21. It is possible, then, that the sayings
are to be regarded as original to the words and statements of Jesus.

In Matthew 5:13f., the logia of salt and light are referred to the disciples and to their mandate. To salt means to make food palatable and
to preserve it from spoiling. This is the commission of the disciples in
respect to men. According to Is. 42:6 and 60:3, Israel, and according to
Is. 49:6, the servant of Yahweh, is the light of the Gentiles. The light
is of God, and is God himself (2 Cor. 4:6). The community of disciples is to effect brightness and clarity in the world and for the world
(Phil. 2:15; Eph. 5:8). The community, therefore, has a mandate to
the whole wide world. The term and concept "ecumene" is found in
Matthew 24:14. The Gospel finds the turning of Jesus to the Gentiles
declared already in Old Testament prophecy. Jesus chooses his abode
in "Galilee of the Gentiles, the people who sat in darkness" (Matthew
4:15f., quoting Is. 9:1f.). As a consequence of wars and foreign occupations of Galilee, that area was scarcely more than a pagan land.

Jesus fulfills what is said of the servant of Yahweh. He will proclaim justice to the nations who hope in him (Matthew 12:17-21, quoting Is. 42:1-4).

Jesus recognizes that he himself is sent ultimately "to give his life as a ransom for the many" (Mark 10:45). His blood, which is poured out for the many, institutes the more extensive new covenant (Mark 14:25; on both these passages, see the present work, Vol. 2, pp. 104f.). The mission and work of Jesus is to Israel and to the Gentiles.

In the parable of the banquet (Matthew 22:2-10; Luke 14:16-24), the first invited decline to accept the invitation. In Matthew 22:7, the destruction of Jerusalem is apparently presupposed. The Jews, therefore, are already lost in disbelief. The messengers are to summon other guests "from the crossways of the streets" (Matthew 22:9). These are undisguisedly the pagan nations.

In the Gospel of Luke (14:21f.), the servant who is the immediate recipient of the first refusals is sent out twice more. First he is to bring in from the streets and squares of the city "the poor and the crippled and the blind and the lame." This corresponds to the special purpose of Luke's Gospel, the Gospel of the sick and the poor. Apparently this invitation is immediately to the poor of Israel. Since there is still room, the servant is to invite and urge guests to come in from the "highways and byways." These, then, are the Gentiles, who are indeed at home on the streets of the world.

In both versions of the parable of the banquet, the Jews, the first invited, are threatened with rejection, because they decline the invitation. Matthew stifles this threat at first primarily for redactional reasons (in view of 22:13), but points it out in 22:14. Luke 14:24, however, declares very strongly: "Not one of those (first) invited will taste of my banquet."

The parable too of the wicked vinedressers (Mark 12:1-12; see above, § 10, 1, b, 1) closes with a threat for Israel and a promise for the Gentiles: "The Lord will destroy those vinedressers and give the vineyard to others." When Matthew 21:41, 43 says twice that the new tenants "will deliver their fruit at the proper time," it thereby expresses to the Gentile Church both the admonition and the hope that it will not reject but will bring forth good works.

In the eschatological discourse, the word of the Lord (Mark 13:9) declares that the disciples will be remanded to the courts, will be scourged in the synagogues, and will be brought before governors and kings for the sake of Christ and to bear witness before the Gentiles. This is already a description of the course and experience of the missions. The apostles had been brought before courts, governors, and kings (Acts 4:7; 5:18; 6:12; 12:1-5; 16:23; 18:12; 21:33; 24:1; 25:6, 23; 2 Cor. 11:23). They had been beaten and scourged (Acts 5:40; 16:22f.; 2 Cor. 11:23f.).

A world-wide mission in an undiscernibly long future of the Church is perfectly presupposed in the words appended: "The gospel must first be preached among all peoples" (Mark 13:10). The saying may have been shaped first by Mark and afterwards accepted by Matthew 24:14. To Mark, the mission is important and essential to the Church (Mark 4:32; 11:17; 15:39); that is why, with a look to the future, Mark 13:5-23 needs to be spoken: "The gospel must first be preached." This need designates the mission as an eschatological-apocalyptic necessity. The perfection of the kingdom, coming from God, is dependent, therefore, upon the prior accomplishment of a human work. This is a later understanding. In Mark 13:10, moreover, the term "gospel" is ecclesiastical language, as also the concept of its "proclamation among the nations" (Rom. 11:25; 16:25f. [post-Pauline]; Col. 1:23, 27; Eph. 3:6; 1 Tim. 3:16).

In the same way, an already successful mission is presumed in the saying extolling the woman with the jar of ointment: "Wherever in the whole world this gospel is preached, there also will be told in her memory what this woman has done" (Mark 14:9 = Matthew 26:13). This woman was the first to surmise the salvational necessity of Jesus' Passion (Mark 14:8). Since this is in fact the gospel, so too will this woman be remembered.

There are no parallels in Luke to correspond to Mark 13:10 and Mark 14:9. Is Luke historian enough to withhold from us logia about the mission of the time and of the Church of the apostles (Acts 1:8)?

The experience of missionary labors is presented collectively in the explanation, placed in the mouth of Jesus, of the parable about the sower (Mark 4:3-9, 13-20).[185] The parable itself (4:3-9) indicates the contrast between minuscule seed and superabundant harvest. It is in these terms that Jesus speaks directly of himself in the parable. His message about the kingdom of God is the seed. The purpose is the whole mounting expectation of the consummation of God's kingdom.

Along with the parable, its meaning is given (Mark 4:13-20), in which the particulars of the parabolic narrative are explained in allegorical fashion. This interpretation does not come from Jesus, but is the oldest of all Christian sermons. In this the history of the gospel in the world is read into the text. "The sower sows the word" (Mark 4:14). The word is simply missionary preaching (Acts 4:4, 6:4; 1 Thess. 1:6). Oppression and persecution hinder the mission (Mark 4:17; 1 Thess. 1:6; 3:3; Rom. 8:35; Phil. 1:27f.; 2 Tim. 1:8). There are obstacles to the word (Mark 4:17; 1 Cor. 1:23; 1 Peter 2:8). Wealth hinders the success of the mission (Mark 4:19; Acts 5:1-11; 2 Thess. 2:10). The word grows, nevertheless, and in spite of all, it bears fruit (Mark 4:20; Acts 19:20; Col. 1:6).

The risen Christ points the Church to her missionary path (Matthew 28:19; Mark 16:15; Acts 1:8). This declares decisively that after Easter the mission becomes possible and begins. The great missionary and baptismal mandate in Matthew 28:19 is founded in the consciousness of the Church that the mission fulfills the task of Jesus of effecting salvation. (On baptism and the command to baptize, see above, § 8, 3, 2).

3. Gospel of John

Just as the harvest is not infrequently an image of the endtime consummation (Joel 3:13; Is. 27:12; Matthew 13:30; Mark 4:8, 29), so too John 4:35-38 probably has to be understood immediately of the mission harvest, but remotely of the endtime. Here too, as, no doubt, in Mark 4:1-9, Christ is the sower, the disciples the reapers. The harvest in the mission is, for sower and reaper alike, joy over the completion of the work (John 4:36).

Here, however, there is no validity to the rule that governs a natural harvest and human efforts. In the divine order, growth can be so swift that the time for sowing and the time for reaping can coincide (John 4:35). In the mission, however, it remains true that a later one reaps what an earlier has sown (John 4:37). It is the culmination of the disciples' labors that they are to harvest what Christ has sown. But it is also the limit of their labor that they only reap. More than this they are unable to do. Another has to do the rest. "Without me you could do nothing" (John 15:5). So too is the mission described in John 4:38: "I sent you out to harvest what you had not worked for; others worked for it and you have entered into their labor." [186]

In John's Gospel, there is no sending out of disciples. It is the resurrected Christ who first sends them off (John 17:18; 20:21). During the earthly life of Jesus, there was no missionary harvest by the disciples. The words of Jesus in John 4:35-38 are spoken from the situation of the later mission, which the Evangelist has already seen bringing in an abundant harvest. The mission harvest must always give thanks to others. The missionary is always in a historical sequence which has its beginning with Jesus. If one sows and another reaps, it is always Jesus who is the one, in contrast to the other: Jesus is the one who sows, the one who has instituted salvation. Each of the "others," the missionaries, is borne along by the series of his predecessors from the beginning of this historical sequence. John 4:35-38 is a significant witness to the consciousness of the Christian mission about the year 100 A.D.

John 10:16 is likewise spoken from a history of the mission: "I have other sheep too, who are not of this fold. Those too I must lead, and they will hear my voice, and there will be one flock and one shepherd." With an image familiar from the Old Testament, Israel is designated as God's flock (§ 11, 2, on Matthew 15:24). The other sheep are the Gentiles. They are indeed Christ's own, because the Father has given him them (John 10:29). Jesus needs only to "lead" them. They hear the voice of Jesus, the Shepherd, through the Church's proclaiming; and they recognize him as their shepherd. Just as there is but one shepherd, so too must there be but one flock. The saying presupposes, as does also and even more intently the prayer of Christ in John 17:20-23 for the unity of the Church, that this Church is already endangered by divisions (see the present work, Vol. 2, pp. 265f.).

In John 11:51f., the Gospel affixes to the prophetic word of the high priest Caiaphas, that one man is to die for the nation, the reflection, "Jesus had to die for the nation and not for the nation alone, but also that he might gather in one the scattered children of God."[187] The people of Israel had to be gathered together again in the plenitude of the twelve tribes (Is. 11:12; Micah 2:12; 4:6; 7:11f.; Jer. 23:3; Bar. 4:36f.; Ezek. 11:17; 20:34; 28:25; 34:12-16). The promise is opened to the whole people of God, who, through the salvific death of Christ are made, as a people, the children of God and are gathered from the world. Again, as in John 10:16, it is emphasized that there is to be but one community of God.

In John 12:20-32 it is recounted that "Greeks, who wanted to worship in Jerusalem on the Passover festival," came to Jesus. It is with this that the passing-over takes place, from Israel to the nations of the world. In that moment Jesus "is troubled in spirit" (John 12:27).

Whether these Greeks were perfect proselytes who assumed circumcision and the whole Law, or were only the "God-fearing," who enjoyed a broad relationship to Judaism (see below, § 11, 4), is not stated; it was not important to the Evangelist. These Greeks approach Jesus in a ceremonious manner through two of the apostles (John 12:21f.). Does this mean that entry to Jesus is imparted to the Greek world through the apostles? The names of the two apostles, Philip and Andrew, are Greek. Was it with them that the Greek world found entry into the circle of the Twelve?

The flocking around of the Greeks means the glorification of the Son of Man. The picturesque saying about the grain of wheat which falls to the earth and dies and thus brings forth much fruit makes clear the depth of the event.[188] The harvesting of the world into the assembly of the community is fruit of the Passion of Jesus (John 12:24). It begins now that Christ, exalted (i.e., lifted up), draws all to himself, after he has freed them from the power of the evil one (John 12:31). The request of the Greeks that they be brought to Jesus is answered with the announcement of the crucified and exalted One, who is the salvation of the world. Titles and texts attest him as the Lord to whom the world belongs. This has to be realized through proclamation and mission. "God so loved the world that he gave his only Son . . . so that the world might be saved through him" (John 3:16-17). Christ is "the Light of the world" (John 8:12; 9:5; 12:46) and the "Savior of the world" (John 4:42).

4. ACTS OF THE APOSTLES

The beginnings of the Church's mission are presented in the Acts of the Apostles.[189] The plan and the goal are described in Acts 1:8: "The Holy Spirit coming upon you, you will receive his power and be my witnesses in Jerusalem and in all Judea and Samaria and even to the ends of the earth." The disciples had asked about the kingdom for Israel (Acts 1:6). Jesus' reply proclaims the world-wide mission. It is not the influence and planning of men that opens and disposes the mission, but God's Spirit and power. The primitive Jewish community had in fact to make every effort to establish a free mission to the Gentiles. That the Spirit impelled it to this is stated repeatedly (see below).

The mission is conducted by witnesses to Jesus who, in the exposition of the Acts of the Apostles, are not all of the Twelve but only some of them (Peter and John especially); but with them also are Barnabas and Paul. The course of the mission is described. It proceeds from Jerusalem, spreads out over Judea and Samaria (Acts 8–9), wins the ecumene, but has first to reach its goal at the ends of the earth, and therefore goes beyond the Acts of the Apostles. After the word of Jesus promises the disciples endowment and mandate, on Pentecost the Spirit opens the Church to the world. Ecstatic speaking in tongues is interpreted as speech in various languages.[190] All peoples hear their own language (Acts 2:8).

The community of Jesus' disciples remains in immediate connection with Israel and the Temple (Acts 3:1). The Christians hope that all Israel will come to acknowledge Jesus as Messiah (Acts 2:36). An initial conflict breaks out between the Jewish community and the Jews of the Diaspora, who, at a distance, take an increasingly freer stance toward Temple and Law. The Jews of the Diaspora had to flee Israel and be dispersed over Judea and Samaria (Acts 8:1). If this first march of the mission came about through natural development, its further progress is the result of divine intervention. An angel (Acts 8:26) and the Spirit (Acts 8:29) stir Philip to the baptism of Queen Candace's chamberlain (Acts 8:38). Peter accepts the pagan Cornelius into the Church, since Cornelius was directed thereto by an angel (Acts 10:3-

6). In a vision Peter is instructed about clean and unclean (Acts 10:9-16), and the Spirit speaks to him (Acts 10:19). In a new Pentecost the Spirit descends upon the pagans, so that the water of baptism can no longer be denied them (Acts 10:44-48).

From Acts 13 on, Saul-Paul is active as the great missionary of the Gentiles. To this purpose, Saul and Barnabas, in the community of Antioch, are singled out and sent forth by the Spirit (Acts 13:2-4). After the institution of the first Gentile Christian Church, an assembly of the apostles and elders in Jerusalem ratifies the principle of the Gentile Christians' freedom from the Law (Acts 15:1-33; see above, § 10, 4).

The passage of the mission from Israel to the Gentiles, as it is so penetratingly presented in the Gospel of Matthew (§ 11, 2, c), repeats itself in the operations of Paul. In all cities the Apostle begins his preaching in the synagogue. Rejected there, he goes to the Gentiles. Barnabas and Paul justify this on principle (Acts 13:46f.): "The word of God had to be proclaimed first to you. But now that you have rejected it and have thought yourselves unworthy of eternal life, behold, we are betaking ourselves to the Gentiles. For this is what the Lord commanded us: 'I have made you the light of the nations, so that you may bring salvation even to the ends of the earth'" (Is. 49:6). Even in his Epistles, Paul acknowledges the preeminence of Israel in salvation history: "The Jews first, then the Greeks" (Rom. 1:16; 2:9f.). "Through Israel's misstep salvation comes to the Gentiles" (Rom. 11:11).

The proclamation among the Gentiles necessarily leads Paul on the path to Rome. On principle he wants to proclaim the gospel only where it is not yet known (Rom. 15:20). Although in Rome there is already a Christian community, Paul wanted to go there anyway. For since he is the Apostle of the Gentiles, he must proclaim the gospel in Rome, the chief city of the world (Rom. 1:15).

In the Acts of the Apostles, Rome is mentioned twice. Of Paul, tarrying in Ephesus, it tells (Acts 19:21): "He intended in the Spirit to journey to Jerusalem through Macedonia and Achaia saying to himself, 'When I have been there, I must see Rome too.'" And when Paul was in prison in the city of Jerusalem, Christ came to him in the night and said: "Just as you have borne witness to me in Jerusalem, so too must you bear witness to me in Rome" (Acts 23:11). In biblical language such a necessity signifies the divine plan of salvation.

Historical speculation may say that the gospel pushed on toward Rome in the same way that other religions had previously made their way to the capital city of the world. In the year 186 B.C. a decree of the senate (*Senatus consultum de baccanalibus*) prohibited and suppressed the abuses of the Dionysian mystery cult in Rome. In Rome was the oldest Jewish community in Europe. Their religious propaganda prompted the Roman praetor in 159 B.C. to expel the Jews from Rome, since they were not Italian citizens. Tacitus (*Histories* 15, 44) says, apropos of his description of Nero's persecution of Christians: "Everything abominable and shameless pours from all sides into Rome and is celebrated there." The Christian community in Rome was probably founded and furthered by Christians who had come to the capital city of the empire for a variety of reasons and had remained there.[191]

That the Church conducted herself well in this new and, as the future would show, abiding locale, is attested in the Apostle Paul's Epistle to the Romans. The Roman Church already enjoyed a high eminence and esteem in the world. "I thank my God through Jesus Christ for you all, because your faith is spoken of in the whole world" (Rom. 1:8).

After the Hellenistic poet Menander (342–291 B.C.) had lauded Rome as the eternal city, Latin literature, Cicero already and afterwards the poets of the Augustan Age, like Tibullus and Vergil, celebrated Rome with the title "Eternal City." Church Fathers like St. Ambrose, St. Augustine, and St. Jerome later transferred the title to Christian Rome. One cannot conceive of the world as existing without the ordering power of Rome at its center. If the Christian religion pressed forward to Rome, it was also to share in the eternal endurance of that city.[192]

5. PAUL, APOSTLE OF THE GENTILES

Paul[193] tells that he was called by God's revelation and the appearance of the exalted Christ "to proclaim the gospel among the Gentiles"; indeed, that he was "chosen thereto from his mother's womb" (Gal. 1:15f.). This does not mean that he would have been distinctly aware of this special commission as an apostle from the very beginning. He turned first (thus in Acts 9:20), and afterwards again and again, to the Jews in their synagogues. According to the Acts of the Apostles (9:15), Paul regarded himself as sent to Israel as well as to the Gentiles. With all his indescribable efforts in his mission to the Gentiles, his goal remained to make Israel jealous and thus to win at least some of his people (Rom. 11:13f.). He always regards himself as obligated ultimately to Israel. Only in the course of his apostolic ministry will he have come to the certain knowledge that his task was "to bring all peoples to obedience to the faith" (Rom. 1:5).

a) Criticism of Paganism

In Rom. 1:18–3:20, Paul points out that Israel as well as the Gentiles[194] lapsed into sin and lost righteousness. In Rom. 1:18-32 he discloses the guilt of the Gentiles, inasmuch as he depicts their religious (Rom. 1:18-23) as well as their moral decadence (Rom. 1:24-32). That religious decadence is blameworthy. God's invisible existence, his eternal power and wisdom, were and are able to be recognized by reasoning from the world. Men did not recognize God because they did not want to recognize him. They exchanged the glory of the immortal God for the shadowy image of mortal men and for the worship of beasts (Rom. 1:20-23).

With this mode of thought Paul is following a broad and lengthy tradition. Greek philosophy and especially the Stoa proved God's existence by reasoning from creation to the Creator; and this proof was taken up also by Hellenistic Judaism (see the present work, Vol. 2, pp. 14f.). Abstract terms in Paul permit recognition of the philosophical background of his reflections: the knowable, the invisible, that which can be concluded by reason, the eternal power and divinity.

Jewish mission preaching likewise concerned itself with these same themes. The witnesses thereto are first of all the canonical Book of Wisdom, called also the Wisdom of Solomon (chs. 11–15), the *Letter of Aristeas*, the Jewish Sibyllines; and even the Hellenistic-Jewish novel *Joseph and Asenath*, in which, in connection with Gen. 41:45, the conversion of the daughter of the pagan priest Potiphera to the Jewish faith is described. In this literature, as also in Rom. 1:23, apparently with reference to the Egyptian religion, the worship of divinized beasts is abominated (Wis. 11:15; 12:23-27; 15:18f.; *Letter of Aristeas* 138f.; *Sibyllines* 3, 551-555; *Testaments of the Twelve Patriarchs: Nephtali* 3:3f.).

Paul supplements and corrects philosophy from biblical thought when he says that it is God who reveals himself to conclusive recognition (Rom. 1:19). Even here God is at work. Consequently Paul declares, and quite unphilosophically, that the denial of the knowledge of God is blameworthy (Rom. 1:18, 20f.). Rational apprehension and apocalyptics are similarly joined in the *Syriac Apocalypse of Baruch* 54:17f.: "You will be severely punished because you have disregarded the apprehension of the Most High. His works have taught you nothing; and the artistic ordering of his creation, which is constantly before you, has not convinced you." There is a comparable passage in the *Testaments of the Twelve Patriarchs: Nephtali* 3:3f. The revelation of God's wrath (Rom. 1:18) is taking place now in the proclamation of the gospel. The eschatological present, however, is revelatory also of times past.

In Paul's judgment, polytheism is not a kind of ignorance or a tragic mistake but an offense, as a lapse from ideal primordial faith.[195] Our history of religion judges otherwise. The worship of many gods is, according to that history, a primitive level of culture and religion, which can gradually refine itself to a high state of religion. Moral judgment can, however, state with Paul, that the history of paganism is not free of guilt.

The scientific study of religions will also recall to mind that the worship of divinities in the form of beasts, as formerly in the Egyptian religion, which might seem so repulsive to the stranger and most especially to the Jews, possibly had its rational origins when man had experience of beasts as excelling in strength or beauty or fidelity, perhaps his own domestic animals; and on that account he represented the divinity in the shape of an animal. No one will lay it to Paul's charge that he did not possess our insight into the history of religion. Yet it may be recalled in this regard that even biblical and Christian belief does, as a kind of simile or metaphor, represent the divine and the holy with the form of a beast. This is the case in Ezek. 1:5-14 (Apoc. 8:6-8) in the mysterious vision of the four animal-like beings, in which our symbols of the four evangelists have their origins. The servant of Yahweh is likened to a lamb (Is. 53:7); and accordingly, Christ is the Lamb of God (John 1:29; Acts 8:32; Apoc. 5:6). The dove is the symbol of the Holy Spirit (Mark 1:10).

Old Testament and Pauline criticism of polytheism follows upon similar pagan reflections. Greek philosophical religious apprehension had long since practiced a severe criticism of mythology. Out of the multiplicity of the gods there was developed a more refined religious feeling of henotheism (see the present work, Vol. 2, pp. 257f.).

Paul depicts in Rom. 1:24-32 the moral decay of paganism. Worship of idols is the tremendous substitution of creatures for the Creator, of lies for the truth (Rom. 1:25). Man first dishonors God and then dishonors himself. Sin, however, is punishment, inasmuch as God abandons men to sin. Paul says this in a thrice repeated "God gave them over" (Rom. 1:24, 26, 28). He gave them over to the sin of lechery, of unnatural relations, and then to immorality in general. Paul enumerates their vices in the form of a traditional catalog of vices (see the present work, Vol. 3, pp. 209f.). In the picture drawn by Paul, it is Jewish deliberation's awareness of the immorality of the surrounding paganism that is speaking. Paul knows and speaks too, of course, of the sins of Israel (Rom. 2:17-24). The rabbinate too judges most critically the conditions prevalent in its own nation (H. L. Strack and P. Billerbeck, *op. cit.*, Vol 3 [1926], pp. 71–74 and 105–115).

b) Acceptance of Gentiles

Paul's severe judgment on the Gentiles in Rom. 1:18-23 is supplemented by Rom. 2:12-16. Here the Apostle says that even the pagans, who do not know the written Law of Moses, possess that law which is written in their hearts and attests itself in their consciences. Paul admits that even pagans who fulfill this law will be justified by God in the judgment.

Paul took the concept of conscience from the outlook and language of popular philosophy (see the present work, Vol. 1, pp. 137–138). He deepens the philosophical apprehension of it when he designates conscience as God's writing (Rom. 2:15; γραπτὸν is a *passivum divinum*) and inasmuch as he adds that the reality of the natural law and of conscience will be revealed in God's judgment (Rom. 2:16).

Paul states further (Rom. 2:25-29) that by fulfillment of the law, uncircumcision is changed to circumcision — to a Jew, a highly offensive assertion. The mentality of circumcision is not that of a legal prescription and an external rite; rather, circumcision is a spiritual reality, a circumcision of the heart. Paul is drawing upon prophetic admonition (Jer. 4:4; see above, § 10, 5, b).

Of his whole ministry as messenger of the gospel, Paul says in Rom. 15:16: "I am minister of Jesus Christ to the Gentiles, performing the priestly duties of the gospel so that the Gentiles may be presented as an acceptable offering, consecrated in the Holy Spirit." In a doubled reference he describes his mission as a ministry of worship. As missionary, Paul is a priest; and the goal of his labors is to prepare the Gentiles as a holy offering. For the Jews, the pagans are unholy and unclean. Now, however, they become a clean and holy offering. Does Paul attest but once and in this place to a deep consciousness, of which he speaks nowhere else (see above, § 4, 2)?

Rom. 10:18 describes the proclamation of the gospel: "Their sound went out to all lands, and their words to the ends of the inhabited world." The Apostle is transferring to the mission Ps. 19:5, according to which the fame of God can be heard everywhere through the glory of the heavens. Christian communities had by this time taken shape in the larger cities at most, and even there they were hardly to be called renowned. One may concede that the countryside was but thinly populated and that with the conquest of the cities, the decision on the culture of the land was determined.

This being his viewpoint, Paul can say, as he does in Rom. 15:19, "I have completed the proclamation of the gospels from Jerusalem to Illyricum, and now I have no more room." In this statement of Paul, an extraordinary awareness is speaking. He already sees as completed the victorious march of the mission through the world (which for him is the world around the Mediterranean Sea). When the fire is ignited, it continues to spread unless it can be contained. But the deepest reason for Paul's conviction is God's word, which must be fulfilled.

This is likewise declared again in Rom. 15:9-12. Paul anticipates the eschatological marvel as a reality. This future is absolutely certain. Paul proclaims it in an ingenious series of Scripture quotations, certainly assembled by tradition, which quotations proceed in broadening circles from the assembly of Israel and the Gentiles (Rom. 15:8, 10) to the totality of the Gentiles (Rom. 15:11), and from time to the eschatological glory of God (Rom. 15:12). The Gentiles are to praise God because of his mercy, as it is written: "For this will I praise you among the Gentiles and sing to your name" (Ps. 18:50). And again: "Rejoice, you nations, with his people" (Deut. 32:43). And again: "Praise the Lord, all you nations" (Ps. 117:1). The Exalted One rules as Lord of the Gentiles: "The root of Jesse will remain; and the Resurrected One will rule over the nations. In him will all peoples hope" (Is. 11:1, 10).

II

THE RULE OF GOD--
ESCHATOLOGY

§ 12. CONCEPTUALITY

1. TERMS AND CONCEPTS

Theological language treats of the endtime largely in the terminology and concepts of eschatology and apocalyptics.[196] Modern practice makes this distinction: eschatology designates the *fact* of the endtime consummation, whereas the term apocalyptics looks to the *how* of the endtime events, both in individual detail and in the aggregate. The New Testament employs both word groupings, ἔσχατος (final time) and ἀποκάλυψις (disclosure, revelation); but it does not distinguish them in the same way that modern practice does.

Biblical concepts and terms can be tabulated as in the following schema (see also the present work, Vol. 1, pp. 70–75), *a*) through *f*).

a) ἔσχατος (*final time, last day*)[197]

This is a term used from the time of the prophets onwards to designate the endtime. The prophets speak of "the last days" (Is. 2:2; Hos. 3:5; Micah 4:1; Jer. 23:20; Ezek. 38:16). The Old Testament conceives time, not as a cyclical succession, but as urgently pushing on toward a goal. The end leads up to salvation and glory for Israel. All nations will be attracted to Israel (Is. 2:2f.; Micah 4:1f.).

Mention of the last days is multiplied in the apocalyptic literature (Dan. 2:28; 10:14; *4 Esdras* 4 [6]:34). The formula "the end of days" is encountered also in the Qumran writings (1 QpHab 2:5f.; *Damascus Document* 4:4). The last day is the day of judgment. Only a small community, "the poor of the flock" (*Damascus Document* 19:9), will be saved. Even now it is the end of days, and now "the final generation" (1 QpHab 7:2). The preaching of the apostles characterizes the present as "eschatological days" (Acts 2:17; Heb. 1:2) and as "eschatological hours" (1 John 2:18).

The pouring out of the Spirit is expected for the messianic endtime (Joel 3:1-5). Since this has now taken place, "the last days" are now present (Acts 2:17). Since Christ is the consummation, he is, in comparison to the first Adam, "the last Adam" (1 Cor. 15:45). The fulfillment of Old Testament prophecy makes the present time the endtime. In times past, God spoke repeatedly through the prophets; "in the present end of days he spoke to us in his son, whom he appointed heir of all things, and through whom also he made the ages" (Heb. 1:1f.). It is the conviction and consciousness of the Church that the course and end of the ages has arrived. Jesus is Messiah as Son of God. The messianic age is the final age. This Sonship embraces the beginning and end of the ages, since all creation is in Christ (see present work, Vol. 1, pp. 24-27).

The present time is the endtime, since revelation and redemption have now taken place for the Church, taken place in Christ, the spotless Lamb, as was promised before the foundation of the world (1 Peter 1:5; 19f.). The conviction that "the last days" are present is indicated by various formulations (James 5:3; Jude 18; 2 Peter 3:3). Things and events of the endtime are characterized as "last"; thus, the eschatological trumpet (1 Cor. 15:42) and the seven last plagues (Apoc. 15:1). As Creator and Consummator (Perfecter), God is above all else, "the first and the last" (Apoc. 1:17; 2:8; 22:13).

The Christ of John's Gospel speaks penetratingly of the resurrection of the dead "on the last day" (John 6:39-40, 44, 54; 11:24) and of the judgment "on the last day" (John 12:48). It is possible, however, that these statements are the insertions of a later redaction (see below, § 17, 2, e).

The end of the ages makes itself known in the breach of the established order. The final times, therefore, are fulfilled with great distress and affliction. That is how the final time is described in the apocalyptic addresses of Jesus (Mark 13:5-27; Luke 17:22-37). Late apostolic Epistles await the final days as "dangerous times" (2 Tim. 3:1). In Jude

18f. and 2 Peter 3:3; the last days are depicted emphatically in this way. "There will be scoffers, behaving in accord with their godless lusts." The two letters are probably not thinking of future heretics; rather, they speak very harshly of the heretics with whom the congregation must already contend. In 1 John 2:18 these opponents are called "antichrists." The endtime will be the time of the "final plagues" (Apoc. 15:1; 21:9). The last days are days of fiery judgment (James 5:3).

b) ἀποκάλυψις (revelation)[198]

In Old and New Testament, the Bible frequently uses the terms "revelation" and "reveal" in reference to past revelation and of revelation still taking place, but seldom enough in regard to the endtime disclosure (see the present work, Vol. 2, pp. 3–5). The Greek Old Testament employs that word group for God's eschatological revelation hardly at all. Early Judaism, however, produced a rich apocalyptic literature. Nevertheless, orthodoxy relegated that literature to a fringe area or rejected it entirely. Early Jewish apocalyptics supported the afterworld, therefore, largely in foreign languages (Syriac, Ethiopic, Armenian, Slavonic).

It is the New Testament that first begins to employ the term *apokalypsis* (= revelation, etc.) with frequency. Paul awaits "the day of wrath and of the revelation of the just judgment of God" (Rom. 2:5). The day of the Lord is revealed in fire (1 Cor. 3:13). On the day of revelation Christ will appear in the fullness of his might (1 Cor. 1:7; 2 Thess. 1:7). In the revelation of Christ (1 Peter 1:13), the salvation of the faithful will also be made apparent (1 Peter 1:5; 4:13; 5:1). Revelation is the grand theme of the Apocalypse of John, which will disclose the revelation of Jesus Christ (Apoc. 1:1). This book was given to apocalyptics its name.

c) ἡμέρα (day)[199]

Israel could speak of a day in its national history on which it had had experience of God's works in a special way, whether for its benefit (Is. 9:3; 49:8) or to its detriment (Lam. 1:21; Ezek. 34:12), as a "day of Yahweh." The nation expects this day as a day of judgment on the Gentiles and of salvation for Israel (Zech. 12:3-14), of purification (Mal. 3:1-3), end of spiritual endowment (Joel 3:1-5). Such prophecy,

however, carries with it warnings against the presumptuous expectation of salvation. "Woe to those who desire the day of Yahweh! What
will the day of Yahweh be for you? Indeed, it is darkness and not
light" (Amos 5:18; similar in Ezek. 7:7). Expectation calls the last
day the "day of Yahweh" (Amos 5:18; Is. 13:6; Ezek. 7:10), the "great
day of Yahweh" (Zeph. 1:14), "his day" (Ps. 37:13; *Syriac Apocalypse
of Baruch* 49:2), the "day of judgment" (Is. 34:8), the "day of wrath"
(Ezek. 22:24; Lam. 1:12), the "day of the Messiah" (*4 Esdras* 11
[13]:52), and "that day" (Is. 2:11; Zech. 2:11 *et passim*).

This language is continued in the New Testament. The eschatological day is called the "day of judgment" (Matthew 11:22; 12:36; 1 John
4:17; 2 Peter 2:9), the "great day" (Jude 6; Apoc. 6:17; 16:14), "that
day" (Matthew 7:22; Luke 10:12; 2 Tim. 1:12), and simply "the day"
(1 Cor. 3:13; 1 Thess. 5:5; Heb. 10:25). In Paul this day is the day of
judgment for the whole world and for the Church (1 Cor. 4:3; Phil.
1:6, 10), but also the day of accountability for the Apostle himself (2
Cor. 1:14; Phil. 2:16). As the day of the parousia, the last day is called
the "day of the Son of Man" (Luke 17:24) and the "day of the Lord"
(1 Thess. 5:2; 2 Thess. 2:2).

d) καιρὸς (*time fulfilled; time arrived at*)[200]

Prophecy and Jewish apocalyptics speak of the eschatological period
of time with the formula "in that time" (ἐν ἐκείνῳ τῷ καιρῷ — Jer. 3:17;
Dan. 12:1). This is the "time of the visitation" (Jer. 6:15), "of wrath"
(Ezek. 7:8), "our time" (Lam. 4:18). In Qumran one expects the
moment of "visitation," already determined by God, when he will
quash outrage and make the truth manifest (1 QS 3:18; 4:18f.).

The term and concept *kairos* are employed also in the New Testament. To the multitude who, in view of advance indications, know
how to judge the coming weather but not the times, Jesus cries out:
"Hypocrites! You know how to interpret the face of the earth and the
heavens. Why, then, can you not interpret the present time?" (Luke
12:56; changed somewhat in Matthew 16:3). The judgment between
salvation and disaster is now inescapable because it is now the messianic-eschatological time. Those who evade this judgment are "hypocrites" — a reproach that comes close to an imputation of godlessness.

The lament over Jerusalem is referred more evidently to Jesus than is the judgment itself. The destiny of Jerusalem must now be fulfilled, because she "has not known the time of her visitation" (Luke 19:44). The time is a time of decision, insofar as in it God's arrival is accepted or rejected. In a programmatic statement (probably formulated by the Evangelist), Jesus says at the beginning of his public life: "The time has been fulfilled and the kingdom of God is at hand" (Mark 1:15). The time has become the time of decision by reason of the fulfillment of the promises.

The Spirit of Christ, preexisting in the old covenant, declared to the prophets the suffering and exaltation of Christ, and the prophets sought to recognize the time of these events (1 Peter 1:11). In the present time God's justice is revealed (Rom. 3:25). "Now is the acceptable time. Now is the day of salvation" (2 Cor. 6:2). The present time is, in its characteristics, in conformity with the endtime. The consummation of *kairos* is not yet made. It is, nevertheless, already certain through Christ. God will make him manifest "at the right time" (1 Tim. 6:15). At that time God will bring to light what is hidden (1 Cor. 4:5). Finally, *kairos* signifies simply the day of judgment (1 Peter 5:6; Apoc. 1:3; 11:18).

e) αἰών (age, world, past and future time)[201]

To the various significations which suit the term and concept eon or age, there belong those of the two ages, the present and the future. Thus age signifies the future world and future time. When age indicates the future world, the concept is significant because of the haziness of its contemplation. It relinquishes any claim to a portrayal of the beyond. The dualistic concept of the two different ages, the present age of sin, suffering, and death, which is under the influence of Satan, and the future age of redemption and salvation ushered in and fulfilled by God, possibly has its origins in Parsiism. The distinction would have been taken up by Jewish apocalyptics. It is present in essence already in Dan. 2 and 7.

The Greek word αἰών indicates, with its frequent occurrence in the Greek Old Testament, past and future time. According to *4 Esdras* 5 [7]:30-33, the new age begins with the resurrection of the dead and the judgment. The expressions "this age" and "the coming age" are employed from the time of the rabbis.

The New Testament follows the linguistic usage of Jewish apocalyptics, insofar as, like the latter, it likewise distinguishes the two ages. This age is entangled in cares (Mark 4:19) and in things far from God (Luke 20:34). The imitation of Christ is promised eternal life in the future age (Mark 10:30). The perfectly righteous are deemed worthy "to participate in that age and in the resurrection of the dead" (Luke 20:35). The future age is presented also as the time of judgment. Blasphemy against the Spirit will find forgiveness "neither in this age nor in that to come" (Matthew 12:32).

In Paul, age (*aiōn*) usually means time (1 Cor. 2:7; 8:13; Rom. 11:36), or lends emphasis to the expression of the present time. Christians must "not conform themselves to this age" (Rom. 12:2). The wisdom of this age is foolishness (1 Cor. 2:6; 3:18). The present age is ruled over by Satan (2 Cor. 4:4) and by the demons (1 Cor. 2:6). Christ can "deliver us from the present wicked age" (Gal. 1:4). Even the Epistle to the Ephesians characterizes the present age as ruled over by the Evil One (2:2). Nevertheless the same Epistle, in a post-Pauline fashion, speaks also of "the overflowing riches of his grace in the future ages" (2:7).

The faithful "have already tasted the powers of the age to come" (Heb. 6:5). These powers are "the Holy Spirit and the good word of God," and also "wonders and deeds of power." These powers originate from the eternal age and lead to it. The new age, already present, was ushered in through Christ, who now, "at the end of the ages, has been made manifest through his sacrifice for the taking away of sins." The sacrifice of Christ, offered one time and once for all time, characterizes the end of the ages (Heb. 9:26).*

*[*Translator's note*: Throughout the foregoing section on the term αἰών, I have consistently used the term "age" where the author simply (and equally consistently) Germanizes the Greek to *Äon* or *Äonen*. If the reader has been in any way conditioned by scriptural language, he will find that in any of the Scripture quotes in the foregoing section he can substitute the term "world" for "age" without changing the obvious meanings in the least. Perhaps it would be of some help to recall that a common liturgical prayer conclusion only continues the language of Scripture when it declares that the duration of the Triune God's existence is εἰς τοὺς αἰῶνας τῶν αἰώνων, which the Western Church has

f) τέλος *(end, consummation)*[202]

Eschatological time is also signified by words with τέλος (end, consummation) for their root. τέλος, and with it συντέλεια, in the Greek Old Testament usually means simply "end" and "completion"; yet, from the time of Daniel (συντέλεια in 8:19; 9:27; 12:13), they indicate also the apocalyptic endtime. The term is used in this way in the *Testaments of the Twelve Patriarchs* (*Levi* 10:2; *Benjamin* 11:3). The end of the ages is a sharply bounded period (*4 Esdras* 1 [3]:14; 10 [12]:9), about which God taught Ezra through revelations.

In the New Testament, τέλος signifies the totality of the endtime events (Mark 13:7). "The end is near," when Christ will turn over the kingdom of God to his Father (1 Cor. 15:24). τέλος also signifies the final destiny of man in destruction and salvation (Rom. 6:21f.). In the New Testament, συντέλεια is employed mostly in the Gospel of Matthew in the phrase συντέλεια τοῦ αἰῶνος (end or fulfillment of time). The formula has its precedents (Dan. 8:19; *Testaments of the Twelve Patriarchs: Benjamin* 11:3). Matthew uses the formula in the explanation of the parable of the weeds among the wheat (Matthew 13:39f., 49). He uses it also in formulating the question of the disciples about the time of the end of the world (24:3) and in the exalted Christ's promise (28:20). Christ has now, "once for all at the end of the ages, been made manifest for the destruction of sin through his sacrifice" (Heb. 9:26).[203]

Eschatological linguistic usage makes it evident — which will now be established and corroborated by numerous themes and references from the content of Scripture — that New Testament eschatology and apocalyptics are determined to a great extent by a tradition from the Old Testament and from early Judaism.[204] The New Testament does not simply parrot these ideas and notions, but explains them as presently to be fulfilled or as already fulfilled. Eschatology is not doctrine and prophecy about distant things, but clarification and proclamation of the present.

rendered *per omnia saecula saeculorum*; and whether these phrases, which mean literally "unto the ages of ages" or "for all ages of ages" or "for all worlds of worlds" be rendered "forever and ever" or "world without end" is of little consequence, since everyone understands that it means, in any case, "eternally," because of the piling up of so many "ages" or "worlds."]

2. Exposition and Interpretation

The exposition of the eschatological and apocalyptic texts of the New Testament has great difficulties peculiar to itself.[205]

Analysis of the texts reveals that New Testament eschatology draws broadly upon Old Testament themes and develops them. The Bible attempts thereby to grasp and make perceptual the utterly unperceptual world beyond space and time. If the Old Testament representations now appear within the canon of the New Testament, they do not thereby become divine revelation, but they remain a human attempt at representation.

It will be a problem, soluble to some degree, for the history of religion and for exegesis to clarify and describe authoritatively the history of these themes, coming in part from the ancient East, thus tracing them from the Old Testament to the New through early Judaism. We cannot, however, arrange the individual themes topographically and put them in a chronological order, and in that way describe the future course of the endtime and the history of the world and of salvation. For this history there is no report and no reporter.

A philosophical explanation of the world can accept a world without beginning and, in consequence, a world without end as well. Both these points are naturally incapable of representation, nor are they comprehensible and conceivable; for all of our ideas and concepts are drawn from the world of space and time, while those eventualities lie before and after time (see the present work, Vol. 1, pp. 59–61).

Apocalyptic themes are to be investigated and explained from the viewpoint of their literary-symbolic sense and of the existential import and intent of their declarations. To interpret the texts as a declaration of revelation is ultimately a further and very difficult task of theological exegesis. Every eschatological and apocalyptic declaration must be approached with some reserve and requires an ever-critical treatment in accord with statements like those of the Apostle Paul: "We hope for what we do not see" (Rom. 8:25). "We look not to things that are seen but to what is unseen. What is seen is temporal. The unseen is eternal" (2 Cor. 4:18). The dimension of hope consists in just this, that the good things hoped for lie beyond experience.

God is not bounded by space and time as man is; rather, he is beyond and above all space and time. The conviction of faith expresses this with the image that God is above the earth in heaven, and with the declaration that he is always there, contemporaneously with all time. He comes forth into time ever from his timelessness, foreshortening and surmounting time. Eschatology is always executed in the faith which lives before God's judgment and salvation. The whole *future* to which faith looks is a future that is God's *be-ing*.*

Like the whole of the New Testament existence and revelation, New Testament eschatology too is "in Christ." Christ and the eternal God manifested through him is the essential content of biblical eschatology. "He [God] shall be our place after this life" (Augustine, *On Psalm* 30:3, in Migne, *PL* 36.252).

13. REIGN OF GOD

1. REIGN OF GOD AND KINGDOM OF GOD

The goal of the final hope of the New Testament is the reign of God. The New Testament uses in part the designation kingdom of God (βασιλεία τοῦ θεοῦ), and in part, kingdom of heaven (βασιλεία τῶν οὐρανῶν).[206] The more primitive formula is probably "kingdom of God." Even Jesus will have used this expression. The formula "kingdom of God" appears in Mark, the oldest of the Gospels, in 1:15; 10:14f.; and 10:24f. It is to be assigned to Source Q along with Matthew 12:28 = Luke 11:20. Also in Luke 6:20 and 9:2, Source Q will have prompted the "kingdom of God." And in Matthew (12:28; 19:24; 21:31, 43), "kingdom of God" occurs four times. In the great majority of cases Matthew employs the formula "kingdom of heaven," whereas in the rest of the New Testament (Mark, Luke, John, Paul, Apocalypse) "kingdom of God" is used regularly.

Out of reverential fear inter-testamental Judaism and the Judaism

---

*[*Translator's note*: If this last statement limps rather badly, it is nevertheless our best attempt at rendering the auhor's pun, which is none too revelatory even in German: *Alle Zukunft, in die der Glaube ausschaut, ist Zu-kunft Gottes.*]

of Jesus' time avoided the use of the name of God. In consequence thereof Matthew says mostly "kingdom of heaven" instead of "kingdom of God." The New Testament in its totality does not share this reluctance to pronounce the name of God. This belongs to the Christian freedom of speech (Eph. 3:12).

Just as in profane and Jewish Greek literature, in the New Testament the term βασιλεία sometimes signifies kingly dignity and kingly rule (as in Mark 11:10; Luke 19:12, 15; 1 Cor. 15:24; Heb. 12:28; Apoc. 17:12), and sometimes the realm ruled over, a kingdom (as in Matthew 4:8; Mark 6:23; Apoc. 16:10). According to the context, in the New Testament βασιλεία τοῦ θεοῦ can be translated either kingdom of God or reign of God. The notion of an empire extended in space and time is bound up with the term kingdom. Either translation, kingdom or reign of God, signifies that God's rule is a state of affairs, and that it is present there where God calls and where faith and love respond to his call It is on this principle that a congregation is formed, and in that sense it can be termed God's province and domain.

The translation of βασιλεία τῶν οὐρανῶν sometimes employed, the kingdom of heaven, is often understood as referring to the domain beyond, into which the pious man hopes one day to enter after his death. The kingdom of heaven in this sense is heaven as the place of eternal blessedness. The exhortation to remain unmarried "for the sake of the kingdom of heaven" (Matthew 19:12) will then be understood as an admonition to remain unmarried in order to be more certain of going to heaven. The unmarried state "for the sake of the kingdom of heaven" really means however, to subordinate everything to the advancement of the reign of God, even to the avoidance of the bond and blessing of matrimony.

2. OLD TESTAMENT AND JUDAISM

In Israel, the expectation of the reign of God reaches far back. Texts found in Asshur and Ugarit indicate that in the Canaanite-Syrian world the highest god, as supreme in the world of the gods, bore the title king. Certainly the familiar name of the divinity Moloch means king. Although Israel fiercely rejected the religion of the original inhabitants of Palestine and likewise the worship of Moloch, Yahweh's designation as King was surely a carryover to Yahweh of pre-Israelitic representations.[207]

In Israel, Yahweh began to be called King (Exod 15:18; 1 Sam. 12:12; Pss. 5:3; 10:16; 29:10) after the earthly kingship had been established in Israel, therefore about the year 1000 B.C. Yahweh is enthroned royally in heaven. Isaiah (6:5), in his vocational vision (to be dated in the eighth century B.C.), sees Yahweh of Hosts on the heavenly throne, surrounded by the hosts of angels, who praise him as Lord of heaven and of earth: "With my eyes I have seen the King, the Lord of Hosts!"

If Israel worships God primarily as King only over his people Israel (Is. 41:21; 44:6), since the time of the prophets he is worshipped more and more as King of the world. Yahweh is King as Creator of the world (Pss. 24; 93:1; 95:3-5). He is "King of the nations" (Jer. 10:7; Ps. 47:3f.). His kingship has dominion over all (Ps. 10:16). He is "King over the whole earth" (Ps. 47:3). The kingship of Yahweh is declared and celebrated in worship, as described in the psalms about ascending the throne (Pss. 47; 93; 96; 97; 99). The earthly king has authority as representative and governor for Yahweh, the divine King. The earthly king is established in his office inasmuch as he is adopted by God as his son (Ps. 2). The royal throne in Jerusalem is "Yahweh's royal throne over Israel" (1 Chron. 28:5).

Israel recognizes, of course, that Yahweh's kingship cannot be realized in this time. Its realization, nevertheless, is an object of hope for the era of salvation, at the end. This kingship is an eschatological kingship. Someday Yahweh will rule over the whole world, enthroned in Jerusalem; and all nations will make pilgrimage to Zion (Is. 24:23; Zech. 14:9; Hos. 1:10f.). The Messiah will be a new King David (Is. 11:1; Ezek. 37:24). This hope is intensified in apocalyptics. Yahweh will establish his kingship. This will be the end of time. "In those days God, the Lord of heaven, will have a kingdom set up which will be indestructible forever" (Dan. 2:44). After the four world empires, which constitute the time of the wicked, the Son of Man (who represents Israel) will establish royal dominion (Dan. 7:14). It is the kingdom "of the saints of the Most High" (Dan. 7:27).

There are early Jewish writings with a temporal proximity to the

New Testament. According to the *Psalms of Solomon* (17), the Messiah-Prince, the Son of David, is to overthrow the foreign oppressors, purify Jerusalem of the Gentiles, create a righteous and holy nation, and rule it in prosperity. God will reign on earth through his Messiah. He himself remains the true and eternal King. Even the community in Qumran recognizes and awaits the kingship of God. God's rule is in heaven: "You, O God, are awesome in the majesty of your kingly rule" (1 QM 12:7). God's kingly rule will be established also on earth, and indeed, as Israel's empire. "To the God of Israel will the kingship belong, and through the holy ones of his people will he demonstrate his power" (1 QM 6:6). "The covenant of the kingly rule of God over his people for eternal generations is given" to the seed of David (4 Q *Blessings of the Patriarchs* 4).

Qumran, like the New Testament, must experience a postponement of fulfillment. The Qumran community recognized itself as "the final generation." Yet the teacher of the community recognized and "explained that the final times were to be lengthened, and must cover all that the prophets had foretold. For the secrets of God are wonderful" (1 QpHab 7:2; 7f.). In the *Prayer of the Eighteen Petitions* or the *Eighteen Benedictions*, which, in its oldest parts, goes back to the time of the New Testament, the eleventh and twelfth petitions read: "Return to us our Judge as before and our Councillor as in the beginning. Be King over us, you alone. . . . Purge out the wicked rule and destroy it quickly in our days." Israel expected the kingly dominion of God, then, as a national and political empire.

Early Jewish apocalyptics, however, stemming from an atmosphere of prophecy, thinks in cosmic proportions. God's kingly dominion will break over the world with a mighty catastrophic stroke. The structure of the world will collapse. The dead will rise. Judgment will encompass all men and the whole world (see below, § 18, 2). Out of terror and woe a new time and a new world will be born (see below, § 20, 1).

God's dominion can also be understood spiritually and morally. "Wisdom showed Jacob God's kingdom and imparted to him a knowledge of holy things" (Wis. 10:10). Israel must "take upon herself the yoke of kingship" (H. Strack and P. Billerbeck, *op. cit.* Vol. 1, pp. 172–178). It is required, therefore, to acknowledge the one true God as King and to follow his Law. The kingly dominion of God is comparable to the Hellenistic notion of virtue. The pursuit of divine law imparts to reason "kingly rule through moderation, righteousness, goodness, and strength" (*4 Maccabees* 2:23). The moral situation of the kingdom is carried further by Philo. "Under kingship I understood wisdom; for the wise man is also king" Philo, (*De migratione Abrahami* 197).

At the time of the New Testament there existed side by side in Israel two orders of apocalyptic expectation, the one of an earthly and national messianic kingdom and the other of a world-wide reign of God. The theological system combined them both in a temporal succession. To come first was a temporally bounded national messianic kingdom. It is described in its riches and in its fullness in the *Syriac Apocalypse of Baruch* 29. Its term of existence is given variously. At the time of the New Testament it occasionally takes a term of a thousand years. The merciful "will proportionately from the first hour partake of a thousand-year meal" (*Testaments of the Twelve Patriarchs: Isaac* 8:20; see also below, note 280). At the end of the messianic kingdom there will be the resurrection of the dead and the judgment. Then the eternal kingly rule of God will be established.

3. NEW TESTAMENT

a) John the Baptist

For centuries Israel had expected the kingly dominion of God. She hoped for it with mounting impatience when she had lost her political independence. With the rule of a foreign power, it was the pagan idols and Satan who ruled. When at this very hour John the Baptist came upon the scene and Jesus succeeded him and both proclaimed the approach of the kingship of God (Matthew 3:2; 4:17), it had to be a truly exciting message. The period of expectation had been completed.

b) Synoptics (*Statements of Jesus; Imminent Expectation*)

The announcement that the kingdom of God was at hand is, according to Mark 1:15, the opening statement of Jesus' preaching. "Jesus came to Galilee, proclaiming the gospel of God. The time is fulfilled, and the kingdom of God is at hand. Turn about and believe in the gospel."[208] The preaching of Jesus is designated as "gospel of God." This is the term and concept of mission, Paul's specialized use of which (Rom. 1:1; 15:16; 2 Cor. 11:7; 1 Thess. 2:2, 8) is already presupposed in the Gospels. Is it not in this sense that Mark 1:1 speaks of "the beginning of the gospel of Jesus," and likewise Mark 1:15, making it apparent that the Book of Mark in its content, the history of the Jesus who is the beginning of salvation, is a gospel which already fills the world?

"The fullness of time" is an Old Testament (1 Kings 8:15; 2 Chron. 36:21f.; — 1 QS 3:16) as well as a New Testament (Gal. 4:4; Eph. 1:10) phraseology. "Near at hand" designates the arrival of the era of salvation (Is. 50:8; 51:5; 55:6). "To believe" has the depth of New Testament salvational faith. God's rule and conversion are related to each other in such a way that God's rule is a turning of God to man, whose conversion he not only makes possible but demands (Mark 1:15; see the present work, Vol. 3, pp. 73–97). Thus Mark 1:15 is probably to be regarded as a perfected and already reflective summary, which the Evangelist, like the Church herself, places as a superscription over the preaching of Jesus. The salvational tidings of the arrival of God's reign is, in Mark, both in word and in deed, really of Jesus.

Further sayings of the Gospels repeat the pronouncement that God's rule has come. The messengers are to go out and announce: "The kingdom of heaven is near at hand" (Matthew 10:7). Just as summer is nigh when the fig tree turns green, so too do the events of the present announce the imminent breakthrough of the kingdom of God (Mark 13:28f.). The kingly dominion of God is near and will, as judgment, suddenly burst forth like the deluge over that generation (Matthew 24:38).

Parables tell of the unexpectedly sudden arrival of the kingdom. It comes like a thief in the night (Matthew 24:43f.), like the householder's returning at an unexpected hour (Matthew 24:46), like a bridegroom's summoning to his wedding (Matthew 25:6). Apparently the kingdom will come in this very generation. "Truly, some of those standing here will not taste death until they see the kingdom of God come in power" (Mark 9:1).

The proximate futurity of God's kingdom is a reality already present.

The demons are overthrown in their expulsion from the possessed; and likewise in the healing of the sick, since sickness and death, as a disturbance and destruction of God's creation, are the work of Satan. Satan had bound the crippled woman (Luke 13:16). The cures are the sign and the beginning of God's dominion, which is a world made whole again. "If I cast out demons by the finger of God, then the kingdom of God has come upon you" (Luke 11:20; see also the present work, Vol. 2, pp. 71–76). The downfall of Satan is an apocalyptic theme (see below, § 14, 3, c and § 19, 2, b). This has now happened: "I saw Satan fall from heaven like a bolt of lightning" (Luke 10:18). This can hardly mean that the pre-existing Christ was watching Satan's downfall (Apoc. 12:8f.), but that Satan is being overthrown now in the activity of Christ and his disciples.

The kingdom that is arriving is indissolubly bound up with the person of Jesus. He is the one "who is to come," that is, the Messiah. In healing the sick, raising the dead, and in proclaiming the gospel, he fulfills the messianic expectations (Matthew 11:5; see the present work, Vol. 2, pp. 177–182). Of the audience present it is true: "Blessed are you poor! For yours is the kingdom of God!" (Luke 6:20). It has pleased the Father "to give the kingdom to the little flock," the community of disciples (Luke 12:32). The kingdom, already present, is resisted: "The kingdom of God suffers violence" (Matthew 11:12f.). So it is correct: "The kingdom of God is in your midst" (Luke 17:21; see below, § 16, 3, a). The decision which his hearers now make in respect to the person of Jesus decides the destiny of his hearers in the eschatological decision (Matthew 7:24-27; 10:32).

The seed that grows of itself (Mark 4:26-29), the mustard seed (Mark 4:30-32), and the leavened dough (Matthew 13:33) are parables that treat of the kingdom of God. They describe the contrast between the hidden littleness of the beginning and the hugeness of the end, which is entirely God's work. Just as fruits come from the earth, the kingdom comes "of itself," without the intervention of man.

The kingdom is God's gift. It is given to the poor who have nothing (Matthew 5:3). Children, therefore, enter into the kingdom (Mark 10:15). There is no talk of childlike innocence which may gain heaven. By children are meant those who know that they can only have things bestowed upon them by adult superiority (see the present work, Vol.

3, pp. 320–322). Because the kingdom is never earned but always bestowed, sinners, prostitutes, and tax collectors enter the kingdom ahead of the righteous (Matthew 21:31). As inheritance (Matthew 25:34), it is always a free bestowal, just as inheritance is always an unearned gift.

The hearers of the message, nevertheless, are called upon to exert themselves for the kingdom of God, in order finally to enter into it. Man comes upon the kingdom like a plowman who uncovers a treasure in a field and sells everything he has in order to buy the field (Matthew 13:44). Or he is like a merchant who finds a precious pearl and sacrifices everything else to acquire it (Matthew 13:45f.).

To find the kingdom is an overpowering joy. What is crucial is that man perceive the preciousness of the kingdom. Then he can surrender everything else for it. For entry into the kingdom, it is always necessary that there be a conversion, as a turning from the world to God (Mark 1:15). Moral endeavor is required: "the keeping of God's commands (Matthew 19:17), the doing of God's will (Matthew 7:21). A new basis of righteousness is required. "If your righteousness is no more than that of the scribes and Pharisees, you will not enter into the kingdom of heaven" (Matthew 5:20). A radical renunciation of everything that can lead a man to evil, whether hand or foot or eye (Matthew 18:8f.) is demanded. The goods and values of the world can be a hindrance to entry into God's kingdom. "With what difficulty will the rich enter into the kingdom of God!" (Mark 10:23).

It is applicable to many, this hard saying that although they do indeed seek to enter, they are unable to do so (Luke 13:24). The kingdom is always bestowed; and yet, entry into the kingdom is tied to the fulfillment of the requirements of moral endeavor. The basic reason is obvious: since God is the Holy One, in his kingdom there can be no sin (see the present work, Vol. 3, pp. 42f.).

In the message of Jesus, any detailed portrayal of the kingdom, such as is attempted in Jewish apocalyptics, is absent. What, then, is the kingly dominion of God? In the promise of Jesus the kingdom is cleansed of all national and material elements. The kingdom is frequently compared to a banquet. This belongs to the body of rabbinic themes (see Strack and Billerbeck, *op. cit.*, Vol. 1, pp. 878f.); but in either instance it is clearly to be understood figuratively. The imagery signifies communion with God and in that, communion with the saints. Insofar as in the Lord's Prayer the individual petitions interpret the chief petition about the arrival of the kingdom, the kingdom of God entails sanctification of the divine Name, fulfillment of God's will, forgiveness of guilt and deliverance from evil (Matthew 6:9-13). These petitions are to be fulfilled now in time, and finally and totally in the eschatological reality of the kingdom.

The concept of the kingdom receives a certain content from parallel concepts. It is acceptance into the Father's house (Luke 15:18-20), entry into joy (Matthew 25:21, 23), participation in light (Luke 16:8) and in majesty (Mark 10:37), entry into life (Mark 9:43-47), inheriting of life (Mark 10:17). But in the final analysis, the kingdom of God is expected as a new creation (see below, § 20). This is entirely God's work, above all human creation and expectation. The future kingdom, therefore, cannot be described.

Along with the parousia (§ 16 below), in the New Testament the kingdom of God is expected with mounting hope as very near. First of all, in three sayings of the Lord Jesus, and, with him, the community speaks of proximate expectation: Mark 13:30 with its parallels, Mark 9:1 with its parallels, and Matthew 10:23. (And to these may be added other hints in sayings of the Lord).

The saying in Mark 13:30 reads: "Truly, I tell you, this generation will not pass away until all this takes place." In its context it says that the destruction of the Temple and the end of the world will come about within Jesus' generation. But is Mark 13:32 uncertain of proximate expectation when it states that no one knows the day and the hour (see below, § 14, 1)?

In contrast to Mark 13:30, the expectation seems to be somewhat softened in Mark 9:1: "Truly I tell you that some of those standing here will not taste death until they see the kingdom of God coming in power." It is no longer stated that the kingdom will be manifest before the generation as a whole, but before some. Has the community already suffered numerous deaths? Was it preparing for a further postponement of the arrival of the kingdom? What is meant by a revelation "in power ($\dot{\epsilon}\nu$ $\delta\upsilon\nu\acute{\alpha}\mu\epsilon\iota$)"? Attempts to interpret it against the transfiguration of Jesus, which took place six days later (Mark 9:2), or against the destruction of Jerusalem do not seem to be possible.

In the Gospels, the miracles of Jesus are termed "deeds of power" (δυνάμεις = Matthew 11:20; Mark 6:2; Luke 4:36). According to Luke 11:20, the kingdom of God is present in the wonders done by Jesus. Can it be understood, then, that some will experience the full revelation of the power of the Messiah and in it the kingdom of God? The other Gospels tried to clarify Mark 9:1. In this way Matthew 16:28 understands it as a statement in reference to the parousia: "Some of those standing here will not taste death until they see the Son of Man coming in his kingdom." And even otherwise in Luke 9:27: "Some of those standing here will not taste death until they see the kingdom of God."

Since even Luke 11:20 sees the kingdom of God coming in the miraculous deeds of Jesus, the saying in 9:27 can, in this formulation, be understood of the full revelation of Christ, "who was a Prophet, mighty in deed and word" (Luke 24:19), and further, of the revelation of God in the Church, in which Luke has seen "signs and great deeds of power" (Acts 8:13) take place. Matthew and Luke give the saying of the Lord its own peculiar form. Is it contained in Mark in all its originality? To what extent has the original sense of the Lord's statement been fixed?

Also difficult to explain is the saying of Jesus to his disciples when he sent them forth: "If they persecute you in one city, flee to another. Truly, I tell you, you will not come to the end of the cities of Israel before the Son of Man comes" (Matthew 10:23).[209] A radically apocalyptic understanding explains that Jesus meant that before the disciples returned, the parousia would begin and he would himself be manifested as the Son of Man. After the disillusionment of this expectation, Jesus hastened to go to Jerusalem, so that — even in the extreme case, by his death — he might bring about the arrival of his kingdom there.

Could Matthew have so understood the saying? The Evangelist would have known that the saying had not been fulfilled in that way. Would he have reported it anyway? His Gospel closes with the missionary mandate, which looks out upon a long further history (Matthew 28:19f.). According to Matthew (16:21; 17:22), the Son of Man always did have to undergo the Passion. If the aforesaid radical eschatological explanation of Matthew 10:23 had come true, then the way of Jesus would have been described otherwise.

Perhaps Matthew 10:23 is to be explained as a later reflection on the failure of the Church's mission to the Jews and as a mysterious announcement of Israel's disbelief (Matthew 23:38f.). Is the saying in Matthew 10:23 a word of comfort to the Church and her missionaries? If it seems that they are without protection and that there is no way out of their distress, the Son of Man will be with them. Perhaps we must resign ourselves to the fact that the original sense of the Lord's saying in Matthew 10:23 remains obscure. Insofar as the saying indicates that there has already been some mission experience, it will allow itself to be acknowledged as a later formulation.

Exegesis expends itself over the clarification of the actual situation. The community of Jesus' disciples expected the kingdom of God as near, and it based its belief on the word of the Lord. Since the originality and precise wording of the adduced apocalyptic sayings of the Lord seem uncertain, or, at least, their meaning seems uncertain, exegesis accepts in part that the community of disciples, having sayings which had originally admonished them to be aware of the nearness of judgment, at some point in time intensified these sayings. The times fixed in Mark 9:1 and 13:30 are later constructions of the community. Acute eschatological expectation would have penetrated Jesus' community from its own milieu (see above, § 13, 2). The sayings handed down, however, probably permit it to be said that Jesus proclaimed the urgent nearness of the kingdom of God. He shared the views of his time and environment. In this too, and precisely in this, he was the Son in whom the Father revealed himself.

In this connection, it would be well to bear in mind that for Jesus the announcement of the day and the hour of the arrival of God's kingdom was of no essential importance. According to his message, the kingdom of God was already projected into the present. Any temporal distance to the kingdom of God and the difference between the here-and-now and the not-yet is thereby suspended. Jesus proclaims the ever-enduring nearness of God's approach to men in judgment and grace. Proximate expectation is to be understood not as temporal but personal.[210]

c) Gospel of John

Outside the synoptic Gospels, the expression "kingdom of heaven," peculiar to Matthew, is never found; and the expression "kingdom of

God" is relatively rare in its occurrence. In the Gospel of John, the term is found in the conversation of Jesus with Nicodemus: "If a man is not reborn, he cannot see the kingdom of God" (John 3:3, 5).[211] Israel's questioning is in the direction of eschatological salvation. The statement of Jesus makes the latter synonymous with the kingdom of God. It is an eschatological gift. In this instance, with the formula "kingdom of God," John's Gospel is using traditional language.

d) Acts of the Apostles

In the Acts of the Apostles, the terminology of the kingdom of God is occasionally encountered (Acts 1:3; 8:12; 14:22; 19:8; 20:25; 28:23). It always means the future kingdom. Jesus, between his resurrection and his ascension into heaven, speaks of the kingdom of God (Acts 1:3). The apostles preach: "It is through many hardships that we must enter the kingdom of God" (14:22). No longer is the arrival of the kingdom awaited, but we hope to enter into it. That the kingdom begins in Christ may be hinted at in 8:12: "But when they believed Philip, who proclaimed to them the gospel of the kingdom of God and of the name of Jesus, they had themselves baptized."

e) Paul

In the collection of Paul's Epistles, the expression "kingdom of God" occurs ten times, and this for the most part in the older and "authentic" Epistles. Unquestionably Paul used the term in his preaching. Like the Synoptics, he employed the prospect of the future kingdom as an admonition to prepare oneself for this kingdom and to live in such a way as to be worthy of it. Five times the formula is repeated, that the Christian is to "inherit the kingdom of God" (1 Cor. 6:9f.; 15:50; Gal. 5:21; Eph. 5:5). The kingdom, therefore, is of the future, and, like every inheritance, is an unmerited gift. The conditions for admission are formulated in a negative way, in which vices are specified which will prevent entry into the kingdom; thus, in 1 Cor. 6:9, "the unjust will have no part in the kingdom of God"; and similarly in Gal. 5:21 and Eph. 5:5.

In regard to the summons to the kingdom, Paul issues a reminder: "We admonish you to conduct your affairs as worthy of God, who called you to his kingdom and to his glory" (1 Thess. 2:12). The summons to the kingdom beyond is likewise a commitment and a pledge of salvation. Entry into the kingdom takes place with the resurrection, "But flesh and blood cannot inherit the kingdom of God nor corruption incorruption" (1 Cor. 15:50). Earthly-human existence must be changed in order to enter into the kingdom, for the kingdom is eschatological-beyond.

In other places it is stated that the kingdom is a reality active in the present. Speaking against such persons as are "puffed up with words," Paul says: "The kingdom of God consists not in speech but in power" (1 Cor. 4:20). Thus the kingdom is described as it must even now be exhibited in the community and in the apostolate. Since in Rome party divisions had arisen over the eating and the not eating of certain foods, Paul explains: "The kingdom of God is not food and drink, but justice, peace, and joy in the Holy Spirit" (Rom. 14:17). Eating or fasting are things of like worth so far as the dominion of God is concerned. That dominion makes itself known and becomes a reality in human and social experience.

Justice, peace, and joy are not simply virtues which are to be won through human efforts; rather, they are eschatological gifts. That is indicated by the appended phrase "in the Holy Spirit," whether it is to be referred to the whole Trinity or to the Third Person alone. Justice or righteousness is, for Paul, the justification bestowed upon faith. Peace is reconciliation with God, who gives it. And more, these gifts are also the pledge of their realization. "Whoever serves Christ in this way is pleasing to God and approved among men" (Rom. 14:18). Peace makes for joy and mutual edification (Rom. 14:19). The kingdom of God has social importance in this time and in the present world.

If Paul intensifies the human aspects of the kingdom, this is but reminiscent of the similar understanding in later Judaism (see above, § 13, 2).

f) Deutero-Pauline Epistles

In the Deutero-Pauline writings, the concept of the kingdom is accentuated very differently. The kingdom is a conversion between here and the beyond, created by God. Through "the just judgment of God" Christians "become worthy of the kingdom of God for which they suffer now" (2 Thess. 1:5).[212] The kingdom is Christ's kingdom beyond. "God has rescued us from the power of darkness and transferred us into the kingdom of his beloved Son" (Col. 1:13). The kingdom belongs to God, insofar as he summons to it and transfers to it. But it is the dominion of Christ, insofar as salvation is mediated through him. This kingdom of Christ is already established and will endure forever. The eschatological reservation of Paul seems, as so often in the Deutero-Paulines, to have been overlooked in Col. 1:13.

The kingdom is the kingdom of Christ, when the Apostle hopes that the Christ will save him "in his heavenly kingdom" (2 Tim. 4:18; similar in 2 Tim. 4:1; 2 Peter 1:11). Here we have reached the later and modern understanding and manner of expression that the Christian will "go to heaven."

The kingdom of God is at last in the later writings of the New Testament no longer so important a concept as it is in the synoptic Gospels. Other terms and concepts make their appearance. With the concept of the Church the kingdom of God is exhibited as already present. The future consummation is specified with new terms: life, salvation, justification (righteousness), grace, glory. In this way terms and values are named which, in the Synoptics, had already been bound up with the kingdom of God (see above, § 13, 3, b). This metamorphosis of conceptuality, and the basis thereof, is visible in the passage of the gospel from Israel to the Greek world, to which the concept of the kingdom of God was foreign.

g) Kingdom of Christ

With the development of Christology, the kingdom of God is understood and proclaimed as the kingdom of Christ. In the history of the Passion, Jesus receives the title King first of all from the mouth of the enemy. But he accepts it and dies as King of Israel (Mark 15:26; see the present work, Vol. 2, p. 90). As David's son, he is the new King David (present work, Vol. 2, pp. 139–141; 159–161). Since any preaching from the basis of the resurrection has to attest that he, as the exalted One, is Lord of the Church and of the world, it must also proclaim that the kingdom of God has its Head in Christ.

This expression penetrates the gospel already when Mark 9:1 speaks of the kingdom of God, but Matthew 16:28 speaks of "the Son of Man in his kingdom." The (later) significance of the parable of the weeds in the field of wheat states similarly: "The Son of Man will send out his angels, and they will gather out of his kingdom all the scandals" (Matthew 13:41). In the preaching of the apostles, the kingdom of God is the kingdom of Christ. This identification is hinted at when the "Gospel" of Philip is designated as the message "of the kingdom of God and of the name of Jesus Christ" (Acts 8:12). The identification is firm when "God transfers (us) into the kingdom of his beloved Son" (Col. 1:13). Now one can speak of the "kingdom of Christ and of God" (Eph. 5:5). From heaven itself it is announced: "The world has really become the kingdom of our Lord and of his Christ" (Apoc. 11:15). Christ receives the saved "into his heavenly kingdom" (2 Tim. 4:18; likewise in 2 Tim. 4:1; 2 Peter 1:11). In the fullness of time Christ gives back to the Father the dominion received from him (1 Cor. 15:25-28). The kingdom of Christ unfolds into the kingdom of God (Apoc. 5:10; 20:4, 6; 22:5).

h) Kingdom of God and the Church

What relationship has the dominion and kingdom of God to the Church of the present time? In the Lord's Prayer, the community of disciples is admonished to pray always: "Thy kingdom come!" (Matthew 6:10). A Church that can pray thus is not already God's kingdom. What is prayed for, rather, is something that is much more of the beyond and of the future, which will first be manifested in the end-time. The kingdom of God, nevertheless, is proclaimed in the Church. It is in the Church that the heavenly kingdom is opened and closed (Matthew 16:19; 18:18). The community of disciples is promised the inheritance of the kingdom: "Fear not, you little flock! It has pleased your Father to give you the kingdom" (Luke 12:32). Toeing the mark to the kingdom is the little community's protection in the world.

Membership in the community, nevertheless, is no guarantee of eventual acceptance into the kingdom. Between the Church in the present and the kingdom in the future stands the decision of God, which he will one day make in the judgment. This is declared in the parable of the net cast into the sea (Matthew 13:47-50) and in the parable of the weeds among the wheat (Matthew 13:24-30, 36-43).

It seems to be a great temptation to the Church to regard herself and to preach herself as the dominion and kingdom of God on earth.

4. In the History of the Church and of Theology

After the New Testament, a pressing expectation of the kingdom of God shows itself broadly in the Church. The *Didache* (10, 5f.; Jurgens, no. 7) expresses its hope for a homecoming into the kingdom: "Remember, O Lord, your Church. Deliver her from every evil and perfect her in your love. Gather her from the four winds, sanctified for your kingdom, which you have prepared for her. For yours is the power and the glory forever. Let grace come, and let this world pass away."

St. Ignatius (*Letter to the Ephesians* 11:1) says in all certainty: "The final times are here." The expectation of an imminent consummation lives on in the fanaticism of Montanism.

Marcion, according to Tertullian (*Against Marcion* 4, 33), made the formulation: "In the gospel, Christ himself is the kingdom of God." Accordingly, Origen says (*Commentaries on Matthew* 14, 7, on Matthew 18:23) that Christ is "the kingdom itself (the αὐτοβασιλεία) of God." Christ is the reigning King over the spirit of him who is no longer ruled by sin, which rules in the mortal body of those who have subjected themselves to it. The heavenly kingdom of Christ is present where righteousness, wisdom, truth, and the other virtues of heaven are realized in a man, since it is thus that a man bears the image of the heavenly (according to 1 Cor. 15:49). Prayer for the kingdom of God is a petitioning of wisdom and knowledge (Origen, *On Prayer* 13). The kingdom, therefore, is an interior, internal, pneumatic dimension. Any eschatological stretch of it is scarcely anymore to be seen. In Augustine's view, the Church is the historical form of the thousand-year kingdom. It will be consummated with the whole of mankind in the "City of God."

The political theology of first the Constantinian and then the Byzantine Empire understands and proclaims the imperial reign of peace as the image and presence of God's kingdom. The monarchy of the emperor represents the monarchy of God. Apocalyptic expectation is no longer either object or goal. The beautiful Bibles presented by the imperial munificence to the great churches did not contain the Apocalypse of John. In a similar manner in the West, Charlemagne understood his dominion as participation in the kingship of God and of Christ.

In the Late Middle Ages, the apocalyptic expectation of the kingdom came alive again in the revolutionary criticism of State and Church by the Spirituals, and with special vigor in the instance of Joachim of Flora. Apocalyptic hopes spurred on the followers of John Hus, as well as those of Thomas Münzer and the Baptist movement, which, however, were quickly stifled one and all by the prevailing views.

Martin Luther taught the second kingdom, the secular empire of the law and the spiritual rule of God, which is constituted in the gospel and justification. Melanchthon equated God's kingdom and the true Church. For Calvin, the kingdom of God was realized through a theocracy in Church and State.

In philosophico-theological schemata of modern times, the kingdom of God is understood as the realm of the Spirit and of morality.[213] In the system of Immanuel Kant, approach to the kingdom of God is achieved in a mankind religiously and morally perfected according to the ideal of Christ. Indeed, in her history the Church is more a reversal than a realization of the kingdom of God. As a human work, the kingdom of God is an ever present reality in the world and in time; but it is not the eschatological work of God. A future movement is accordingly reserved, as the consummation has not yet come and must constantly be striven for, but which is also to be effected by God. Kant's understanding had broad and deep aftereffects, especially in Protestant theology.

For Hegel, the kingdom of the divine Spirit is realized in history. Eschatological world judgment has a total convergence with history. "May the kingdom come and our hands be not idle" (Hegel to Schelling).

The idea of the kingdom of God has been secularized in the theoretical utopian states of Marxism and socialism.[214] As in biblical eschatology, the dimension of the future is of essential importance. This, however, comes not from a divine largesse, but is man's own achievement.

The Kantian concept of the kingdom of God has had its effect also on Catholic theology, as witnessed by the "Tübingen Catholic School."[215] According to J. S. Drey, the kingdom of God is "the central idea of Christianity." The kingdom of God has appeared in Christ as a reality and, under grace, will perfect history. J. B. von Hirscher outlined Christian morality as the "doctrine of the realization of the divine kingdom in humanity." He sought thereby to unite the biblical doctrine of the kingdom of God with the "realm of truth, goodness, the sublime, the beautiful, and blessedness" (*Moral*, Vol. 1, 5th ed., Tübingen 1851, pp. 101–103).

Contrary to this development, exegetic biblical theology, especially in the thought of J. Weiss and A. Schweitzer,[216] brought the rigidly eschatological character of the kingdom of God again to validity. The kingdom of God comes, not as human achievement and virtue, but as an action of God. Karl Barth drafted his dogmatics as a doctrine of the kingdom of God which unites biblical and systematic conceptions. "A Christianity that is not totally and absolutely eschatology has totally and absolutely nothing to do with Christ" (K. Barth, *Der Römerbrief*, 2nd ed., Zürich-Zollikon 1921, p. 298).

A work of significance to the renewal of biblical eschatology is Jürgen Moltmann's *Theologie der Hoffnung* (8th ed., Munich 1969 [an earlier edition was translated under the title *Theology of Hope*, New York 1967]). "God is essentially not just the God over us or in us, but the God before us."

In the visions of the future of Teilhard de Chardin, "God Forward" operates in the onward marching world process. The world flows onward to the omega point (drawn from Apoc. 1:8) as to an eschatological conclusion (see the present work, Vol. 3, pp. 97–113).

The concept of the dominion and kingdom of God, which is of fundamental importance to the New Testament, is of relatively little significance in modern systematic Catholic theology. Dogmatics employs the concept, perhaps, in the theology of the Church, inasmuch as the Church is conceived as present realization of the kingdom of God, which, however is possible only with some reservation (see above,

§ 13, 3, h). Or "heavenly kingdom" describes the eternal blessedness of the righteous, which does not answer to the original biblical significance of the term. In moral theology there may be talk of "the building up of God's kingdom" in the Church and in the world. The kingdom of God, however, does not depend on man's enactments; rather, it is God's promised eschatological work.

§ 14. ENDTIME

1. Threats against the Temple

The New Testament characterizes the time leading up to the end as crammed full of apocalyptic miseries.[217] Detailed portrayals are given in discourses placed in the mouth of Jesus in Mark 13:1-37 (= Matthew 24:1-36; Luke 21:5-36).[218] The descriptions are supplemented by texts in the late apostolic Epistles and the Apocalypse of John. The themes, and first of all in the synoptic texts, are to be isolated and discussed according to their origin and history. Also, one must examine the composite import of the discourses of Jesus. To this end Mark will be taken as the basis for the common synoptic texts. According to the preponderant view, exegesis considers, in respect to Mark 13, that this chapter, and, indeed, the whole of Mark's Gospel, apart from possible later addenda, was written under the threatening imminence of the Jewish-Roman war, but before the destruction of Jerusalem and the Temple in the year 70 A.D.[219]

The predictions of Mark 13 do not correspond precisely to the actual events. The Temple was not destroyed by razing, as seems to be presupposed by Mark 13:2; rather, it was demolished by burning. The profanation of the Temple did not take place, as would seem to have been announced mysteriously in Mark 13:14 (see below). The possibility of a flight in winter (Mark 13:18) is still left open. The destruction of the Temple and the afflictions in Jerusalem on the one hand, and the cosmic catastrophe proceding the parousia on the other hand, are not yet temporally separated from each other in Mark 13:24, as they are in Matthew 24:29 and Luke 21:25. The historicity of the threats uttered against the Temple can be established (see below). The announcements and predictions in Mark 13 cannot be explained simply as fictitious prophecies after the course of events.

With the threat against the Temple in Mark 13:2, Jesus contributes to a prophetic criticism of worship. The Gospels tell repeatedly, as also with this admonitory warning, of Jesus' criticism of the Temple and of worship. The city and the Temple will one day be desolate and abandoned (Matthew 23:38). Jesus is more than the Temple, which will come to an end (Matthew 12:6). The conflict is displayed historically in the narrative of Jesus' purifying of the Temple (Mark 11:15-18).

Taking offense at the commercialization that attended worship, the prophets criticized the same and threatened that worship and Temple would come to an end. As at Shiloh, where earlier the name of God dwelt and which was now abandoned, so too would it be with Jerusalem. "With this house which is called after my name, and on which you set your hopes, and with the place which I have given to you and to your fathers, I will do as I did to Shiloh" (Jer. 7:14). "Because of you Zion shall be ploughed as a field and Jerusalem shall be as a pile of stones and the mountain of the Temple a highland forest" (Micah 3:12). Other threats are found in Jer. 26:6, 18.[220]

From the time of Ezekiel (40–44), the fall of the Temple was transfigured by the expectation of the new and heavenly temple, which was afterwards taken up and preserved in Apoc. 7:15 and 21:22. Jesus' saying about the Temple in Mark 14:58 will also have been originally in this latter frame of reference.

The uttering of threats against the Temple is continued even in the apocalyptic writings. *Ethiopic Henoch* 90:28 foresees the discontinuance and destruction of the old Temple. Josephus (*Jewish War* 6, 5, 3) knows of such threats, as also do the rabbis (H. Strack and P. Billerbeck, *op. cit.*, Vol. 1, pp. 1045f.). The Qumran community is of the conviction that in Jerusalem an unholy priesthood performs an unholy service (1 QS 5:10-19; 1 QpHab 9:4-11; *Damascus Document* 6:12-18). The community keeps its distance from the Temple in Jerusalem and expects a new sanctuary (1 QM 2:4f.). It will not be a temple of stone, but will constitute a new community (1 QS 9:6).[221]

Jesus' threat uttered against the Temple appears also as an accusation against him in his trial in Mark 14:58: "We heard how he said: 'I will destroy this Temple built with hands and in three days build another not built with hands.'" His enemies recall it to jeer at the Crucified (Mark 15:29). John 2:19 mentions the saying in explanation of Jesus' purifying of the Temple. This multiple tradition is an indication of its historicity. The community preserved the saying and waited for its fulfillment, watching for the threatened fall of the Temple. The statement was, for the Jews, a blasphemy against God's sanctuary, and withal a burdensome thing to the Christian community. While in Mark 14:58 Jesus says that he will destroy the Temple, in Matthew 26:61 the saying has come to the point that it says he could do this, but not that he will. In John 2:19 the saying has been allegorized. Luke omits it. It was not possible to deny the saying; one could only attempt to dull it.

Which form of the saying is original, Mark 13:2 or 14:58? The latter form seems to be developed further, with its contrast of "made with hands" and "not made with hands" (similar in Acts 7:48 and 17:24). The time period of the three days (Mark 14:58) is probably indicative of the Easter experience.

2. SYNOPTICS

In Mark 13:1-3, the discourse of Jesus is prefaced with a statement of place and time. According thereto, Jesus voiced his threat against the Temple when he was leaving the Temple for the last time, after a final visit there two days before his death. On the next day he celebrated the Passover meal with his disciples, after which he was seized by the arresting officers.

In Luke 21:5-7 the whole matter is portrayed otherwise. The Evangelist omits the beginning of the discourse with the threat against the Temple. Indeed, he seems to locate the whole apocalyptic discourse in the Temple itself or in the forecourt of the Temple (21:37-38).[222]

Often the Evangelists shape the circumstances of Jesus' discourse with great freedom. Are the time and place of Jesus' discourse depicted thus by Mark also in this instance? That Jesus expressed the threat against the Temple at the very hour when he was leaving the Temple for ever (although the latter fact was something not yet known) is highly significant. It is also historical? The significance of this dating of the event may pertain to the Evangelist. Is its allocation to place also the work of the Evangelist? Jesus sits on the Mount of Olives, opposite the mighty Temple, when he voices his threat (Mark 13:3). Perhaps there is an influence here of Zech. 14:2-4, "The city of Jerusalem shall be taken, its houses shall be plundered. . . . Half its population shall be driven away. . . . Then shall Yahweh go forth against those nations. . . . On that day his feet shall stand on the Mount of Olives, which lies opposite Jerusalem toward the east."

a) Mark 13

In Mark 13:5-27, apocalyptic events are introduced in their broad and cosmic course. There will be war (13:7), earthquakes and famine (13:8), martyrdom (bearing witness) even to death (13:9-13), flight of the distressed inhabitants (13:14), shaking of the heavens, darkening of the sun, falling of the stars (13:24), and finally the arrival of the Son of Man (13:26).

This is also the apocalyptic sequence of Apoc. 6:1-16. Three terrible riders go forth; they bring war, famine, and death (6:4-8). To this passage too belong mortal martyrdoms (6:9-11), earthquakes, darkening of the sun, falling of the stars (6:12-14), and the flight of men (6:15-16). Is the first rider, the victor on the white horse, Christ the King (as in Apoc. 19:11)?

The themes in Mark 13 are the same as in Apoc. 6, and they are quite similarly arranged. What we have running through both places is a schema of apocalyptic notions. It would be a mistake to try to lay out, in accordance therewith, an apocalyptic calendar of events and days.

Mark 13:5-13 depicts the community oppressed in its surroundings and in the world. In 13:7f. there are apocalyptic events: wars between nations, famine, and earthquakes. Such apocalyptic signs are frequently mentioned in Old Testament and later representation; thus wars in Is. 13:2-5; 19:2; *4 Esdras* 11 [13]:30f.; famine in Is. 8:21; 14:30; war, famine, and plague in Is. 21:7; Jer. 14:12; Jer. 14:12; Ezek. 5:12; 1 Kings 8:37; *Ethiopic Henoch* 102:2. In the Qumran writings, the endtime is depicted as a "war of the sons of light with the sons of darkness" (1 QM 1–11). Other themes pertain to the history of the Christian community and mission. The warning against being led astray by false prophets in the community is heard also in Apoc. 12:9; 13:3-10; Acts 20 29f.; 2 Thess. 2:3f.; 1 John 2:26; 3:7.[223]

The community of disciples must, according to Mark 13:9-13; prove itself in *martyrium* before Jews and pagans. The experiences of the community of disciples as well as of the mission seem to be already presupposed.[224] The report of the disciples in the missions is similarly described in Matthew 10:17-22; so too, Acts 5:17-41. The Spirit himself attests to the martyrs, as in Mark 13:11, so too in Luke 12:11f.; Acts 4:8; Phil. 1:19. In Mark 13:13, the community of disciples is hated in the world because of the name of Jesus, as in John 15:18 and 1 Peter 4:14. This manifestly presupposes a later period.

In Mark 13:14-20, the distress in Judea is described. The verses repeat in reference to Judea a tradition of Jewish apocalyptics, in distinction to Mark 13:8-10, where the discourse is about the nations, and Mark 13:24-27, about the world. Mark 13:14-20 is not to be regarded as temporally arranged between the other traditional accounts.

The passage is introduced with the enigmatic challenge: "Let him who reads take note" (Mark 13:14). To what writing, which he is to read with understanding, is the reader and listener referred? The Evangelist cannot mean that it is his own book which is to be read attentively. Still less can he be so clumsy as to put a reference to the written Gospel in the mouth of Jesus. Is it a marginal note of a reader, written in at that place, which was at a later time incorporated into the text? In Mark 13:14, the "abomination of desolation" is a quote from Dan. 9:27. Does it mean that in reading the Book of Daniel it is to be remembered that the saying is again validated? In Dan. 9:27, 11:31, and 12:11, "abomination of desolation" means the desecration of the Temple by Antiochus IV, who, according to 1 Macc. 1:54 and 2 Macc. 6:2, had an altar with the image of Zeus erected in the Temple. A similar desecration of the Temple was feared in the year 40 A.D., when an image of the divine emperor Caligula was about to be set up in the Temple by the Romans, an undertaking that was abandoned, however, when the emperor was assassinated.

In exegesis, the conjecture has long since been made that the note

"Let him who reads" refers to a short apocalypse or apocalyptic pamphlet which Mark had before him. It would perhaps have been written close to 40 A.D., when the desecration of the Temple by Caligula was threatening. Its intent was to warn the Jews, in the face of the expected disorders, to flee to the mountains (13:14). A new edition of the pamphlet may have been circulated during the Jewish-Roman war of the year 70 A.D.[225] It would have invited the Jewish Christians to take flight now, when it announced that the enemy of God (the Antichrist) would take possession of the Temple and from there direct the struggle against God and the community. In 2 Thess. 2:3f., the Antichrist is expected: "The son of perdition, the opponent . . . , is seated in the Temple of God and gives it out that he is God." If this were meant, the destruction of the Temple in the year 70 A.D., in view of this prophesying and expectation, would not yet have taken place.

The inhabitants of Judea are not to flee, perchance, to the fortified capital city of Jerusalem but to the mountains. The admonition follows the history of the Maccabean wars in accord with 1 Macc. 2:28 and 2 Macc. 5:27.

In depicting the distress of the poor and helpless, Mark 13:15-18 has no parallel in Jewish apocalyptics. "That the central focus is not on the desecration of the Temple but on the bitter misery of the weak and of mothers can scarcely be understood apart from the influence of Jesus."[226] As an apocalyptic theme, however, the declaration is probably to be understood as meaning that this distress will be the greatest the world has ever known (13:19). Dan 12:1 says likewise of the end-time: "It will be a time of such distress as there never was from the time that nations began until that time"; similarly in 1 QM 1:11f.: "There never yet was such affliction from the outset until the consummation of eternal redemption."

God has determined the time of affliction in his schedule of times. But he has shortened the duration of that time for the sake of the righteous and the elect (Mark 13:20). This schedule of God is mentioned also in Wis. 8:8 and in *4 Esdras* 2 [4]:36-39. For the sake of the pious, the era of godlessness will be shortened (*Apocalypse of Abraham* 29:13).

False messiahs and lying prophets will make their appearance and attempt to lead astray with their assertions and dictates (Mark 13:21f.).

The Acts of the Apostles (5:36; 21:38) tells of the appearance of false messiahs, as does profane history (Josephus, *Antiquities of the Jews* 18, 1, 1; 5, 5). The Christian community expects a teacher of error in the final age (Acts 20:29f.; Jude 4; 2 Peter 3:3f.). The great seducer is designated Antichrist (1 John 2:18f.). That false prophets identify themselves through signs and wonders is known already to Exod. 7:11f. and Deut. 13:2-4.

The apocalyptic statements and themes transmitted by tradition are referred comprehensively in Mark 13:23 to Christ and the community of disciples. "But be on your guard! I have told you all things beforehand." The word of Christ explains to the Church her ever-present actuality. The eschatological events reach their goal and terminus in the appearance of the Son of Man (Mark 13:24-27). Cosmic upheavals will precede that appearance. The sun and moon will be darkened. The stars fixed on the firmament will plummet to earth. "The Powers in the heavens will be shaken." Probably these are spirit powers who dispose the heavenly bodies. At the approach of the Son of Man the latter will slip into tumult and abandon their set paths.[227] The Son of Man will step forth from the tumbled cosmic powers.

In other apocalyptic literature, too, such catastrophes herald the day of judgment. Earthquakes, darkening of sun and moon, and plummeting of stars are adduced in Is. 13:10; 34:4; Joel 2:10; 3:15; *Ethiopic Henoch* 80:4-7; 1 QH 3:13-17, 27-34. Similar themes are encountered in Apoc. 6:12-14. For rabbinic references, see H. Strack and P. Billerbeck, *op. cit.*, Vol. 1, pp. 995f.

Amid the collapse of everything, the Son of Man appears, escorted by the angels (Mark 13:26f.), just as the Son of Man is expected according to Dan. 7:13f. (see the present work, Vol. 2, pp. 189–191). Angels are the assistants of the judgment. The call of the archangels heralds the beginning of the parousia (1 Thess. 4:16). Angels gather men to judgment (Matthew 13:39-41). The Son of Man leads "his elect together from the four winds, from the extremity of the earth to the extremity of the heavens" (Mark 13:27). The gathering of Israel from her dispersal among the nations is expected in the endtime (Deut. 30:4f.; Is. 60:4-9; Micah 4:1-8). In the New Testament, this expectation is fulfilled in part in the gathering in of the Gentiles through the mission of the Church (Rom. 15:16; John 11:52) and in part in the future homecoming in the kingdom of God (Mark 13:27; *Didache* 9:4 [Jurgens, no. 6]).

In Mark 13:27, the elect are seen gathered on the highest mountain in the world. From there they will be enraptured to the pinnacle of heaven, where the Son of Man is enthroned at the right of God. There is nothing in the passage about a universal resurrection of the dead, nothing of a judgment of the world; neither is there anything about a temporal and earthly empire of the Son of Man with his community. With the enrapturing of the elect into heaven the consummation has taken place. Everything else is swallowed up. God, the Son of Man, and the elect are with each other in eternity.

In Mark 13:28-37, a mixed lot of sayings and declarations of Jesus are collected as a kind of appendix of his apocalyptic address. It contains admonitions to the community on the expectation of the parousia (13:28f., 33-37) and revelations as to the time of the parousia (13:30-32). The attached admonitions show that the sense of the whole apocalyptic discourse is that of an admonition to the community.

If the apocalyptic discourse employs Jewish tradition to a great extent, its utilization in exhortation now lies very near to the heart of the gospel and to the Christian community. And even here original sayings of Jesus will be voiced. A parable about a fig tree (Mark 13:28f.) invites recognition of the nearness of the eschatological consummation. The parable stood originally in another context. "When you see these things come to pass, know then that it [the parousia or the Son of Man?] is near." Immediately before (Mark 13:26f.), the consummated parousia was described. Now "these things" will be a sign only that the parousia is near. "These things" probably meant in the original sense the sign-filled works of Jesus in general (as in Luke 11:20).

In Mark 13:30-32 are revelatory statements, characterized as such by the formula: "Truly, I tell you. . . ." The three sayings treat of the time of the parousia. They offer, therefore, an answer to the question posed in 13:4. Such questions on calculations were undertaken in Jewish apocalyptics (see above, § 16, 3, a). In Mark 13:20, a terminus seems to be designated: "This generation will not pass away until all this happens." This declaration is not verified, if by "this generation" is understood what currently constitutes a generation, embracing about thirty years. It will scarcely be possible to avoid giving offense if one understands by the collective "all this" the prior signs of the parousia, especially the destruction of the Temple (13:2) and wars and martyrdoms (13:7-11), but not the parousia itself (13:25-27). "All this," therefore, must undoubtedly be taken in reference to all the preceding; and the parousia too will take place in this generation.

Alternatively, "this generation" is understood of the Jews of that time, or of mankind as the ever wicked generation (Matthew 12:39). This would mean, then, that Israel will remain in existence to the end of the world, or that mankind will be until then ever wicked. This interpretation, however, is hardly convincing. The statement in Mark 13:30 speaks rather of the impending nearness of the consummation, which did not in fact take place so soon. The explanation of the saying must be sought in the context of other similar sayings (Mark 9:1; Matthew 10:23 — see above § 13, 3, b).

Mark 13:30 and 31 are joined externally primarily by the catchword "pass away." The saying in 13:31 is a superlative declaration on the teaching of Christ. Jesus is more than the teacher of Israel (Matthew 12:41). His word remains as the word, revelation, and salvation of God. He has divine power and eternity. The Law will endure until heaven and earth pass away (Matthew 5:18). But the word of Jesus endures even beyond the Law. What is most firm, the world, and what is most fleeting, the word, are juxtaposed to each other. What is most firm will pass away. But this thing most fleet, as the word of Christ, will not pass away. In the context of Mark 13:31, what is said is that the word of Jesus is given to the community until he returns. It can depend on it, confident even amid all the terrors that may come. Does the promise of the parousia need to be strengthened because the community finds it difficult, in the face of the delay in its coming, to hold fast to the faith? (See below, § 16).

The assurance in Mark 13:32 that no one knows the day, not even the angels, not even the Son, but God alone, seems to be a supplementation to 13:30. It remains true that the day of the consummation is near. Nevertheless, the day is not to be computed as a calendar day. It is an ever biblical conviction that decisive days are known to God alone (Zech. 14:7; likewise Acts 1:7). Even the angels who cooperate toward that day have no full knowledge of it (Eph. 3:10; 1 Peter 1:12; *4 Esdras* 2 [4]:52).

The clause that states that even the Son of Man does not know the day has become important to Christological exposition. Christ speaks of himself as the Son, which, in the Synoptics, is rare (Mark 12:6; Matthew 11:27), even if it is common enough in the developed Christology of John's Gospel (see the present work, Vol. 2, pp. 193–203). In the context of Mark's Gospel, the dictum of revelation says that the Church does indeed have the word of Christ (Mark 13:31), but knows no information on the plans of God and cannot attempt to proceed therefrom in making any apocalyptic calculation. The Church cannot, with the help of God's revelation, take possession of God himself. Christ himself directs away from himself to the Father (Mark 10:18; 1 Cor. 15:28).

Following from this is the warning attached in Mark 13:33. The time of the consummation cannot be reckoned. Nevertheless, and for that very reason, this time is approaching man always and directly. Therefore the warning: "Watch ye." This is the posture in which the disciples are ever responsible before the Lord. The present determines the future. Expectation of nearness engenders constant expectation.

The parable of the returning householder in Mark 13:33-37 admonishes watchfulness. Two images are mixed together. The one parable (13:34) treats of a master journeying away from home, leaving behind for his servants for the meantime his instructions, which the servants must carry out in all fidelity. The theme is developed further in the parable of the talents in Matthew 25:14-30 (= Luke 19:11-26). But if in Mark 13:35 it is emphasized that the master returns unexpectedly in the night, it is presupposed that he was away only a short time, perhaps at a dinner party. With this in mind, the mention of the gate-keeper and his service of watching through the night are pregnant with meaning. This is brought out again in the parable in Luke 12:35-48. Here watchfulness is demanded. Both of the themes of Mark 13:33-37 are eschatologically ordered. With the expectation of the parousia, the stressing of fidelity, as in 13:34, must be emphasized more and more.[228]

The apocalyptic address, which instructed primarily some of the disciples (Mark 13:4), finally breaks out in Mark 13:37 into an admonition to all. "But what I say to you, I say to all: 'Be watchful!'" The exalted Lord speaks to the whole community. The discourse ends with a remarkable absence of any local or temporal orientation, and without any connection to the history of the Passion beginning at Mark 14:1. The discourse is directed to the Church, outside any historical context.

Mark 13 is, in this Gospel, the parting address of Jesus to his disciples. It must be viewed in the broader context of its form-critique. The words of a departing person constitute a particular literary genre in biblical, late Jewish, and ancient literature in general. In the Old Testament, examples of this genre are had in the blessing of Jacob in Gen. 47:29–49:33; the address of Moses in Deut. 29 and 30; and that of the seven Maccabean brothers in 2 Macc. 7. Outside the canon of Scripture, the testamentary literature is of this genre (Testament of Abraham, of Moses, of the twelve sons of Jacob). Of more recent discovery at Qumran are "the words of Moses from Mount Nebo" (1 QDM = 1 Q 22). In the New Testament, belonging to this genre are the farewell discourses of Jesus at the Last Supper, especially in Luke 22:15-37 and John 13:31–17:26. Farewell discourses of the apostles are in Acts 20:18-35 and, of an epistolary character, in 2 Timothy and 2 Peter.[229]

Like other extensive discourses of Jesus in the synoptic Gospels, the apocalyptic address in Mark 13 is a composite. The Evangelist had groups of sayings already at hand, which he supplemented and united. The joints are still discernible. The question posed in 13:4 about the destruction of the Temple is not answered in the discourse. In any case, 13:14 is perhaps a mysterious prophecy on the fate of the Temple, which, however, has not been fulfilled in just that way. In 13:27 the parousia is consummated, in 13:29 it is "near, before the door." The themes of the discourse of Mark 13 are found in part also in Jewish apocalyptics,[230] and in part they belong to the theology of Scripture (13:8, 14, 19, 24-27). Elsewhere they provide a view of the experience of the mission (13:9-13). That there are statements of Jesus from his preaching to be found here, and that the whole discourse repeats the sense of Jesus' eschatological preaching is not to be contested. This is certainly the case especially with the hortatory section (13:28-32).

If Mark 13 is designated as apocalypse, the way in which it differs from Jewish apocalyptics must not be overlooked. It lacks the hallmark of Jewish apocalyptics, as found in the Book of Daniel and in the post-canonical apocalypses of Abraham, of Baruch, and of Henoch, in which the history has already taken place up to what is the present time for the author of the book is placed fictitiously under the form of prophecy in the mouth of a holy man of earlier times.

In Mark 13, there is no interest in intrinsic prophecy of future events nor in disclosure about the world beyond. Even the calculations of times, so dear to Jewish apocalyptics, are refused (13:33). The themes of national Jewish expectation are lacking: holy war, exaltation and glorification of Israel in the face of the Gentile nations, the overthrow of Rome, Jewish world domination centered in a new Jerusalem, sensual portrayal of life in the new era. There is no talk of the majesty of the Temple, but only of its downfall. Of essential importance thereto is the appeal to the community. A desire of prophetism, from which apocalyptics arose, is renewed. This desire was the conversion of Israel.

In Mark 13, apocalypse is referred to God and Christ. God is the Lord of history. As the Creator, he remains sympathetic to the world, to its things and events great and small (13:14-20). The center of the apocalypse is Christ (13:9, 13, 23, 26, 37). In him God is manifested for the Church and in the Church. As in him God has shown himself sympathetic to the world, so too he is the sign in which the future brightens.

In the discourse in Mark 13, there is an absence of the important events which are specified in other New Testament eschatologies: resurrection of the dead, judgment of the world, fall of Satan, consummation of the rule and kingdom of God. The Evangelist does not intend to give a dogmatic summation of the "last things," a task of which he was incapable. A calculated systematization is not yet available.

According to Mark 13:30, all these things are to take place in the generation of the hearers of the Gospel. The end of the generation is the end of time and of the world. Within Mark 13, the whole history of the community of disciples, the whole history of the Church, will take place. Her history is a history of eschatological distress. The Church, however, is secure in the plan of God (13:20), firmly based on the word of Jesus (13:31), looking forward in the hope and expectation of soon being gathered home (13:27), in an attitude of watchfulness and fidelity (13:34).

b) Matthew 24

Matthew and Luke accept the apocalyptic discourse from Mark and include it in their respective Gospels. In Matthew 24:3 (as in Luke 21:7), the disciples ask in the same way about the downfall of the Temple, as also about the parousia of Christ and the consummation of the world. These events are still closely bound up with and in each other in Mark 13:4. Matthew and Luke make it clear that they separate the downfall of the Temple and the end of the world, since in the course of history they have had direct experience of this separation.

Mark 13:9-13 appears already in Matthew in the commissioning discourse in 10:17-23. What the community of disciples experiences in the time of Jesus and with him is afterwards already an endtime history. In Matthew 24:9-14, however, a series of sayings similar to Mark 13:9-13 is given once again, probably the peculiar creation of Matthew. These sayings of the Lord speak of the persecution and destiny of the community in the Gentile world (24:9) and in the ecumene (24:14; also 24:30). The horizon has broadened beyond that which Mark knew. The expectation of the end is extended until all of this will be fulfilled. On that account, however, inner conflicts are elucidated and depicted as increasing (24:10-12). Love grows cold in the community (24:12). The preservation of the community is the work of God alone. In spite of this distress and in the midst of it, this gospel must be proclaimed (24:14). It is this gospel that is already proclaimed in the Church (and also already written down?).

The obscure statement in Mark 13:14 about the abomination of desolation standing where it ought not is clarified in Matthew 24:15. The Evangelist refers it back to the prophecy of Dan. 9:27 and 12:11, and designates the Temple as the place of the abomination. Does Matthew 24:15 — "When you see the abomination . . . standing in the holy place" — indicate that the events have already taken place?

Matthew 24:26-28 (= Luke 17:23-25, 28) is taken by the Evangelist from Source Q. The Church of Matthew, accordingly, is endangered

by heretical teachers. The disciples must not let themselves be led
astray to seek for the messianic Son of Man in the desert nor in seclu-
sion — both of which were Jewish expectations. His arrival will be in-
escapably evident. The portrayal of the appearance of the Son of Man
in Matthew 24:30f. is supplemented by other apocalyptic themes (sign
of the Son of Man, lamenting of nations, blasting of trumpets).

Matthew 24:37-42 (= Luke 17:26f., 30, 34f.) describes from Source
Q the unconcern of men at the return of the Son of Man. That return
will indeed produce a change. The disciples, however, expect the Son
of Man and are prepared at any moment. The parable of the watchful
servant in Matthew 24:45-51 is similar to that in Mark 13:33-37. Matthew adds further sayings and parables which admonish watchfulness
and fidelity. He takes them largely from Source Q. There is the saying
about the master of the house who does not allow a thief to enter in
the night season (Matthew 24:42-44 = Luke 12:39f.),[231] the parables
of the wise and faithful servant (Matthew 24:45-51 = Luke 12:42-46),
of the ten virgins (Matthew 25:1-13) and of the master who turned
over to his servants the talents for their usufruct (Matthew 25:14-30 =
Luke 19:12-27).

c) Luke 21:5-36

In a first apocalyptic address (17:22-37; see below, § 16, 3, a), Luke
speaks of the sudden bursting forth of the days of the Son of Man.
The second apocalyptic address (Luke 21:5-36) describes the time preceding the days of the Son of Man. Here Luke follows Mark 13, while
accommodating this prototype to his own later time. It is an unre-
solved question whether Luke may perhaps have used a special source.
While according to Mark 13:3 Jesus delivered his eschatological address on the Mount of Olives, Luke 21:5f. locates it in the Temple or
in the Temple courtyard.

In Luke, the disciples do not ask about the end of the Temple. The
association of the destruction of the Temple and the end of the world
as co-features of the endtime is dissolved. A longer period of time between the two events is already accepted. The assertion that the endtime is at hand is an erroneous teaching against which the community
is warned (Luke 21:8). Wars and uprisings must take place first; and
even then the end will not follow immediately (21:9). Earthquakes,

plague, famine, and terrible things will take place. They are not designated, however, as the beginning of apocalyptic woes (21:11). Before the end, the history of the Church must have a certain extension; and in Luke 21:12-17 it is depicted in accord with the Acts of the Apostles. The community is admonished to perseverance, a thing which may well be needful for a long time (Luke 21:19).

The mysterious prophecy of the abomination of desolation is replaced in Luke 21:20-24 by a portrayal of the end of Jerusalem under the pressure of the events of the Jewish-Roman war. Perhaps use is made of other threatening sayings against Jerusalem. Israel's time is cut off by the times of the Gentiles.

Following Mark 13:24-27 but without any temporal determination, Luke 21:25-28 portrays the cosmic catastrophe. He describes the anxieties of men and, in contrast thereto, the consolation of the community, which is afforded by its expectation of redemption. When Luke 21:32, following Mark 13:30, says that "this generation will not pass away until all these things take place," he may be thinking of the Church or, indeed, of the human race, which is to be saved in spite of the distress of the endtime. Luke 21:34-36 concludes with an admonition to sobriety and watchfulness. "Be on the alert for that time." From expectation of nearness a constant expectation has developed.

3. TIME OF THE APOSTLES AND THE ANTICHRIST

The apocalyptic endtime is given further description in the writings of the apostolic age.[232] The themes of the synoptic apocalypses are repeated and developed further. The postponement of the parousia is frequently emphasized.

The endtime blasphemer of Mark 13:14 is now the "Antichrist."[233] Ancient mythical notions are contained in the expectation of the Antichrist. In primordial times, God's creating conquered inimical figures and powers (Amos 9:3; Pss. 74:13f.; 104:6f.; Job 3:8; 7:12; see the present work, Vol. 1, pp. 6f.). Primordial time is recapitulated in the endtime, when once more the powers inimical to God will be brought into a final combat. Contemporary notions also find entry, since Judaism too expected for the final era an assault led by a political domination inimical to God (*Psalms of Solomon* 17:6-8; *Syriac Apocalypse of Baruch* 39f.; *Ascension of Moses* 8). Accordingly, the preaching even of the Church announced the endtime enemy (2 Thess. 2:3f.; 1 John 2:18).

In 2 Thess. 2:3f., this enemy of God is called "the great blasphemer, the son of perdition, the adversary"; in 1 John 2:18; 4:3; and 2 John 7 he is the "Antichrist." This term is evidently a new Christian construction. In the retinue of the Antichrist are the apocalyptic powers opposed to God: the beast from the sea (Apoc. 13:1) and the beast from the land (Apoc. 13:11), both of whom have their power probably from Satan and are probably incarnations of pagan Rome.

a) Pauline Epistles

Paul awaits the closely approaching endtime as a period of oppressive "distress" (1 Cor. 7:26). Zephaniah (1:15) has already designated Yahweh's judgment day as a "day of affliction and distress." The messianic-eschatological oppression demands an aloofness from earthly relationships and values (1 Cor. 7:29-31). This is especially true of marriage (1 Cor. 7:32; see the present work, Vol. 3, pp. 256f.). With an image employed in the Old Testament (Is. 26:17f.) as well as in the Synoptics (Mark 13:8), Paul designates in Rom. 8:22 the distress of the endtime as labor pains. "All creation groans and is in travail until now." The travail is a cosmic event.

1 Cor. 7:26 speaks of the ἐνεστῶσα ἀνάγκη. In accord with the basic meaning of ἐνεστῶσα as "that which is entering [that which is in-standing]," the distress might be interpreted as being said to be imminent or as already present. But since in 1 Cor. 3:22 and Rom. 8:38 τὰ ἐνεστῶτα means the present, it must be so interpreted also in 1 Cor. 7:26. The endtime has already begun.

b) Late Apostolic Epistles

The persecutions and miseries of the community of disciples are understood in 2 Thess. 1:4-7 as a necessary test in the period preceding the parousia of Christ. They will bring to the oppressors the just God's retaliatory punishments, but to those now oppressed, freedom and glory (Luke 21:28).

2 Thess. 2:1-12 presents a proper apocalypse. The parousia will bring

"union with Christ." But it belongs still to the future. They are heretical teachers who maintain that "the day of the Lord is already here." Proximate expectation is designated straight out as heresy. Prior to the end there must be the appearance of the "great blasphemer, who establishes himself in the temple of God and gives it out that he is God" (Mark 13:14). The blasphemer is already at work. But he is still bound.[234] At the end he will come forth with deceptive wonders and lead many astray.

The last days will be characterized by the appearance of people who have fallen away from the faith and cling to erroneous spirits and demoniacal teachers. "They bear their brand on their consciences" (1 Tim. 1:4f.). The charge about the immorality of the heretical teachers is repeated often. The last days will be difficult. Men full of wickedness will bring about great disorders (2 Tim. 3:1-9). In the late apostolic age the Church's unity was in danger from new teachings. Strange doctrines are to be accounted as signs and distresses of the endtime.

The "final hour," according to 1 John 2:18, is characterized by heretical teachers in great numbers, who are called "Antichrists." The mythical figure of the Antichrist is represented in history.

Affliction and distress of the community make known that the "end of all things" is at hand (1 Peter 4:7). "Judgment begins in the house of God." just as for the prophets (Jer. 25:29; Ezek. 9:6) the judgment of God begins with his people. Even the Church is subject to the judgment, because of disobedience (i.e., disbelief — 1 Peter 4:17). Nevertheless, after a short time God will bring to a close the pains of his community (1 Peter 5:10).

Heretical teachers, as "scoffers who walk after the lusts of godlessness" are announced for the endtime also in Jude 18f.

The warning about false teachers is repeated in 2 Peter 2:1-3. The heretical teachers disavow in particular "the promise of the arrival" of the Lord and the future judgment of the world.

c) Apocalypse of John

The eschatological consummation is, in John's Apocalypse, the theme throughout. In the vision of the four apocalyptic horsemen (6:1-8), the endtime is filled with dissension, war, famine, and death. Heaven and earth, sun, moon, and stars are convulsed and thrown into confusion prior to the coming of the day of the great wrath (6:12-17). The servants of God, however, are signed and protected (7:3-8). The community of those who bear witness to Christ is persecuted by the dragon (12:13-17). The antichristic and satanic powers appear in the form of the two beasts (13) and the false prophets (16:13). At the very end Satan will come forth again with all his power, but then he will be cast into the pool of fire and brimstone for all time (20:7-10).

d) Didache

The *Didache*, in 16:1-7, closes with an apocalypse (Jurgens, no. 10). As in the credal formulas of the Church already taking shape and belonging as yet to the future, the "last things" portray the end of ecclesiastical doctrine. The *Didache's* apocalypse is clearly much dependent upon Matthew 24. The *Didache* admonishes to communion and fidelity, which, in the trials and temptations of the final hour, will be especially necessary. Lying prophets and corrupters will be numerous in the last days. Love will be turned to hate. With signs and wonders the deceiver of the world will come forth as a Son of God. Many will be ruined. Those who endure will be saved. Trumpets will blast; the dead will arise. "The Lord will come on the clouds of heaven." In place of the one sign in Matthew 24:30, there are three designated "signs of the truth" that will appear: the "sign spread out in the heavens"; the "sign of the sound of the trumpet"; and "the resurrection of the dead." Does "the sign of the spreading out" (namely, of the hands) mean the appearance of the effulgent Cross?

§ 15. DEATH AND LIFE

1. Immortality of the Soul in Philosophy

The common consciousness of the Christian, and of Christian theology as well, conceives and describes death as the separation of the immortal soul from a mortal body.[235] The Christian notion of death can certainly be so formulated. Such a formulation, however — evidently, in any case, in its terms and form — is co-determined by that understanding of man and of death which has its basis in Greek thought. The latter understands man as a duality, and as a unity composed of a mortal body and an immortal soul. This unity is dissolved in death.

The Orphic mysteries, like the Eleusinian, were confident in their belief in the immortality of the soul. Under the influence of these religious convictions, Plato expounded the philosophical doctrine of the immortality of the soul in several of his dialogues, notably in the *Phaedo*, that writing in which the death of Socrates provides the occasion for the development of a basis for the philosophy of immortal life. Plato even defines death as "separation of the soul from the body" (*Phaedo* 64 C). "What is mortal in man dies in death, the immortal passes along to a state of hale and hearty well-being" (*Phaedo* 106 E). A body bound to the delusive and ephemeral hinders the soul in its chief duty, the achieving of a knowledge of truth. The soul is unchangeable and immortally devoted to the eternal truth and to participation therein. Death is a freeing and a perfecting. The arguments for the immortality of the soul come to the conclusion that "God and the idea of life, and whatever else is immortal, never perish" (*Phaedo* 106 D). Life after death is assigned after the judgment of the dead. The wicked fall into Tartarus. The good attain to holy places in which are not merely images of the gods, but the very gods themselves. Eternal life is granted to men in a companionship with the gods (*Phaedo* 111 C; 113 D–114 C; see below, § 18, 1). The soul is not absolutely immortal, living in a self-assured existence; rather, it is dependent upon the eternal Godhead.[236]

The idea of the immortality of the soul, as an inheritance from the Greek spirit, took on an even deeper significance for Christian thought. Certainly Christianity modified what it had inherited. The soul is immortal not of its own nature and inherent stability, but is supported by God's creating will. That is how the account of creation in Gen. 2:7 was explained: God shaped the man from earth and breathed into him a soul (see the present work, Vol. 1, pp. 85f.).

Christian philosophy does not, however, in consideration of the doctrine of creation, and as Greek teaching declared, regard the body as a prison or tomb for the soul. The soul is the vivifying and forming principle of the body (*anima forma corporis*). The body is the vehicle of the soul, through which the soul lives in relationship and in mutual efficacy with nature and with the human interaction of body and soul. Death concerns this whole man. It is the living man who dies, and not only his mortal body.

The teaching of the Enlightenment on the immortality of the soul is otherwise. Death does not properly affect man at all. He lives on in a better life. In the consciousness of his indestructible immortality, man elevates himself into the eternal and divine world.[237] For some decades past, there has been a sharp reaction to the Enlightenment's doctrine of immortality on the part of Protestant theology, which asserts the radical mortality of man, unless God protect man's life and give it to him anew in death. The hope of eternal life has its basis in the resurrection of Christ from the dead (see below, § 17, 2).[238]

2. Old Testament

The Old Testament acknowledges God as the Eternally Living One, and as absolutely the only Living One (Deut. 5:26; 2 Kings 19:4; Ps. 42:3). He is the Source of all Life (Ps. 36:10). God creates all life, and so too, the life of man (Gen. 2:7). If God takes back this life, it is the whole living man that dies, and not just the mortal body.

Only gradually did Israel perceive the difficulties of death and all the questions it raised. God's relationship to Israel was experienced at first and for a long time as a covenant between God and the whole chosen people, not as a relationship between God and the individual man. In the course of time, the individual life in the nation was elevated. A man lived on in his progeny (Gen. 22:17f.; Ps. 25:13). Thus his name remains (Ps. 72:17; Is. 66:22). Israel accepts life enthusiastically (Ps. 115:17f.; Job 2:4; Qoh. 9:4). Life is the highest good (Gen. 15:15; Job 42:17). Life is a blessing, death is a curse (Deut. 30:19). For the era of salvation a long and happy life is expected (Is. 65:20, 22).

A man recognizes, nevertheless, that death is his natural boundary; and he accepts it as his destiny (Ps. 89:48f.; Sir. 41:3). Man is dust, and to dust he returns when God takes back the breath of life he loaned him (Ps. 90:3; Job 34:14f.; Qoh. 12:7). If a man achieves the fullness of a long life, he departs thankfully and contentedly (Ps. 91:16; Sir. 3:6), "old and full of days" (Gen. 25:8; 35:29; Job 42:17).

But still, a man must experience and bemoan the shortness and uncertainty of life (Ps. 39:6f.). He laments at a life broken off early and prematurely, "in the midst of his days" (Ps. 102:25; Jer. 17:11), as also over sickness and misery that blight his life (Ps. 116:3, 8). Illness and death can be understood as punishments (Pss. 37; 109; Prov. 2:21f.). The departed will, in the chambers of the grave, "be gathered to the fathers."

Epitaphs are unusual in early Israel. A name belongs to the living. The names of the dead will be, after a time, forgotten by men; but they are forgotten, too, by God (Ps. 88:11-13). Certainly it is a sorrowful thing that life in the lower world, which man expects, is far removed from Yahweh (Pss. 6:6; 30:10f.; 88:11f.). "The lower world does not praise you, death lauds you not; they that go down into the pit do not expect your constancy. The living, only the living praise you" (Is. 38:18f.; see also Ps. 6).

The Yahwist's account of creation, in Gen. 2:17 and 3:19, posits a connection between death and sin. The text, nevertheless, combines various strata of tradition. The threat of death uttered in Gen. 2:17, "As soon as you eat thereof, you must die," is not carried out immediately upon the lapse into sin; rather, as punishment man is expelled from Paradise. In Gen. 3:19, the destiny of death is taken rather as one's natural fate: "Earth you are, and to earth you must return." The uniting of Gen. 2:17 and 3:19, however, understands the whole of life as death. In any case, it is the foreshortening of the span of life that is experienced as punishment (Gen. 6:3).

Hellenistic Judaism acquires from Greek philosophy the idea of the immortality of the soul. "Obedience to the precepts is security of immortality. Immortality achieves life in nearness to God" (Wis. 6:18f.). The saying: "The corruptible body is a load upon the soul, and the earthly habitat burdens the thoughtful spirit" (Wis. 9:15) is reminiscent of Greek dualism. In death the soul is separated from the body (*4 Esdras* 5 [7]:78). Philo, too, unites biblical tradition and Greek thought. The soul, ever lively, belongs to God (*De incorruptibilitate mundi* 84). Here the soul finds itself in a strange place; in the divine world it is at home (*De somniis* 1, 181).

For centuries Gen. 2 and 3 were hardly considered at all in Israel's theological tradition. Only after the Exile, and in particular only shortly before and after the settling of the Old Testament canon, was any attention and consideration given to those first chapters of Genesis. Then certainly death came to be understood as punishment for sin. "Through the Devil's envy did death come into the world; and all who belong to him experience it" (Wis. 2:24). Now too it is said: "The beginning of sin has its origin in one woman, and because of her we all die" (Sir. 25:24). Adam became the beginning of the calamity of death. Afterwards, nevertheless, all entered into the stream of that calamity on their own responsibility and by their own guilt. "Adam bears the guilt only and solely for himself. We all became an Adam, each man for himself" (*Syriac Apocalypse of Baruch* 54:19; see the present work, Vol. 1, pp. 92–95).

Death is now experienced as something hard and oppressive: "O death, how bitter is the very thought of you for the man who dwells peacefully in his home" (Sir. 41:1). Its contemplation can be without solace. Men and beasts share death as their common lot. "Who knows if the breath of man mount upward, while the breath of beast fall back to earth?" (Qoh. 3:19-21). Still, a possible solution presents itself. If death is understood no longer as a natural destiny but as a punishment for sin, there can be a hope of a forgiveness of guilt and an overcoming of death through Yahweh's salvation (Is. 26:19). This hope grows in the developing belief in a resurrection (see below, § 17, 1).

3. New Testament

For the New Testament, death is an incontrovertible reality. Adamitic mankind is subject to death (Rom. 5:12; 1 Cor. 15:42-49). Certainly life [239] is of irreplaceable value (Mark 8:36; Luke 12:16-21; 16:19-31; see the present work, Vol. 3, pp. 226–230). The Gospel knows about the sorrow and grief which have their origin in death. It makes mention of the lamentation in the house of Jairus (Mark 5:38). Luke, himself somewhat moved, tells of the especially difficult instance of death's having taken the only son of the widow. At the grave of Lazarus, his sister weeps, as also do the Jews. Jesus himself weeps. And from the fact of Jesus' weeping, the Jews recognize the loving friendship which bound him to the dead man (John 11:33-36).

Ultimately man can make no disposition of his life and death. For a man cannot — as Jesus recalls in the parable of the foolish farmer — by all his wealth make his life secure. It can be taken from him at any moment (Luke 12:16-21). God is the Lord of man's life and death. That he is such a Lord is made manifest also by the fact that he alone possesses immortality (1 Tim. 6:16). Although God is Lord of life and death, this does not imply that he is the Creator of death. He is, rather, the Creator and Lord of life; death, however, is ruin. Death, therefore, is not directly the work of God, but a work of the destroyer which God permits. Sickness is the work of Satan, who kept the woman bound for eighteen years (Luke 13:16). Death has its deepest origin in sin (Luke 13:1-5).

But there is something even worse than physical death. "Do not fear those who kill the body but cannot kill life. Fear those, rather, who can plunge life and body together into hell" (Matthew 10:28). Death remains, nevertheless, the greatest evil of a man's lifetime. Only the inconceivable terrors of the endtime can be so great that against them man can regard death as a lesser evil (Luke 23:30). Because of the constant threat of death, human life is lived not in the light but in darkness. Men are characterized as those "who sit in darkness and in the shadow of death" (according to Is. 8:23; Matthew 4:15f; Luke 1:78f.).

Jesus himself did not die the calm and beautiful death of the philosopher, but the holy death of the martyr. He suffered the pangs of death (Mark 14:34) and died with an agonizing cry (Mark 15:37).

In the manner of reporting on resurrections from the dead, the Gospels say that Jesus is the one who overcomes death when he confronts it (Mark 9:25; Luke 7:14; John 11:44; see also the present work, Vol. 2, pp. 80–81). Life is present in Christ, and to him who believes, it will be given (Mark 5:36; John 5:25). Finally Christ conquers death in the all-surpassing marvel that he rises up again in the power of God (see the present work, Vol. 2, pp. 131–136).

In the writings of the apostles, death is certainly treated as inevitable

(Heb. 7:8; 9:27), but still not simply as among the consequences of nature. The Epistles give a considered answer to the question of the origin of death, stating more clearly and more concretely what the Gospels presuppose or intimate. In this way Paul says (Rom. 5:12-21) that death is a consequence of sin. Through Adam's sin death found entry into the world. For Adam's descendants death is an inheritance, but not a mere inheritance, since each man, by his own personal sin, earns death as his lot. "Death passed over to all men, because all sinned" (see the present work, Vol. 1, pp. 114–126).

Sin, however, grew powerful in the world through the Law, since the prohibiting Law aroused man's appetite for wickedness (Rom. 7:7-25; 1 Cor. 15:56). The Law increased sin beyond all measure, thus it is the Law that kills (Rom. 7:10). But since the Law has its seat and potential in the flesh of man, it can further be stated that the flesh effects death (Rom. 7:24). And behind all this, it is still the destructive power of Satan that is operative. "The Devil is a murderer from the very beginning" (John 8:44). Christ, by his death, wanted to dispose of him who held the power of death, that is, the Devil (Heb. 2:14). Fear of death holds man in a lasting servitude throughout his life (Heb. 2:15).

Now, however, through Christ, God has frustrated death. Christ has borne that death which is the punishment of sin. But as the sinless One, he was not forfeit to death. He bore it, therefore, not for himself but for others. "He made him who knew no sin, to be sin, so that in him we might become righteousness of God" (2 Cor. 5:21). The death of Christ is a saving death for others and for us (Rom. 8:3f.; Gal. 3:13f.; see the present work, Vol. 2, pp. 100–112). From death, however, Christ has come alive again (Phil. 2:6-11). While the life of man leads to death, Christ's life comes forth out of death. "Our Savior Christ Jesus has frustrated death and, through the gospel, has brought life and incorruptibility to light" (2 Tim. 1:10; present work, Vol. 2, pp. 131–136).

As the first-born from the dead, Christ is life for all (Col. 1:18; Apoc. 1:5). Faith already has the victory. "Death is swallowed up in victory. O Death, where is thy victory? O Death, where is thy sting?" (1 Cor. 15:5f.). The Christian must now, each for himself, make his own the way of Christ from death to life. He must be conformed with the death and with the resurrection of Christ (Rom. 6:5). Baptism is effective of death and resurrection with Christ (Rom. 6:3f.). In obedient conduct the baptized must realize the sacramental event of the death and life of the Lord. "You are to recognize yourselves as being dead to sin, but alive to God in Christ" (Rom. 6:11). Christians have "come alive, from the dead" (Rom. 6:13).

The Gospel of John expresses this certitude with the declaration that he who believes will not die. "I am the resurrection and the life. Whoever believes in me will live, even if he die. And everyone who lives and believes in me shall not die in eternity" (John 11:25f.). Faith has passed from death into life (John 5:24).

4. LASTING REALITY

In the unity of the Christian with Christ, death is overcome. Death has lost its frustrating power to annihilate, and with it, its terrors. The believer lives and dies in the same way as the Lord (Rom. 14:7f.). The dead are "dead in Christ" (1 Thess. 4:16). Even in death Christians cannot be removed from their union with their Lord. Nothing can part them from the love of Christ and from the love of God manifested in Christ, nothing, "neither death nor life" (Rom. 8:38). This certitude is the solace that "we shall evermore be with the Lord" (1 Thess. 4:17). Paul, therefore, is able to say that life and death, present and future, belong to the Christian (1 Cor. 3:22); and, indeed, for him, to die is gain, since it means being with Christ (Phil. 1:23).

This is New Testament. The God of the old covenant has to do only with the living and with life. He is separated from death and from the dead (Is. 38:18f.). Death is unclean and makes one unclean. Its province is apart from that of God (Lev. 21:1; Num. 19:16). Now God is in life and in death. This has its true basis in the fact that in the death of Christ, God comes into contact with death and is concerned with it, indeed, that he took death upon himself and overcame it in the raising up of Christ. "For to this end did Christ die and come alive again, that he might rule over the dead and the living" (Rom. 14:9).

In all confidence and in the certitude of the overcoming of death, the New Testament sees that the reality of death continues to exist. Paul says, in respect to his existence as an apostle and in regard to every aspect of his living the faith, that he bears about in his body the death of Christ (2 Cor. 4:10f.). In point of fact, the community is in deep peril: "For your sakes we are put to death all the day long. We are regarded as sheep for the slaughter (Rom. 8:36 = Ps. 44:23). Paul tells how he was in the most urgent danger of death. And he thanks God for having saved him and bids the community to join with him in prayers of thanksgiving (2 Cor. 1:10f.). Death is the distress of those who live. Paul announces also that his beloved Epaphras had been mortally ill. "But God had mercy on him, and not on him only but on me as well, that I might not have sorrow heaped on sorrow" (Phil. 2:27). Death brings grief and sorrow. We wished, not to be unclothed, but to be clothed over, so that without sorrowful death what is mortal might be swallowed up by life (2 Cor. 5:4).

The Acts of the Apostles tells of the death of Stephen. Dying, he saw heaven open and Christ standing at the right of God (Acts 7:55f.). "God-fearing men buried Stephen, and raised a great lamentation over him" (Acts 8:2). The Church experiences the death even of her saints as a sorrow and breaks forth in lamentation.[240]

The Apocalypse of John portrays death in ugly visions as the terror of mankind. He rages over earth, with the lower regions, hell, following him. He kills with every means available — with the sword, with famine, with plague, and with the wild beasts of the earth (Apoc. 6:8). Death remains the enemy of mankind to the end. Not until the final day will he be conquered and undone (1 Cor. 15:26). Only then will Death and Hades be cast into the sea of fire (Apoc. 20:14). Only in the perfected kingdom of God will there no longer be any death. "And he will wipe away every tear from their eyes, and death will be no more, and neither grief nor lamentation nor sorrow (Apoc. 21:4).

Christian faith is confident that in death we are not confined and taken up by nothingness, but by God, who, as Creator, is also the Perfecter of each and every life. He is merciful and strong, to rescue the life of man in the direst straits and to bring him safely through death. The "great Shepherd of the sheep" (Heb. 13:20) promises: "No one shall ever snatch them from my hand" (John 10:28).

§ 16. PAROUSIA

Parousia [241] is the term used in the New Testament to designate the coming of Christ at the end of time.[242]

1. OLD TESTAMENT

The Old Testament rarely employs the word parousia, and never with a special significance related to salvation history. Yet the reality which it specifies is certainly an intensive theme of the Old Testament, since it bears witness in all its parts to the coming of God into the history of Israel, and to the hope that God will, in the messianic endtime, appear in all his might and establish his reign.

2. GREEK MILIEU

In the Greek language, the term parousia is current in its everyday meaning of "arrival." In the sacral and political spheres of Hellenism, and in the imperial age in Rome, the word has newer significance with a special emphasis.[243] The two spheres can, as for example in the worship of the ruler, become intermixed. Here parousia means the visit of the ruling potentate or of a high official as his deputy. In papyri and on monuments, there is talk of the parousia of kings, even if only because such a parousia called for a gift, for which special taxes had to be levied. For a parousia special coins were struck. Sometimes a new era was dated from a parousia; thus, in an inscription: "sixty-nine years after the first parousia of the god Hadrian in Greece." On the occasion of a parousia, a potentate distributed tokens of his favor. For city and country, then, a parousia is occasion for festive celebration.

There is likewise talk of the charitable parousias of the gods. Asclepius, on the way home, heals a woman. "Thus did he make his parousia known." In the mysteries, the parousia of Dionysius takes place. In the *Corpus hermeticum* (1, 22), the divine Nous says: "My parousia will be of assistance to them."

3. New Testament

a) Synoptics

Without using the term itself, Christ speaks of the parousia of the Son of Man. He will come "in the glory of his Father with the holy angels." If someone is contemptuous of Jesus and of his word, the Son of Man, on his arrival, will not know him (Mark 8:38). In his discourse on the parousia, Jesus says that at the collapse of the world the Son of Man will appear "on the clouds of the heavens with great power and majesty" (Mark 13:25-27). Before his judges, Jesus finally confesses himself as Messiah and Son of God, and he adds that they (i.e., their offspring) will "see the Son of Man sitting at the right of the Power and coming with the clouds of heaven" (Mark 14:62). Undoubtedly it is of set purpose that Luke 22:29 changes the statement to: "From now on the Son of Man will sit at the right of the power of God." This is no more than an announcement that the appearance of the Son of Man is near at hand.

For the expected arrival of Christ, Matthew uses the word parousia (παρουσία); thus in Matthew 24:3, where the apostles speak of the parousia of Jesus. In Matthew 24:27 and 37, Jesus speaks of the parousia of the Son of Man. These verses are found also in Luke (17:24, 26), and stem, therefore, from Source Q. Luke, however, speaks of the "days of the Son of Man," not of his parousia. This will have been the linguistic usage of Source Q. There is no question but that in all the passages mentioned, the Gospels, since for them Jesus is the Son of Man whose return is expected, refer to the parousia of Christ. Since in these texts Jesus speaks of the Son of Man as if he were speaking of another, exegesis debates whether or not the equating of the Son of Man with Christ is contained in the original form of the passages. Was it perhaps the community of disciples that first promoted this understanding of the passages, when it declared that the present Jesus and the future Son of Man were one and the same? (See the present work, Vol. 2, pp. 185–193).

In an eschatological discourse in Luke 17:20-37 (with 18:1-8), the Evangelist offers an exhortational passage on the parousia of the Son of Man.[244] The discourse can be interpreted in detail. The Evangelist employs in his composition additional sayings, found also in Source Q (Luke 17:23, 26f., 31, 33, 34f., 37), and special tradition, which seems to be primary (thus Luke 17:20f., 22, 24, 28f.). Three groups of sayings are brought together on the theme of the parousia. Luke 17:20f. treats of the coming of the reign of God; 17:22-37, of the coming of the Son of Man; 18:1-8, of praying for his coming.

Luke 17:20f. is without synoptic parallel, even if Mark 13:21 = Matthew 24:23 is comparable. The Pharisees ask Jesus when the kingdom of God is to come.[245] Jesus replies: "The kingdom of God does not come in such a way that men could notice it. . . . The kingdom of God is within you." In Luke, the Pharisees are in no way the constant opponents of Jesus, always thoroughly at odds with him (Luke 7:36). As with rabbinism and apocalyptics, the Pharisees occupy themselves with the question of the coming of the kingdom of God. The results of such questions and calculations are seen in Dan. 9:2-27, if here the seventy years which are to constitute the time of the exile according to Jeremiah (25:11; 29:10) are being extended to sevently weeks of years, that is, seven times seventy years. In the time of the New Testament the expectation was especially urgent, since Israel expected the reign of God as a liberation from the foreign rule of Rome. Thus in the *Eighteen Benedictions* 10f.: "Blow loud the trumpet at our liberation. Bring back our judges as before. Rule over us, you alone." Judaism recognized, however, that man cannot circumscribe God's freedom by such computations. Thus a rabbi states (*ca.* 150 A.D.,): "Whoever calculates the end has no share in the future world."

Moreover, the place of God's reign was debated, and the expectation was that it would be established in Jerusalem. It was from here that God would exercise his messianic-eschatological rule. Jesus denies not only the assertion of a date, but even the idea that one can calculate the period of God's kingdom. He does seem, however, to ascribe to it a place. "The kingdom of God is within you." What does "within you" mean?[246] Linguistically possible would be the interpretation: The kingdom of God is inside of you, it has no measurable external dimension. But never elsewhere does Jesus designate the workings of God within a man as the kingdom of God. The explanation of the passage is sometimes supplemented from its context: "Someone will say that the kingdom of God is there. While men were attempting to compute its arrival, the kingdom of God slipped in quietly under the door and was already there."

Mostly, however, the passage is interpreted as meaning: "The kingdom of God is in your midst." Then the saying of the Lord is understood as meaning that the kingdom of God is present among those to whom the Lord is speaking. According to Luke 4:21, the messianic promise is being fulfilled at that very time. According to Luke 11:20, wherein Jesus overcomes the demons, the eschatological kingdom is present in the works and in the person of Jesus — hidden, it is true, but nonetheless real. It is in this sense, then, that Luke 17:21 is to be understood. The saying diverts the questioners from an apocalyptic future time and cautions them to recognize and grasp hold of the present.

In Luke 17:22-37, revelations about the days of the arrival of the Son of Man are brought together. The sayings are grouped according to the title Son of Man, apocalyptically understood. The temporal sequence intended is probably that the days of the Son of Man are to precede the kingdom of God (Luke 16:21). The suturing of the composition is recognizable in Luke 17:22 through the new clause: "But he said to his disciples." Before it was the Pharisees who were addressed (Luke 17:20), but now he is speaking to his disciples. There is no longer any talk of the glory of the reign of God. Those days are much more days of terror. As Israel's expectation of the "days of the Messiah" speaks of the time from the arrival of the Messiah to the beginning of God's kingdom, so Luke speaks of the "days of the Son of Man." The disciples will yearn for a day of being together with the Son of Man, certainly not in the remembrance of times past, which they spent with Jesus, but yearning after a future day of the messianic kingdom, which is to begin with the arrival of the Son of Man.

Is the saying addressed to the community, anxious in its expectations, a community which awaits the revelation or at least a sign of the glorified Son of Man? Because that is the direction of the disciples' gaze, the announcement of false prophets may deceive them (Luke 17:23). The disciples are not to heed announcements that the Messiah is here or there. When the Son of Man really comes, he will appear suddenly and unmistakably before all the world (Luke 17:24). This is indicated by the image of the lightning. The image may seem to be peculiarly appropriate, because the Son of Man is anticipated in an image of light (as in Luke 9:29).

Perhaps, too, the saying is polemically addressed to the Jewish point of view, according to which the Messiah must be in an obscurity, out of which he is to be sought and discovered. Before the Son of Man is made manifest in glory, he must suffer much (Luke 17:25). The Son of Man is equated with Jesus, whose Passion is announced beforehand. Here the prediction of his Passion is, compared to the others (Mark 8:31; 9:31; 10:33f.), short and undeveloped, and probably the earliest original (see the present work, Vol. 2, p. 108).

To the community of disciples, however, it must be said that, oppressed in the world, they are necessarily included in the sufferings of their Lord. The days which precede the arrival of the Son of Man are, in a duplex example, compared to the days of Noah and of Lot (Luke 17:26-29). In the days of Noah, men had abandoned themselves to their grossest dissolute impulses. They had forgotten God and the impending judgment. The deluge came suddenly and destroyed all. The time of Lot is depicted as one of a richly developed culture. Judgment came down from heaven unexpectedly and destroyed all. Unexpectedly and unaccountably, the Son of Man will appear in a foolishly careless generation (Luke 17:30). The community must be admonished to a truly eschatological stance: to be always prepared and never to lose itself in earthly cares. The catastrophe comes so suddenly that one must save himself as quickly as possible without hesitation or delay.

It is a genuinely Lucan admonition, no longer to take any trouble for possession or treasures, which means in general to give up one's possession (Luke 17:31); see also the present work, (Vol. 3, p. 309). Luke 17:31 seems to be similar to Mark 13:15f. = Matthew 24:17f. Here, however, the statement is an admonition to flight in the upheaval of the endtime; in Luke, since one certainly cannot flee before the parousia, the admonition is to a turning away from the world.

The history of Lot is referred to once more (Luke 17:32). Lot's wife could have been saved like the other members of the household. She turned to look back and thus forfeited her salvation. On the apocalyptic day one must abandon the past and devote oneself entirely to what is coming. The meaning of the history of Lot is expressed in Luke

17:33 with a saying that is found in another context in Mark 8:35 = Matthew 16:25 = Luke 9:24. It means that the surrender of everything earthly must extend itself even to earthly life. The saying is probably in reference to a period of severe dangers, but not actually to judgment day itself.

Is it an originally profane proverb that is used? The explanation is sought in various ways. Perhaps it is that the vultures gather where the corpse is, and therefore, where deaths occur. Those not chosen, those left behind, are forfeit to death. Or, the place of the parousia will be as unlikely to be overlooked as is a corpse by the vultures. Or, everywhere there is a corpse, the vultures circ'e. They find every corpse. So too the judgment finds every man, and everywhere there are men, there is judgment. Or finally, and less likely, when the world, through its sins, is as dead as a corpse, then will the Son of Man come. The saying appears also in Matthew 24:28. Here its meaning is probably that the arrival of the Son of Man will be as little hidden from men as is a corpse from the vultures.

The eschatological discourse of Luke 18:1-8 calls forth the parable of the godless judge, which constitutes an admonition to pray without cease. God will finally grant justice to his elect. Through Luke 18:7f., the parable is ordered to the parousia and interpreted as prayer for the parousia. The Son of Man will bring God's judgment and his justice. But it is uncertain whether or not the Son of Man, at his arrival on earth, will find faith. This seems like a mute applied to the loud call for the arrival of the Son of Man. It could be turned against the petitioner himself.

The apocalyptic discourse in Luke 17:20-37 emphasizes by contrast that the arrival of the Son of Man will break forth suddenly from heaven upon unsuspecting men below. Any counting on prior signs is denied. By contrast, in the great synoptic apocalypse according to Mark 13:5-23 and Luke 21:8-36, an endtime peril of a long period of historical earthly distress is introduced. Luke 21 opens to the Church, before the end, a path through history. The admonitions to perseverance in the shorter apocalypse of Luke (Luke 17:21f., 25, 31, 33; 18:7f.) may be Luke's own joinings. Similar hortatory passages belong to the style of Luke's Gospel (11:49-51; 13:23f.; 21:34, 36).

The emphasizing of the suddenness of the arrival of the Son of Man will be the earlier form and the older content of the New Testament apocalyptics. There are also some synoptic parables that emphasize this theme (Matthew 24:43, 50; 25:10; Mark 13:35; see § 14, 1 above). The protracted period of prior signs demonstrates patient waiting in the face of the deferred parousia, and the beginning of the Church's history. Just as Luke 17:20-37 proves to be earlier in respect to Luke 21:8-36, so too is 1 Thess. 4:15; 5:2f., with its declaration of the nearness of the parousia, earlier in respect to the (deutero-Pauline) text in 2 Thess. 2:1-12, which adduces what must take place before the parousia.

In the Apocalypse of John, finally, the prior signs are broadly expanded temporally in groups of seven: the seven angels, the seven trumpets, the seven vessels of wrath.

b) Acts of the Apostles

The Acts of the Apostles expects the parousia at the end of time. God "has determined the day on which he will judge the world in justice through a Man whom he has appointed thereto." In accord with its basically Lukan stance, the point of it is perhaps not the nearness of judgment, but only its future certitude. Christ is appointed to be the universal Judge. The judgment will take place after the resurrection of the dead (Acts 17:32) and will manifest the justice of God in reward and in punishment.

c) Gospel of John

The Gospel of John does not use the word parousia; the concept, however, is indicated as "that day."[247] It has an internal harmony with the Old Testament expectation of the eschatological day of Yahweh, which is judgment and salvation (see above, § 12, 1, c). According to the eschatology of the Gospel of John, the eschatological day is always understood in its presentness. "Abraham rejoiced that he was to see my day" (John 8:56). Abraham's hope was ordered to the endtime salvation. The historical day of Jesus is the eschatological day of messianic salvation, which is all-embracing.

In his parting discourse, Jesus announces his return; nevertheless, not as a distant event, but as a day soon to come (14:3, 18, 23, 28). The return takes place first of all, of course, in his resurrection (14:19;

16:16-23), but it takes place constantly in the experiencing of the Spirit (14:16-18). Resurrection of Christ, gift of the Spirit, and parousia are one. Thus the old term "day of Yahweh" is brought to the present. "On that day you will recognize that I am in my Father, and you in me and I in you" (14:20). In the eschatological consummation, faith and understanding are at their end point. "On that day you will ask me nothing" (16:23). The disciples will no longer have any questions. It is the hour of unveiled discourse by the Father (16:25). In their eschatological existence, everything will be clear to the disciples. It is the day on which the disciples are taken up into the love of the Father, so that every prayer is fulfilled (16:28f.). With the making of the parousia an ever-present reality, is the question answered that was agitated within the community in consequence of the non-appearance of a parousia understood as future event?

d) Epistles of Paul

Paul speaks often of the expected arrival of Christ and describes it in representations rich in content. It will be the content of the "day of the Lord." Paul often designates this arrival of Christ as parousia (1 Thess. 2:19; 3:13; 4:15; 5:23; 1 Cor. 15:23; and the probably post-Pauline 2 Thess. 2:1, 8). The congregation will be the Apostle's crown of glory "before our Lord Jesus Christ at his parousia" (1 Thess. 2:19). The congregation should be "blameless in holiness before God our Father, at the parousia of our Lord Jesus, with all his saints" (1 Thess. 3:13). The saints, with whom Jesus appears, are, according to Old Testament evidence (Zech. 14:5), probably not some perfected Christians, but the heavenly court of God. Paul repeats his wish (1 Thess. 5:23) that Christians "may be blameless at the coming of Christ."

In 1 Thess. 4:13-5:11, the parousia of Christ is depicted as an apocalyptic revelation in glory.[248] Paul gives this detailed eschatological exhortation with a positive inducement. The deaths of its members perplexed the community. Christians hoped to live to witness the parousia. Triumph over death was first begun in the resurrection of Christ; the parousia would make it manifest and consummate that victory. But now the dead would have no share in it. In a comparable way, *4 Esdras* laments over those generations which could not participate in the messianic era; thus, in *4 Esdras* 11 [13]:17-19, "Whoever does not live to behold those days must be sorrowful. Certainly they know the joys which are prepared for that time, but they themselves shall not come to them. But woe even to those who shall remain, for they shall experience great affliction and much distress"; similarly, *4 Esdras* 3 [5]:41f.

In the face of mortalities in the community, Paul surely did not call upon a philosophical doctrine of immortality. Such a philosophical belief was undoubtedly confined to narrow circles. Despair was vulgar (1 Thess. 4:13). Neither did Paul call upon the Jewish hope of a resurrection. In Israel it was only in part alive, while in Gentile Christian circles probably it was scarcely known. Paul did not even reassure the Christians with the conviction that the dead are with the Lord (Phil. 1:23). Did he himself become certain of this conviction only later? It was the expectation of a parousia soon to take place that he confided to Christians (1 Thess. 1:10). They hoped that their generation might yet live to see the parousia (1 Thess. 4:15). Paul therefore strengthened the community in this hope. Paul does not pose the obvious question of one's status in the (short) time between death and parousia. Or does he accept a "sleep of death" (1 Thess. 4:15)?

Paul appeals to a "word of the Lord" (1 Thess. 4:15). Is this a saying of the historical Jesus such as Paul customarily adduces (1 Cor. 7:10; 9:14; see also Acts 20:35)? Is it a saying of the glorified Christ, such as Paul did in fact adduce in other instances (2 Cor. 12:8f.; [also 1 Cor. 15:51?])? Does this saying of the Lord embrace the whole text of 1 Thess. 4:15-17? One cannot imagine that Jesus should have predicted apocalyptic particulars. In Mark 13:32 Jesus denies such knowledge.

A saying like 1 Thess. 4:15 has something of an apocryphal ring to it, rather like a passage from the *Epistula apostolorum* 16 (27) [*Epistula Apostolorum. Nach dem äthiopischen und koptischen Texte herausgeben*, H. Duensing, Bonn 1925]: "I will come like the sun that shines . . . , while I am borne, in its sparkling, on the wings of the clouds . . . , and I will come down to earth that I may judge the living and the dead." One might very easily believe that 1 Thess. 15-17 originates in an apocalypse which placed the statement in the mouth of Jesus, like Mark 13:5-37 or Apoc. 1:1, the "apocalypse of Jesus Christ." The saying of the Lord in Matthew 24:30f. comes close. Comparable also is the apocalypse in *Didache* 16, 3-7 (Jurgens, no. 10).

The parousia of the Lord is announced by a "command" ($\kappa \acute{\epsilon} \lambda \epsilon \upsilon \sigma \mu a$ — 1 Thess. 4:16). The word Paul uses is a technical term of military and sporting language. Who gives the command? God or an archangel? Is the "voice of the archangel" the same as the "trumpet of God" (1 Thess. 4:16)? Trumpets blow in war, in worship, and on festal occasions in general.[249] They proclaim the appearance of God (on Sinai, in Exod. 19:16, 19; also, Pss. 47:6; 81:4). Blasts of the horn proclaim judgment day in Is. 27:13; Joel 2:1; Zeph. 1:16. In *4 Esdras* 4 [6]:23, the trumpet blast is an eschatological sign. According to the *Apocalypse of Moses* 22, the judgment is to be announced by Michael's trumpet, and according to the rabbis, by the voice of Gabriel (H. Strack and P. Billerbeck, *op. cit.*, Vol. 3, p. 635). In the Qumran book, *The War of the Sons of Light with the Sons of Darkness* the trumpet is often a signal for battle. The *Eighteen Benedictions* (10) implores: "Blow loud on the trumpet for our liberation." The trumpet is blown also as an eschatological sign in Matthew 24:31 and 1 Cor. 15:52.

Christ comes down from heaven. In the older expectation, the Messiah is a son of the earth. In late Judaism the representation of the Messiah is elevated beyond human dimension. Before all time he is in heaven, and it is from there that he comes (Dan. 7:13f.; *Ethiopic Henoch* 62:7). John (6:33-51) designates the incarnation of Christ as his descent from heaven.

"The dead in Christ" will rise again. Is Paul speaking of a resurrection only of the just (see below, § 17, 1)? The arisen and the living will be enraptured on the clouds to Christ.[250] Clouds are God's carriage (Ps. 104:3; Is. 4:5; 19:1; 2 Macc. 2:8). Christ too appears on the clouds (Mark 9:7; 13:26; 14:62; Acts 1:9). Christ, coming from heaven, is "met." Meeting ($\dot{a}\pi\dot{a}\nu\tau\eta\sigma\iota\varsigma$) is a term of biblical origin (Exod. 19:10-18), which, in Hellenistic Greek, often describes a political ceremonial. Both meanings may apply here.[251] What direction is taken after this meeting or encounter? First of all, one can probably assume that it is an absorption into heaven. Or do they return to earth, where the messianic kingdom is then established?

As a further question, Paul must treat in 1 Thess. 5:1-10 of the time of the parousia. To that end Paul appeals to the knowledge of Christians. He wants the common representations and expectations of Jewish-Christian apocalyptics to be borne in mind. The parousia will make a precipitate entry (1 Thess. 5:2f.). Paul emphasizes, therefore, an expectation that is taught in a penetrating manner in the apocalypse in Luke 17:20-37, as well as in the comparisons employed in apocalyptic discoursing (Matthew 24:37–25:13), whereas the synoptic apocalypse (Mark 13:4-27) accepts a longer prior period of tribulations (above, § 14, 1). The Lord comes like a thief in the night (1 Thess. 5:2, 4). Paul uses an image employed in apocalyptics (Matthew 24:43; see above, § 14, 2, a-b). Traditional, too, is the image of the sudden eruption of the pangs of childbirth (1 Thess. 5:3; Mark 13:8).

Paul then develops the terminology and theme of the night (1 Thess. 5:2, 4-8, 10), which the Apostle employed also in eschatological exhortation in Rom. 13:11-13. The image appears first of all in 1 Thess. 5:2 in its ordinary sense, and then, without losing its usual sense, in a transferred meaning also. Christians are not in darkness; they will not, therefore, be overtaken and made ashamed in the brightness of the day of the parousia (1 Thess. 5:4). Christians are sons of the day, not of night. They dare not sleep, they must be watchful and sober (1 Thess. 5:5-8). Here again a familiar theme of eschatological warning is employed (Mark 13:33-37; see above, § 14, 2, a). What is essential is not the knowledge of the precise day of the parousia, but the attaining of the salvation that is promised and introduced in the saving death of Christ (1 Thess. 5:9-11).

Motivated by questions in the congregation at Corinth, in 1 Cor. 15 Paul develops in a detailed manner the doctrine of the Christian hope of resurrection (see below, § 17, 2, c). In 1 Cor. 15:22-28, 51-55, Paul described the parousia (15:23) of Christ. The dead who belong to Christ will arise at his parousia. The victory of Christ is manifested in events of increasing moment. These events are his resurrection, his parousia, the overthrow of all powers, and finally the restoring of the kingdom of God, the Father.

It is a witness to the eschatological expectation of the Church and of of the Apostle himself when, according to Paul, in the celebration of the Eucharistic Meal "the death of the Lord is proclaimed until he comes" (1 Cor. 11:26). The Eucharistic Meal, in its action as in its accompanying explanatory statement, calls to mind the death of the Lord as salvational event and makes it present. The Eucharistic Meal also takes place, however, in the expectation of the parousia of the

Lord as the full revelation of his majesty as Lord, which in communion in the Eucharistic Meal is acknowledged and experienced, and at the parousia is to be made manifest. The Crucified and the Glorified is the One who is to come. The Meal of the Corinthian Church is in the eschatological tradition and hope which invests that Meal in accord with the very word of the Lord (Mark 14:25).

The eschatological expectation of the Church is heard in the call "Maranatha!" (1 Cor. 16:22).[252] The word (Aramaic, *maran atha* or *marana tha*) probably does not mean the linguistically possible "The Lord has come" (i.e., into the world or into the worshipping community), but "Come, O Lord!" The exclamation, originating in the primitive Aramaic-speaking Christian community, will have had its place in the liturgy, and even in the celebration of the Eucharistic Meal. Christ the Lord is entreated to be present at the Meal, and at the same time his parousia is petitioned. The community would not have separated the two, seeing that for it the sacramental Meal was a prefigure of the eternal banquet.

Paul speaks also of the expected parousia of Christ in Phil. 3:20f.: "Our country[253] is in heaven, where also we await the Savior, the Lord Jesus Christ. He will refashion the body of our lowliness, that it may be of like form to the body of his majesty." The coming Lord will accomplish in the bodies of those who are his own that which has already taken place in the glorified body of the resurrected One. The great transformation will take place, as is declared also in Rom. 8:11 and 1 Cor. 15:42-44, 52f.

A question sometimes debated is whether or not the forms and shapes of Paul's endtime expectations were changed on the basis of his experiences and reflections. A part of the texts are indicative of an urgent expectation of an imminent parousia of Christ. The time left for the world is short (1 Cor. 7:29). It was Paul's conviction that he would be among those who would live to see the parousia. The parousia will unite with their Lord the living as well as those raised from the dead (1 Thess. 4:15). Not all will fall asleep before the parousia, but all will be transformed at the parousia (1 Cor. 15:51). Before Christ the Judge, the Apostle will be the glory of the congregation, and the congregation will be the Apostle's glory (2 Cor. 1:14). The hour is at hand, so that, just as the sun suddenly brightens the morning sky, so too the glory of Christ is soon to appear (Rom. 13:12).

Other texts seem to say that Paul, considering his possible death before the parousia, expects communion with Christ immediately after death. Probably this is presupposed in 2 Cor. 5:1-10, since 5:1f. and 5:6-8 are hardly to be understood of the parousia, but of personal death. Certainly we desired to experience this not as a violent divesting, but as a prompt clothing over with the heavenly body. But if the "becoming clothed over" were perhaps to take place at the parousia (as in 1 Cor. 15:52), then Paul would be declaring his desire not to die before the parousia. But death, ever sorrowful, is, for all of that, a "going home to the Lord." Everyone is, immediately after death, summoned before the judgment seat of Christ. With this statement, is Paul considering the possibility of death before the parousia, inasmuch as he had just now been rescued from the jaws of death (2 Cor. 1:9f.)?

In Phil. 1:23, Paul writes that for him departure would mean "being with Christ." Is this declaration called forth by circumstances? It cannot be decided with certainty whether the Epistle to the Philippians is to be dated early or late in Paul's time. But Paul writes as a prisoner facing a possible condemnation of death. He is convinced that death itself cannot disrupt his communion with Christ, but will in fact induce it (likewise in Rom. 8:38). Even in the Epistle to the Philippians (1:6, 10; 2:16; 4:4f.), Paul speaks most penetratingly of the parousia, in which the transition to glory will take place (3:20f.).

Since the expectation of the parousia in the Epistle to the Romans (13:12), certainly a late Epistle, is still quite undiminished, the difference between declarations cannot be explained on so simple a basis as the supposition that in the later years of his life Paul would have reckoned with the possibility of his dying before the parousia. The questions which we have in reference to the eschatological times do not present themselves to Paul in the same way that we see them. He has no conception then of the vast periods of time until the parousia. The one Lord, the Resurrected and Glorified, comprehends the times and their contents up to a soon to come consummation.

The question is also raised of the interim state between death and resurrection. Paul employs various representations that are drawn from

Jewish apocalyptics as well as from universal Christology. They are valid side by side, and to some extent flow into each other. That the Greek notion of the immortality of the soul had an additional influence therein is improbable. Perhaps Paul wanted to say of the attempt to bring the departed into a system that only a fool would seek a precise knowledge of the course and details of the eschaton (1 Cor. 15:36).

e) Deutero-Pauline Epistles

The Second Epistle to the Thessalonians gives detailed instructions "on the parousia of Christ and our reunion with him" (2:1). The Lord will manifest himself, "appearing from heaven with the angels of his power in flaming fire," to punish the disobedient and to free the afflicted righteous (1:6-10). Nevertheless, the parousia is not yet present (2:2). Many prior signs must first come to pass. The great apostasy must take place. The man of lawlessness must first appear, who makes his entry with lying signs and filthy wonders (2:3-12). Jesus, at his own epiphany, will slay this blasphemer "with the breath of his mouth" (2:8). The Epistle employs, instead of the term "parousia," the Hellenistic and not characteristically Pauline term "epiphany" (as in 1 Tim. 6:14; 2 Tim. 4:1, 8; see below).

Jewish (and New Testament) apocalyptics expects similar advance signs. Here too there is talk of a great apostasy before the end (*Ethiopic Henoch* 91:7; *Book of Jubilees* 23:14; *4 Esdras* 3[5]:1f.). This apostasy is likewise depicted in Matthew 24:10-12; *Didache* 16:3 (Jurgens, no. 10). The "son of perdition" is designated as precursor of the end also in Is. 57:4; the eschatological adversary of God, in the *Apocalypse of Elijah* 34f. He is the Antichrist of 1 John 2:18, 22; 4:3; 2 John 7 (see above, § 14, 3). In blasphemous arrogance he settles himself in the Temple (Mark 13:4; above, § 14, 2). He gives it out that he is God (*Ascension of Isaiah* 4:6; *Didache* 16:4 [*Jurgens*, no. 10]). The mystery of lawlessness is already at work; but it is still restrained (2:6f.). What the restraining power is, is uncertain (see above, § 14, note 234). Is it God's will and plan in general? The blasphemer works great wonders (2:9-11), which also is in accord with Jewish expectations (*Ascension of Isaiah* 4:5; *Apocalypse of Elijah* 33:1f.; 38:1; also *Didache* 16:4 [Jurgens, no. 10]). The end of the Antichrist (2:8) is painted in Old Testament colors. Thus "God strikes the violent with the staff of his mouth and he kills the blasphemous with the breath of his lips" (Is. 11:4 in the Septuagint). Thus too "the man" destroys his opponent (*4 Esdras* 11 [13]:10).

In the portrayal of the parousia, significant differences are noticed in the accounts of the two Epistles to the Thessalonians. In the first Epistle, the parousia is expected as very near. According to the second Epistle, it is still at an undetermined distance. In this second Epistle, the parousia of Christ and the stature of the blasphemer are depicted in apocalyptic-mythological strokes. As compared to the first Epistle, this is all a later development.

Colossians 3:4 says of the parousia: "When Christ, our life, is made manifest, then will you too be made manifest with him in glory." In the parousia the glory of the exalted Lord will be made manifest before the world. Then the life hidden until now (Col. 3:3), and the already real but as yet veiled glory of those who are his, will be made manifest. This short and merely intimational reminder of the parousia in the (probably post-Pauline) Epistle to the Colossians already betrays a certain ecclesiastical tradition.

The Pastoral Epistles do not use the term parousia, employing instead the word epiphany,[254] by which is understood both the first coming of Christ in his incarnation (2 Tim. 1:10) and his final eschatological coming (1 Tim. 6:14; 2 Tim. 4:1; Titus 2:13; see also the present work, Vol. 2 pp. 151f.) Like parousia, epiphany too is a word from the Hellenistic religious milieu. The term describes the becoming visible of the otherwise hidden divinity, in history and in worship (also in biblical Greek, as in 2 Sam. 7:23; 2 Macc. 2:21; 3:24; 12:22; 15:27; further, in Josephus and Philo). Thus in the Pastoral Epistles (as already in 2 Thess. 2:8) the coming of Christ is designated an epiphany. "I entreat you before God and Christ Jesus, who will judge the living and the dead, and by his epiphany and by his kingdom" (2 Tim. 4:1). Is the term epiphany a polemic usage, since Hellenistic princes (like Antiochus Epiphanes, for example) and Roman emperors caused themselves in their titles to be celebrated as an epiphany of the gods? Is it stated that Christ is and will be the only true Epiphany of God, and is the endtime epiphany understood as his enthronement as King?

Now is the time "to keep the commandment untarnished and unbroken until the epiphany of our Lord Jesus Christ, which at the proper time will let us see the blessed and only Sovereign" (1 Tim. 6:14). There is no more talk of the event's being near at hand; but neither is it suggested in any way that its postponement might have been perceived as trying to anyone's faith.

"We look forward to the blessed hope and the epiphany of the glory of our great God and [of our] Savior Jesus Christ" (Titus 2:13; see also the present work, Vol. 2, p. 216). The parousia will be the happy and glorious consummation of the Church. But if the already effected as well as the yet expected appearance of the Lord is conceived as an epiphany, the significance of a future parousia diminishes. Faith is already in possession; hope no longer presses. The expectation of return is becoming the formalized conclusion of the tidings of salvation, as soon it will be, in the Creed that is already taking shape.

f) Epistle to the Hebrews

In the Epistle to the Hebrews, the expectation of the parousia is unbroken. "Only a very short time yet, then he who is to come will come, and will not delay" (10:37). The Epistle takes up Is. 26:20. In general, in the Old Testament the Messiah is called "He who is to come" (Ps. 118:26). The prophecy will be fulfilled in the imminent parousia of the Lord. Then too will the righteous receive the eschatological promise (10:38f.).

g) Catholic Epistles

The Epistle of James bears witness to the conviction of the nearness of the parousia: "Wait patiently, strengthen your hearts. For the parousia has drawn near" (James 5:8). As so frequently, here too the Epistle speaks with assurance of the now short period of waiting, in the form and spirit of the humble piety of the Old Testament (Ps. 37:10f; Sir. 35:16-24). The expectation of the parousia is sure, as certain, in fact, as "the farmer patiently awaiting the precious fruits of his field" (5:7). This certitude is only the more remarkable when we consider that the Epistle of James is probably to be dated in late Apostolic times.

The First Epistle of John uses the word parousia: "Abide in him, so that when he appears, we may have confidence and not be ashamed in his presence at his parousia" (2:28). The Epistle bears witness to uninterrupted imminent expectation. "It is the final hour." Antichrists are abroad (2:18). The Epistle includes the incarnation of the Son of God (1:2; 3:5, 8) and his parousia under the term "be made manifest" ($\phi\alpha\nu\epsilon\rho o\tilde{\upsilon}\sigma\theta\alpha\iota$).[255] If the incarnation was a manifesting of God's love (4:9), then Christ will at the end be made manifest as Judge (2:28). That first and this last manifestation are but a single manifestation of God in the earthly-human realm. The Epistle speaks not only of the future judgment but also of the already perfected present determination. "We know that we have passed over from death into life, since we love the brothers" (3:14; similar in 5:12). The report is quite similar to that which is found in John's Gospel. There, too, the future resurrection is emphasized alongside a passage from death to life that has already taken place (John 5:24-29; 11:23-26). The hypothesis is established that the doctrine of a future resurrection is inserted in the Gospel in a later redaction (see below, § 17, 2, e). What must be considered, then, is whether the prospect of the future parousia in 1 John 2:28 does not likewise provide evidence of later redaction.[256]

The First Epistle of Peter, in view of its expectation of the parousia, offers the admonition: "The end of all things has drawn near. Be prudent, therefore, and sober, in prayer" (4:7). In the foreknowledge of the Lord's imminent return and of the end of all things, the Christian in the world is truly prudent. Because he knows the ephemeral quality of the world, he is sober in respect thereto (1:13). The nearness of judgment gives him an appreciation of the fact that his life is menaced. This turns him into a man of prayer (4:7). In the imminent judgment, love will save, love which "covers over a multitude of sins" (4:8). Thus we have a picture of the Christian in the service of love in the community. Those who share in the Passion of Christ can be jubilant, full of joy, at his parousia, the manifestation of his glory (4:13; similar in 5:10).

In the Second Epistle of Peter, which is probably to be dated at the beginning of the second century, the word parousia is found, along with questions about its expectation. "It was not in following tenuous myths that we made known to you the might and parousia of our Lord Jesus Christ; rather, we were eyewitnesses of his grandeur" (1:16). That might or power is the divine power which the exalted One will make known at the parousia. The gospel of the parousia is no myth, but future history, guaranteed by a past history which had its eyewitnesses. Probably the mentioning of myths refers to Gnostic errors. The Epistle, however, must defend the expectation of the parousia. "In the last days deceitful scoffers will arise, who walk according to their own lusts and say: 'Where now is the promise of his parousia? Ever since the fathers fell asleep, everything remains as it was from the beginning of creation'" (3:3f.)

These scoffers are probably Gnostic heretics. The generation which expected the coming of Christ (Mark 9:1; 13:30) is dead. The Epistle means to counteract the assertion of its opponents that since the beginning of creation nothing has taken place, by calling to mind the destruction of the world in the deluge (3:6). So too will the present world come to an end. In fire, it will pass away "with a sizzle. Burning, the elements will be melted together" (3:12).

Besides biblical terms, the Epistle also employs secular philosophical concepts of its time which predict the great world conflagration. The Epistle says, however, that the word of God determines the history of the world (3:7). The day of the world's end is "the day with the Lord" (3:8). Those who in expectation await the judgment must "live in holy behavior and piety" (3:11). The world is not nature but history. But there is no human measure of time that is valid for this history. "With the Lord a thousand years are as a single day" (3:8; Ps. 90:4). Apocalyptic calculations, therefore, are precluded. The end, however, is not destruction and dissolution, but new creation (3:13; see below, § 20, 2). Just as the creation narratives of Genesis interpret Oriental myths biblically for the word of God, so too 2 Peter employs the mythological and scientific traditions of its time in order to depict God's operations.

h) Apocalypse of John

The Apocalypse of John means to unveil "what must soon take place" (1:1). "The time is near" (1:3). The necessity of what is to happen has its basis in the plan and will of God. The book, written toward the end of the first century, presents throughout an urgent eschatological expectation. The Church is the Church of the martyrs, and it expects, as arriving soon, God's comfort and redemption. In two visions the Apocalypse represents the parousia of Christ, as Judge and

King: 14:14-20 and 19:11-16. The two visions are independent and describe the same event in different ways.

In the first vision (Apoc. 14:14-20), Christ appears as Son of Man (as in Mark 13:26), enthroned on a white cloud, on his head a golden crown and in his hand a sharp sickle. An angel emerges from heaven and calls to the Son of Man: "Put forth your sickle and reap. The harvests of the earth is overripe." As so frequently in John's Apocalypse, the vision employs and combines compact Old Testament themes. The Son of Man is as in Dan. 7:13. The term and image of the harvest draw upon Joel 3:13a, Is. 17:5; and Jer. 51:33. The harvest is depicted first as a reaping of grain by the Son of Man (14:16), and then as a gathering of grapes by an angel, who also works the wine press (14:18-20). If the first harvest image signifies the gathering of the pious, then the second depicts the judgment on the world. The wine press is an image of divine wrath, as in Joel 3:13b; Is. 63:2-4; Lam. 1:15. The judgment is wrought outside the city (i.e., in the Valley of Gehinnom, outside the city of Jerusalem; see below, § 19, 2 a) as a horrible bloodbath (depicted as in Is. 34:3-5; *Ethiopic Henoch* 100:1-3; *4 [6] Esdras* 15:35f.). Here too it is the angels who carry out the judgment (as in Mark 13:27; Matthew 13:41; 25:31).

In the second vision (19:11-16), the heavens are standing open and Christ comes forth from there as a rider on a white horse. The heavenly armies follow him on white horses. He wears many crowns and his eyes are like flames of fire (see Dan. 10:6). His name is "The Word of God." His weapon is the destroying word of the Judge, just as in Wis. 18:15f., where the Word of God, like a sharp sword leaping down from heaven, works judgment and fills all things with death. The King pastures the nations with an iron staff (see Ps. 2:9) and treads the wine press of God's wrath (see Joel 3:13 and Is. 63:3). It is thus that he is manifested as "King of Kings and Lord of Lords" (Apoc. 19:16).

The Apocalypse closes (22:20) with a cry of yearning: "Amen! Lord Jesus, come!" Again, this seems to be, like the prayer of similar import, "Maranatha," in 1 Cor. 16:22 (see above, § 16, 3, d), a liturgical cry, which in the present instance is in reply to the promise of the exalted One: "Yes, I am coming soon!" (22:20). That call, therefore, of the primitive community of Aramaic-speaking people seems to have

been translated in the Greek-speaking Church. After all the images
and mythologizations, tensions and conflicts, now at last, in this cry,
the eschatological hope that fills the whole book declares itself in plain
language and with great fervor!

4. MEANING OF THE PAROUSIA

What does the gospel of the parousia mean? The parousia presupposes the ancient and mythical concept of the world as heaven above
the earth and the throne of God above the world. If the ascension of
Christ, described according to this same conception, is a portrayal circumscribed by a presupposed imagery (see the present work, Vol. 2,
pp. 127f.), it is thus too with the parousia. The proclaiming of the
parousia bears witness to the faith of the Church and that salvation is
still hidden from the world. The Church does not claim to be a "perfected society." She awaits the raising of herself in the perfection of
God. "Return of Christ is the entry of the Indispensable into the self-
sufficient ghetto of our absolute attachment to our present existence.
To keep this absolute concern with the present world open to the creative power of the Indispensable God is the hazardous undertaking of
Christian existence."[257]

§ 17. RESURRECTION OF THE DEAD

1. OLD TESTAMENT AND JUDAISM

In Israel's older philosophy and outlook on the world and on life,
death leads irretrievably to the underworld of Sheol, which is remote
from God.[258] Here the dead live an extremely diminished and shadowy
existence, which probably ceases entirely after a time. "The underworld does not praise you, nor does death laud you; those who go
down to the grave do not look for your fidelity" (Is. 38:18f.; see above,
§ 15, 2). God's friends Henoch (Gen. 5:24) and Elijah (2 Kings 2:11)

were enraptured before death, because beyond death there is no longer any hope.

In certain of the psalms, probably later ones, the conviction begins to be heard that one whom God favors is not deprived of his companionship even in death. Faith acknowledges: "Your favor is better than life" (Ps. 63:4). The temporal and natural life is gift of God. And still there is grace as a greater gift. The hope raises itself that the pious man is never excluded from God's realm and from life, if he but once can tarry therein. "You lead me with your counsel, and afterwards you take me into your glory" (Ps. 73:24). God embraces all realms. "If I mount up to heaven, you are there. If I make my bed in the land of the dead, you are there too" (Ps. 139:8).

Quite otherwise than in the pagan religions, in the faith of Israel the land of the dead has no other ruler than the one God (Amos 9:2; Job 26:6; Prov. 15:11). Man is never outside the realm and sway of this God. The dead are at his disposal. Finally, the God of Israel is the God who loves. Valid here in all its consequences is the saying: "Love is strong as death" (Cant. 8:6). Israel's faith in God arrives at the hope and intuition of a life beyond death, in the companionship of God.

The certainly postexilic apocalypse in Isaiah (Is. 24–27) rises to new certainties and declarations.[259] "Your dead are to live, my corpses to rise again. Awake and rejoice, you inhabitants of dust" (Is. 26:19). In a portrait of apocalyptic distress (Is. 26:7-21), that verse, in which the resurrection of the dead is declared as divine promise, is probably a later insertion. Whoever added the verse, and probably a circle of followers about him, had the ability to produce a powerful representation of the resurrection of the dead.

In a description of future salvation, again probably the insertion of a later hand, there is a passage drawing the essentially correct conclusion that God will remove death in general: "He will destroy death forever" (Is. 25:8). The New Testament takes up this verse and declares with it the hope of eternal life (1 Cor. 15:54; Apoc. 21:4).

The expectation of a resurrection of the dead is conceived in terms of the Old Testament notion of man. Man is a unity of body and soul, created by God (see the present work, Vol. 1, pp. 85f.). It looks to the restoration and perfection of the whole human being, which would not be conceivable without corporeality, the latter, of course, transfigured. It is quite possible or even probable that Israel, in here development of a belief in resurrection, drew ideas and conceptions from the Iranian religion, which had a richly developed doctrine of the beyond (see below, § 18, 1).[260]

Belief in the resurrection is further elucidated. For the end of time and the establishment of the kingdom of God, Daniel (12:2) proclaims a resurrection of the dead: "Many of those who sleep in the land of dust will awake, some to eternal life and others to disgrace and eternal rejection." Daniel does not yet speak of a universal resurrection. "Many" will arise. Are these the exemplars of goodness, who arise to their reward, and the exemplars of wickedness, who arise to their punishment? The rest remain in death. The Maccabean martyrs (2 Macc. 7:9-14) declare their conviction that they will later be raised up by God. For the blasphemous king who orders their death, there will, however, be "no resurrection to life."

In later apocalyptic books, the testimonies to the resurrection, at least of the righteous, are numerous and clear. Especially notable among them are *Ethiopic Henoch* 51; 92; *Testaments of the Twelve Patriarchs: Judah* 25; *Zebulon* 10:1-3. Shortly before the time of the New Testament, the *Psalms of Solomon* (3:13-16) states that while sinners will remain in corruption, the God-fearing will rise to eternal life.

In the Qumran scrolls, the hope of a resurrection has a multiplicity of witnesses; thus, in 1 QH 11:12f.: ". . . that this worm of the dead may be raised up out of the dust to eternal counsel and from a perverse spirit to your understanding, and that he might come into your company in your presence, with the everlasting host and the spirits of knowledge, . . . to be renewed with all things that are."

The universal resurrection of the dead is taught unequivocally in the apocrypha that are contemporaneous with the New Testament. According to *4 Esdras* 5 [7]:31, the whole world awakes to a final judgment. The resurrection seems to be represented in such a way that souls, returning from the chambers of the dead, are united with their bodies, rising up from the dust. "The earth gives back those who rest therein, the dust lets loose those who sleep therein, the chambers return those confided to them" (*4 Esdras* 5[7]:32). According to the

Syriac Apocalypse of Baruch 50:2-4 and 51:1-5, the dead are raised up
in their former condition. The appearance of sinners is wrapped in
gloom, that of the righteous is transfigured.[261]

2. NEW TESTAMENT

a) Synoptics

In the New Testament, the resurrection of the dead appears as a disputed question, with the Pharisees supporting it and the Sadducees
contending against it (Mark 12:18-27; Acts 23:6-9). In the disputation
with the Sadducees, Jesus teaches the resurrection of the dead (Mark
12:18-27). The Sadducees invent — according to the levirate law of
Deut. 25:5f. — the history of a woman who married seven brothers one
after another; and the question the Sadducees propose is: "To whom
will the woman belong at the resurrection?" The question is prompted,
perhaps, by the rabbinic notion that in the future life marriage will
continue and will be endowed with a wonderful fruitfulness. The Sadducees, with the case they advance, hope to draw forth a contradiction
to belief in resurrection. Jesus' reply affirms the reality of the resurrection and explains its manner. The resurrected will be beyond married life "like the angels in heaven."

Jewish apocalyptics is capable of similar teaching. *Ethiopic Henoch*,
in 15:6f. and 51:4, and the *Syriac Apocalypse of Baruch*, in 51:3-5, say
that the resurrected are transformed to the brightness of the angels. If
"in heaven" were a circumlocution of God's name (see below, § 19, 1
a), it would be a statement to the effect that the existence of the resurrected is maintained in the companionship and in the life of God. Jesus
finds the fact of eternal life and therefore of the resurrection of the
dead declared in the word of God to Moses: "I am the God of your
father, the God of Abraham, the God of Isaac, and the God of Jacob"
(Exod. 3:6). The statement originally declared that God once dealt
with the fathers during their lifetime, and not that they are living forever in God. Jesus interprets the Old Testament passage in this latter
sense when he explains: "He is not the God of the dead but of the
living."[262] God is always the same Being, and with him are always

his elect. The Sadducees err because they know "neither the Scriptures nor the power of God."

In this disputation Jesus shares and defends the belief in the resurrection of the dead, expressly, in any case, the resurrection of the righteous. But he manifestly criticizes the misunderstanding to which a gross mentality can subject it. Resurrection of the dead is not a restoration of earthly life, but a renewal of life in a form superior to that of the earth.

In this conversation Jesus uses the scriptural technique after the fashion of the schools of the rabbis. Was he such a rabbi? Have scriptural debates or dogmatic altercations of the community with Israel or within the community itself perhaps found expression in this disputation of Jesus with the Sadducees? What exegesis is asking, then, is whether this disputation can be affirmed as being strictly historical.

A further saying of the Lord in Luke 14:14 speaks of the resurrection. A good deed "will be repaid you at the resurrection of the just." The saying could be interpreted in accord with the late Jewish belief that only the righteous will be raised up. Nevertheless, it can also proceed from the self-evident presupposition that the resurrection will be a happy consummation only for the righteous.

The parable of the rich reveler and poor Lazarus (Luke 16:19-31) employs the late Jewish notion of the chambers of the underworld, in which, after death, the righteous and sinners abide, separated from each other (*Ethiopic Henoch* 22:1-13). The possibility of the resurrection is intimated when the rich man finally begs Abraham to send a messenger to his father's house. Abraham declines: "If they do not listen to Moses and the prophets, they will not allow themselves to be convinced even if someone should be raised from the dead." Does this statement look back to the resurrection of Jesus and to its effects? Israel, not having listened to the word of God in Old Testament revelation, would not be converted even by the resurrection of Jesus.

b) Preaching of the Apostles

Early Jewish expectation of the resurrection achieves its certitude in the New Testament through the resurrection of Jesus Christ (see the present work, Vol. 2, pp. 112–136). "God has raised the Lord, and will raise us up also by his power" (1 Cor. 6:14; further, in Rom. 8:11; 1 Cor. 15:15f., 20; 2 Cor. 4:14).

That the resurrection of Christ is the basis of the universal resurrection of the dead is the substance of Paul's preaching in Athens (Acts 17:31f.). The spiritual situation is rightly assessed when the Acts of the Apostles tells that the Athenians did not understand the gospel of the resurrection. The Hellenism that, determined largely by Plato, regarded the body as the prison of the soul had no interest in a raising up of the dead to life, and no understanding of this Judeo-Christian hope. Other New Testament preaching, too, had to contend with this same philosophical outlook (1 Cor. 15:35; 2 Tim. 2:18).

c) Paul

Paul brings a quite penetrating reflection to bear on the New Testament doctrine of the universal resurrection. This is preeminently notable in 1 Cor. 15. The discussion of the theme was occasioned by false opinions in Corinth, of which Paul had learned. "Some say there be no resurrection of the dead" (15:12). This could be Greek philosophy speaking, be it a skepticism that doubted and denied any further life after death, or the attitude that did indeed believe in the immortality of the soul but looked upon the body as a burden to the soul, and for that reason would not accept a reuniting of the soul with the body. Or is it an expression of the error that "the resurrection has already taken place" (2 Tim. 2:18), insofar as the gift of the Spirit has already bestowed divine life upon men? Is a dualistic Gnosticism, inimical to the flesh, at work in Corinth, or is it that the same enthusiasm which was scandalized by the hard reality of the Cross (1 Cor. 1:18-25; 3:18-23) now likewise denies the corporeality of the resurrection?

Paul introduces the deliberation and discussion with a statement of the gospel of the resurrection of Christ, wherein he repeats the primitive Christian kerygma, already formulated as a confession of faith (1 Cor. 15:3-5; see the present work, Vol. 2, pp. 113–115). For Paul, the doctrine of the resurrection does not have its basis in philosophy or outlook on life, but in belief in the God who has been made manifest in the raising up of Christ (1 Cor. 15:12-19, 34). The reality of the resurrection of the dead passes judgment on the reality of Christian faith and life (1 Cor. 15:12-34). The resurrection of Christ is the beginning and basis of the universal resurrection. Whoever denies the one must deny the other also. The gospel is tidings of redemption from sin (1 Cor. 15:17) and of the initiation of salvation. But this has its beginning with the raising up of Jesus, as if with the beginning of new life.

Without resurrection of the dead, preaching, faith, and hope are deceptions (1 Cor. 15:17-19). Then all the trouble and danger of an apostle's life are senseless, and the only sensible thing would be the daily enjoyment of life (1 Cor. 15:32f.). The resurrection of Christ is the beginning of the movement toward the consummation. Paul points out the relation between the resurrection of Christ and his parousia. Christ is the "Firstling of those who have fallen asleep" (1 Cor. 15:20, 23). At his parousia Christians will be raised up. All powers and forces, and finally death itself, will be subject to the sovereign Christ. He will then subject the kingdom and himself to the Father, so that God may be "all in all" (1 Cor. 15:28). This is the consummate or perfected kingly rule of God.

Paul describes (1 Cor. 15:35-58) the manner of existence of the world of the resurrection and of the resurrected. Here the Apostle wants to answer those who deny the resurrection, and whose questions were intended only to demonstrate the impossibility of the corporeal resurrection. Paul says that on the other side of death God bestows a body as he will (1 Cor. 15:38). Paul sees a similarity between this and the rising up of the new plant from a grain of seed. God's creative power is boundless. There is a fullness of forms of bodies and of life; there are earthly bodies and there are heavenly bodies (the stars). "Thus a psychic body is sown, and a spiritual body is raised up" (1 Cor. 15:44).

A psychic body is the earthly body that dies. Since, in Paul, the Spirit is almost always the divine Spirit, a spiritual body is a body that God's power of life creates. The resurrection is new creation, therefore a wonder beyond all human expectation and possibility.

Paul does not teach an immortality and eternity of the soul, which is parted in death from the earthly body, and which lives on without a body, and through which man even then participates in the eternal and divine world. Nor does he follow Greek mysticism which thinks to possess the eternal in the divinization of man, who enters into the pantheistically conceived divine All. For Paul, man is always a being of corporeal existence, even in the world of the resurrection. The whole man, who is God's creation, dies and achieves salvation in God's new creation.

In 1 Cor. 15:21f., 45-49, Paul explains the relationship between creation and redemption in the figures of Adam and Christ, just as in Rom. 5:12-21 he draws a comparison of contrasts between Adam and Christ. Adam as the first man and Christ as the ultimate eschatological man are ever the image and embodiment of the whole of mankind. Adam is the earthly-psychic man, Christ is "life-creating Spirit." As earthly men we have borne the image of Adam; in the consummation we will bear the image of the heavenly Christ.

Paul is probably entering into speculations on the creation of men in accord with the history of creation. Therein the creation of Adam is spoken of twice (Gen. 1:26f. and 2:7). According to our exegesis, this has its basis in the hypothesis that two different accounts, the Priestly narrative and the Yahwist account, have been joined together. Jewish interpretation explained it quite otherwise, as for example in Philo (*Allegory of the Laws* 1, 31f. and the *Creation of the World* 1, 34), under the utilization of older notions about the primordial man and heavenly Son of Man, as pursued in the Platonic doctrine of ideas. Accordingly, the first account in Gen. 1:26f. would be speaking of the creation of the primordial man and ideal man, who is a divine being, and the second account in Gen. 2:7 of the earthly-real man.

Paul certainly says that the first man was the earthly-psychic Adam, and the second man is the Christ, with pneumatic power. The new life is not transmitted by a nature to which it is bound; rather, it is an ever spiritual existence. While death by sin is present reality, the new life is of the future and a hope (1 Cor. 15:22). This is the Pauline eschatological reservation or postponement.

Just as Paul keeps apart from the spiritualistic Greek outlook, so too he separates himself from the materialistic Jewish conception of the beyond (1 Cor. 15:50-53), according to which the resurrection is the restoration and continuation of earthly life. In Mark 12:18-27, Jesus had already rejected this notion as resulting from a lack of knowledge of God and Scripture. Paul confirms as his doctrine that "flesh and blood"—that is, man in his earthly corporeality—"cannot inherit the kingdom of God." In death man passes through a mysterious transformation into a new life, which is entirely a creative action of God.

Even the Old Testament (Dan. 12:3) and Jewish apocalyptics expect such a transformation to heavenly glory. For the living this will take place at the parousia. Trumpets (as already in 1 Thess. 4:16; see Matthew 24:31 and above, § 16, 3, d) will signal the resurrection of the dead. The corruptible must put on incorruption (1 Cor. 15:53; similar in 2 Cor. 5:4). Condensing his thoughts on the union of Law, sin, and death, which are treated more fully in Rom. 7, Paul concludes by giving praise to God, by whose grace and power sin and death are overcome in the victory of life (1 Cor. 15:54-57).

Paul utilizes the notions and insights of a long tradition. But he gives them a new basis by anchoring them in a Christology. The universal resurrection of the dead takes place in consequence of the resurrection of the dead (1 Cor. 15:3-22). Like Adam, and incomparably more than with him, Christ is life and spirit (1 Cor. 15:22, 45-47). Beyond Christ, salvation history leads back to God (1 Cor. 15:28). Tradition is directed and concentrated in an eschatological and theological fashion. In all, Paul's use of the traditional doctrines of faith is a critical one. Even in the description and development of eschatological hope, sober consideration must not be lacking (1 Cor. 15:34, 58). Resurrection and eternal life are a mystery inaccessible to human understanding. Anyone who thinks he can investigate or know everything is a fool (1 Cor. 15:36).

Paul has a predilection for dialectical passages. We can, no doubt, say that all things will be otherwise than they are now; but we cannot say how they will be (1 Cor. 15:39-49). The earthly and the heavenly body are not at all identical (1 Cor. 15:35-38). However well Paul can depict the apocalyptic scene in the broad strokes of traditional images (1 Thess. 4:14-17), now he says only that all will take place "in an instant, in the blink of an eye" (1 Cor. 15:52). Where is there time for the course of the events described? Have they no temporal dimension? Creation and redemption are the work of a powerful God, rich in mercy. Man cannot take the measure of God's real and possible plans and actions.

The event of resurrection is treated also in 2 Cor. 5:1-10. Paul spoke before of the certainty of the hope of resurrection with Jesus (2 Cor. 4:14) and of "eternal abundance of glory" (2 Cor. 4:17). This hope, nevertheless, tends not to the visible but to the invisible. "For the visible is temporal, the invisible is eternal" (2 Cor. 4:18). This leads into the passage in 2 Cor. 5:1-10, which treats in detail of eschatological expectation. He describes therein the hope itself and its blessings in numerous graphic images: earthly home and tent (2 Cor. 5:1-4); clothing and nakedness (2 Cor. 5:2f.); homeland and exile (2 Cor. 5:6-9); and finally, judgment seat and recompense (2 Cor. 5:10).

Whereas Paul said before that in daily dying union with the Lord only becomes ever stronger (2 Cor. 4:16), now he says that living in love means separation from the Lord (2 Cor. 5:6-9). Before he spoke of the conquest of death as already accomplished (2 Cor. 4:16f.), but now of the dread of death as yet to be overcome (2 Cor. 5:2-5). By this contrariety the texts declare that Paul is not to be pinned down to too great a literal understanding of his own imagery. In the images employed, Paul makes use of biblical tradition, and perhaps also the content of other (Gnostic?) traditions — thus with earthly home and tent (Is. 38:12; Wis. 9:15; 2 Peter 1:13); clothing (Apoc. 3:18; 4:4; 6:11; *Ethiopic Henoch* 62:16; *Ascension of Isaiah* 9); homeland (Phil. 3:20; Heb. 12:22).

The heavenly home which we are to possess is already prepared in heaven, just as the good things of the salvation in the messianic era have been readied from time immemorial (2 Cor. 5:1). Of an identity between the present and the future body, which our dogmatics teaches, there can scarcely any more be any discussion.

What is meant to be said with these images is a question for exegesis. Paul is arguing, or so it appears, against opponents in Corinth who deny a bodily resurrection. They think that after death the soul mounts up to the world of light, freed from the body as from fetters, designated in images as a confining house or as clothing. But Paul, in accord with biblical-Jewish anthropology, cannot conceive of disembodied life. His manner of thought is not at all Greek when he conceives the disembodied as naked, and nakedness as degrading. It is not that the body is evil, which could probably indicate a dualist philosophy, but it is sin that is evil (Rom. 8:10). Paul's hope awaits a new, transfigured body (as in 1 Cor. 15:35-38), with which he is to be clothed over. The earthly body, if it is so clothed over, will be wonderfully transformed. The mortal will be swallowed up by the immortal (1 Cor. 15:53-55).

When is this clothing-over to take place? At death, or at parousia and resurrection? And if the latter, is the interim period between death and parousia to be understood as one of being naked? Then Paul would wish to live until the parousia, or at least, that the interim state between death and parousia might be as short as possible.

Yet, in Phil. 1:23 the interim is a state of happy existence with Christ. In 2 Cor. 5:1-10, Paul speaks expressly neither of parousia nor of resurrection. If in 2 Cor. 5:4, he speaks of the "clothing-over" that pertains to the heavenly house; and if, according to 1 Cor. 15:53, at the parousia "the corruptible puts on the incorruptible," it still does not follow that in 2 Cor. 5:4 he is alluding to the parousia. The not infrequently employed image of being clothed-over simply indicates the reception of a new manner of existence. Thus in 2 Cor. 5:4; Paul probably refers to the ever personal experience of death, or even the end condition ushered in along with death, which is transfigured corporeality.

We would wish that transfiguration might be achieved in immediate passage from life without a transition through death. Thus it appears that in this text Paul is expressing the universal human wish to experience death, not as death, but as a transformation. He conceives death as a power, as a reality inimical to God. The Apostle articulates what lies within the nature of man, who hopes not to have to relinquish life, but to achieve a new and true life. God has created him for the consummation of this perfection. The gift of the Spirit, which is an installment towards the whole gift, prepares its consummation in advance. The Spirit is the beginning of the new, heavenly existence (2 Cor. 5:5).

Again and again Paul says that the resurrection of Christ is the basis for the Christian's hope of resurrection (see above, present section). The salvation event is the same for Christ and for Christians. Paul yearns "to know Christ and the power of his resurrection and the fellowship with his suffering, conformed alike to his death, so that in the end I might attain to the resurrection from the dead" (Phil 3:10f.). The "coming to know" of which he speaks will have manifold expressions: obedience, doctrine, faith, sacraments, life.

In the resurrection of Christ, the power of God is made manifest, as also the personal power of Christ. The divine power becomes the power of the Apostle. It is operative even now, especially in the conquest of suffering, and it will become efficacious in participation in the resurrection from the dead. If the Christian is conformed with the death of Christ, he hopes to achieve, also with Christ, the resurrection (1 Cor. 15:30-32; 2 Cor. 4:10f.).

Does the uncertainty expressed in "so that *in the end* I might attain to the resurrection from the dead" negate a false doctrine to the effect that resurrection has already taken place in this life (2 Tim. 2:18)? Paul, too, knows the power of the resurrection as effective even now, but he emphasizes that the totality of the eschatological perfecting is still to be awaited as gift of God.

The power of the resurrection of Christ become effective in faith and sacrament, inasmuch as baptism accomplishes in the faithful the death and resurrection of Jesus (Rom. 6:2-11). Thus for Paul the eschatological reservation holds good again. For the present, Christians must ratify their baptism in being dead to sin but alive to God (Rom. 6:11). The consummation of resurrection is promised for the future. "If we have died with Christ, we believe that we shall also live with him" (Rom. 6:8).

d) Deutero-Pauline Epistles

In the Deutero-Pauline Epistles — and this is surely characteristic of them — this eschatological reservation or postponement diminishes. "Buried with him in baptism, you were also raised up with him through faith in the power of God, who raised him from the dead" (Col. 2:12). Being raised up with Christ is something that has already happened to the believer; and certainly this is something that is effective only through faith, so it is not some event of natural necessity. Only at the manifestation of Christ in the parousia will the as yet hidden life of redemption be made manifest (Col. 3:3f.).[263]

Toward the end of the apostolic age, the resurrection of the dead is a firm doctrinal article of faith. Belonging to the "foundation" are "the doctrine on baptism and laying on of hands, resurrection of the dead, and eternal judgment" (Heb. 6:1f.). Even Israel can learn these articles of faith. The catechesis of the Church includes, however, a Christology, even if the name of Christ is not mentioned here, since the universal resurrection has its basis in the resurrection of Christ, and since Christ is Judge in the general judgment (see below, § 18, 3, f-g).

The Pastoral Epistles, too, account the denial of the future resurrection as destruction of the foundation of the faith. "They have strayed from the truth, who say the resurrection has already taken place" (2 Tim. 2:18). The erroneous teaching probably arises from Greek philosophy, which depreciated the body as prison of the soul, and even from the spiritualistic gnosis, which accorded a value only to the spirit. It is from these that the assertion might be drawn that the resurrection has already taken place in the gift of spirit and in the spiritual awakening through faith.

e) Gospel of John

In the Gospel of John, the whole eschatology, and with it the resurrection of the dead, is graphically presented. The eschatological decision begins now; indeed, it has already taken place in the person and manifestation of Christ. And it takes place continually in the faith. Faith means to know and experience the end of the world and time. In the decision between faith and disbelief the judgment now takes place (John 3:18f., 36; 9:39). Even the resurrection has already taken place and takes place now. "The hour is coming, and is now here, when the dead will hear the voice of God, and those who hear it will live" (John 5:25). The resurrection to life is not the endtime resurrection of the dead on a distant day; rather, it takes place now as the awakening of men from spiritual death at hearing and accepting the gospel. Standing at the tomb of Lazarus, Martha says: "I know that the dead will rise at the resurrection on the last day." Jesus answers her: "I am the resurrection and the life. Whoever believes in me, even if he dies, shall live; and each one who believes in me will not die for ever" (John 11:24-26). One who believes "has already passed over from death into life (John 5:24).

The same Gospel of John speaks also of the last day as future event: "The hour is coming in which all who are in their graves will hear the voice of the Son of Man, and those who have done good will enter into the resurrection of life, those who have done evil, into the resurrection of judgment (John 5:28f.). In the discourse about the bread of life, which states that Jesus gives and is the true Bread (John 6:27, 35), the statement is repeated like a refrain: "I will raise him up on the last day" (John 6:39f., 44, 54).

Are the two series of declarations, about the present and future resurrection, of any possible significance side by side? Traditional exegesis has sought to unite the two series to each other. It may be said that the decision has already been made, but will be manifest and ratified only in the final judgment.[264]

Rudolf Bultmann has given an explanation conclusively and of more far-reaching effectiveness. He thinks the two series of declarations permit of no uniting among themselves. He supposes the Evangelist has taught an eschatology realized in the present, and thus the futurity of it would be in relation to believing men today. All statements that were speaking of the eschatology as future event will have been the insertions of a later redactor who wanted to assimilate the Gospel of John to the common ecclesiastical teaching, and thereby make possible the acceptance of the Gospel in the Church.

Critical analysis shows, for Bultmann, that the texts which teach future eschatology are secondary not only by reason of their content, but are proved to be later insertions even from literary-stylistic indices. Even John's Gospel expects a consummation. This, however, is not a cosmic history, but a consummation of the faith of the disciple in eternal life. It is also the consummation of the salvational community. Christ is present in his work and in the faith, in the world and in the Church. That is where the apocalyptic parousia is to be sought. The gospel no longer describes the apocalyptic world-theater. Eschatology is demythologized and existentially interpreted.[265]

3. Dogmatic Questions

The usual presentation and teaching of the resurrection on the last day is to a considerable extent historically conditioned, since it uses the imaginal descriptions and presentations of Old Testament Jewish apocalyptics. This holds good also for the representation of the judgment⋅ (see below, § 18), as well as of heaven and hell (below, § 19).

Paul and John accepted traditional eschatology, but with independent reflection and reductive criticism. As so often, so here too, for us the problem that arises seems to be one of winning the old truth for ourselves anew. Modern theology will have to recognize questions of natural science, which arise from the propositions of the conservation and movement of matter. The doctrine of the material identity of the dead and risen body is ultimately confronted by apologetics only in a minimal way.[266] The attempt to harmonize natural science and Bible in the eschatology calls to mind the unfortunate attempt to balance the biblical history of creation and the teaching of natural science on the origin of the world.

More recent Protestant theology broadly denies the (philosophical) doctrine of the natural immortality of man (see above, § 15, 1). God, however, bestows life on man at man's death, and thus gives him immortality. This is new creation. Resurrection, then, after a long interim period, would be meaningless;[267] on the other hand, that new creation would in fact be a resurrection. Even modern Catholic theology considers the idea that the resurrection takes place in the instant of death, in which God accepts and perfects the man.

The new Dutch Catechism (*De nieuwe Katechismus*, translated by Kevin Smyth as *The New Catechism*, Herder and Herder, New York 1972, p. 474, says ". . . *existence after death is already something like the resurrection of the new body.* . . . Man begins to awake as a new man."[268]

Is there no respite at all, then, no foregoing of presumptions and declarations on what God will do? Do we not thereby create a new mythology?

§ 18. JUDGMENT

1. EXTRA-BIBLICAL REPRESENTATIONS

That man stands under divine judgment and must justify himself before it is the belief of ancient peoples as well as of the Bible, Old Testament and New.[269]

Egyptian religion bears witness, as far back as the third century before Christ, to representations of a judgment after death. This is the case with papyrus texts from the tombs of the kings of the old kingdom, in mummy-case texts of the middle kingdom, and in the *Book of the Dead*, as, in the new kingdom, this information was imparted to the dead, on sheets of papyrus.[270]

The Iranian religion has broad and rich perceptions of judgment, punishment, and reward in a world beyond, which developed from the century of Zoroaster (Zarathustra — *ca.* 600 B.C.) up to Christian times. After death the soul comes before the judgment conducted by three angels. The good attain to the place of life, the wicked plunge headlong into the darkness of hell, where they are tormented by devils. After the universal resurrection of the dead, world judgment passes sentence forever with punishment or reward. Purifying fire is the means of divine justice. After the judgment the earth will be renewed as paradise, where the blessed will dwell.

Jews belonged to the Persian Empire from the conquest of Babylon by Cyrus until its end (539–331 B.C.,). That Judaism was variously influenced by Persian (Iranian) culture is not contested. To what extent, however, and from precisely what period onwards the Jewish religion, and especially Old Testament apocalyptics, experienced Iranian influences is a difficult and much disputed question. In any case, for later Judaism it can hardly be denied.[271]

In Greek religion, law and morals had divine dignity and godly sanction. Dikē, the goddess of the law, is the daughter of Zeus and his enthroned companion. Homer's Odysseus (11, 20-640) and Vergil's Aeneas (6, 262-892) describe the kingdom of Hades, with examples of punishment and reward in the beyond. Plato portrays in three dialogues (*Gorgias* 523 A–527 A; *Phaedo* 113 D–114 A; *Republic* 614 B–615 D) the judgment held over the dead by three demigods. The guilty must take a road to the left, leading to Tartarus, while the righteous take the road to the right, on which they attain to the Isles of the Blessed. That Plato again and again employs splendid visions and wonderful myths to portray the world beyond clearly indicates that these things transcended all conceptual thought.

With the development of its representations of the beyond, especially of the judgment of the dead and of the destinies of souls, possibly

Hellenism underwent Egyptian and Oriental influences on its Orphic mysteries, to which even Plato repeatedly refers, but which also old, primitive folk-religions have preserved.

2. OLD TESTAMENT AND JUDAISM

For the Old Testament, it is certain that God, as Creator of the world, is also its Lord and Judge. His judgment follows from the history of men and nations. Nevertheless, Israel expects also the universal final judgment.

Yahweh judges the nations. The great judgment will take place on the "Day of Yahweh" (see above, § 12, 1, c). A text common to Is. 2:2-4 and Micah 4:1-3 says: At the end of days all peoples will stream to the mountain of the Lord, which towers over all mountains, and to the house of the God of Jacob. Among the peoples he will judge, and over the nations he will pass sentence. Then the great reign of peace will begin. Exegesis is not certain to whom or to what time the verses are to be attributed. Do Isaiah and Micah quote some older prophet, or were the verses inserted by a prophet of the exilic period? Yahweh will pour out his indignation and wrath upon the peoples, and the fire of his zeal will consume the earth (Zeph. 3:8). "He judges the world with justice, and for the peoples he makes things right with equity" (Ps. 9:9). Yahweh appears as Judge of peoples in the undoubtedly postexilic Psalms 94 and 96–99.

Yahweh is Judge also over Israel. Israel expects that the Day of Yahweh will bring judgment upon the Gentile peoples, but for Israel herself it will be a day of joy. Nevertheless, the Prophet has to announce: "Woe to those who desire the Day of Yahweh. What is the Day of Yahweh to you? It is darkness and not light" (Amos 5:18). Israel will be judged with special severity. "You alone have I chosen before all the tribes of the earth. Therefore will I visit upon you all your guilt" (Amos 3:2). Yahweh will punish the disobedient among his people (Is. 1:19f.), the greed of the rich (Micah 2:1-4), all immorality, murder, violence, and adultery (Hos. 4:1-6; Mal. 3:2-5). Yahweh protects the rights of the downtrodden and avenges the blasphemy of the godless (Ps. 94).

To the extent that the individual in Israel gains importance as an individual apart from the nation, the judgment begins to be understood more and more as being of personal concern. Yahweh is salvation for the pious, damnation for the godless (Ezek. 18). Individual responsibility is accentuated in the later Old Testament books (Wis. 4:20–5:23; Sir. 16:17-23). The judgment of God is represented as a process after the style of human judgment. God sits in judgment over men, angels, and demons. "Then thrones were placed and the Ancient of Days sat. . . . Judgment was held, and books were opened" (Dan. 7:9-14).

The representations of judgment were further developed in late Jewish apocalyptics. The great world judgment is depicted in *Ethiopic Henoch* 1–5; 45–47; 55; 90. The judgment day is called "the last day," because it forms the end of the present age. "What can they say at the judgment? What answer can they make on the last day?" (*4 Esdras* 5 [7], 73). The Judge is God, who appears surrounded by the heavenly hosts (*Ethiopic Henoch* 1:4-9). The Son of Man too will judge (*Ethiopic Henoch* 45f.; 55; 71). Sentencing follows the verdict. "The undertaking goes on, recompense appears. Good deeds awake, wicked deeds fall asleep no more" (*4 Esdras* 5 [7]:35). The special or particular judgment after death brings an immediate decision between blessedness and damnation (*4 Esdras* 5[7]:78-99).

"On the day of judgment God will destroy from the earth the godless and all who adore idols" (1 QpHab 13:2-4). The holy men of Qumran are convinced that in the judgment God will lead their cause to victory. "The sword of God will come swiftly in the time of the judgment, and all the sons of his truth will prepare themselves to destroy the sons of blasphemy and the sons of guilt will be no more" (1 QH 6:29f.).[272]

3. NEW TESTAMENT

That God is the Judge is likewise the conviction of the whole New Testament. The message is more intense because of the proclamation of the impending nearness of the judgment. It becomes a message of salvation through the promise of deliverance in the judgment.

a) John the Baptist

In continuation of the early Jewish apocalyptic expectation, John the Baptist proclaims the imminent judgment (Matthew 3:7-10 = Luke 3:7-9, from Source Q). The conviction that "God's wrath" is coming makes John a preacher of conversion. The prophets' threatened "Day of the Lord" and "Terror of the Lord" (Amos 5:18-20; Is. 2:6-21; Zeph. 1:14-18) has drawn near.

b) Synoptics

Statements and discourses of Jesus predict the rewarding and punishing judgment of God (present work, Vol. 3, pp. 36f.). The distinction is brought into prominence in the contrast of the statements of blessing and threats of woe in Luke 6:20-26. The Jesus of the Sermon on the Mount according to Matthew 5:21f., 22-27 speaks of God's judgment after the manner of the Old Testament (Exod. 20:13f.) and even heightens its exactions. Man is ever on the way to God's judgment. He ought therefore always reconcile himself with his opponent — man or God — so that he will not be brought before the judgment and be vanquished there (Matthew 5:25).

The statements on admission warn that while the many walk the road to perdition, one must exert himself to travel the close path and pass through the narrow gate in order to gain life (Matthew 7:13f.). One must not be like the worthless tree that is threatened with being cut down and cast into the fire. Man must account for the fruits of his life (Matthew 7:17-19). In regard to the expected judgment, the disciples are warned not to judge others, because judging belongs to God's judgment (Matthew 7:1). (In Mark 7:2, the absolute prohibition of judging is tempered to the necessities of life; it is mellowed with an admonition to just and charitable judgment.)

The disciples are not to fear men, who can do no more than kill the body. They must fear him who has the power to destroy in hell the whole man, body and life together. In the narrative example of the rich reveler and poor Lazarus, the decision follows immediately upon death (Luke 16:19-31). The rich man is buried, the poor man is brought into the bosom of Abraham (see below, § 19, 2, b). In all these statements of Jesus, a judgment is indicated of such kind that it will pass sentence on each individual man. If we are to reckon here with the dogmatic distinction of particular and general judgment, we would have to recognize that it is consistently the particular judgment that is spoken of in these statements.

Further statements of Jesus treat of the general and public judgment. All those statements which announce the parousia of Jesus are predicated on this general judgment (see above, § 16, 3, a). The one who returns in the parousia will be the Judge in the great judgment. It is this judgment that is meant when Jesus threatens the cities of Israel with a day of judgment "on which it will be more tolerable for Sodom and Gomorrha" (Matthew 10:15). In accord with Gen. 19, Sodom and Gomorrha are, in biblical tradition (Jer. 23:14; Ezek. 16:48-50; Rom. 9:29; Jude 7) as well as in extra-biblical (*3 Macc.* 2:5; *Testaments of the Twelve Patriarchs: Nephtali* 3:4; 4:1; Philo, *Life of Moses* 2, 56), examples of divine punishment. Jesus warns the cities privileged to have witnessed his deeds about the judgment, which, for them, will be even more terrible than that which is to overtake the worst pagan cities like Tyre and Sidon (Is. 23; Ezek. 26-28; Matthew 11:21f.). His threat predicts that at the final judgment the people of Nineveh and the Queen of the South will come forward against the lack of faith of the generation to whom he is speaking. These statements signify that generations long past will, by means of the resurrection, rise up from the dead, and they will accuse Israel on the apocalyptic day of judgment. The judgment ponders and graduates punishments. The history of the Old Testament is displayed as an example, after the manner of the Wisdom literature (Sir. 44-50; Wis. 10-19).

The parable of the weeds among the wheat (Matthew 13:24-30) teaches that after the present time and its message of salvation, a general final judgment will pass sentence on participation in God's kingdom. The messianic community is not yet sufficiently pure and perfect. Perhaps Jesus emphasizes this in opposition to Pharisaic zelotism. The certainly later explanation of the parable in Matthew 13:36-43 interprets the parable in reference to the world judgment. The harvest is the consummation of the world. The Judge is the Son of Man, who sends out his angels so that they will bring about the world harvest. The judgment separates the good and the wicked. The wicked are thrown into the oven of fire, the righteous shine in the kingdom of the Father (see below, § 19). In its explanation the parable becomes a declaration warning of judgment for the Church.

The parable of the fish taken in a net (Matthew 13:47-50) has a similar content. God's tendering of grace aims to gather all; now, in time, his patience yields a mishmash of just and wicked. But finally the judgment will distinguish between them. Again it is the angels who are the servants of the judgment which casts the wicked into the fiery oven. In both parables it is said of the final judgment that future and judgment are planned in the present decision of man, for which an accounting must be made.

The parable about the man without a wedding garment (Matthew 22:11-14) is a warning about the judgment. The parable was originally independent. Probably it was united redactionally with the parable of the marriage feast (Matthew 22:1-10). The seams still show. According to Matthew 22:9f., the guests were brought in off the streets. How, then, can the host demand that the person invited appear in a wedding garment? The parable of the wedding garment was attached in order that one might, with no efforts of his own, find entry to the banquet, that is, to the kingdom. The garment signifies festive beauty and is a biblical image for eschatological justification (Is. 61:10; Apoc. 19:18). The parable of the wedding garment emphasizes the requirement of worthiness through moral conduct. The condemnation to the punishment of damnation bursts the seams of the parable.

In Matthew 7:21-23, the final judgment is anticipated. The immediately prior statements in Matthew 7:13-20 summon up moral endeavor, which alone gives hope to the one who stands in judgment. In Matthew 7:21-23, this is depicted as world judgment. The judgment is activated "on that day," that is, on the day referred to in the Old Testament as the "Day of Yahweh." Jesus is the Judge who passes sentence on entry into the kingdom of heaven. He is addressed as "Lord, Lord." He is already the exalted Lord (see the present work, Vol. 2, pp. 210–214). He speaks as the Son when he says that the fulfillment of his Father's will decides entry into the kingdom. The Son is one with the Father (see the present work, Vol. 2, pp. 193–203).

Those to be judged will insist in vain that they made predictions, drove out demons, and worked wonders in the name of Jesus. The name of the "Lord" Jesus is already a confession of faith that sets the community apart from the world. The deeds mentioned are capacities that are treasured in the community as charisms (1 Cor. 12:8-10). For Jesus (Matthew 25:40, 45f.), however, and for the community, the determining factor is the fulfilling of the commandment of love (1 Cor. 12:31–13:13). In the statements of Matthew 7:21-23, the community is in judgment before its exalted Lord. The statements are a later construction. They are developed from their short form in Luke 6:46, where it is stated that the word of Jesus included in itself eschatological determination. This can be a saying of Jesus, if it is understood that "Lord, Lord" was an address to the Teacher.

A detailed exposition of the world judgment is given in Matthew 25:31-46.[273] The pericope is in its entirety the peculiar property of Matthew. Parallels even of individual verses are not to be identified. In tradition, no source for the pericope can be designated nor even surmised. The Evangelist deliberately situates the passage at the conclusion of chapters 24 and 25 of the Gospel. Both chapters treat of the eschatological judgment. To begin with, Matthew 24:1-31, following Mark 13, tells of the end of the Temple and of the city of Jerusalem, and of the end of the world. Matthew 25:1-30 follows with two parables about the judgment: the parables of the ten virgins and the parable of the talents. These parables are finally concluded by the discourse on the great universal judgment (Matthew 25:31-46).

In Matthew 25:31f., judgment is held by the Son of Man, who, in the import of the Gospel, is the exalted Christ who has returned (see the present work, Vol. 2, pp. 185-193). In late Jewish apocalyptics, the Judge is traditionally God himself, accompanied by the angels, and not the Son of Man. Nevertheless, in *Ethiopic Henoch* (45f.; 55; 71), it is in fact the Son of Man who is Judge. The Gospel transfers to Christ, along with the function of Judge, a note of God's grandeur. "All nations are gathered before him" (Matthew 25:32). Judgment is held over all men of all times, Jew and Gentile alike. Israel believed that as God's chosen people she would be judged in the last judgment according to the measure of mercy, while the Gentiles would be damned. Of this the Gospel knows nothing.

The account presupposes that a general resurrection of the dead has taken place beforehand. The Judge is represented as a shepherd, just as in the Old Testament, God is shepherd (Ps. 23), and in antiquity, the kings are called shepherds (Ezek. 34). Sheep and rams (or goats?) are separated.[274] Right and left (Matthew 25:33) differ as signs of good fortune and misfortune.[275] The Judge is the messianic king (Matthew 25:34; see the present work, Vol. 2, pp. 89–90, 181f.). The righteous are the "blessed of the Father." The royal power of the Judge is not tyrannical, but acknowledges the Father (Matthew 20:23; John 17:24; Eph. 1:4f.).

When did the righteous become the blessed? From now on and forever? Or were they already before time the blessed, and did they choose and do what is good in the power of God's blessing? Perhaps this is indicated in the declaration that the kingdom has been prepared for them from the creation of the world. God's plan and action of salvation is from eternity. When the good people chosen are addressed as "righteous" or "just" (Matthew 25:37), this might not mean that they are righteous by reason of their own virtuous conduct, but that their justification is, by God's word, eschatological gift and consummation. The granting of salvation is founded in works of charity (Matthew 25:35f.).[276]

According to Israel's belief and piety, works of charity are highly esteemed and widely practiced (Is. 58:6f.; Ezek. 18:8, 16; Sir. 7:32-35; see also H. Strack and P. Billerbeck, *op. cit.*, Vol. 4, part 1, pp. 536–610). Even outside Israel (in Egypt, in Iran, in Greece), works of mercy are highly regarded. One who is ever helping his neighbor and does good works is carrying out Christ's will. Indeed, the works of mercy are not tendered or denied to men but to the Son of Man himself, who is Judge (Matthew 25:34-45).

In word and in deed, Jesus took to himself in a very special way the ill and the sinners, the despised and the abandoned, and treated them as his equals, making their cause his own. So too he says now that whatever was done to the helpless was done to him. Yet the righteous certainly did not know this, especially since all people of all times are judged in this judgment. Is there, then, an anonymous Christianity, which neither would nor could call itself such? If God's love, even his love in Christ, embraces all men, then is, if not every man, at least every man who responds to this love, a Christian?[277]

Appealing to Gen. 1:26f., according to which man is God's image and therefore God's representation in the world, Israel too says that what is done to men is done to God. A rabbinic statement explains: "If you have given something to the poor to eat, I account it in your regard as if you had given me something to eat." Is a Jewish representation of the judgment held by God transferred to Christ in the Gospel? In the rabbinic statement, God would be saying, as Judge of the world, that every good deed is as if done to him. Since among men a universal consciousness of God can be presupposed, such a verdict of God as Judge would be reasonable to all the righteous in judgment, just as the condemned would have to understand their respective repudiation.

Another question yet. According to the discourse in Matthew 25:31-46, is not charitable action, sympathy for one's fellow-man, the sole essence of Christianity? Is Christianity simply humanitarianism?[278] On this point, it would be well to say that certainly according to the New Testament human submission or humanitarian conduct is an essential condition of the gospel. But the commandment of love is a new commandment (John 13:34), because it has its basis and possibility in the revelation of God's love for men in Christ (see the present work, Vol. 3, pp. 124-131).

The decision of the Judge is pronounced (Matthew 25:46). Some go into the kingdom of eternal life (Matthew 25:34), others into the punishment "of the eternal fire, which was prepared for the devil and his angels" (Matthew 25:41). On heaven and hell, see below, § 19.

The portrait of the world judgment in the Gospel of Matthew is not historiography of a future event and of the end of the world. Here too the hermeneutics of the eschatological texts of the Bible must be considered. The portrait is sometimes designated parabolic discourse.[279] The action of the Judge is compared to that of a shepherd (Matthew 25:32). The description is a portrait of judgment, as it is usually found in early Jewish literature. It is a portrait like other frequently grandiose paintings of the last judgment, as found in all periods of Christian art. It must be considered, moreover, that these judgment discourses of the Gospel are to be understood and supplemented from the totality of biblical and New Testament revelation. There is no guilt and no condemnation without a tendering of clemency and forgiveness. The God of Jesus Christ is first and always the Father, who seeks out the lost, not the unmerciful Judge whose only satisfaction is to damn.

The question presents itself of whether and to what extent the discourse in Matthew 25:31-46 is an apocalyptic revelation of Jesus himself. The discourse gives evidence of a broadly developed Christology. Jesus is the Son of Man (Matthew 25:31), the messianic Shepherd and King (Matthew 25:32, 34), the Son of the Father (Matthew 25:34), the exalted Lord (Matthew 25:37, 44) — in all, the eschatological Judge. Did Jesus in this way apply Christological titles of majesty to Himself? Or are they not much more likely to be the Church's confession of faith? (See the present work, Vol. 2, p. 177). Does the discourse, furthermore, not presuppose a later Christology so clearly that it can hardly be understood as an original statement of Jesus? Does not this confession transfer to Christ a temporal-historical apocalyptic, in which God or the Messiah is represented as Judge?

c) Gospel of John

The eschatological judgment is represented in the Gospel of John. Its primary message is: "God sent his Son into the world, not that he might judge the world, but that the world might be saved through him" (John 3:17). Jesus says, therefore: "You judge according to the flesh. I judge no one" (John 8:15). Jesus does not judge anyone after the inadequate manner of men. Rather, he judges according to truth.

It is said quite properly, therefore, in the Johannine dialectic: "If I judge, My judgment is true, because I am not alone, but he that sent me is with me" (John 8:16). Jesus will judge, because it is not himself alone, but the Father also, with whom he is one, who has been disavowed: "Whoever believes in him is not judged; but whoever does not believe is already judged, because he has not believed in the name of the only-begotten Son" (John 3:18).

God's love, which sent the Son, will judge, because the world rejected the Son. The judgment itself takes place as an already present separation between belief and unbelief. "Judgment consists in this, that the light has come into the world, and men loved darkness more than the light" (John 3:19). The judgment takes place when the word and its manifestation are denied. "Whoever denies me and does not receive my word has his judge. The word, which I have spoken, will judge him" (John 12:48). This judgment takes place now in respect to the word of Jesus. "Whoever hears my word and believes him who sent me has eternal life and does not come to judgment; rather, he has passed over from death into life" (John 5:24). The "wrath of God's judgment" is on the unbelievers (John 3:36). Judgment on the world is already carried out. "Now is the judgment on this world" (John 12:31).

Thus the claim holds good in John's Gospel, as in the rest of the New Testament, that the Son is the Judge. "The Father judges no one; rather, he has given all judgment over to the Son, so that all may honor the Son even as they honor the Father" (John 5:22f.). Since the eschatology is present, any portrayal of a cosmic apocalyptic is lacking (see above, § 17, 2, e).

d) God as Judge in the Preaching of the Apostles

Drawing information from the word of Jesus as also from the faith of Israel, the apostles continue the preaching of the judgment. That God is the just Judge stands firm as an article of faith (Rom. 2:2-11; 3:4-6). God's judgment is standing at the ready (James 5:9). As Judge, God governs by the law that he himself has given. "One only is the Lawgiver and Judge, who is able to save and to destroy" (James 4:12). The Epistle concludes from this (like Matthew 7:1 and Rom. 2:1) that it is not permitted a man to pass judgment on another. "Who are you that you should judge your neighbor" (James 4:12).

The First Epistle of Peter speaks penetratingly of the judgment. God, the Father and Judge, will "judge each man's works without respect of persons" (1 Peter 1:17). Christ himself, in his suffering, "submitted the judgment to him who judges justly" (1 Peter 2:23).

The Church, too, stands under judgment. So much the more will the pagans, who defame the Christians, have to submit to the accounting which stands ready to judge the living and the dead. "For to this end was salvation proclaimed even to the dead, so that they may indeed be judged after the manner of men in the flesh, but may live after the manner of God in the spirit" (1 Peter 4:6).

At his descent into the underworld (1 Peter 3:19), Christ proclaimed redemption to the dead. They had indeed experienced death, the universal judgment on mankind (Rom. 5:12; 6:23;), but the gospel of Christ was for them the salvational word which raises them up to life. It was offered to all, and if to the dead, so much the more to the living, if only they would accept it. Therefore all will come to the judgment that is held over the living and the dead — the dead, after their resurrection. God the Judge holds himself in readiness for the judgment. It is expected soon. "Salvation stands ready" (1 Peter 1:5). "The end of all things is at hand" (1 Peter 4:7). The primitive Christian expectation of imminence is unbroken.

The Second Epistle of Peter describes the parousia with the cosmological conceptions of its own time (see above, § 16, 3, g). The world will vanish in fire. This event of nature, however, is the "power of God's word, . . . the day of the judgment and destruction of godless men" (2 Peter 3:5-7). The severe judgment of teachers of error as godless men is indicative of a later period when parties and doctrinal quarrels had arisen within the Church. "The earth and the works that are in it will be found out in the judgment" (2 Peter 3:10). The works on the earth are probably the creations of civilization and culture. They will vanish in the judgment. Is this the voice of a later time, culturally exhausted, and of a mood of collapse that is speaking?

e) Apocalypse of John

The Apocalypse of John looks upon the judicial office of God in a visionary manner. The world judgment begins with the final blast of the angel's trumpet. God's wrath judges all, the prophets, the saints, and the corrupters of the earth (Apoc. 11:18). The angel proclaims judgment for all peoples of the earth at the same time, and calls out as a final message of penance and salvation: "Fear God and give him honor, for the hour of his judgment has come" (Apoc. 14:7). To the Church, which awaits redemption, the visions proclaim the judgment as now present. God is he "who is and who was and who is coming" (Apoc. 1:4; 4:8). For him all times are the present, and he is contemporary to all ages.

f) Christ as Judge in the Acts of the Apostles

If already in the Synoptics, Christ, as Judge, had passed over to God (Matthew 7:21-23; 25:31), the preaching of the apostles now says this same thing. It proclaims (with Ps. 110:1) Christ as the Resurrected and Exalted (Acts 2:33-36). He will return at the "restoration of all things" (Acts 3:21). At the reception of the Gentile Cornelius into the

Church, Peter declares that Christ is "appointed by God to be the Judge of the living and of the dead." Attached immediately thereto is the statement that "everyone who believes in him attains, by his name, to the forgiveness of sins" (Acts 10:42f.).

To the Areopagus, Paul preaches Christ as Judge of the world, while explaining that the Day of Yahweh proclaimed in the Old Testament has come. "God has arranged a day on which he will judge the ecumene in justice through a Man whom he has appointed; and him he has guaranteed to all by raising him from the dead" (Acts 17:31). Certainly Greeks could understand the representation of a personal judgment of the dead (see above, § 18, 1), but the news of a general judgment after a resurrection had to be foreign to their way of thinking (Acts 17:18, 32). The resurrection is the exaltation, an investiture as Lord, and therefore as future Judge (Acts 2:34-36). It is in that capacity that Christ will judge.

It should be noted, and probably it bespeaks a Lukan frankness with the history of the Church, that in both discourses the reality of the judgment is emphasized, while nothing is said of its nearness.

g) Christ as Judge in the Epistles

Paul sees the community at and in God's eschatological judgment. The agent of the judgment is Christ. "Who will condemn the elect of God? Christ Jesus, the one who dies, and still more, the one who rose again — he is at the right hand of God, he intercedes for us" (Rom. 8:33f.). According ot 2 Cor. 5:10, Christ is the Judge: "For we must all be made manifest before the judgment seat of Christ, so that each one may receive recompense for what he has done in the body, be it good or be it evil."

Christ, then, is shown as the enthroned Judge (as in Matthew 19:28). This is the situation of the general and final judgment, in which each individual has to justify himself. The judgment is judgment according to works. The Christian lives always in a responsibility before God. The body is the implement of one's behavior. According to biblical understanding, man is in the body, he exists as body. Body is life of the body, period of life.

Other texts, soon to be formalized, declare that Christ will hold world judgment in God's mandate. Thus in 2 Tim. 4:1, "I entreat you before God and Jesus Christ, who will judge the living and the dead, and by his return and by his kingdom." The Lord Jesus, appearing at the judgment, will, as just Judge of the Apostle and of all who await his coming, award the crown of justification (2 Tim. 4:8). One may well ask whether such a conviction, which amounts almost to certitude, does not reveal the later image of Paul, in which the Apostle becomes a holy martyr and the prototype of martyrdom.

The Epistle to the Hebrews repeats the articles of faith. "To man it is appointed once to die, and thereupon follows the judgment" (Heb. 9:27). "The Lord will judge his people" (Heb. 10:30, quoting Ps. 135:14). The judgment will be terrifying. "A fearful thing it is, to fall into the hands of the living God" (Heb. 10:31). "Our God is a consuming fire" (Heb. 12:29). In prior prospect of the resurrection, the Christian trusts in Christ, who sacrificed himself for sin, and who, at his returning for the judgment, will appear "as salvation for those who wait upon him" (Heb. 9:28).

Communion with Christ is the conviction of Christians, when Christ will appear at his parousia for the judgment (1 John 2:28). "We have confidence in the day of judgment. For as he is, so too are we, already in the world" (1 John 4:17). Faithful Christians know Jesus, the heavenly Judge, already before his parousia. They have experienced God's love and have realized it in Christ (1 John 3:16). They have walked the way of Christ (1 John 2:6) and have fulfilled his justice (1 John 2:29). They are already formed to the image of Christ and are already withdrawn from the world. The judgment will but make manifest the separation between good and evil that has now already taken place.

h) Chiliasm or Millenarianism and the Apocalypse of John

In the Apocalypse of John, the apocalyptic events are redoubled. In a first resurrection of the dead, the souls of the martyrs are raised up, and then in judgment and in triumph they are justified and glorified. These rule with Christ as kings and priests for a thousand years. "This is the first resurrection" (Apoc. 20:4-6).

In early Jewish apocalyptics, the messianic kingdom is reckoned as a final epoch, sometimes specified as lasting for a thousand years, prior to the eternal kingdom of God (*4 Esdras* 5 [7]:28; *Syriac Apocalypse of Baruch* 29:3-6). The temporally reduced messianic interim kingdom is a calculated compromise between the national and secular hope in the kingdom of the Messiah and a universal eschatology in the beyond. The messianic interim kingdom is inserted ahead of the eternal kingdom of God (see above, § 13, 2). The chiliasm of the Apocalypse of John is devoid of any material and sensual description, such as is proper to the Jewish representations. In the revelation of John, the thousand years are a period of earthly perfection heralding in advance the eternal kingdom of God.[280]

The second judgment is depicted as the world judgment in Apoc. 20:11-15. Even those who had no part in the first resurrection will be raised up. "Death and Hades give up their dead." The enthroned God is Judge of the world. "Before his face, heaven and earth fled away." The horizon of the world is sunken. Everything takes place in room that is limitless.

The ancient and traditional concept of the eternal books (Dan. 7:10; *4 Esdras* 4 [6]:20; *Ethiopic Henoch* 47:3; 103:2f.; *Syriac Apocalyse of Baruch* 24:1; Luke 10:20; Phil. 4:3) is used in a double fashion. The works of the dead stand recorded in books, and the judgment is conducted on the basis of these works. Another book, the "book of life," contains the names of the elect. The New Testament tension between grace and works remains impenetrable even here. The condemned are, like Death and Hades, cast into the pool of fire. The death of Death is truth.

4. JUDGMENT AND CHURCH

If the faith hopes, on the basis of the salvational work of Christ, to be able to come through the judgment, the Church, nevertheless, does not reckon herself as in any way secured. On the contrary, she expects that she has to experience the special rigors of the judgment. The Church must now accept the judgment of God, and she must now straighten up in self-judgment so that she need not eventually suffer condemnatory judgment.

The earnest already know from Old Testament prophecy that on his chosen people God will visit all their guilt with special zeal (Amos 3:2). The judgment will commence in the Holy City (Jer. 25:29) and in God's sanctuary (Ezek. 9:6). Jesus threatened the unfaithful of his own generation with God's judgment (Mark 8:12; Matthew 12:45; 17:17). The encounter with Christ does not guarantee salvation; indeed, it can turn to doom (Matthew 11:21-24). Matthew 7:21-23 brings the community of disciples under the judgment (see above, § 18, 3, b).

The judgment of God falls even now on Christians as punishment of their guilt in respect to the Sacrament of the Body and the Blood of the Lord, as well as in his Body, which is the Church. Whoever participates unworthily in the Sacrament draws judgment upon himself. The participants must put themselves to the test. This present judgment is to guard the community against being judged with the world (1 Cor. 11:27-32).

The judgment begins now in a hidden way, recognizable only to the faith. If Christians are tried now in persecutions and tribulations, it is so that they may thereby be made worthy of God's kingdom. Their oppressors will get their just deserts in the final and public judgment. For the believer it is certain that God will acknowledge his own before the world (2 Thess. 1:4-10).

Even the Church of the First Epistle of Peter (4:12-18) lives in a period of beginning persecutions. Christians now have a share in the suffering of Christ, so that they can rejoice at the revelation of his glory. "The judgment is beginning now in the house of God," so that the pious will be able to stand the final judgment. The judgment is rigorous, so much so that "the righteous man can scarcely be saved. Where then will the godless and sinners appear?"

5. Judgment and Works

In the preaching of judgment, the question is broached as to the place of works in judgment (see the present work, Vol. 3, pp. 178-192). This question is posited especially by Paul. He says emphatically: "We infer that man is justified by faith [alone] without works of the Law" (Rom. 3:28). "For him who has no works, but has faith in him who justifies the godless, his faith is credited to him as righteousness" (Rom. 4:5). Jesus Christ is "the end of the Law. Whoever believes in him, the same is just" (Rom. 10:4). Faith [alone] justifies. But this faith is never alone, if it is otherwise true and genuine; it is "active in charity" (Gal. 5:6).The Christian must do good toward every man (Gal. 6:10). Righteousness must bear its "fruits" (Phil. 1:11). Now the just requirements of the Law can and must be fulfilled (Rom. 8:4).

The mission of the Apostle himself is operative through Christ (Phil. 1:6), it is the "work of the Lord" (1 Cor. 16:10). The genuineness of this righteousness will be made manifest in the judgment. "For it is not the hearers of the Law who are just before God; rather, the doers of the Law shall be justified" (Rom. 2:13). Even this justification is not their own work. Of this too it holds good: "All are justified by a grace, after the manner of a gift" (Rom. 3:24). Justification by faith is a reality even now.

Nevertheless, justification is also a future good, inasmuch as it is implanted in the final judgment. "In the Spirit, we await, by the power of faith, the realization of the hope of justification" (Gal. 5:5). The work of the Christian will "obtain its reward" in the judgment (1 Cor. 3:14). The justification proclaimed by Paul is not something quite apart from justification by grace and justification by works. The preaching of Paul is an invitation to an onging encounter with God's judgment and with God's grace. To undertake works earnestly, therefore, is genuinely Pauline. Certainly un-Pauline is that self-discipline of the man who supposes he can achieve his redemption by his own powers.

In between the prior (Apoc. 14:6-12) and subsequent visions of the wrath of the divine judgment (Apoc. 14:14-20), the seer has a promise to announce: "Write! 'Blessed are the dead who die in the Lord from now on!' Yes, the Spirit speaks: 'They are to rest from their labors, for their works follow after them'" (Apoc. 14:13).

The faithful who die from now on — which means, first of all, as martyrs — are with the Lord, to whom they belonged in faith and in life, united in eternal communion with him and having escaped the judgment. Salvation is promised them. The works which follow them are the internal works of faith and the external works of charity. There is mention of works which follow one before the judgment throne of God, and of a stored up treasure of good works also in *4 Esdras* 5

[7]:35, 77. But here the works are to be the deciding factor in the judgment, while in Apoc. 14:1 the faithful are already withdrawn from the judgment. Works are simply the fruit and the eschatological manifestation of a Christian life.

§ 19. HEAVEN AND HELL

1. HEAVEN

a) Old Testament

According to the belief of Israel, God created the heavens and the earth (Gen. 1:1; Is. 42:5; Pss. 33:6; 104).[281] Having come into existence, both are ephemeral, and both will pass away. The heavens so created are as a firmament, or the visible upper part of the world. In its power and beauty, it makes God's glory known (Ps. 19:2; Sir. 42:15–43:33). Beyond the visible heavens is God's dwelling (Ps. 115:16), and in its elevated majesty it is called the "heaven of heavens" (Deut. 10:14; 1 Kings 8:27; Ps. 148:4). Theological casuistry concluded from the misunderstood plural to the existence of numerous heavens (*Slavonic Henoch* 3–8; also 2 Cor. 12:2).

In accord with earthly imagery, heaven is described as room, city, palace, and kingdom. God's throne is there (Pss. 11:4; 103:19; Wis. 18:15). From heaven God descends to earth (Gen. 11:5; Is. 64:1). From heaven he calls (Deut. 4:36), blesses (Gen. 49:25), and punishes (Gen. 19:24). In heaven God is surrounded by his court of angels and powers (1 King 22:19; Is. 6:1f.; Dan. 7:10). According to the ancient conception of Job 1:6 and Zech. 3:1, there is also a place below God for Satan as the accuser of men.

The elect of God can be enraptured to him in heaven (Gen. 5:24; 2 Kings 2:11; Is. 53:8). The concept of heaven as the domicile of the blessed, and contrariwise of hell as the prison of the damned, could have originated when the representation of Sheol as the universal resort of the dead (see above, § 15, 2) became differentiated in accord with the belief of a recompense for good and evil. The concepts separate and clarify themselves only gradually. At first, for example, the spirits of the just and of sinners lived apart in subterranean areas until the judgment (*Ethiopic Henoch* 22; see also Luke 16:26).

In the Wisdom literature, the representation of heaven takes shape. "The souls of the just are in the hands of God" (Wis. 3:1-9; 4:7). "The just will receive the kingdom of glory and the crown of beauty from the hand of the Lord" (Wis. 5:16). "The gates of heaven stand open to you" (*Ethiopic Henoch* 104:2). The place of the blessed is represented also as Paradise (*Ethiopic Henoch* 60:8; 70:4; accordingly also Luke 23:43; 2 Cor. 12:4).

In the Qumran scrolls, eternal life is depicted thus: "The Sons of Truth will receive eternal joy in everlasting life and a crown of glory with a splendid garment in eternal life" (1 QS 4:7f.).[282]

Even the Old Testament knows that the heavens cannot contain God, as Solomon says already at the dedication of the Temple: "Heaven and all heavens of heaven are unable to contain you, and so much the less this house which I have built" (1 Kings 8:27). God fills both heaven and earth (Jer. 23:24). He is all-present (Is. 66:1; Ps. 139:7-12; 2 Chron. 2:6; 6:18). Figuratively, "heaven" is used as a word for God himself. In formulas of prayer and oath-taking, "heaven and earth" are called upon in invoking God and men (Deut. 4:26; Ps. 73:9; 1 Macc. 3:18). We do this even in English when we say, "Heaven knows. . . ." But God is more than heaven. "Whom might I have in heaven besides you? And if I have you, I desire nothing on earth" (Ps. 73:25).

b) New Testament

The New Testament employs the traditional representations based on imagery of the world. God is Creator and Lord of heaven and earth (Matthew 11:25). He dwells in heaven (Matthew 5:16, 34, 45; Apoc. 4f.), which, as in the Old Testament, is described as a kingdom ("kingdom of heaven"; see above, § 13, 1), or even as a holy city (Heb. 12:22; Apoc. 21:2).

Heaven is the place of light (1 John 1:7; Apoc. 22:5) and of the divine glory (Luke 2:14; John 12:41; 1 Thess. 2:12; Jude 24; Apoc. 21:6f.). God is surrounded by his angels (Matthew 18:10; Mark 12:25; Luke 2:15; John 1:51; Eph. 3:15; Apoc. 7:11 *et passim*). Heaven designates God himself (Matthew 5:3, 10; Luke 15:18; John 3:27). The place of God can be described entirely in terms of negations. "He that alone is immortal, who dwells in unapproachable light, whom no man has seen nor is able to see" (1 Tim. 6:16). Here the biblical image of God, who is light inasmuch as he is man's salvation (see the present work, Vol. 2, pp. 277–281), is turned into a description of God's place, which is in turn a veiled description of his Being. (The attempt in *Ethiopic Henoch* 14:15-22 is comparable: God's glory is enthroned in a house of blazing fire).

The pre-existing Christ came down from heaven (John 3:13). He is taken back up again in order now to be enthroned as Lord, to the right of God (Matthew 28:20; Acts 1:11; Eph. 1:20; 1 Peter 3:22). There the true High Priest performs his work of offering sacrifice (Heb. 8:1-3). From thence the Exalted will appear again at the end of time (Mark 8:38; 14:62; 1 Thess. 4:16; Heb. 9:28). If the Old Testament says that Yahweh fills heaven and earth (Jer. 23:24), now the New Testament says likewise that Christ is the fullness of all things (Eph. 1:23; 4:10).

Blessed men are received into heaven. The heavenly glory is still hidden to the redeemed (Col. 3:3). They are still admonished to seek what is above (Col. 3:1-4). They have, nevertheless, the promise of eternal reward in heaven (Matthew 5:12). Their heavenly inheritance is reserved for them there (1 Peter 1:4). They are citizens of the heavenly kingdom (Phil. 3:20). Their names are inscribed in the heavenly books (Luke 10:20; Heb. 12:23; Apoc. 20:12). Their heavenly body is already prepared for them in heaven (2 Cor. 5:1). Indeed, Christians have already risen with Christ (Eph. 2:6). Here the eschatological proviso, which holds good always for Paul (Rom. 6:8), seems to have been exceeded. The Apocalypse (7:9-17; 14:1-5) finally beholds the incalculably great multitude of the perfected in heaven.

c) Contemplation of God (Seeing God)

The term and notion of the "contemplation of God"[283] is known to both the Old and the New Testaments. After the Old Testament had told quite inconceivably of the appearances of God in human form (Gen. 18; 32:24-31), it became conscious of the rigid beyondness of God. Not once did Moses, the friend of God and prince of Israel, dare to gaze upon the glory of God. "No man can see God and remain alive" (Exod. 33:20; 1 Kings 19:11-13; Is. 6:5). With the depicting of the ideas of the heavenly world, there arose in apocalyptic literature also the theme of a contemplation of God by the blessed. "They hasten ahead, to gaze upon the countenance of him whom they have faithfully served" (*4 Esdras* 5 [7]:98; similarly in the *Apocalypse of Abraham* 29:20; for rabbinic references, see H. Strack and P. Billerbeck, *op. cit.*, Vol. 1, pp. 207–215).

The New Testament strengthens the eschatological expectation of seeing God. Now on earth, God is seen, manifested in Christ (John 12:45; 14:9). Immediate looking upon God is not possible. On the contrary, it holds good that "no one has ever seen God" (John 1:18; 1 John 4:12). "We walk by faith, not by sight" (2 Cor. 5:7). But the sight of God is an eschatological possibility. Jesus himself teaches: "Blessed are the pure of heart. For they shall gaze upon God" (Matthew 5:8). Only the pure and holy dare approach the holy God (Pss. 15; 24:4). This sight is a potentiality of the heart, that is, of the inner and hidden man, and not some sort of philosophical end or mystical exercise. The hiddenness of God manifests itself to the hiddenness of man.

Paul, too, speaks of the expectation of the eschatological sight of God. Faith now beholds "the glory of God on the face of Christ" (2 Cor. 4:6), who is "God's image," that is, God's revelation or manifestation (2 Cor. 4:4; Col. 1:15; see also the present work, Vol. 2, pp. 215f.). "Now we see enigmatically in a mirror; then, however, face to face" (1 Cor. 13:12).[284] We do not now see directly, but only in an intervening image. Here Paul does not name the object of our seeing. He does not say expressly that we shall see God. It could probably also refer to the intellectual vision of an understanding of salvation history. That the seeing, nevertheless, is to be understood as seeing God, is inferred from the formula "face to face," (i.e., from the Old Testament formula of the vision of God in Gen. 32:30, Judg. 6:22, and Exod. 33:11), as well as from the description of a mutual and personal recognition (1 Cor. 13:12f.).

In this life, the sight of God is not attainable by man by means of gnosis or mystic cult, but is first an eschatological promise and then the gift of God. "I shall know entirely, even as now I am known" (1

Cor. 13:12; cf. 1 Cor. 8:2f.; Gal. 4:9). Only if man is first known by God, can he then know God.

The Epistle to the Hebrews (12:14) specifies (like Matthew 5:8; see above, § 13, 3, b) the moral stipulation for the contemplation of God: "Strive for peace with men and for the holiness without which no one can see God."

The First Epistle of John (3:2) says of the consummation: "We will be like him. For we shall see him as he is." Now we are children of God. From being children of God we are to be elevated to a condition of similarity to God. This similarity is achieved through contemplation of God, and at the same time we will, in our contemplation, recognize our similarity to him.

Speaking of the perfected community of the heavenly Jerusalem, Apoc. 22:4 says: "They shall see his face, and his name shall be on their foreheads."

The doctrine of the contemplation of God came already into Judaism through Philo, by means of Platonic and Stoic philosophy, and afterwards was developed and deepened in the patristic and subsequent theology of the Church. Here Greek philosophy had an even broader influence, especially the Platonic teaching of the contemplation of ideas.

Heaven is not a place, but rather a historical event, when man comes to God and God to man. This happened perfectly in the obedience of Jesus and in the ratification of this obedience in the resurrection and exaltation of Christ. To be in heaven, therefore, means to be with Christ (Luke 23:43; 1 Thess. 4:16f.; Phil. 1:23).

2. HELL

If the place of God and of the blessed is the world of light, the world of heaven, above the earth, so too do Death and the dead have a place and area beneath the world inhabited by men. The kingdom of Death is described in earthly imagery as a land ("land of no return," in Job 10:21) or house (Job 17:13), eternal house (Qoh. 12:5), house with chambers (Prov. 7:27), and house with gates (Job 38:17; Ps. 9:14).

a) Old Testament

The Greek Old Testament designates the underworld by the terms abyss (ἄβυσσος), Hades (ᾅδης), and hell (γέεννα).[285]

Abyss indicates the primordial depths, referred to in the phrase "face of the deep" in Gen. 1:2, the world of the dead in Ps. 71:20, the prison of the apostate spirits in the *Book of Jubilees* 5, 6 and in *Ethiopic Henoch* 10:4 and 18:11-16.

The current Greek word Hades served as a rendering of Sheol, the underworld which received all the dead. It is a land of gloom and darkness (Job 10:21f.). Here one does not remember Yahweh (Pss. 6:6; 30:10; 115:17), and Yahweh does not remember the dead (Ps. 88:6). Hades is the preparatory place of residence of all souls until the resurrection (*Ethiopic Henoch* 51:1).

The term γέεννα is used in biblical Greek only as a rendering of the Hebrew *ge-hinnom*. This was originally the name of a valley at Jerusalem, shunned as having been a place where children had been sacrificed (2 Kings 16:3; 21:6). It is regarded afterwards as the locale of the final divine judgment (Jer. 7:32; 19:6). It is there that the corpses of idolaters will lie after the judgment. "Their worm does not die, and their fire is not quenched: they are a thing of disgust to all" (Is. 66:24). Two concepts are combined: that of a huge pile of corpses, not buried but decaying; and that of a fire which destroys all (such as is mentioned already in Is. 30:33 and 34:9f.). The terminology and the imagery of Is. 66:24 are employed again in Judith 16:17; Sir. 7:17; Dan. 2:2 and Mark 9:47f. The word itself takes on the character of a proverb. According to Jewish apocalyptics, the hell of fire was to open up in the valley of Gehinnom (*Ethiopic Henoch* 90:26f.; *4 Esdras* 5 [7]:36). Finally Gehenna became forthrightly the interim or endtime place of punishment (and thus in the New Testament).

Early Jewish (and, accordingly, early Christian) writings bear witness to manifold representations about the beyond, and especially about hell. Such portrayals are found in the *Book of Jubilees* 5:6-10; *Psalms of Solomon* 14:7 and 15:11; *Ethiopic Henoch* 10:4-14; 18:11-16; 22; 27:1f.; 90:23-27; *Syriac Apocalypse of Baruch* 59:10; 85:13; *4 Esdras* 5 [7]:78-87; *Vision of Esdras* 1-66 (in P. Riessler, *Altjüdischer Schrifttum ausserhalb der Bibel*, 1928, pp. 350–354). Hell is a place of dark-

ness (*Psalms of Solomon* 15:11; *Ethiopic Henoch* 10:4f) and of the
pool of fire (*Ethiopic Henoch* 10:6; 63:10; 90:26f.; *Sibyllines* 4:178;
Vision of Esdras 13-58). The damned lie on pointed stones (*Ethiopic
Henoch* 10:5). A dragon devours their flesh (*Greek Apocalypse of
Baruch* 4:4f.). A worm swallows sinners and vomits them out again
(*Vision of Esdras* 35).

In the Qumran writings, hell is conceived as a deep pit (1 QH
17:13). Sinners are tortured in everlasting torments in darkness and
fire, by the devil (1 QS 2:7f., 14-17; 4:11-14). The blasphemous priests,
enemies of the community, are condemned in burning brimstone (1
QpHab 10:5; 12f.). The place of punishment and damnation for the
wicked and for Belial is ghastly (1 QH 3:26-36).[286]

b) New Testament

The authors of the New Testament probably accepted completely
the notions of their time about the beyond. The New Testament declarations thereon, however, are not particularly strong. They want to
admonish and warn consciences, but they have no interest in describing hell, apart, perhaps, from a few texts in John's Apocalypse. Without the New Testament authors having been themselves aware of it,
the apocalyptic world was forced into the background by something
more important, the proclamation of which was entrusted to them —
the gospel. In the period immediately after the New Testament, to be
sure, the underworld was described in a quite fanciful and horrible
manner. Such is the case with the *Apocalypse of Peter*. A late fruit
of such a portrayal, first passing through many intermediaries, is
Dante's *Divina Commedia*.

For the New Testament, following previous localization, it is self-
evident that the place of punishment of the wicked is under the earth.
One descends into it (Matthew 11:23; Luke 10:15; 16:23; Rom. 10:7;
Eph. 4:9; Apoc. 20:13).

The New Testament still employs the traditional terms for the underworld. The "abyss" is the prison of the demons (Luke 8:31). John's
Apocalypse has considerable to say about it. From a ravine the smoke
of the subterranean fires mounts up (Apoc. 9:2). A king rules over
that world (Apoc. 9:11). Monstrous beastlike beings inhabit hell, com-

ing up from there to destroy the world (Apoc. 9:3-10). From thence come the apocalyptic "beasts" (Apoc. 11:7; 17:8). Satan is bound there during the thousand-year kingdom (Apoc. 20:1-3).

Hades is a subterranean city or stronghold (Matthew 16:18), a prison (1 Peter 3:19; Apoc. 20:7). Hades is also thought of personally, as a powerful ruler (Apoc. 20:13). The dead abide in Hades until the resurrection (Acts 2:27; Luke 16:23). The spirits of the godless are in Hades forever (1 Peter 3:19).

Gehenna was created before the world (Matthew 25:41), as an abyss of eternal fire (Matthew 5:22; 13:42; 18:8f.). It is the place of eternal punishment after the general judgment (Matthew 25:41; 23:15, 33). Satan and his helpers are then cast into this abyss (Apoc. 20:10, 14f.).

Hellfire and the abyss are the present and the future eternal place of the powers of evil (Matthew 25:41; Luke 8:31; Apoc. 20:10, 14). The idea that Satan abides in heaven (Job 1:6; see above, § 19, 1, a) was long since untenable. Satan can still try to be active on earth and work evils there (1 Cor. 7:5; 2 Cor. 2:11).

In contrast to its contemporaneous Judaism, which taught an extensive demonology, the New Testament declares the power of evil has been vanquished by the redemptive work of Christ. Midway between proclamation and salvational works, Jesus speaks a word of revelation: "I saw Satan fall like a lightning bolt out of the heavens (Luke 10:18). The saying does not describe some experience of the pre-existing Christ. The headlong fall of Satan is the result of Christ's salvational work. The imagery of the saying makes use of Jewish concepts of a fallen angel, who was thrust out of heaven (H. Strack and P. Billerbeck, *op. cit.*, Vol. 1, pp. 136–139; Vol. 2, pp. 167f.). The saying makes no declaration on any residing of Satan in heaven prior to that time, but only compares his downfall to lightning coming down from the heavens. In Apoc. 12:5-12, the downfall of Satan is a consequence of the coming of Christ into the world. If Satan was or is the prince of this world, he is now overthrown by the operation of Christ (John 12:31). He is already judged (John 16:11).

According to another view, the demons can yet dwell in the regions of the air between heaven and earth (Eph. 2:2; 6:12). They were vanquished, however, by Christ, ascending up to heaven (Phil. 2:10; Eph.

4:8; 1 Peter 3:12). If it be that there are yet many gods and lords, they nevertheless have no longer any power over those who have the one God as Father and the one Lord Jesus Christ (1 Cor. 8:5f.). The Evil One has power only in that place where it is granted to him.

The New Testament description of hell is formalized. Damnation is depicted: "Where their worm dies not, nor is their fire quenched" (Mark 9:48). The saying goes back to Is. 66:24 and was current in tradition (see above, 19, 2, a). The Gospel of Matthew employs the following characterization, as if in a refrain: "They will be cast forth into outer darkness. In that place there will be weeping and gnashing of teeth" (Matthew 8:12; 22:13; 24:51; 25:30). "And they will cast them out into the hell of fire. In that place there will be weeping and gnashing of teeth" (Matthew 13:42, 50).

In the foregoing sayings, hell is perhaps localized in the darkness at the outermost rim of the world. Weeping and gnashing of teeth may be intended as expressive of powerless rage. The portrait employs themes known after the manner of proverbial sayings; for it speaks of a known weeping and a known gnashing of teeth.

In Matthew, all the damnation sayings are placed in the mouth of Christ. But since, with the exception of Luke 13:28, they are all found in Matthew only, they manifestly pertain to the Evangelist's own redacting. In Matthew 8:12 and Luke 13:28, the saying threatens Israel with exclusion from salvation. Here the statement may be drawn from a source of sayings. We will not be able to attribute the statement of damnation to the original discourse of Jesus.

Without description, Paul speaks of a place or condition of eternal rejection, calling it destruction (1 Thess. 5:3) and downfall (Rom. 9:22; 1 Cor. 1:18; 2 Cor. 2:15).[287]

Strictly speaking, it is only by inference from the fact that the New Testament makes mention of notions of a devilish counterworld that it can be said that it refers in any way to powers undone by the salvation of Christ.[288] Inasmuch as Christ came through death and won life in the resurrection, he has become Lord over the living and the dead (Rom. 14:9). Nothing, not even death, can keep one apart from the love of God in Jesus Christ (Rom. 8:38f.). Death has lost its "sting," its power to torture and kill (1 Cor. 15:55). In his death Christ has frustrated Death and the Devil, who exercised his power in death; and he has freed those who were enslaved by the fear of death (Heb. 2:14f.). Christ frees from death. He has the key to Hades (Apoc. 1:18).

In the First Epistle of Peter, the depicting of the conquest by Christ of the world of death makes use of mythological conceptions. Between death and resurrection Christ goes to "the spirits in prison, who once were disobedient," in order to preach salvation even to them (1 Peter 3:19f.). These spirits are not the righteous of antiquity; for those now spoken of were "disobedient." Those referred to are either the sinners from the generation of the deluge, who, according to Jewish tradition, are to be banished forever to hell; or more probably they are the sons of God from Gen. 6:1-6, who consorted with the daughters of men and with them begot the giants. According to Jewish apocalyptics (*Ethiopic Henoch* 10:16; 19; 21; also Jude 6f.), they are to be kept chained in the subterranean prison until the final judgment. Henoch is afterwards commissioned by God to announce to them that they will find no forgiveness.

The First Epistle of Peter, however, has for its message that the redeeming and royal power of Christ reaches to the depths of the underworld. He proclaims and brings salvation there even to the damned. It is, no doubt, of this same journey of Christ to the underworld that 1 Peter 4:6 says once more that the Redeemer proclaimed salvation to the dead, "that they may live in the spirit."

Wherever else in the New Testament the tradition of the descent of Jesus into the underworld is indicated (Rom. 10:7; Eph. 4:8-10; Heb. 13:20), there too it is not mythology that is intended, but always the declaration of the saving power of Christ.

§ 20. NEW CREATION

The announcement of the end of the world in judgment is not the last declaration of New Testament eschatology. On the contrary, it promises a new world.[289] With this promise, the New Testament accepts an expectation drawn from Old Testament apocalyptics.

1. Old Testament

In the Old Testament, belief in creation prepared by God in the beginning carries on in the conviction that he constantly creates anew. Certainly there develops and remains a traditional expectation of the "Day of the Lord," on which the world will vanish in the judgment (Is. 24:1-27; Zech. 12:1-14, 21; Joel 3:1-21; see above, § 12, 1 c). Nevertheless, though heaven and earth pass away, God's righteousness and salvation remain forever (Is. 51:6). New creation follows on the chaos (Is. 51:15f.). In this new world, instead of a sun and a moon, Yahweh will be the eternal light and the glory of the new mankind (Is. 60:19). Godlessness passed away in the judgment (Is. 57:20f.). In the new creation, justice (Is. 62:2) and peace (Is. 65:25) hold sway. "Behold, I create a new heaven and a new earth. . . . I create for Jerusalem a rejoicing" (Is. 65:17f.). New creation is new covenant (Jer. 31:31-34), new hearts, new spirit (Ezek. 36:26f.; Ps. 51:12). Man, therefore, will be newly created.

Apocalyptics takes up the expectation from prophecy. It coins the term "new creation" (*Book of Jubilees* 1:29; 4:26; *Ethiopic Henoch* 72:1; *Syriac Apocalypse of Baruch* 32:2, 6). The new creation is depicted thus: "The first heaven will fade and pass away; then a new heaven appears, and all the powers of heaven will then be brightened sevenfold forevermore. There will be countless weeks into eternity, in goodness and righteousness, and sin will be mentioned no more" (*Ethiopic Henoch* 91:16f.).

Even the community of Qumran expects new creation and new mankind through God's holy Spirit (1 QS 4:2-25).[290] In intertestamental Judaism, "there is a general notion of a total renewal of the cosmos, be it that it comes about through this modern world's being destroyed and a new one's rising up in its place, or that this present world is to be radically changed. Both notions are forthcoming."[291]

2. New Testament

The New Testament takes up the Old Testament expectation, inasmuch as it speaks in its own time of the new creation. The new creation can be expected as a transformation of existing creation (primarily Rom. 8:19-23; 2 Cor. 5:17; Gal. 6:15) or as expectation of a completely new creation after the disappearance of the existing world (Apoc. 21:1-27; 2 Peter 3:7-13).

a) Synoptics

Jesus speaks of the present as the old and of the future as the new, in a way that precludes mixing of old and new (Mark 2:21f.). The new covenant is established in the blood of Jesus (Luke 22:20). At the Last Supper, Jesus points in advance to the eschatological banquet of joy, which will be celebrated with "new wine" (Mark 14:25). The goal of the history of the world is, after the endtime judgment, the "rebirth" ($\pi\alpha\lambda\iota\gamma\gamma\epsilon\nu\epsilon\sigma\iota\alpha$ — Matthew 19:28) of the world. The Evangelist employs with this word a term created by the Stoa and used also by Jewish Hellenism in the persons of Philo and Josephus. The difference in meaning in the Evangelist's use of the term, however, is not to be overlooked. In the Stoa, the rebirth of the world takes place in an eternal succession of the world's passing away and arising anew, whereas rebirth in its biblical understanding belongs to a once-only eschatological history that has already begun.

b) Paul

According to the announcement of Paul, the "old man" destroyed by sin is in the "newness of life" (Rom. 6:4). Now there is "new creation." Paul uses this formula twice (Gal. 6:15; 2 Cor. 5:17), each time drawing different conclusions. "Neither circumcision nor uncircumcision is of any account, but new creation" (Gal. 6:15). New creation means that the Jewish and pagan systems of religion are finished; what counts now is "faith, which is operative in love" (Gal. 5:6), or even "the keeping of God's commandments" (1 Cor. 7:19).

In 2 Cor. 5:17, Paul repeats: "If any man is in Christ, he is a new creation. The old has passed away and the new has come to be." In the death of Christ all have died, and in his resurrection life has begun for all (2 Cor. 5:15). The new creation is "in Christ." Just as through Adam death came to all, so through Christ life came (Rom. 5:12-21). The Church, as the "new covenant," is the new, all-embracing creation (1 Cor. 11:25; 2 Cor. 3:6).

Paul is no fanatical dreamer who never saw reality. He says that "the shape of this world is (now at last) passing away" (1 Cor. 7:31). Christians still live in the flesh (2 Cor. 10:3), Satan still prowls about (2 Cor. 2:11), death still rules (1 Cor. 15:26). At the same time, neither is Paul a mere prophet who might be predicting future salvation; rather, he is the herald of a salvation already brought about. This salvation is real "in Christ." It is starkest reality, even if it is still hidden. The new creation can and must be ratified. The Christian must "walk in a new life" (Rom. 6:4), in the "newness of spirit" (Rom. 7:6). "If the outer man is being destroyed, the inner man, nevertheless, is being renewed day by day" (2 Cor. 4:16). Thus did Paul live in the suffering and the resurrection of Jesus (2 Cor. 4:10).

c) Deutero-Pauline Epistles

In the spirit and mentality of Paul, Col. 3:3f. says: "You have died, and your life is hidden with Christ in God. When Christ, our life, is made manifest, then you too will be made manifest with him in glory." The new life is truly in the death and life of Christ, but it is not given in a demonstrable and visible nature, but in a double hiddenness. The Christian has the life in which he lives "with Christ," and he is hidden in God's spiritual reality. The Christian, however, is confident in his expectation of the eschatological consummation with the parousia of Christ.

In Col. 3:9f., it is made explicit that the new life is given, and must be won through Christian living. The new life has its foundation in baptism. That is the teaching of Paul (Rom. 6:3f.), which afterwards is deepened in the Deutero-Pauline Epistles. "He has led us to salvation . . . according to his mercy, through the bath of rebirth in the Holy Spirit" (Titus 3:5; see Col. 2:11-13).

d) New Life

The new life is both a gift and a giving up. It is required now that we "put off the old man, be renewed in the spirit of your mind, and put on the new man who is created according to God" (Eph. 4:22-24). In Christ, Jew and Gentile "are made into one new man" (Eph. 2:15). The new creation is the one new community. The Epistle to the Hebrews (8:8-13; 9:15; 12:24) points out how much greater than the old covenant is the new covenant established through the Mediator Christ. It is "eternally valid" (Heb. 13:20).

The Johannine writings say that the new existence is love, as the new commandment (John 13:34; 1 John 2:7).

e) Final Observations

As Col. 3:4 predicts about the eschatological consummation of the new creation, so too Paul says that the new creation, which has already taken place, is the promise and beginning of a still future divine creative action, as it is described in Rom. 8:19-30. "The yearning expectation of creation waits on the revelation of the future glory of the sons of God."

Paul recognizes anxiety and yearning as primordial phenomena of all created life. He hears the same yearning in the prayer of those in the community, oppressed by the world, who cry "Abba, Father." In this prayer it is the Spirit himself, given to the community, who cries out (Rom. 8:15). These manifold cries do not go unheard. Paul explains the basis and meaning of this yearning as the restless waiting of the creature for redemption and glorification. "Creation will be set free from the bondage of corruption, into the freedom of the glory of the sons of God" (Rom. 8:21). The thoughts of the Apostle become clearer in the light of the long tradition in which he shares and which he reflects in the New Testament.

Israel's prophets expected the messianic era of salvation as a time of new creation (Is. 65:17). Jewish apocalyptics say that by reason of human guilt, creation would be made subject to nullity. Along with man, it will be redeemed in a consummational perfecting (see the present work, Vol. 1, pp. 57–61). "The mythical features of this message are not to be overlooked. Still less can one fail to recognize how near it comes to the world in its deep estrangement. Demythologizing, at least in the measure of the previous century, has to be on its guard, and it must take present experience no less seriously than that of the Enlightenment. Thus Christianity, which testified to adoption and which, in the communion of suffering, looked to Christ as the coming Lord of the world, was seen by Paul as a grand promise to all creatures, even to those of the non-human realm." [292]

If such texts of the New Testament speak of a purification and renewal of the existing world, there are others that speak of a new creation after the collapse of the old. The Apocalypse of John describes the
new world in overpowering visions (Apoc. 21:1-22). Before the face
of the judging God, "earth and heaven fled away, and no places any
more were found for them" (Apoc. 20:11). The new creation comes
about by the word of God enthroned, the word which, just as it called
the first creation into existence, now likewise brings forth the new.
His words "are certain and true."

And John "saw a new heaven and a new earth." The sea, ever the
image of the chaos, from which the satanic beast came forth (Apoc.
13:1), is no more. The new Jerusalem coming down from heaven is
"the dwelling place of God with men." There will no longer be any
death nor any distress. The first creation, the earth, which endured the
deluge (Gen. 3:17-19), has passed away and is redeemed in new creation.

The Second Epistle of Peter (3:7, 10, 12) depicts the passing of the
world in a great world conflagration, employing thereby themes of
contemporary world views (see above, § 18, 3, d). "We await, in accord
with his promise, new heavens and a new earth, wherein justice
dwells" (2 Peter 3:13). Echoes are heard of texts like Is. 65:17 and
66:22. Perhaps the Epistle sees even in those texts the promise of God.
God's powerful and regulating will is, according to Second Peter, the
basis of what is to happen, and not some natural law of passing away
and becoming. Eschatology is understood not mythically but historically. The new world is depicted without any indebtedness of sensual
images to mythology. Justice dwells in this new world.

According to the Old Testament (Jer. 23:5f.; Mal. 3:20) and other
writings (*Psalms of Solomon* 17:25; *Ethiopic Henoch* 38:2), justice is
the hallmark and essence of the messianic era. Justice opens the era of
salvation (Rom. 3:21). Heaven and earth will then be as God wills:
righteous in his eyes. According to the expectation of new creation,
the world will experience, not an annihilating end, but an all-embracing divine perfecting or consummation.

This hope of the consummation or perfecting is accepted by modern
political-revolutionary conceptions. Man is destined and desires to ex-

perience the consummation not as a foreign work; rather, he himself is destined and desires to cooperate in its planning and in its being carried out. The believer expects God's future, inasmuch as he recognizes himself as called to cooperate in effecting it and to be included in it. His mandate is to cooperate in introducing this future into time and world, on an earth on which the Cross stands, but in which also the resurrection of Christ has brought the Cross to fulfillment. Man is summoned to assist in the conquest of poverty, guilt, ruin, and death.

That the future is always God's future and God is the whole future may be implied in the very name Yahweh, if his name is interpreted as meaning that God is he who always is coming and is always there, Helper and Redeemer (Exod. 3:14).

NOTES

[In regard to general bibliography on New Testament theology and on dogmatics, the following works, most of which have appeared only since the publication of the earlier volumes of our *Theology of the New Testament*, ought to be considered in connection with note 1 in Vol. 2 of the present work, with note 1 in Vol. 3, and along with the subject matter of Vol. 3, pp. 18–21: L. Goppelt, *Theologie des Neuen Testaments: I. Jesu Wirken in seiner theologischen Bedeutung*, Göttingen 1975. E. Lohse, *Grundriss der neutestamentlichen Theologie*, Stuttgart 1974. O. Merk, *Biblische Theologie des Neuen Testaments in ihrer Anfangszeit, Ihre methodischen Probleme bei Johann Philipp Gabler und Georg Lorenz Bauer und deren Nachwirkungen*, Marburg 1972. G. Strecker (ed.), *Das Problem der Theologie des Neuen Testaments*, Darmstadt 1975. P. Stuhlmacher, *Schriftauslegung auf dem Weg zur biblischen Theologie*, Göttingen 1975. And more particularly on the doctrinal teaching of the Church: L. Dullart, *Kirche und Ekklesiologie*, Munich and Mainz 1975. F. Feiner and M. Löhrer (eds.), *Mysterium salutis*, Vols. 4/1 and 4/2: *Das Heilsgeschehen in der Gemeinde*, Einsiedeln 1972 and 1973. Jürgen Moltmann, *Kirche in der Kraft des Geistes*, Munich 1975. M. Schmaus, *Katholische Dogmatik*: Vol. 3/1, *Die Lehre von der Kirche*, 3rd to 5th ed., Munich 1958.]

[1] H. Schlier, Art. αἱρέω, in the *Theol. Dict. N. T.*, Vol. 1, 1964, pp. 180–185. W. Michaelis, Art. ὁδός, in the *Theol. Dict. N. T.*, Vol. 5, 1967, pp. 42–96. L. Goppelt, *"Kirche und Häresie bei Paulus,"* in *Gedenkschrift D. W. Elert*, Berlin 1955, pp. 9–23. H. Köster, *"Häretiker im Urchristentum als theologisches Problem,"* in E. Dinkler (ed.), *Zeit und Geschichte (Festschrift R. Bultmann)*, Tübingen 1964, pp. 61–76.

[2] R. Meyer and H. F. Weiss, Art. Φαρισαῖος, in *Theol. Dict. N. T.*, Vol. 9, 1974, pp. 11–48. G. Baumbach, *Jesus von Nazareth im Lichte jüdischer Gruppenbildung*, Berlin 1971. Leo Baeck, *The Pharisees and Other Essays* (trans.), New York, 1966. Also of Baeck, *Paulus, die Pharisäer und das Neue Testament*, Frankfurt 1961. C. Gruber-Margitot, *Jésus et les Pharisiens*, Paris 1959. M. Hengel, *Die Zeloten*, Leiden 1961. Also of Hengel, trans. J. Bowden, *Judaism and Hellenism*, Philadelphia 1974. R. T. Herford, *The Pharisees*, New York 1924. R. Hummel, *Die Auseinandersetzung zwischen Kirche und Judentum im Matthäusevangelium*, 2nd ed., Munich 1966. M. Limbeck, *Die Ordnung des Heiles, Untersuchungen zum Gesetzesverständnis des Frühjudentums*, Düsseldorf 1971. H. Merkel, *"Jesus und die Pharisäer,"* in *New Testament Studies*, Vol. 14 (1967/68), pp. 194–208. R. Meyer, *"Tradition und Neuschöpfung im antiken Judentum. Dargestellt an der Geschichte des Pharisäismus,"* in *Sitzungsbericht der Sächs-*

ischen Akademie der Wissenschaften, Philological-historical Section, Vol. 110, Part 2, Berlin 1965, pp. 9–88. F. Mussner, *"Jesus und die Pharisäer,"* in *Praesentia salutis,* Düsseldorf 1967, pp. 99–112. Hugo Odeberg, *Pharisaism and Christianity,* trans. J. M. Moe, St. Louis 1964. N. Oswald, *"Grundgedanken einer pharisäisch-rabbinischen Theologie,"* in *Kairos,* Vol. 6 (1963), pp. 40–58. D. Rössler, *Gesetz und Geschichte, Untersuchungen zur Theologie der jüdischen Apokalyptik und der pharisäischen Orthodoxie,* 2nd ed., Neukirchen 1962. K. Schubert, *Die jüdischen Religionsparteien in neutestamentlicher Zeit,* Stuttgart 1970. Ph. Seidensticker, *"Die Gemeinschaftsform der religiösen Gruppen des Spätjudentums und der Urkirche,"* in *Studii biblici Franciscani liber annuus* 9 (1959), pp. 94–108. M. Simon, *Jewish Sects at the Time of Jesus,* trans J. H. Farley, Philadelphia 1967. K. Thoma, *"Der Pharisäismus,"* in J. Maier and J. Schreiner (eds.), *Literatur und Religion des Frühjudentums,* Würzburg and Gütersloh 1973, pp. 254–272. H. F. Weiss, *"Der Pharisäismus im Lichte der Überlieferung des Neuen Testaments,"* in *Sitzungsbericht der Sächsischen Akademie der Wissenschaften,* Philological-historical Section, Vol. 110, Part 2, Berlin 1965, pp. 91–132.

[3] J. Becker, *Das Heil Gottes, Heils- und Sündenbegriffe in den Qumrantexten und im Neuen Testament,* Göttingen 1964. H. Braun, *Qumran und das Neue Testament,* 2 vols., Tübingen 1966. A. Dupont-Sommer, *The Essene Writings from Qumran,* trans. G. Vermes, Oxford 1961. G. Jeremias, *Der Lehrer der Gerechtigkeit,* Göttingen 1963. O. Klinzing, *Die Umdeutung des Kultus in der Qumrangemeinde und im Neuen Testament,* Göttingen 1971. E. Lohse, *Die Texte aus Qumran, hebräisch und deutsch,* Darmstadt 1964. J. Maier, *Die Texte vom Toten Meer,* 2 vols., Munich and Basel 1960. R. Mayer and J. Reuss, *Die Qumranfunde und die Bibel,* Regensburg 1959. K. H. Schelkle, *Die Gemeinde von Qumran und die Kirche des Neuen Testaments,* 2nd ed., Düsseldorf 1965. A. Vögtle, *Das öffentliche Wirken Jesu auf dem Hintergrund der Qumranbewegung (Freiburger Universitätsreden 27),* 1958.

[4] The texts tell nothing of the passing of the teacher of righteousness. That he was crucified and rose again and that his return was expected was read into the texts quite irresponsibly. His death on the cross was supposedly intimated (1 QpHab 9:8-12; 11:4-8; 4 QpNah 1:6-8), as also his exaltation and the expectation of his return (*Damascus Document* 6:10f.; 19:35–20:1). Today this view is universally abandoned; see H. Braun, *Qumran und das Neue Testament,* Vol. 2, pp. 54–63.

[5] K. L. Schmidt, Art. ἐκκλησία, in *Theol. Dict. N. T.,* Vol. 3, 1965, pp. 501–536. W. Schrage, Art. συναγωγή, *ibid.,* Vol. 7, 1971, pp. 798–852. O. Linton, Art. *Ekklesia,* in *Reallexikon für Antike und Christentum,* Vol. 4, 1959, pp. 905–921. Also of Linton, *Aux Origines de l'Église (Recherches Bibliques 7),* Bruges 1965; and *L'Église dans la Bible (Studia Montreal 13),* Bruges 1962. J. Blank, *"Der historische Jesus und die Kirche,"* in *Wort und Wahrheit,* Vol. 26 (1971), pp. 291–307. L. Cerfaux, *The Church in the Theology of St. Paul,* trans. G. Webb

and A. Walker, New York 1959. J. Daniélou, *L'Église des apôtres,* Paris 1973.
G. Delling, *"Merkmale der Kirche nach dem Neuen Testament,"* in *New Testament Studies,* Vol. 13 (1966/67), pp. 297–316. E. Finke, *"Jesus und die Kirche,"* in M. Roesle and O. Cullmann (eds.), *Begegnung der Christen (Festschrift O. Karrer),* Stuttgart and Frankfurt 1959, pp. 54–81. J. Finkenzeller, *Von der Botschaft Jesu zur Kirche Christi,* Munich 1974. K. Haacker, *"Jesus und die Kirche nach Johannes,"* in *Theol. Zeitschr.,* Vol. 29 (1973), pp. 179–201. W. G. Kümmel, *"Jesus und die Anfänge der Kirche,"* in *Heilsgeschehen und Geschichte,* Marburg 1965, pp. 289–309. Also of Kümmel, *Kirchenbegriff und Geschichtsbewusstsein in der Urgemeinde und bei Jesus,* 2nd ed., Göttingen 1968. P. S. Minear, *Images of the Church in the New Testament,* Philadelphia 1960. R. Schnackenburg, *The Church in the New Testament,* trans. W. J. O'Hara, New York 1965. W. Schrage, *" 'Ekklesia' und 'Synagoge,' Zum Ursprung des urchrislichen Kirchenbegriffs,"* in *Zeitschrift für Theologie und Kirche,* Vol. 60 (1963), pp. 178–202. E. Schweizer, *Church Order in the New Testament,* trans. F. Clarke, London 1961 and 1963. Also of Schweizer, *Matthäus und seine Gemeinde,* Stuttgart 1974.

[6] A. Loisy, *L'Évangile et l'Église,* Paris 1902 (5th ed., 1929), p. 155 (in English as *The Gospel and the Church,* Philadelphia 1976); also of Loisy, *Autour d'un petit livre,* Paris 1903 (2nd ed., 1904), p. 159. D. Baader, *Der Weg Loisys zur Erforschung der christlichen Wahrheit,* Freiburg 1974. J. Hulshoff, *Wahrheit und Geschichte, Alfred Loisy zwischen Tradition und Kritik,* dissertation, Münster i. W., Essen 1973.

[7] *Das Zweite Vatikanische Konzil, Konstitutionen, Dekrete und Erklärungen,* Vol. 1, Freiburg, 1966, pp. 137–347.

[8] In his *Kommentar zum Zweiten Vatikanischen Konzil,* Karl Rahner explains on pp. 213f.: "The text [of the decree] naturally does not want to prejudice the more minute historical questions about the manner and establishment of the circle of the Twelve. . . . The question of what further elements in the development of a Church can be referred back historically to Jesus is neither alluded to nor decided (Pastoral Epistles!). The Scripture citations can constitute a dogmatic argument in this area, but they cannot easily be seen as a historical one."

[9] J. Hainz, *Ekklesia, Strukturen paulinischer Gemeindetheologie und Gemeindeordnung,* Regensburg 1972. H. Schlier, *"Zu den Namen der Kirche in den paulinischen Briefen,"* in *Besinnung auf das Neue Testament,* Freiburg 1964, pp. 294–306.

[10] H. Schlier, Art. κεφαλή, in *Theol. Dict. N. T.,* Vol. 3, 1965, pp. 673–682. E. Schweizer and F. Baumgärtel, Art. σῶμα, *ibid.,* Vol. 7, 1971, pp. 1028–1094. H. Schlier, Art. *Corpus Christi,* in *Reallexikon für Antike und Christentum,* Vol. 3 (1957), pp. 437–453. K. M. Fischer, *Tendenz und Absicht des Epheserbriefes,* Göttingen 1973. E. Käsemann, *Leib und Leib Christi, Eine Untersuchung zur paulinischen Bergrifflichkeit,* Tübingen 1933; also of Käsemann, *"The Theological Problem Presented by the Motif of the Body of Christ,"* in his *Perspectives*

on Paul, trans. M. Kohl, Philadelphia 1971, pp. 102–121. H. Merklein, *Das kirchliche Amt nach dem Epheserbrief*, Munich 1973. J. Reuss, *"Die Kirche als 'Leib Christi' und die Herkunft dieser Vorstellung bei dem Apostel Paulus,"* in *Biblische Zeitschrift*, new series, Vol. 2, 1958. In addition to the above, see also the commentaries on the Epistle to the Romans (E. Käsemann, 3rd ed., Tübingen 1974; O. Michel, 12th ed., Göttingen 1963); on the Epistle to the Colossians (J. Lähemann, Gütersloh 1971; E. Lohse, Göttingen 1968); and on the Epistle to the Ephesians (J. Gnilka, Freiburg 1971; H. Schlier, 6th ed., Düsseldorf 1968).

[11] F. van der Horst, in his *Das Schema über die Kirche auf dem I. Vatikanischen Konzil*, Paderborn 1964, recalls the reservations that were voiced in this Council and even more broadly to the concept of the Church as "Mystical Body." In the decrees of the Second Vatican Council, the concept of the Mystical Body of Christ is diminished.

[12] G. Quell and J. Behm, Art. διαθήκη, in *Theol. Dict. N. T.*, Vol. 2, 1964, pp. 106–134. H. Pohlmann, Art. *Diatheke*, in *Reallexikon für Antike und Christentum*, Vol. 3 (1957), pp. 982–990. L. Krinetzki, *Der Bund Gottes mit den Menschen nach dem Alten Testament und dem Neuen Testament*, Düsseldorf 1963.

[13] The corresponding Hebrew word is *bᵉrith*. The Septuagint usually translates the term, when used in a secular way, with συνθήκη = contract between or among equally empowered partners, and when used in a sacral way, with διαθήκη = arrangement and enactment on the part of God.

[14] H. L. Strack and P. Billerbeck, *Kommentar zum Neuen Testament aus Talmud and Midrasch*, Vol. 3, 1926, pp. 89–91, 704.

[15] H. Strathmann and R. Meyer, Art. λαός, in *Theol. Dict. N. T.*, Vol. 4, 1967, pp. 29–52. N. Dahl, *Das Wort Gottes*, Olso 1941. B. Hanssler, *Das Gottesvolk der Kirche*, Düsseldorf 1960. E. Käsemann, *Das wandernde Gottesvolk*, 3rd ed., Göttingen 1959. F. Mussner, *"Das 'Volk Gottes' im Neuen Testament,"* in *Praesentia salutis*, Düsseldorf 1967, pp. 244–252. A. Oepke, *Das neue Gottesvolk in Schrifttum, Schauspiel, bildender Kunst und Weltgestaltung*, Gütersloh 1957.

[16] See the commentary thereto of A. Grillmeier in *Das Zweite Vatikanische Konzil, Konstitutionen, Dekrete und Erklärungen*, Vol. 1, Freiburg 1966, pp. 176–209.

[17] Some exegetes regard the mention of the sacraments as an insertion through ecclesiastical redaction. The evidence seems hardly sufficient to provide any security in such a judgment (see § 8, 3, c, 10).

[18] Besides the current commentaries, see also J. Jeremias, Art. θύρα, in *Theol. Dict. N. T.*, Vol. 3, 1965, pp. 173–180; same author, Art. ποιμήν, *ibid.*, Vol. 6, 1968, pp. 485–502; H. Preisker and F. Schulz, Art. πρόβατον, *ibid.*, pp. 689–692; K. Haacker, *"Jesus und die Kirche nach Johannes,"* in *Theol. Zeitschr.*, Vol. 29 (1973), pp. 179–201; E. Schweizer, *"Der Kirchenbegriff im Evangelium und in den Briefen des Johannes,"* in *Neotestamentica*, Zürich 1963, pp. 254–271; A. J. Simonis, *Die Hirtenrede des Johannesevangeliums*, Rome 1967.

[19] Th. Klauser, "*Studien zur Entstehungsgeschichte der christlichen Kunst,*" I and VIII, in *Jahrbuch für Antike und Christentum*, Vol. 1 (1958), pp. 20–51, and 8/9 (1965/1966), pp. 126–170. A. Legner, *Der gute Hirt*, Düsseldorf 1959.

[20] J. Behm, Art. ἄμπελος, in *Theol. Dict. N. T.*, Vol. 1, 1964, pp. 342–343; same author, Art. κλῆμα, *ibid.*, Vol. 3, 1965, p. 757. R. Borig, *Der wahre Weinstock, Untersuchungen zu Jo 15, 1-10*, Munich 1967. A. Jaubert, "*L'image de la vigne (Jean 15),*" in F. Christ (ed.), *Oikonomia (Festschrift O. Cullmann)*, Hamburg-Bergstedt, 1967, pp. 93–99.

[21] G. Stählin, article φιλέω, in *Theol. Dict. N. T.*, Vol. 9, 1974, pp. 113–171. H. Leroy, *Nicht Knechte, sondern Freunde*, Zürich 1973.

[22] E. Käsemann, *Jesu letzter Wille nach Johannes 17*, 3rd ed. Tübingen 1971. M. Lattke, *Einheit im Wort. Die Spezifische Bedeutung von* ἀγάπη, ἀγαπᾶν *und* φιλῶ *im Johannesevangelium*, Munich 1975. U. Luck, "*Die kirchliche Einheit als Problem im Johannesevangelium,*" in *Wort und Dienst*, new series, Vol. 10, 1969, pp. 51–67. J. F. Randall, "The Theme of Unity in John 17, 20-23," in *Ephemerides theologicae Lovanienses*, Vol 41 (1965), pp. 373–394.

[23] H. Conzelmann and W. Zimmerli, Art. χάρις, in *Theol. Dict. N. T.*, Vol. 9, 1974, pp. 372–402. U. Brockhaus, *Charisma und Amt*, Wuppertal 1972. J. Brosch, *Charismen und Ämter in der Urkirche*, Bonn 1951. H. von Campenhausen, *Kirchliches Amt und geistliche Vollmacht in den ersten drei Jahrhunderten*, Tübingen 1953 [*Ecclesiastical Authority and Spiritual Power in the Church of the First Three Centuries*, trans. J. A. Baker, Stanford, California, 1969]. Also of von Campenhausen, "*Recht und Gehorsam in der ältesten Kirche,*" in *Aus der Frühzeit des Christentums*, Tübingen 1963, pp. 1–29. G. Friedrich, "*Geist und Amt,*" in *Wort und Dienst*, new series, Vol. 3 (1952), pp. 61–85. F. Grau, *Der neutestamentliche Begriff Charisma, seine Geschichte und seine Theologie*, typed dissertation, Tübingen 1946. G. Hasenhüttl, *Charisma, Ordnungsprinzip der Kirche*, Freiburg 1969. Also of Hasenhüttl, *Herrschaftsfreie Kirche*, Düsseldorf 1974. M. Hengel, *Nachfolge und Charisma*, Berlin 1968. O. Knoch, *Der Geist Gottes und der neue Mensch*, Stuttgart 1975. F. J. Leenhardt, "*Les fonctions constitutives de l'Église et épiscopé selon le Nouveau Testament,*" in *Revue d'Histoire et de Philosophie religieuses*, Vol. 47 (1967), pp. 111–149. K. Rahner, *Das Dynamische in der Kirche*, Freiburg 1958 [trans. W. J. O'Hara, *The Dynamic Element in the Church*, New York 1964]. Also of Rahner, "*Löschet den Geist nicht aus,*" in *Schriften zur Theologie*, Vol. 7, 1966, pp. 77–90 [trans. D. Bourke as "Do Not Stifle the Spirit!" in *Theological Investigations*, Vol. 7, London 1971, pp. 72–87]. J. Ratzinger, "*Bemerkungen zur Frage der Charismen in der Kirche,*" in G. Bornkamm and K. Rahner (eds.), *Die Zeit Jesu (Festschrift H. Schlier)*, Freiburg 1970, pp. 252–272. U. Schnell, *Das Verhältnis von Amt und Gemeinde im neueren Katholizismus*, Berlin 1975. H. Schürmann, "*Die geistlichen Gnadengaben,*" in *Ursprung und Gestalt*, Düsseldorf 1970, pp. 236–267. H. Schütte, *Amt, Ordination und Sukzession im Verhältnis evange-*

lischer und katholischer Exegeten und Dogmatiker der Gegenwart sowie in Dokumenten ökumenischer Gespräche, Düsseldorf 1974.

[24] When St. Ignatius of Antioch says, in his *Letter to the Magnesians* 2 [Jurgens, no. 43a], that one who obeys the bishop obeys the grace of God, it probably means that the bishop procures the grace of God, and it is through the bishop that that grace is imparted to others.

[25] The opposition between charisms, law, and office is emphasized in significant and long influential works of R. Sohm, *Kirchenrecht,* Vol. 1, *Die geschichtlichen Grundlagen,* Leipzig 1892 (p. 700: "The nature of canon law is in contradiction to the nature of the Church"), and of Adolf von Harnack, *Entstehung und Entwicklung der Kirchenverfassung und des Kirchenrechts in den zwei ersten Jahrhunderten,* Leipzig 1910. See also U. Brockhaus, *Charisma und Amt,* Wuppertal 1972, pp. 15–46; W. Böckenförde, *Das Rechtsverständnis der neueren Kanonistik und die Kritik Rudolf Sohms,* dissertation, Münster 1969; E. Käsemann, "*Sätze heiligen Rechtes im Neuen Testament,*" in *Exegetische Versuche und Besinnungen,* Vol. 2, Göttingen 1964, pp. 69–82 ["Sentences of Holy Law in the New Testament," in the selections translated by W. J. Montague, under the general title *New Testament Questions of Today,* Philadelphia 1969, pp. 66–81]; W. Maurer, "*Die Auseinandersetzung zwischen Harnack und Sohm und die Begründung eines evangelischen Kirchenrechts,*" in *Kerygma und Dogma,* Vol. 6 (1960), pp. 194–213.

[26] For the designations and titles, see the usual dictionaries. G. Delling, Art. ἄρχω, in *Theol. Dict. N. T.,* Vol. 1, 1964, pp. 478–484; W. Förster, Art. ἐξουσία, *ibid.,* Vol. 2, 1964, pp. 562–574; also of Förster, Art. κύριος, ibid., Vol. 3, 1965, pp. 1039–1098; J. Schneider, Art. τιμή, ibid., Vol. 8, 1972, pp. 169–180.

[27] H. W. Beyer, Art. διακονέω, in *Theol. Dict. N. T.,* Vol. 2, 1964, pp. 81–93. Th. Klauser, Art. *Diakon,* in *Reallexikon für Antike und Christentum,* Vol. 3, 1957, pp. 888–909 (see also § 4).

[28] Analysis reveals two sources: the one, Mark 6:7-13 = Luke 9:1-6; the other, Source Q, in Luke 10:1-16 and Matthew 9:36–11:1, in which, in Matthew, the sayings from Mark and Source Q are combined. See P. Hoffman, *Studien zur Theologie der Logienquelle,* Münster 1972, pp. 235–331. G. Theissen, "*Wanderradikalismus. Literatursoziologische Aspekte der Überlieferung von Worten Jesu im Urchristentum,*" in *Zeitschrift für Theologie und Kirche,* Vol. 70 (1973), pp. 245–271; and also of Theissen, "*Legitimation und Lebensunterhalt: Ein Beitrag zur Soziologie urchristlicher Missionäre,*" in *New Testament Studies,* Vol. 21 (1974/75), pp. 192–221.

[29] By no means to be excluded is the other possibility, that the text of Mark 6:8f., as we have it today, was tempered somewhat at a later time, in the face of the originally more rigid demands which were contained in Matthew = Luke in accord with Source Q. In the more rigid demands perhaps the directive to temple pilgrims has found a voice: "One is not to go up the temple hill with a

staff, nor in shoes, nor with a money-belt, nor with dusty feet" (see H. L. Strack and P. Billerbeck, *Kommentar zum Neuen Testament,* Vol. 1, 1922, p. 565).

³⁰ The meaning of the term καθηγητὴς in Matthew 23:10, which we have rendered "master," is really quite uncertain. Is the term a Hellenistic translation of "rabbi," or does it designate, as it sometimes does in profane Greek, a leader or guide?

³¹ H. von Campenhausen, *"Die Begründung kirchlicher Entscheidungen beim Apostel Paulus,"* in *Aus der Frühzeit des Christentums,* Tübingen 1963, pp. 30–80. Also of Campenhusen, *"Das Problem der Ordnung im Urchristentum und in der alten Kirche,"* in *Tradition und Leben,* Tübingen 1960, pp. 157–179. M. Limbeck, *Von der Ohnmacht des Rechts,* Düsseldorf 1972, pp. 84–107.

³² H. Goldstein, *Das Gemeindeverständnis des Ersten Petrusbriefes,* dissertation, Münster i. W. 1973; also of Goldstein, *Paulinische Gemeinde im Ersten Petrusbrief,* Stuttgart 1975. W. Nauck, *"Probleme des frühkirchlichen Amtsverständnisses (1 Peter 5,2f.),"* in *Zeitschr. f. d. neutest. Wissensch.,* Vol. 48 (1957), pp. 200–220. K. H. Schelkle, *Die Petrusbriefe. Der Judasbrief,* Freiburg, 3rd ed., 1970, pp. 127–130.

³³ 1 Peter 5:3 uses the term κατακυριεύειν to designate the abuse of power in the Church, the same term by which Jesus refers, in Mark 10:42, to the violent exercise of power in the world.

³⁴ E. Lohse, Art. χείρ, in *Theol. Dict. N. T.,* Vol. 9, 1974, pp. 424–437; also of Lohse, *Die Ordination im Spätjudentum und im Neuen Testament,* Göttingen 1951.

³⁵ P. Bläser, *"Amt und Gemeinde im Neuen Testament und in der reformatorischen Theologie,"* in *Catholica,* Vol. 18 (1964), pp. 167–192. H. von Campenhausen, same references as in note 23 above. J. Delorme (ed.), *Le ministère et les ministères selon le Nouveau Testament,* Paris 1974. P. V. Dias, *Vielfalt der Kirche in der Vielfalt der Jünger, Zeugen und Diener,* Freiburg 1968. H. Greeven, *"Propheten, Lehrer, Vorsteher bei Paulus,"* in *Zeitschr. f. d. neutest. Wissenschaft,* Vol. 44 (1952/53), pp .1–43. J. Guyot (ed.), *Das apostolische Amt,* trans., Mainz 1961. E. Käsemann, *"Amt und Gemeinde im Neuen Testament,"* in *Exegetische Versuche und Besinnungen,* Vol. 1, 4th ed., Göttingen 1965, pp. 109–134. K. Kertelge, *Gemeinde und Amt im Neuen Testament,* Munich 1972. Ph. H. Menoud, *L'Église et les ministères selon le Nouveau Testament,* Neuchâtel 1949. W. Trilling, *"Amt und Amtsverständnis bei Matthäus,"* in A. Descamps and A. de Halleux (eds.), *Mélanges Bibliques en hommage au R. P. Béda Rigaux,* Gembloux 1970, pp. 29–44.

³⁶ K. H. Rengstorf, Art. ἀποστέλλω, in *Theol. Dict. N. T.,* Vol. 1, 1964, pp. 398–447; also of Rengstorf, Art. δώδεκα, *ibid.,* Vol. 2, 1964, pp. 321–328. P. Bläser, *"Zum Problem des urchristlichen Apostolats,"* in *Unio Christianorum. Festschrift L. Jaeger,* Paderborn 1962, pp. 92–107. H. von Campenhausen, *"Der urchristliche Apostelbegriff,"* in *Studia theologica,* Vol. 1 (1948), pp. 96–130. B. Gerhardsson,

"*Die Boten Gottes und die Apostel Christi*," in *Svensk Exegetisk Arsbok*, Vol. 27 (1962), pp. 89–131. R. Groscurth (ed.), *Katholizität und Apostolizität* (*Kerygma und Dogma*, Subsidiary Vol. 2), Göttingen 1971. F. Hahn, "*Der Apostolat im Urchristentum*," in *Kerygma und Dogma*, Vol. 20 (1974), pp. 54–77. E. Käsemann, "*Die Legitimität des Apostels*," in *Zeitschrift für die neutestamentliche Wissenschaft*, Vol. 41 (1942), pp. 33–71. K. Kertelge, "*Die Funktion der Zwölf im Markusevangelium*," in *Trierer theologische Zeitschrift*, Vol. 78 (1969), pp. 193–206. G. Klein, *Die zwölf Apostel*, Göttingen 1961. E. M. Kredel, "*Der Apostelbegriff in der neueren Exegese*," in *Zeitschrift für katholische Theologie*, Vol. 78 (1956), pp. 169–193; 257–305. W. Marxsen, "*Die Nachfolge der Apostel*," in *Der Exeget als Theologe*, Gütersloh 1968, pp. 75–90. K. H. Rengstorf, *Apostolat und Predigtamt*, 2nd ed., Stuttgart 1954. B. Rigaux, "*Die 'Zwölf' in Geschichte und Kerygma*," in H. Ristow and K. Matthiae (eds.), *Der historische Jesus und der kerygmatische Christus*, 2nd ed., Berlin 1961, pp. 468–486. J. Roloff, *Apostolat, Verkündigung, Kirche. Ursprung, Inhalt und Funktion des kirchlichen Apostelamtes nach Paulus, Lukas und den Pastoralbriefen*, Gütersloh 1965. G. Schille, *Die urchristliche Kollegialmission*, Zürich and Stuttgart 1967. G. Schmahl, *Die Zwölf im Markusevangelium*, Trier 1974. W. Schmithals, *Das kirchliche Apostelamt*, Göttingen 1961 [trans. J. E. Steely, *The Office of Apostle in the Early Church*, Nashville 1969]. R. Schnackenburg, "*Apostel vor und neben Paulus*," in *Schriften zum Neuen Testament*, Munich 1971, pp. 338–358.

[37] O. Schmitz, Art. θρόνος, in *Theol. Dict. N. T.*, Vol. 3, 1965, pp. 160–167. J. Dupont, "*Le logion des douze trônes (Mt 19,28; Lk 22,28-30)*," in *Biblica*, Vol. 45 (1964), pp. 355–392.

[38] R. Baumann, *Mitte und Norm des Christlichen*, Münster 1968 (see references to Paul in index). T. Holtz, "*Zum Selbstverständnis des Apostels Paulus*," in *Theologische Literaturzeitung*, Vol. 91 (1961), pp. 321–330. K. Kertelge, "*Das Apostelamt des Paulus, sein Ursprung und seine Bedeutung*," in *Biblische Zeitschrift*, new series, Vol. 14 (1970), pp. 161–181.

[39] U. Wilckens, Art. στῦλος, in *Theol. Dict. N. T.*, Vol. 7, 1971, pp. 732–736. Of the commentaries, see especially F. Mussner, *Der Galaterbrief*, Freiburg 1974, pp. 132–167. Also, J. Dupont, *Pierre et Paul à Antioche et à Jérusalem — Études sur les Actes des Apôtres*, Paris 1967, pp. 185–215. H. Feld, " '*Christus Diener der Sünde*'. *Zum Ausgang des Streites zwischen Petrus und Paulus*," in *Theologische Quartalschrift*, Vol. 153 (1973), pp. 119–131.

[40] According to K. H. Rengstorf, in his article ἀπόστολος, in *Theol. Dict. N. T.*, Vol. 1, 1964, pp. 407–447, and in his *Apostolat und Predigtamt*, 2nd edition, Stuttgart 1954, the acceptance often expressed of ἀπόστολος as translation of the Hebrew *shaliach*, as the messenger in the service of the synagogue was called, has recently been made questionable. The institution of these messengers is first witnessed in the post-New Testament era. Besides, their duties involved only commissions in respect to the Law and its administration.

[41] The texts (in Mandaean and Manichaean writings and in Gnostic fragments

preserved in patristic writings) are, however, post-Christian; and here it is a question only of New Testament influence. J. P. Miranda, *Der Vater, der mich gesandt hat,* dissertation, Tübingen, Bern, and Frankfurt 1972, pp. 9f., 275–278. W. Schmithals, *Das kirchliche Apostelamt,* Göttingen 1961, pp. 121–126.

[42] G. Schrenk, Art. ἱερός, in *Theol. Dict. N. T.,* Vol. 3, 1965, pp. 221–283. J. Blank, *"Kirchliches Amt und Priesterbegriff,"* in F. Hentrich (ed.), *Weltpriester nach dem Konzil,* Munich 1969, pp. 11–52. H. von Campenhausen, *"Die Anfänge des Priesterbegriffes in der alten Kirche,"* in *Tradition und Leben,* Tübingen 1960, pp. 272–289. L. Cerfaux, *"Regale sacerdotium,"* in *Recueil Lucien Cerfaux,* Vol. 2, Gembloux 1954, pp. 283–315. G. E. Ebeling, *"Das Priestertum in protestantischer Sicht,"* in *Wort Gottes und Tradition,* Göttingen 1964, pp. 183–196. H. Schlier, *"Grundelemente des priesterlichen Amtes im Neuen Testament,"* in *Theologie und Philosophie,* Vol. 44 (1969), pp. 161–180. E. Schüssler-Fiorenza, *Priester für Gott,* Münster 1972. H. Volk, *Priestertum heute,* Rodenkirchen 1972. K. Weiss, *"Paulus, Priester der christlichen Kultgemeinde,"* in *Theologische Literaturzeitung,* Vol. 79 (1954), pp. 355–364. R. Zollitsch, *Amt und Funktion des Priesters. Eine Untersuchung zum Ursprung und zur Gestalt des Presbyterats in den ersten zwei Jahrhunderten,* Freiburg 1974.

[43] Since the New Testament uses the designation ἀρχή (above, § 3, 2, a) for office in the Church and avoids the use of the word ἱερὸς to designate holiness, some reservations ought to be had about our accustomed usage of the term "hierarchy" for ecclesiastical offices.

[44] O. Michel, *Der Brief an die Hebräer,* 6th ed., Göttingen 1966, pp. 165–169. S. Nomoto, *"Herkunft und Struktur der Hohepriestervorstellung im Hebräerbrief,"* in *Novum Testamentum,* Vol. 10 (1968), pp. 10–25. H. Zimmerman, *Die Hohepriester-Christologie des Hebräerbriefes,* Paderborn 1964.

[45] H. J. Elliott, *The Elect and the Holy. An Exegetical Examination of 1 Peter 2:4-10 and the Phrase* βασίλειον ἱεράτευμα, Leiden 1966. H. Goldstein, *Das Gemeindeverständnis des Ersten Petrusbriefes,* dissertation, Münster i. W. 1973. J. Michl, *"Die Presbyter des ersten Petrusbriefes,"* in H. Fleckenstein (*et. al.,* eds.), *Ortskirche Weltkirche (Festschrift J. Döpfner),* Würzburg 1973, pp. 48–62.

[46] H. Strathmann and R. Meyer, Art. λειτουργέω, in *Theol. Dict. N. T.,* Vol. 4, 1967, pp. 215–225. In profane Greek, ἱερουργέω signifies "liturgical celebration," "sacrifice"; in Philo and Josephus, "sacrifice"; in *4 Macc. 7:6,* "to fulfill the Law in martyrdom." See G. Schrenk, Art. ἱερουργέω, in *Theol. Dict. N. T.,* Vol. 3, 1965, pp. 251–252. C. Wiener, " Ἱερουργεῖν *(Röm 15,16),"* in *Studiorum Paulinorum congressus internationalis catholicus 1961,* 2 vols. (*Analecta biblica* 17–18), Rome 1963, Vol. 2, pp. 398–404.

[47] λατρεύω (Rom. 1:9) means to carry out a ministry, priestly and otherwise; H. Strathmann, Art. λατρεύω, in *Theol. Dict. N. T.,* Vol. 4, 1967, pp. 58–65.

[48] G. Bornkamm, Art. πρέσβυς, in *Theol. Dict. N. T.,* Vol. 6, 1968, pp. 651–683. W. Michaelis, *Das Ältestenamt der christlichen Gemeinde im Lichte der Heiligen Schrift,* Bern 1953.

[49] Perhaps the Gothic terms were not accepted, as was the case with the Greek ἱερεύς, because they had about them an overtone of magic. F. Kluge, *Etymologisches Wörterbuch der deutschen Sprache*, 20th ed., Berlin 1967, p. 565. R. von Raumer, *Die Einwirkung des Christentums auf die althochdeutsche Sprache*, Stuttgart 1845, pp. 295–302.

[50] H. Krämer, R. Rendtorff, R. Meyer, and G. Friedrich, Art. προφήτης, in *Theol. Dict. N. T.*, Vol. 6, 1968, pp. 781–861. Th. M. Crone, *Early Christian Prophecy*, dissertation, Tübingen, Baltimore 1973. G. Dautzenberg, *Urchristliche Prophetie*, Stuttgart 1975. H. Greeven, "*Propheten, Lehrer, Vorsteher bein Paulus*," in *Zeitschrift für die neutestamentliche Wissenschaft*, Vol. 44 (1952/53), pp. 1–43. B. Henneken, *Verkündigung und Prophetie im 1. Thessalonicherbrief*, Stuttgart 1969. U. B. Müller, *Prophetie und Predigt im Neuen Testament*, Gütersloh 1975. J. Panagopoulos, *Der Prophet aus Nazareth*, Athens 1973 (in modern Greek). F. Schnider, *Jesus der Prophet*, Göttingen 1973.

[51] K. Rahner, *Das Dynamische in der Kirche*, Freiburg 1958, pp. 38–73.

[52] K. H. Rengstorff, Art. διδάσκω, *Theol. Dict. N. T.*, Vol. 2, 1964, pp. 135–165. G. Friedrich, Art. εὐαγγελιστής, *ibid.*, pp. 737f. H. W. Beyer, Art. κατηχέω, *ibid.*, Vol. 3, 1965, pp. 638–640. E. Lohse, Art. ῥάββι, *ibid.*, Vol. 6, 1968, pp. 961–965. H. Flender, "*Lehren und Verkündigung in den synoptischen Evangelien*," in *Evangelische Theologie*, Vol. 12 (1965), pp. 701–714.

[53] J. Jeremias, article ποιμήν, in *Theol. Dict. N. T.*, Vol. 6, 1968, pp. 485–502. O. Kiefer, *Die Hirtenrede, Analyse und Deutung von Jo 10,1-18*, Stuttgart 1967. A. J. Simonis, *Die Hirtenrede im Johannesevangelium*, Rome 1967. W. Tooley, "The Shepherd and Sheep Image in the Teaching of Jesus," in *Novum Testamentum*, Vol. 7 (1964–65), pp. 15–25.

[54] H. W. Beyer, Art. ἐπισκέπτομαι, in *Theol. Dict. N. T.*, Vol. 2, 1964, pp. 599–622. H. W. Beyer and H. Karpp, Art. *Bischof* in *Reallexikon für Antike und Christentum*, Vol. 2, 1954, pp. 394–407. P. Benoit, "*Les origines de l'Épiscopat dans le Nouveau Testament*," in *Exégèse et Théologie*, Vol. 2, Paris 1961, pp. 107–153. F. Nötscher, "*Vorchristliche Typen urchristlicher Ämter? Episkopos und Mebaqqer*," in *Vom Alten zum Neuen Testament*, Bonn 1962, pp. 188–200.

[55] H. W. Beyer, Art. διακονέω, in *Theol. Dict. N. T.*, Vol. 2, 1964, pp. 81–93. Th. Klauser, Art. *Diakon* in *Reallexikon für Antike und Christentum*, Vol. 3, 1957, pp. 888–909. J. Schütz, *Der Diakonat im Neuen Testament*, typed dissertation, Mainz 1952.

[56] B. Reicke, Art. προΐστημι, in *Theol. Dict N. T.*, Vol. 6, 1968, pp. 700–703.

[57] F. Büchsel, Art. ἡγέομαι, in *Theol. Dict. N. T.*, Vol. 2, 1964, pp. 907–909. O. Michel, *Der Brief an die Hebräer*, 6th ed., Göttingen 1966, pp. 487–490, 526f.

[58] A. Oepke, Art. γύνη, in *Theol. Dict. N. T.*, Vol. 1, 1964, pp. 776–789. H. L. Strack and P. Billerbeck, *Kommentar zum Neuen Testament*, Vol. 2, 1924, p. 438; Vol. 3, 1926, pp. 467f., 558–561; Vol. 4, 1928, pp. 157f., 196f., 1073f.

[59] G. G. Blum, "*Das Amt der Frau im Neuen Testament*," in *Novum Testamentum*, Vol. 7 (1963), pp. 142–161. H. Cancik (*et al.*), *Zum Thema Frau in*

Kirche und Gesellschaft, Stuttgart 1972. A. Feuillet, *"La dignité et le rôle de la femme d'après quelques textes pauliniennes*," in *New Testament Studies*, Vol. 21 (1974/75), pp. 157–191. G. Fitzer, *"Das Weib schweige in der Gemeinde*," Munich 1963. J. Galot, *Mission et ministère de la femme*, Paris 1973. E. Kähler, *Die Frau in den paulinischen Briefen*, Zürich 1960. H. van der Meer, *Priestertum der Frau?*, Freiburg 1969. I. Raming, *Der Ausschluss der Frau vom priester-lichen Amt — gottgewollte Tradition oder Diskriminierung?*, Cologne 1972. F. Schüssler, *Der vergessene Partner*, Düsseldorf 1964.

[60] H. Conzelmann, *Der erste Brief an die Korinther*, Göttingen 1969, pp. 222–226, 289f. [trans. J. W. Leitch, *First Corinthians: A Commentary*, Philadelphia 1975, pp. 181f.]

[61] O. Cullmann, Art. πέτρα, in *Theol. Dict. N. T.*, Vol. 6, 1968, pp. 95–99; also of Cullmann, Art. Πέτρος, Κηφᾶς, ibid., pp. 100–112. J. Blank, *"Petrus — Typol-ogie und Petrusamt*," in *Concilium*, Vol. 9 (1973), pp. 173–179. R. E. Brown and K. P. Donfried (eds.), *Peter in the New Testament*, Minneapolis 1973. *"Contributi Petriani*," in *Miscellanea Francescana*, Vol. 74 (1974), pp. 273–432, (issued also as *Pietro nelle Sacra Scrittura*, Florence 1975). O. Cullman, *Petrus, Jünger, Apostel, Märtyrer*, 2nd ed., Zürich 1960 [trans. F. V. Filson, *Peter: Dis-ciple, Apostle, Martyr: A Historical and Theological Study*, Philadelphia 1962]. M. Didier, *L'Évangile selon St. Matthieu, Rédaction et Théologie*, Gembloux 1972. W. Dietrich, *Das Petrusbild in den lukanischen Schriften*, Stuttgart 1972. E. Dinkler, *"Die Petrus-Rom-Frage, Ein Forschungsbericht*," in *Theologische Rundschau*, new series, Vol. 25 (1959), pp. 189–230; Vol. 27 (1961), pp. 33–64. P. Gaechter, *Petrus und sine Zeit*, Innsbruck 1958. D. Gewalt, *Petrus, Studien zur Geschichte und Tradition des frühen Christentums*, dissertation, Heidelberg, 2 vols., 1966. G. Klein, *Rekonstruktion und Interpretation*, Munich 1969 (pp. 11–128): *"Die Berufung des Petrus*," *"Die Verleugnung des Petrus*," *"Galater 2, 6-9 und die Geschichte der Jerusalemer Urgemeinde*"). F. Refoulé, *"Primauté de Pierre dans les Évangiles*," in *Revue des Sciences Religieuses*, Vol. 38 (1964), pp. 1–41. B. Rigaux, *"Der Apostel Petrus in der heutigen Exegese*," in *Concili-um*, Vol. 3 (1967), pp. 585–600. G. Schulze-Kadelbach, *"Die Stellung des Petrus in der Urchristenheit*," in *Theologische Literaturzeitung*, Vol. 81 (1956), pp. 1–14.

[62] R. Pesch, *Der reiche Fischzug Luke 5,1-11 / John 21,1-14*, Düsseldorf 1969: that Luke 5:1-11 is a duplication, backdated into the life of Jesus, from the paschal history in John 21:1-14.

[63] It is hardly correct to translate πίστις in Luke 22:32 by "constancy" or "fidel-ity." This meaning is very uncommon in the New Testament (Matthew 22:23; Gal. 5:22; Titus 2:10) and would be of singular occurrence in Luke and Acts. In any case, the Evangelist would have understood the word in the sense of "faith"; see R. Bultmann, Art. πίστις, in *Theol. Dict. N. T.*, Vol. 6, 1968, pp. 203–204. Also of Bultmann, *Geschichte der synoptischen Tradition*, 4th ed., Gott-tingen 1971, pp. 287f. [trans. John Marsh, *The History of the Synoptic Tradi-

tion, 2nd ed., New York 1968, is of the 2nd German edition, of 1931; see pp. 266f. for corresponding place].

[64] Paul refers to Simon mostly by the surname Kephas (Gal. 1:18; 2:9, 11, 14; 1 Cor. 1:12; 3:22; 9:5; 15:5), and only exceptionally with the surname Peter, in Gal. 2:7f. Here Peter and Paul stand opposed to each other, Peter as Apostle of the Jews, Paul as Apostle of the Gentiles. In such circumstances, a formula "Kephas and Paul" woul not be possible.

[65] J. Jeremias, Art. ᾅδης, in *Theol. Dict. N. T.*, Vol. 1, 1964, pp. 146–149. F. Büchsel, Art. δέω, *ibid.*, Vol. 2, 1964, pp. 60–61. J. Jeremias, Art. κλείς, *ibid.*, Vol. 3, 1965, pp. 744–753. O. Procksch and F. Büchsel, Art. λύω, *ibid.*, Vol. 4, 1967, pp. 328–337. J. Jeremias, Art. πύλη, *ibid.*, Vol. 6, 1959, pp. 920–927. O. Michel, Art. *Binden und Lösen*, in *Reallexikon für Antike und Christentum*, Vol. 2, 1952, pp. 374–380. O. Betz, "*Felsenmann und Felsengemeinde*," in *Zeitschrift für die neutestamentliche Wissenschaft*, Vol. 48 (1957), pp. 49–77. G. Bornkamm, "*Die Binde- und Lösegewalt in der Kirche des Matthäus*," in G. Bornkamm and K. Rahner, *Die Zeit Jesu (Festschrift H. Schlier)*, Freiburg 1970, pp. 83–107. R. Bultmann, "*Die Frage nach der Echtheit von Mt 16,17-19*," in *Exegetica*, Tübingen, 1967, pp. 255–277. G. Denzler *(et al.), Zum Thema Petrusamt und Papsttum*, Stuttgart 1970. Also of Denzler, as editor, *(et al.), Das Papsttum in der Diskussion*, Regensburg 1974. P. Hoffman, "*Der Petrus-Primat im Matthäusevangelium*," in J. Gnilka *(et al.*, eds.), *Neues Testament und Kirche (Festschrift R. Schnackenburg)*, Freiburg 1974, pp. 94–114 (also in G. Denzler's *Das Papsttum in der Diskussion*, pp. 9–35). F. Obrist, *Echtheitsfragen und Deutung der Primatsstelle Mt 16,18f. in der deutschen protestantischen Theologie der letzten 30 Jahre*, Müsnter 1961. J. Ringger, "*Das Felsenwort: Zur Sinndeutung von Mt 16,18, vor allem im Lichte der Symbolgeschichte*," in M. Roesle and O. Cullman (eds.), *Begegnung der Christen*, Stuttgart and Frankfurt 1959, pp. 271–347. J. Schmid, "*Petrus der 'Fels' und die Petrusgestalt der Urgemeinde*," in M. Roesle and O. Cullmann (eds.), *Begegnung der Christen*, Stuttgart and Frankfurt 1959, pp. 347–359. A. Vögtle, "*Messiasbekenntnis und Petrusverheissung*," in *Das Evangelium und die Evangelien*, Düsseldorf 1971, pp. 137–170. Also of Vögtle, "*Zum Problem der Herkunft von 'Mt 16,17-19',*" in F. Hoffmann *(et al.*, eds.), *Orientierung an Jesus (Festschrift J. Schmid)*, Freiburg 1973, pp. 372–393. W. Trilling, "*Zum Petrusamt im Neuen Testament*," in *Theologische Versuch*, Vol. 4, Berlin 1972, pp. 27–46.

[66] The rather common explanation of the "gates of hell" as the powers of the underworld, inimical to God, is hardly correct. J. Jeremias defended this meaning at first in his article ᾅδης in *Theol. Dict. N. T.*, Vol. 1, 1964 (original German edition appeared, however, already in 1938), pp. 146–149; but in the article πύλη in the same *Theol. Dict.*, Vol. 6, 1968 (1959 in the original German edition), pp. 921–928, he defends the idea that the "gates of hell" means the world of death; likewise in the more recent commentaries.

[67] J. Jeremias, Art. λύω, in *Theol. Dict. N. T.*, Vol. 4, 1967, pp. 328–337. O.

Michel, Art. *Binden und Lösen,* in *Reallexikon für Antike und Christentum,* Vol. 2, 1952, pp. 374–380. See also H. L. Strack and P. Billerbeck, *Kommentar zum Neuen Testament aus Talmud und Midrasch,* Vol. 1 (1922), pp. 738–744.

[68] A. Vögtle, in his *"Messiasbekenntnis und Petrusverheissung,"* in *Das Evangelium und die Evangelien,* Düsseldorf 1971, pp. 137–170, and in his *"Zum Problem der Herkunft von 'Mt 16,17-19',"* in *F. Hoffman's Orientierung an Jesus (Festschrift J. Schmid),* Freiburg 1973, pp. 372–393, explains Matthew 16:17 as shaped by the Evangelist, who wanted to provide a transition from Peter's confession of the Messiah in Matthew 16:16 to the traditional saying of the Lord in Matthew 16:18f. Among the authors who agree with this explanation is P. Hoffmann, in his *"Der Petrus-Primat im Matthäusevangelium,"* in J. Gnilka's *Neues Testament und Kirche (Festschrift R. Schnackenburg),* Freiburg 1974, pp. 94–114, published also in G. Denzler's *Das Papsttum in der Diskussion,* pp. 9–35.

[69] This is the case with P. Hoffmann and A. Vögtle, in their works cited above in note 65, with W. Trilling in his *"Zum Petrusamt . . ."* cited in the same note, as well as Hans Küng in his *Fehlbar?,* Zürich 1973, pp. 403–410. O. da Spinetoli, *"La portata ecclesiologica di Mt 16,18-19,"* in *Antonianum,* Vol. 42 (1967), pp. 357–375, comes to the conclusion that Matthew 16:18f. is not the point of departure for a doctrine, but that what is formulated here is already a long and rich experience of the Church.

[70] Instances are pointed out especially in Strack and Billerbeck, *op. cit.,* Vol. 1, 1922, pp. 730–747, and also in the articles in *Theol. Dict. N. T.* as cited in note 65 above.

[71] Thus with E. Dinkler in his article in *Theologische Rundschau,* new series, Vol. 27 (1961), p. 37; and E. Schweizer, *Das Evangelium nach Matthäus,* Göttingen 1973, p. 220 [trans. David E. Green, *The Good News According to Matthew,* Atlanta 1975, pp. 340f.].

[72] Thus with P. Hoffman and A. Vögtle, in their works cited in note 65 above. See also E. Dinkler, article in *Theologische Rundschau,* new series, Vol. 27 (1961), p. 36. E. Käsemann, *"Die Anfänge christlicher Theologie,"* in *Exegetische Versuche und Besinnungen,* Vol. 2, Göttingen 1964, p. 104.

[73] Thus with G. Bornkamm in his *Die Binde- und Lösegewalt,* cited above in note 65, and W. Trilling, same place. See also the commentaries on the Gospel of Matthew, of W. Grundmann, Berlin 1958, pp. 419f., and E. Schweizer, *Das Evangelium nach Matthäus,* Göttingen 1973, p. 242 (pp. 371f. in the English edition noted above in 71).

[74] J. Ludwig, *Die Primatsworte in der altkirchlichen Exegese,* Münster 1952, pp. 31–34, 63f.

[75] A. Debrunner, H. Kleinknecht, O. Procksch, and G. Kittel, Art. λέγω, in *Theol. Dict. N. T.,* Vol. 4, 1967, pp. 69–143. Hans Urs von Balthasar, *Verbum Caro,* Einsiedeln 1960 [trans. A. V. Littledale, *Word and Redemption,* New York 1965]. Đ. Barsotti, *Christliches Mysterium und Wort Gottes* (translation from Italian), Einsiedeln 1957. A. Card. Bea, *The Word of God and Mankind,* trans.

D. White from Italian, Chicago 1967. G. Ebeling, *Wort und Glaube*, 2nd ed., Tübingen 1962 [*Word and Faith*, trans. J. W. Leitch, Philadelphia 1963]. H. Fries (ed.), *Wort und Sakrament*, Munich 1966. P. Grelot, *La Bible, Parole de Dieu*, Paris 1965. W. Heinen, *Bild, Wort, Symbol in der Theologie*, Würzburg 1969. E. Lohse, "*Deus dixit: Wort Gottes im Zeugnis des Alten und Neuen Testamentes*," in *Die Einheit des Neuen Testaments*, Göttingen 1973, pp. 9–28. E. Repo, *Der Begriff* ῥῆμα *im Biblisch-Griechischen*, 2 vols., Helsinki 1951 and 1954. L. Scheffczyk, *Von der Heilsmacht des Wortes*, Munich 1966. K. H. Schelkle, "*Wort Gottes*," in *Wort und Schrift*, Düsseldorf 1966, pp. 11–56. H. Schlier, *Wort Gottes*, 2nd ed., Würzburg 1962. Also of Schlier, *Das Ende der Zeit*, Freiburg 1971, pp. 16–36: "*Grundzüge einer neutestamentlichen Theologie des Wortes Gottes*,"; and pp. 151–168: "*Die Stiftung des Wortes Gottes nach dem Apostel Paulus.*" O. Semmelroth, *Wirkendes Wort*, Frankfurt 1961.

[76] A memorable example of a lesser esteem for the word is the speech of Faust in Goethe's tragedy:

> In the beginning was the word!
> At this I balk! Who will assist my need?
> No, I could never treasure speech so much.
>
> . . .
>
> The spirit helps me! Now the truth I see
> And write: In the beginning was the deed.

[77] L. Dürr, *Die Wertung des göttlichen Wortes im Alten Testament und im antiken Orient*, Leipzig 1938. O. Grether, *Name und Wort Gottes im Alten Testament*, Giessen 1934. K. Koch, "*Wort und Einheit des Schöpfergottes in Memphis und in Jerusalem*," in *Zeitschrift für Theologie und Kirche*, Vol. 62 (1965), pp. 251–293.

[78] F. Buri, in his "*Entmythologisierung oder Entkerygmatisierung der Theologie*," in H. W. Bartsch (ed.), *Kerygma und Mythos*, Vol. 2 Hamburg-Volksdorf, 1952, pp. 85–101, asks also for a demythologizing of the term "word of God." "We cannot and must not, however, allow ourselves to be so dedicated to a word that we can no longer inquire about its legitimacy" (p. 98).

[79] A. Hufnagel discusses the question of the analogy of the word of God in his article "*Wort Gottes. Sinn und Bedeutung nach Thomas von Aquin*," in H. Feld and J. Nolte (eds.), *Wort Gottes in der Zeit*, Düsseldorf 1973, pp. 236–256. Thomas Aquinas emphasizes in significant and critical reflection that the word handed down in Scripture cannot be understood simply as the word of God. In the biblical word the human constituent must be distinguished from the divine word. Jesus Christ alone is the Word of God in the perfect sense.

[80] F. Bormann, *Die Heilswirksamkeit der Verkündigung nach dem Apostel Paulus*, Paderborn 1965.

[81] O. Michel, *Der Brief an die Hebräer*, 12th ed., Göttingen, 1966, 196–203.

[82] *Das Zweite Vatikanische Konzil, Konstitutionen, Dekrete und Erklärungen*

1: *Konstitution über die heilige, Liturgie*, with introduction and commentary by J. A. Jungmann, Freiburg 1966, pp. 20–23.

[83] On the relationship between word and sacrament: J. Betz, *"Wort und Sakrament,"* in Th. Filthaut and J. A. Jungman (eds.), *Verkündigung und Glaube (Festschrift F. X. Arnold)*, Freiburg 1958, pp. 76–99; W. Kasper, *"Wort und Sakrament,"* in O. Semmelroth (ed.), *Martyria, Leiturgia, Diakonia (Festschrift H. Volk)*, Mainz 1968, pp. 260–285; K. Rahner, *"Wort und Eucharistie,"* in *Schriften zur Theologie*, Vol. 4, Einsiedeln 1960, pp. 313–355 [trans. Kevin Smyth, *"The Word and the Eucharist,"* in *Theological Investigations*, Vol. 4, Baltimore 1966, pp. 253–286.

[84] J. Behm, Art. θύω, in *Theol. Dict. N. T.*, Vol. 3, 1965, pp. 180–190. H. Strathmann and R. Meyer, Art. λειτουργέω, *ibid.*, Vol. 4, 1967, pp. 215–225. G. Bornkamm, Art. μυστήριον, *ibid.*, Vol. 4, 1967, pp. 802–828. E. Jüngel and K. Rahner, *Was ist ein Sakrament?*, Freiburg 1971. M. Köhnlein, *Was bringt das Sakrament? Disputation mit Karl Rahner*, Göttingen 1971. K. Rahner, *Kirche und Sakramente*, 3rd ed., Freiburg 1968. M. Raske, *Sakrament, Glaube, Liebe, Gerhard Ebelings Sakramentsverständnis: eine Herausforderung an die katholische Theologie*, Essen 1973. E. H. Schillebeeckx, *Christ, the Sacrament of the Encounter with God*, trans. Paul Barrett, New York 1963. O. Semmelroth, *Die Kirche als Ursakrament*, Frankfurt 1953; also of Semmelroth, *Vom Sinn der Sakramente*, Frankfurt 1960.

[85] E. Lohse, Art. σάββατον, in *Theol. Dict. N. T.*, Vol. 7, 1971, pp. 1–35; also of Lohse, *"Jesu Wort über den Sabbat,"* in *Die Einheit des Neuen Testaments*, Göttingen 1973, pp. 62–72.

[86] In the pericope of Mark 2:23-28, several themes are joined together: the example from the Scriptures (2:25-26), the rule of love of neighbor (2:27), and the decisive majesty of the Son of Man (2:28). If this piling up of principles were to be explained as a growing of the narrative out of the discussion of the Christian community with Israel, it must be in its entirety a witness to a later problematic and its solution.

[87] Ch. Mohrmann, *"Sacramentum dans les plus anciens textes chrétiens,"* in *Harvard Theological Review*, Vol. 47 (1954), pp. 141–152. A. Kolping, *Sacramentum Tertullianeum*, Regensburg and Münster 1948.

[88] J. Dournes, *"Die Siebenzahl der Sakramente,"* in *Concilium*, Vol. 4, 1968, pp. 32–40. J. Finkenzeller, *"Die Zählung und die Zahl der Sakramente,"* in L. Scheffczyk (*et al.*, eds.), *Wahrheit und Verkündigung (Festschrift M. Schmaus)*, Vol. 2, Munich, 1967, pp. 1005–1033.

[89] A. Oepke, Art. βάπτω, in *Theol. Dict N. T.*, Vol. 1, 1964, pp. 529–546; also of Oepke, Art. λούω, *ibid.*, Vol. 4, 1967, pp. 245–307. E. Schweizer, Art. πνεῦμα, *ibid.*, Vol. 6, 1968, pp. 332–455. L. Goppelt, ὕδωρ, *ibid.*, Vol. 8, 1972, pp. 314–33. K. Aland, *"Zur Vorgeschichte der christlichen Taufe,"* in H. Baltensweiler and B. Reicke, *Neues Testament und Geschichte (Festschrift O. Cullman)*, Zürich and Tübingen 1972, pp. 1–14. H. J. Auf der Maur and B. Kleinheyer (eds.),

Zeichen des Glaubens (Festschrift B. Fischer), Zürich and Freiburg 1972. K. Barth, *Die Taufe als Begründung des christlichen Lebens (Die kirchliche Dogmatik, Vol. 4/4)*, Zürich 1967. W. Bieder, *Die Verheissung der Taufe im Neuen Testament*, Zürich 1966. G. Delling, *Die Taufe im Neuen Testament*, Berlin 1963. N. Gäumann, *Taufe und Ethik: Studien zu Röm 6*, Munich 1967. H. Schlier, *"Die kirchliche Lehre von der Taufe,"* in *Die Zeit der Kirche*, 3rd ed., Freiburg 1962, pp. 107–129. E. Schlink, *Die Lehre von der Taufe*, Kassel 1969.

[90] L. Goppelt, article ὕδωρ, in *Theol. Dict. N. T.*, Vol. 8, 1972, pp. 314–333. R. Wolf, *Aqua religiosa. Die religiöse Verwendung von Wasser im frühen Christentum und seiner Umwelt*, typed dissertation, Leipzig 1956.

[91] H. Braun, *Qumran und das Neue Testament*, Vol. 2, Tübingen 1966, pp. 1–29. O. Betz, *"Die Proselytentaufe der Qumransekte und die Taufe im Neuen Testament,"* in *Revue de Qumran*, Vol. 1 (1958/59), pp. 216–220. J. Gnilka, *"Die essenischen Tauchbäder und die Johannestaufe,"* in *Revue de Qumran*, Vol. 3 (1961/62), pp. 185–207.

[92] J. Daniélou, *Sacramentum futuri*, Paris 1950, pp. 69–94. P. Lundberg, *La typologie baptismale dans l'ancienne église*, Uppsala 1942. O. Michel, *"Zum Thema Paulus und seine Bibel,"* in H. Feld and J. Nolte (eds.), *Wort Gottes in der Zeit*, Düsseldorf 1973, pp. 114–126.

[93] On the theology of the sacraments in John's Gospel, see especially the commentaries of R. Bultmann, 19th ed., Göttingen 1968; R. Schnackenburg, 2 vols., Freiburg 1965 and 1971; S. Schulz, Göttingen 1972. See also H. Klos, *Die Sakramente im Johannesevangelium*, Stuttgart 1970; E. Lohse, *"Wort und Sakrament im Johannesevangelium,"* in *Die Einheit des Neuen Testaments*, Göttingen 1973, pp. 193–208. R. Bultmann (p. 98) wants (with others) to separate from John 3:5 the words ὕδατος καὶ as a secondary addition. He accepts as fact that John's Gospel was originally a purely oral Gospel. The references to the sacraments (3:5; 6:51b-58; 19:34b, 35) stemmed from a later redaction, which, by these corrections, made possible the acceptance of the Gospel in the Church. Notwithstanding the question of this interpretation in general, it must be maintained in regard to John 3:5 that the nearly unanimous text tradition provides hardly any basis for the exclusion of the words ὕδατος καὶ. To be sure, the words ὕδατος καὶ are lacking in John 3:6 and 8. But in any case, John 3:3-8 does presuppose in the Church a long-practiced baptism by water and Spirit. For the authenticity of the words ὕδατος καὶ, there is H. Klos (pp. 69–74); R. Schnackenburg (Vol. 1, p. 383), S. Schulz (p. 56); likewise, H. Leroy, *Rätsel und Missverständnis*, Bonn 1968, pp. 124–136. E. Lohse agrees with R. Bultmann, likewise J. Becker, *"Jo 3,1-21 als Reflex johanneischer Schulddiskussion,"* in H. Balz and S. Schulz (eds.), *Das Wort und die Wörter (Festschrift G. Friedrich)*, Stuttgart 1973, pp. 85–95. F. Porsch, *Pneuma und Wort*, Frankfort 1974, pp. 91f., thinks the words ὕδατος καὶ may be an elucidation attached in a later redaction.

[94] H. Frankemölle, *Jahwebund und Kirche Christi*, Münster 1973, pp. 42–72. K. Kertelge, *"Der sogenannte Taufbefehl Jesu (Mt 28,19),"* in H. J. Auf der

Maur and B. Kleinheyer, *Zeichen des Glaubens (Festschrift B. Fischer)*, Zürich and Freiburg 1972, pp. 29–40. J. Lange, *Das Erscheinen des Auferstandenen im Evangelium nach Matthäus, Eine traditions- und redaktionsgeschichtliche Untersuchung zu Mt 28,16-20*, Würzburg 1973. A Vögtle, *"Ekklesiologische Auftragsworte des Auferstandenen: Das christologische und ekklesiologische Anliegen von Mt 28, 18-20,"* in *Das Evangelium und die Evangelien*, Düsseldorf 1971, pp. 243–272.

[95] See R. Schnackenburg, *Schriften zum Neuen Testament*, Munich 1971, p. 461. A. Vögtle, *Das Evangelium und die Evangelien*, Düsseldorf 1971, p. 226; also of Vögtle, *"Wie kam es zur Artikulierung des Osterglaubens?"* in *Bibel und Leben*, Vol. 15 (1974), pp. 174–193.

[96] E. Helzle, *Der Schluss des Markusevangeliums (Mk 16,9-20) und das Freer-Logion (Mk 16,14 W)*, typed dissertation, Tübingen 1959.

[97] J. J. von Allmen, *"Notizen zu den Taufberichten in der Apostelgeschichte,"* in H. J. Auf der Maur and B. Kleinheyer, *Zeichen des Glaubens (Festschrift B. Fischer)*, Zürich and Freiburg 1972, pp. 41–60.

[98] H. Bietenhard, Art. ὄναμα, in *Theol. Dict. N. T.*, Vol. 5, 1967, pp. 242–283. G. Delling, *Die Zueignung des Heils in der Taufe*, Berlin 1961.

[99] A. Oepke, Art. λουτρόν, in *Theol. Dict. N. T.*, Vol. 4, 1967, pp. 295–307. See also the usual commentaries.

[100] The laying on of hands for the imparting of the Spirit was made independent in the later sacrament of confirmation. It is accorded New Testament foundation through Acts 8:14-17 and 19:1-7. The form and import of both accounts are the same. Communities initially independent taking shape in Samaria in the one instance, in Ephesus in the other, had to be incorporated in order to prevent any division within the collective body of the Church. This took place in a natural way through the apostles. As a rite, the imposition of hands for the conferring of the Spirit is pregnant with meaning. This, at any rate, is the interpretation of E. Käsemann, *"Die Johannesjünger in Ephesus,"* in *Exegetische Versuche und Besinnungen*, Vol. 1, 3rd ed., Göttingen 1964, pp. 158–168 [translation by W. J. Montague, selections, under title *Essays on New Testament Themes*; "The Disciples of John the Baptist in Ephesus," pp. 136–148]. See also J. Amougou-Atangana, *Ein Sakrament des Geistempfangs?*, Freiburg 1974.

[101] G. Fitzer, Art. σφραγίς, in *Theol. Dict. N. T.*, Vol. 7, 1971, pp. 939–953. He contests, however, that Eph. 1:13 and 4:30 are to be referred directly to baptism.

[102] A. Oepke, Art. δύω, in *Theol. Dict. N. T.*, Vol. 2, 1964, pp. 318–321.

[103] F. Büchsel and K. H. Rengstorff, Art. γεννάω, in *Theol. Dict. N. T.*, Vol. 1, 1964, pp. 665–675. J. Dey, Παλιγγενεσία, Münster 1937.

[104] M. Rissi, *Die Taufe für die Toten*, Zürich 1962. About two hundred different explanations of the passage have been tallied by K. C. Thompson, "1 Corinthians, 15,29 and Baptism for the Dead," in F. L. Cross (ed.), *Studia evangelica*, Vol. 2 (*Texte und Untersuchungen*, Vol. 87), Berlin 1964, pp. 647–659.

[105] As literary parallels, dictionaries cite Ps. 41:8 in the Septuagint version: "Your waves went over me"; Libanius, *Discourse* 64, 115 (4th century A.D.): "the soul is strengthened, which is immersed (baptized) in sorrow (ψυχὴν λύπῃ βεβαπτισμένην)."

[106] The supposition that Paul starts from the execution of baptism as an immersion in water and a reappearance therefrom must be regarded as questionable. It would seem to presuppose later liturgical usage. E. Stommel, " '*Begraben mit Christus*' (*Röm 6,4*) *und der Taufritus*," in *Römische Quartalschrift*, Vol 49 (1954), pp. 1–20; also of Stommel, "*Das 'Abbild seines Todes' (Röm 6,5) und der Taufritus, ibid.*, Vol. 50 (1955), pp. 1–21.

[107] Deserving of special mention among the commentaries are: E. Käsemann, *An die Römer*, 3rd ed., Tübingen 1974, pp. 150–161; O. Kuss, *Der Römerbrief*, Regensburg 1957/59, pp. 292–381; O. Michel, *Der Brief an die Römer*, 12th ed., Göttingen 1966, pp. 148–165. H. Frankemölle, *Das Taufverständnis des Paulus*, Stuttgart 1970. E. Lohse, "*Taufe und Rechtfertigung bei Paulus*," in *Die Einheit des Neuen Testaments*, Göttingen 1973, pp. 228–244. R. Schnackenburg, *Baptism in the Thought of St. Paul*, Oxford 1964.

[108] H. Braun, "*Das 'Stirb und Werde' in der Antike und im Neuen Testament*," in *Gesammelte Studien zum Neuen Testament und seiner Umwelt*, 3rd ed., Tübingen 1971, pp. 136–158. K. Prümm, *Religionsgeschichtliches Handbuch für den Raum der altchristlichen Umwelt*, Rome 1954, pp. 268–294. B. Neunheuser, Art. *Taufe*, in *Sacramentum Mundi* (theological lexicon), Vol. 4, 1969, pp. 815–833. V. Warnach, "*Die Tauflehre des Römerbriefes in der neueren theologischen Diskussion*," in *Archiv für Liturgiewissenschaft*, Vol. 5 (1958), pp. 274–332; also of Warnach, "*Taufe und Christusgeschehen nach Röm 6*," in *Archiv für Liturgiewissenschaft*, Vol. 3 (1954), pp. 284–366. E. Käsemann says in his *An die Römer* (see note immediately above) on p. 150: "The question of the influence of the Hellenistic mystery religions on the baptismal teaching of the Apostle is disputed to this very day." O. Kuss, in his *Der Römerbrief*, pp. 319–381, reckons with a dependency at least as to terminology. G. Wagner, in *Das religionsgeschichtliche Problem von Röm 6,1-11*, Zürich 1962, disputes any influence of the mystery religions on Paul. [Wagner's work has been translated by J. P. Smith, under the title *Pauline Baptism and the Pagan Mysteries*, Edinburgh and London 1967.]

[109] O. Casel, "*Mysteriengegenwart*," in *Jahrbuch für Liturgiewissenschaft*, Vol. 8 (1928), pp. 145–224. Also of Casel, *Das christliche Kultmysterium*, 3rd ed., Regensburg 1948.

[110] Of the commentaries, see especially H. Schlier, *Der Brief an die Epheser*, Düsseldorf, 6th ed., 1968, pp. 240–242; and J. Gnilka, *Der Epheserbrief*, Freiburg 1971, pp. 257–263.

[111] Of the commentaries, see especially J. Lähnemann, *Der Kolosserbrief*, Gütersloh 1971, pp. 120–122; E. Lohse, *Die Briefe an die Kolosser und an Philemon*, 14th ed., Göttingen 1968, pp. 153–159.

[112] Of the commentaries, see especially R. Bultmann, *Das Evangelium nach Johannes*, 19th ed., Göttingen 1968, pp. 524–526; S. Schulz, *Das Evangelium nach Johannes*, Göttingen 1972, pp. 239f. J. Herr, *Der Durchbohrte*, dissertation, Rome 1969, pp. 99–122; F. Porsch, *Pneuma und Wort*, Frankfurt 1974, pp. 332–337. H. Klos, in his *Die Sakramente im Johannesevangelium*, Stuttgart 1970, pp. 74–81, explains that in John 19:34 only "the salvational significance of the death of Jesus is broadly represented"; G. Richter, *"Blut und Wasser aus der durchbohrten Seite Jesu,"* in *Münchener theologische Zeitschrift*, Vol. 21 (1970), pp. 1–21, finds in John 19:34 "nothing else but an (antidocetist) testimony to the true humanity and the real corporeality of Jesus."

[113] R. Schnackenburg, *Die Johannesbriefe*, 2nd ed., Freiburg 1963, pp. 260–263.

[114] H. Leroy, *Vergebung und Gemeinde nach dem Zeugnis der Evangelien*, typed habilitation paper, Tübingen 1971; also of Leroy, *Zur Vergebung der Sünden: Die Botschaft der Evangelien*, Stuttgart 1974. H. Thyen, *Studien zur Sündenvergebung im Neuen Testament und seinen alttestamentlichen und jüdischen Voraussetzungen*, Göttingen 1970 (p. 50: "We have found no proof for the endtime forgiveness of sin by the Messiah, of which there is so often discussion in the literature.").

[115] K. Kertelge, *"Die Vollmacht des Markus zur Sündenvergebung (Mk 2-10),"* in P. Hoffman (*et al.*, eds.), *Orientierung an Jesus (Festschrift J. Schmid)*, Freiburg 1973, pp. 205–213. J. Maisch, *Die Heilung des Gelähmten (Mk 2,1-12)*, Stuttgart 1971.

[116] The words of the resurrected Christ are probably to be understood as a formulation by prophets from the Spirit of the Church (see note 95 above).

[117] Examples in H. Schlier, Art. ἀλείφω, in *Theol. Dict. N. T.*, Vol. 1, 1964, pp. 229–232; also of Schlier, Art. ἔλαιον, *ibid.*, Vol. 2, 1964, pp. 470–473; and the usual commentaries.

[118] J. Behm, Art. αἷμα, in *Theol. Dict. N. T.*, Vol. 1, 1964, pp. 172–177; Art. ἄρτος, *ibid.*, pp. 477–478; Art. δεῖπνον, *ibid.*, Vol. 2, 1964, pp. 34–35; Art. ἐσθίω, *ibid.*, pp. 689–695; and still of Behm, Art. κλάω, *ibid.*, Vol. 3, 1965, pp. 726–743. E. Schweizer and F. Baumgärtel, Art. σῶμα, *ibid.*, Vol. 7, 1971, pp. 1024–1094. L. Goppelt, Art. τράπεζα, *ibid.*, Vol. 8, 1972, pp. 209–215. H. Conzelmann, Art. εὐχαριστέω, *ibid.*, Vol. 9, 1974, pp. 407–415. P. Benoit, *"La Dernière Cène,"* in *Exégèse et Théologie*, Vol. 1, Paris 1961, pp. 163–261. J. Betz, *Die Eucharistie in der Zeit der griechischen Väter*, 2 vols., 2nd ed., Freiburg 1964, and 1st ed., 1955; also of Betz, *"Eucharistie als zentrales Mysterium,"* in J. Feiner and M. Löhrer (eds.), *Mysterium salutis*, Vol. 4/2, Einsiedeln 1973, pp. 185–313. A. Bittlinger, *Das Abendmahl im Neuen Testament und in der frühen Kirche*, Wetzhausen 1969. A. C. Cochrane, *Eating and Drinking with Jesus: An Ethical and Biblical Inquiry*, Philadelphia 1974. H. Feld, *Das Verständnis des Abendmahles*, Darmstadt 1976. R. Feneberg, *Christliche Passafeier und Abendmahl*, Munich 1971. A. Gerken, *Theologie der Eucharistie*, Munich 1973. F. Hahn, *"Die alttestamentlichen Motive in der urchristlichen Abendmahlsüberlieferung,"* in *Evan-*

gelische Theologie, Vol. 27 (1967), pp. 337–374. J. Jeremias, *Die Abendmahls-worte Jesu,* 4th ed., Göttingen 1967 [earlier edition translated by N. Perrin, *The Eucharistic Words of Jesus,* New York 1966]. W. Marxsen, *Das Abendmahl als christologisches Problem,* Gütersloh 1963 [trans. L. Nieting, *The Lord's Supper as a Christological Problem,* Philadelphia 1970]. H. Patsch, *Abendmahl und historischer Jesus,* Stuttgart 1972; also of Patsch, *"Abendmahlsterminologie aus-serhalb der Einsetzungsberichte,"* in *Zeitschrift für die neutestamentliche Wissen-schaft,* Vol. 62 (1971), pp. 210–231. B. Sandvik, *Das Kommen des Herrn beim Abendmahl im Neuen Testament,* Zürich 1970. H. Schürmann, *Der Paschamahl-bericht Lk (7-14) 15-18,* 2nd ed., Münster 1970; *Der Einsetzungsbericht Lk 22,19-20,* Münster 1955; *Jesu Abschiedsrede Lk 22,21-38,* Münster 1957: "Das Mahl des Herrn," in *Ursprung und Gestalt,* Düsseldorf 1970, pp. 77–196; and still of Schürmann, *Jesu Abendmahlshandlung als Zeichen für die Welt,* Leip-zig 1970. E. Schweizer, *"Das Herrenmahl im Neuen Testament,"* in *Neotesta-mentica,* Zürich 1963, pp. 344–370.

[119] F. Bammel, *Das heilige Mahl im Glauben der Völker,* Gütersloh 1950. Franz Cumont, *The Mysteries of Mithra,* trans. T. J. McCormack from 2nd revised French edition, 2nd ed. reprint, Dover, New York 1956.

[120] H. Braun, *Qumran und das Neue Testament,* Vol. 2, Tübingen 1966, pp. 29–54. J. Gnilka, *"Das Gemeinschafsmahl der Essener,"* in *Biblische Zeitschrift,* new series, Vol. 5 (1961), pp. 39–55. K. G. Kuhn, *"Über den ursprünglichen Sinn des Abendmahls und sein Verhältnis zu den Gemeinschaftsmahlen der Sektenschrift,"* in *Evangelische Theologie,* Vol. 10 (1950), pp. 508–527.

[121] The texts have preserved Semitisms, which permit the conjecture of their great age and origin in the Jewish-Christian community. See J. Jeremias, *Die Abendmahlsworte Jesu,* 4th ed., Göttingen 1967, pp. 165–179; H. Schürmann, *"Die Semitismen im Einsetzungsbericht bei Markus und Lukas (Mk 14,22-24 / Lk 22,19-20),"* in *Zeitschrift für katholische Theologie,* Vol. 73 (1951), pp. 72-77.

[122] M. Rese, in his *"Zur Problematik von Kurz- und Langtext in Luk XXII. 17ff.,"* in *New Testament Studies,* Vol. 22 (1975/76), pp. 15–31, recently reminds us that the questions about the short or long text are not easy to decide. If one accepts that the long text is original, it remains to explain the almost verbal agree-ment of Luke 22:19(b)-20 and 1 Cor. 11:24f., since Luke did not know the Epistles of Paul.

[123] That the Last Supper of Jesus was a Passover meal is expressly defended by J. Jeremias, Art. πάσχα, in *Theol. Dict. N. T.,* Vol. 5, 1967, pp. 896-904. See also his *Die Abendmahlsworte Jesu,* pp. 35-82 [pp. 41–62 in Perrin's translation, *The Eucharistic Words of Jesus*]. For others, this is questionable: R. Feneberg, *Christ-liche Passafeier und Abendmahl,* Munich 1971, pp. 15–41, and H. Patsch, *Abend-mahl und historischer Jesus,* Stuttgart 1972, pp. 33–36, think that Jesus' Last Supper took place "in the atmosphere of a Passover meal," the conditioning fac-tors of which Jesus made use.

[124] Thus A. Jaubert, *La date de la Cène: Calendrier biblique et liturgie chré-*

tienne, Paris 1957; and also of Jaubert, *"Jésus et la calendrier de Qumrân,"* in *New Testament Studies*, Vol. 7 (1960/1961), pp. 1–30. The hypothesis quickly gained much support, but is more recently regarded as questionable; see H. Braun, *Qumran und das Neue Testament*, Vol. 2, Tübingen 1966, pp. 43–54.

[125] The symbolic nature of the offering of bread and wine is admitted again and again. See the account of H. Lessig, *Die Abendmahlsprobleme im Lichte der neutestamentlichen Forschung seit 1900*, typed dissertation, Bonn 1953. The symbolic sense is acknowledged for example by H. Schürmann, *"Das Mahl des Herrn,"* in *Ursprung und Gestalt*, Düsseldorf 1970, pp. 93–99. H. Patsch, however, in his *Abendmahl und historischer Jesus*, Stuttgart 1972, pp. 40–50, is more inclined to reject it.

[126] H. Lietzmann, *Messe und Herrenmahl*, Bonn 1926 (3rd ed., 1955). E. Lohmeyer, *"Vom urchristlichen Abendmahl,"* in *Theologische Rundschau*, new series, Vol. 9, (1937), pp. 168–227, 273–312; Vol. 10 (1938), pp. 81–99. R. Bultmann, *Theologie des Neuen Testaments*, 6th ed., Tübingen 1968, pp. 61f., 146–153. F. Hahn, *"Die alttestamentlichen Motive in der urchristlichen Abendmahlsüberlieferung,"* in *Evangelische Theologie*, Vol. 27 (1967), pp. 337–374.

[127] J. Schniewind, Art. καταγγέλλω, in *Theol. Dict. N. T.*, Vol. 1, 1964, pp. 68–71.

[128] H. Bornkamm, *"Herrenmahl und Kirche bei Paulus,"* in *Studien zu Antike und Christentum*, 2nd ed., Munich 1963, pp. 138–176. H. Conzelmann, *Der erste Brief an die Korinthier*, Göttingen 1969, pp. 200–206, 226–240. E. Käsemann, *"Anliegen und Eigenart der paulinischen Abendmahlslehre,"* in *Exegetische Versuche und Besinnungen*, Vol. 1, 3rd ed., Göttingen 1964, pp. 11–34. P. Neuenzeit, *Das Herrenmahl. Studien zur paulinischen Eucharistieauffassung*, Munich 1960.

[129] J. Betz, *Die Eucharistie in der Zeit der griechischen Väter*, Vol. 1/1, pp. 86–139. M. Schmaus, *Katholische Dogmatik*, Vol. 4/1, 6th ed., Munich 1964, pp. 331–342.

[130] M. Schmaus, as in note 129, pp. 501–507.

[131] L. Goppelt, Art. πίνω, in *Theol. Dict. N. T.*, Vol. 6, 1968, pp. 135–160; also of Goppelt, Art. τρώγω, *ibid.*, Vol. 8, 1972, pp. 236–237. P. Borgen, *Bread from Heaven*, Leiden 1965. H. Klos, *Die Sakramente im Johannesevangelium*, Stuttgart 1970. J. R. Nearon, *My Flesh for the Life of the World*, dissertation, Rome 1973. R. Schnackenburg, *Das Johannesevangelium*, Vol. 2, Freiburg 1971, pp. 41–102. I regard the discourse of John 6:28-59 as a cohesive unit; but R. Bultmann, in his *Das Evangelium des Johannes*, 19th ed., Göttingen 1968, pp. 174–177, judges that John 6:51b-58 is a later interpolation in accord with the sacramental theology of the Church; and E. Lohse, *"Wort und Sakrament im Johannesevangelium,"* in *Die Einheit des Neuen Testaments*, Göttingen 1973, pp. 193–208, agrees with Bultmann.

[132] H. Leroy, *Rätsel und Missverständis*, Bonn 1969, pp. 100–124, 191f.

[133] H. Denzinger and A. Schönmetzer, *Enchiridion Symbolorum, Definitionum*

et Declarationum de rebus fidei et morum, 35th ed., Freiburg 1974, No. 802 (p. 206) and No. 1642 (p. 387).

[134] K. Rahner, *"Die Gegenwart Christi im Sakrament des Herrenmahles,"* in *Schriften zur Theologie*, Vol. 4, Einsiedeln 1960, pp. 357–385. E. Schillebeeckx, *Die eucharistische Gegenwart*, translation, 2nd ed., Düsseldorf 1968. T. Schneider, *Gewandeltes Eucharistieverständnis?*, 2nd ed., Einsiedeln 1969. Pope Paul VI, in the encyclical *Mysterium fidei*, insists upon both the concept and the very term "transubstantiation," in connection with which, however, the terms *"nova significatio"* and *"novus finis"* may also be used. *Transelementatio* is appearing as a substitute term for *transsubstantiatio*; W. Beinert, *"Die Enzyklika 'Mysterium Fidei' und neuere Auffassungen über die Eucharistie,"* in *Theologische Quartalschrift*, Vol. 147 (1967), pp. 159–176.

[135] This explanation could, no doubt, make appeal to the theology of the Fathers. Again and again the Greek Fathers designate the elements of the Eucharist as symbol or as type of the Body and Blood of Christ. [*Translator's note*: But St. Cyril of Jerusalem, in the *Catechetical Lectures* 23, 20, says plainly that we do not eat of the bread and wine, the type, "but of the antitype, of the Body and Blood of Christ." (See Jurgens, no. 853j, with its footnote no. 142)]. In the West, Augustine describes the symbolism of the Eucharist. He calls it *signum, figura, similitudo* of the Body and Blood of Christ. The sacrament is a sign in the Platonic sense. Just as the individual things delineate the idea without comprising it, so too the Sacrament of the Meal refers back to the proper reality: the Body and Blood of Christ and spiritual union with Christ. J. Betz, *Die Eucharistie in der Zeit der griechischen Väter*, Vol. 1/1, pp. 217–242; also of Betz, *"Eucharistie als zentrales Mysterium,"* in J. Feiner and M. Löhrer (eds.), *Mysterium salutis*, Vol. 4/2, Einsiedeln 1973, pp. 226–229. J. Lemmens, *"De Sakramenten en het Vleesgewoordenen Woord volgens Augustinus,"* in *Augustinianum*, Vol. 14 (1964), pp. 5–71. L. J. van der Lof, *"Eucharistie et présence réelle selon S. Augustin,"* in *Revue des Études Augustiniennes*, Vol. 10 (1964), pp. 295–304.

[136] G. von Rad, K. G. Kuhn, W. Gutbrod, Art. Ἰσραήλ, in *Theol. Dict. N. T.*, Vol. 3, 1965, pp. 356–391. G. Fohrer and F. Lohse, Art. Σιών, *ibid.*, Vol. 7, 1971, pp. 292–338. W. Schrage, Art. συναγωγή, *ibid.*, pp. 798–852. G. Baum, *Is the New Testament Anti-Semitic?*, Glen Rock, N.J., 1965 (originally published under the title *The Jews and the Gospel*). W. P. Eckert, N. P. Levinson, and M. Stöhr (eds.), *Antijudaismus im Neuen Testament?*, Munich 1967. L. Goppelt, *Christentum und Judentum im ersten und zweiten Jahrhundert*, Gütersloh 1954; also of Goppelt, *Die apostolische und nachapostolische Zeit*, 2nd ed., Göttingen 1966. D. R. A. Hare, *The Theme of Jewish Persecution of Christians in the Gospel according to St. Matthew*, Cambridge 1967. R. Hummel, *Die Auseinandersetzung zwischen Kirche und Judentum im Matthäusevangelium*, Munich 1963. D. Judant, *Judaisme et Christianisme*, Paris 1969. Ch. Klein, *Theologie und Anti-Judaismus*, Munich 1975. J. Maier and J. Schreiner (eds.), *Literatur und Religion des Judenchristentums*, Würzburg and Gütersloh 1973. M. Limbeck, *Von*

der Ohnmacht des Rechts, Düsseldorf 1972. Ch. Plag, *Israels Weg zum Heil,* Stuttgart 1969. H. J. Schoeps, *Theologie und Geschichte des Judenchristentums,* Tübingen 1949; also of Schoeps, *Urgemeinde, Judentum, Gnosis,* Tübingen 1956. G. Strecker, *"Christentum und Judentum in den ersten beiden Jahrhunderten,"* in *Evangelische Theologie,* Vol. 16 (1956), pp. 458–477. K. Thoma, *Kirche aus Juden und Heiden,* Vienna 1970.

[137] G. Bornkamm, G. Barth, and H. J. Held, *Überlieferung und Auslegung im Matthäusevangelium,* 2nd ed., Neukirchen-Vluyn 1961. H. Frankemölle, *Jawebund und Kirche Christi: Studien zur Form- und Traditionsgeschichte des 'Evangeliums' nach Matthäus,* Münster 1974. Jules Isaac, *Jésus et Israël,* Paris 1948. A. Sand, *Das Gesetz und die Propheten: Untersuchungen zur Theologie des Evangeliums nach Matthäus,* Regensburg 1974. G. Strecker, *Der Weg der Gerechtigkeit: Untersuchungen zur Theologie des Matthäus,* 2nd ed., Göttingen 1966. W. Trilling, *Das wahre Israel: Studien zur Theologie des Matthäusevangeliums,* 3rd ed., Munich 1964. R. Walker, *Die Heilsgeschichte im ersten Evangelium,* Göttingen 1967.

[138] A. Sand, *"Wie geschrieben steht . . .', Zur Auslegung der jüdischen Schriften in der urchristlichen Gemeinde,"* in J. Ernst, *Schriftauslegung,* Paderborn 1972, pp. 331–357.

[139] The *Gospel of Thomas* (65 and 66) provides a form of the parable or similitude in which allegorical elements are almost lacking. Nevertheless, it is hardly an earlier form of the parable (thus, W. Grundmann, *Das Evangelium nach Matthäus,* Berlin 1968, p. 461; and J. Jeremias, *Die Gleichnisse Jesu,* 7th ed., Göttingen 1965, pp. 67–75 [6th ed. translated by S. H. Hooke, *The Parables of Jesus,* 1963, pp. 66–89]). More probably it is a carefully considered Gnostic recasting: W. Schrage, *Das Verhältnis des Thomas-Evangeliums zur synoptischen Tradition und zu den koptischen Evangelienübersetzungen,* Berlin 1964, pp. 137–146. See also R. A. T. Robinson, "The Parable of the Wicked Husbandmen," in *New Testament Studies,* Vol. 21 (1974/75), pp. 443–461.

[140] Κεφαλὴ γωντίας in Mark 12:10 can just as easily designate the foundation stone bearing the weight of the building, the cornerstone, as the keystone holding together the arches of the building (K. H. Schelkle, Art. *Akrogoniaios,* in *Reallexikon für Antike und Christentum,* Vol. 1, 1950, pp. 233f.).

[141] H. L. Strack and P. Billerbeck, *Kommentar zum Neuen Testament aus Talmud und Midrasch,* Vol. 1, 1922, pp. 875f.

[142] U. Wilckens, article ὑποκρίνομαι, in *Theol. Dict. N. T.,* Vol. 8, 1972, pp. 559–571.

[143] H. L. Strack and P. Billerbeck, *op. cit.,* Vol. 1, 1922, pp. 931f. H. Braun, *Spätjüdisch-häretischer und frühchristlicher Radikalismus,* Vol. 2, Tübingen 1957, pp. 80–83.

[144] J. Jeremias, *Heilengräber in Jesu Umwelt,* Göttingen 1958.

[145] Today I would no longer say, as I did in Vol. 2, p. 32 of the present work, that in Matthew 23 "the opposition between the old and the new righteousness

is exposed . . . entirely in the spirit of Jesus." A very critical judgment of Matthew 23 is given by W. G. Kümmel, in his *"Die Weherufe über die Schriftgelehrten und Pharisäer,"* in W. P. Echert (*et al.*), *Antijudaismus im Neuen Testament?*, Munich 1967, pp. 135–147.

[146] O. Betz *Offenbarung und Schriftforschung in der Qumransekte*, Tübingen 1960, 92 to 99. K. Schubert, *Die Gemeinde vom Toten Meere*, Munich 1958, pp. 36–41.

[147] F. Christ, *Jesus Sophia: Die Sophia-Christologie bei den Synoptikern*, Zürich 1970.

[148] In Matthew 23:35, Zechariah is erroneously designated, in view of Zech. 1:1, as son of Barachiah, whereas the murdered Zechariah, of 2 Chron. 24:20-22, was a son of Yehoiada. The confusion is found elsewhere also; see H. L. Strack and P. Billerbeck, *Kommentar zum Neuen Testament*, Vol. 1, 1922, pp. 940f.

[149] O. Michel, Art. οἶκος, in *Theol. Dict N. T.*, Vol. 5, 1967, pp. 119–131.

[150] A considerable body of commentary, nevertheless, regards Matthew 23:39 as referring to the judgment. Thus, with W. G. Kümmel, *"Die Weherufe über die Schriftgelehrten und Pharisäer,"* in W. P. Eckert (*et al.*), *Antijudaismus im Neuen Testament?*, pp. 135–147; H. van der Kwaak, *"Die Klage über Jerusalem (Mt 23,37-39),"* in *Novum Testamentum*, Vol. 8 (1966), pp. 156–170; S. Schulz, *Q, die Spruchquelle der Evangelisten*, Zürich 1972, pp. 346–360; O. H. Steck, *Israel und das gewaltsame Geschick der Propheten*, Neukirchen-Vluyn 1967, pp. 297f.; G. Strecker, *Der Weg der Gerechtigkeit*, 2nd ed., Göttingen 1966, pp. 113f.; W. Trilling, *Das wahre Israel*, 3rd ed., Munich 1964, pp. 87f.

[151] H. J. Schoeps, *"Die jüdischen Prophetenmorde,"* in *Aus frühchristlicher Zeit*, Tübingen 1950, pp. 126–143. O. H. Steck, as in note 150.

[152] Christian tradition, and so too the Fathers, has taken up these charges and increased them. O. Michel, *Der Brief an die Hebräer*, 6th ed., Göttingen 1966, pp. 418f.

[153] According to Luke 23:34, Jesus, on the Cross, prayed for his murderers. That account, though it stands only in a part of the manuscripts, is presupposed by Acts 7:60. Certainly it is not a later addition, but was expunged, or so it would appear, when anti-Semitism could no longer bear it, that Jesus had prayed for the Jews. The anti-Semitic tendency grew stronger in post-canonical tradition. In the apocryphal *Gospel of Peter*, Pilate is entirely innocent, while the Jews are accused so much the more. It is stated therein: "Of the Jews, however, no one washed his hands, neither Herod nor any of his judges" (1:1). King Herod gives the order to take Jesus away for execution (1:2). The Jews "took the Lord and hurried him out and said, 'Let us destroy the Son of God' " (3:6). All that took place in the Passion was carried out by the Jews. Pilate finally says: "I am innocent of the blood of the Son, you have done this" (11:46). (J. Denker, *Die theologiegeschichtliche Stellung des Petrusevangeliums*, Bern and Frankfurt 1975, pp. 58–78). The paschal homily of Melito of Sardes, 72–99, laments over Israel, that she has without reason killed her Messiah. Indeed, "God has been killed"

(96). It is probably here that one encounters for the first time the pernicious charge of deicide against the Jews (B. Blank, *Meliton von Sardes, Vom Passa,* Freiburg 1963).

[154] J. Eckert, *"Paulus und die Jerusalemer Autoritäten nach dem Galaterbrief und der Apostelgeschichte,"* in E. Ernst (ed.), *Schriftauslegung,* Paderborn 1972, pp. 281–311. E. Haenchen, *"Quellenanalyse und Kompositionsanalyse in Act 15,"* in W. Eltester (ed.), *Judentum, Urchristentum, Kirche (Festschrift J. Jeremias),* Berlin 1960, pp. 153–164; also of Haenchen, *"Tradition und Komposition in der Apostelgeschichte,"* in *Gott und Mensch,* Tübingen 1965, pp. 206–226.

[155] D. Georgi, *Die Geschichte der Kollekte des Paulus für Jerusalem,* Hamburg-Bergstedt 1965.

[156] The historicity of the circumcision of Timothy is contested by some on the suspicion that notice of it is a pro-Semitic construction; thus H. Conzelmann, *Die Apostelgeschichte,* Tübingen 1963, pp. 88f.; E. Haenchen, *Die Apostelgeschichte,* 3rd ed., Göttingen 1961, pp. 424–428.

[157] V. Hasler, *"Judenmission und Judenschuld,"* in *Theologische Zeitschrift,* Vol. 24 (1968), pp. 173–190. R. Lichtenhan, *"Paulus als Judenmissionar,"* in *Judaica,* Vol. 2 (1946), pp. 56–70. C. Müller-Duvernoy, *"L'Apôtre Paul et le problème juif,"* in *Judaica,* Vol. 15 (1959), pp. 65–91. See also note 164, below.

[158] On anti-Semitism in antiquity, see I. Heinemann, Art. *Antisemitismus,* in A. Pauly and G. Wissowa, *Real-Enzyklopädie der classischen Altertumswissenschaft,* Supplement 5, 1931, pp. 3–43; J. Leipoldt, Art. *Antisemitismus,* in *Reallexikon für Antike und Christentum,* Vol. 1, 1950, pp. 469–476; J. N. Sevenster, *The Roots of Pagan Anti-Semitism in the Ancient World,* Leiden 1975.

[159] E. Bammel, *"Judenverfolgung und Naherwartung,"* in *Zeitschrift für Theologie und Kirche,* Vol. 56 (1959), pp. 294–315. W. Schmithals, *"Die historische Situation der Thessalonicherbriefe,"* in *Paulus und die Gnostiker,* Hamburg-Bergstedt, 1965, pp. 89–157. Since the time of F. Chr. Baur, *Paulus,* 1845, p. 482, the Paulinian authenticity of 1 Thess. 2:14-16 has been contested again and again; and thus quite recently with Ch. Demke, *"Theologie und Literaturkritik im 1. Thessalonicherbriefe,"* in G. Ebeling (ed.), *Festschrift für E. Fuchs,* Tübingen 1973, pp. 103–124; K. G. Eckert, *"Der zweite echte Brief des Apostels Paulus an die Thessalonicher,"* in *Zeitschrift für Theologie und Kirche,* Vol. 58 (1961), pp. 30–44; and B. A. Pearson, *"1 Thess 2,13-16: A Deuteropauline Interpolation,"* in *Harvard Theological Review,* Vol. 64, (1971), pp. 79–84.

[160] Our interpretation follows for the most part the commentaries of H. Mussner, *Der Galaterbrief,* Freiburg 1974, and of H. Schlier, *Der Brief an die Galater,* Göttingen 1949. See also U. Borse, *Der Standort des Galaterbriefes,* Cologne 1972, pp. 32–41. J. Eckert, *Die urchristliche Verkündigung im Streit zwischen Paulus und seinen Gegnern nach dem Galaterbrief,* Regensburg 1971. H. Feld, *" 'Christus Diener der Sünde', Zum Ausgang des Streites zwischen Petrus und Paulus,"* in *Theologische Quartalschrift,* Vol. 153 (1973), pp. 119–131. W. Schmithals, *"Die Häretiker in Galatien,"* in *Paulus und die Gnostiker,* Ham-

burg-Bergstedt 1965, pp. 9–46. J. B. Tyson, "Paul's Opponents in Galatia," in *Novum Testamentum*, Vol. 10 (1968), pp. 241–254.

[161] H. von Campenhausen, *"Ein Witz des Apostles Paulus und die Anfänge des christlichen Humors,"* in *Aus der Frühzeit des Christentums*, Tübingen 1963, pp. 102–108.

[162] O. Michel, Art. κύων, in *Theol. Dict. N. T.*, Vol. 3, 1965, pp. 1101–1104. R. Meyer, Art. περιτέμνω, *ibid.*, Vol. 6, 1968, pp. 72–84. H. Köster, Art κατατομή, *ibid.*, Vol. 8, 1972, pp. 109–111. J. Gnilka, *Der Philipperbrief*, Freiburg 1968, pp. 184–188.

[163] G. Delling, Art. στοιχεῖον, in *Theol. Dict N. T.*, Vol. 7, 1971, pp. 670–687. J. Lähnemann, *Der Kolosserbrief*, Gütersloh 1971, pp. 63–107. E. Lohse, *Die Briefe an die Kolosser und an Philemon*, Göttingen 1968, pp. 140–191.

[164] R. Bring, *Christus und das Gesetz*, Leiden 1969. H. Luz, *Das Geschichtsverständnis des Paulus*, Munich 1968. F. W. Marquardt, *Die Juden im Römerbrief*, Zürich 1971. Ch. Müller, *Gottes Gerechtigkeit und Gottes Volk, Eine Untersuchung zu Römer 9–11*, Göttingen 1964. J. Munck, *Christus und Israel, Eine Auslegung von Röm 9–11*, Copenhagen 1956; also of Munck, *Paulus und die Heilsgeschichte*, Copenhagen 1954. P. Stuhlmacher, *"Zur Interpretation von Röm 11,25-32,"* in W. Wolf (ed.), *Probleme biblischer Theologie (Festschrift G. von Rad)*, Munich 1971, pp. 555–570. D. Zeller, *Juden und Heiden in der Mission des Paulus, Studien zur Römerbrief*, Stuttgart 1973. M. Zerwick, *"Drama populi Israel secundum Röm 9–11,"* in *Verbum Domini*, Vol. 46 (1968), pp. 321–338.

[165] H. L. Strack and P. Billerbeck, in their *Kommentar zum Neuen Testament aus Talmud und Midrasch*, Vol. 3, 1926, pp. 96–118, like other commentators, point out that Paul shares not only in the prominent phenomenon of Jewish self-confidence, but also in the self-consciousness and self-criticism of rabbinic Judaism. Even Jews bewailed the moral collapse in the revolutionary movements prior to the final outbreak of the Jewish-Roman war. The early Church Fathers at least did not take such texts as an occasion to condemn either themselves or the Jews, but as a warning to the Church. Thus Origen, commenting on Rom. 2:21-24 (Migne, *PG* 14:897 A), says: "More than to the Jews, this blame attaches to all those who have only the name of religion and piety, but those works are lacking in wisdom and faith"; K. H. Schelkle, *"Kirche und Synagoge in der frühen Auslegung des Römerbriefes,"* in *Wort und Schrift*, Düsseldorf 1966, pp. 282–299.

[166] S. Lyonnet, " *'La circoncision du coeur, celle qui relève de l'Esprit et non de la lettre' (Rom 2,29),"* in *L'Évangile hier et aujourd'hui (Mélanges F. J. Leenhardt)*, Geneva 1968, pp. 87–97.

[167] E. Käsemann, *An die Römer*, 3rd ed., Tübingen 1974. K. H. Schelkle, *Paulus, Lehrer der Väter*, 2nd ed., Düsseldorf 1959, pp. 331–334. W. Thüsing, *Per Christum in Deum*, 2nd ed., Düsseldorf 1969, pp. 147–150.

[168] Paul says in Rom. 9:22f., and apparently quite deliberately, that God pa-

tiently endured the vessels of wrath which were prepared for destruction and that he has predestined for glory the vessels of mercy. He does not say that God prepared the vessels of wrath for destruction. But they are prepared. By whom? By God? By man himself? Paul teaches a predestination to salvation, but not to damnation. Nor does the latter proceed from the former as logical consequence. The possibilities open to God are not to be calculated by human logic. They are the secrets of his might.

[169] From the Fathers on, efforts have been made to interpret the promises of Paul as valid for all of Israel. In Rom. 11:26, "all Israel" ought to apply only to the whole of Israel's faithful, and therefore only to a part of Israel. Rom 11:29, "The gifts of grace and election by God are without repentance" (i.e., without revocation), is reduced by the Fathers so as to refer only to the faithful, the true Israel. Or they explain that God gives his gifts without man's prior repentance. See K. H. Schelkle, Paulus, *Lehrer der Väter*, 2nd ed., Düsseldorf 1959, pp. 400–406; and C. Spicq, "ΑΜΕΤΑΜΕΛΗΤΟΣ *dans Rom., XI 29*," in *Revue Biblique*, Vol. 67 (1960), pp. 210–219.

[170] C. K. Barret, *Das Johannesevangelium und das Judentum*, Stuttgart 1970. J. Blank, *Krisis*, Freiburg 1964, pp. 231–251. C. H. Dodd, "*A l'arrière-plan d'un dialogue johannique (Jo 8,33-58)*," in *Revue d'histoire et de philosophie religieuses*, Vol. 37 (1957), pp. 5–17. E. Grässer, "*Die antijüdische Polemik im Johannesevangelium*," in *New Testament Studies*, Vol. 11 (1964/65), pp. 74–90. J. Jocz, "*Die Juden im Johannesevangelium*," in *Judaica*, Vol. 9 (1953), pp. 129–142. R. Leistner, *Antijudaismus im Johannesevangelium?*, Bern and Frankfurt 1974. J. L. Martyn, *History and Theology in the Fourth Gospel*, New York 1968.

[171] Attempts are occasionally made to interpret this finding, apparently with the purpose of dulling it, in such a way that the Jews in their totality are not presented by the Gospel as enemies of Jesus, but as if "the Jews" were to mean, in John's Gospel, the leaders of Israel. With some of the texts, in any case, this is possible. But the Gospel does not say, when it speaks of the Jews, that it means only their leaders. "The Jews" are the whole responsible people. The high priests and the Pharisees are not separate from the Jews, but are their representatives. See G. Baum, *The Jews and the Gospel* (note 136, above); R. Leistner, *Antijudaismus im Johannesevangelium?*, pp. 47–51.

[172] H. Leroy, *Rätsel und Missverständnis: Ein Beitrag zur Formgeschichte des Johannesevangeliums*, Bonn 1968.

[173] This is probably how John 8:44 is to be understood. A literal translation could be: "You are from the father of the devil." This may be an abbreviated manner of expression (or a mistranslation from the Aramaic) for: "You are from the devil, your father." See E. Grässer, "*Die Juden als Teufelssöhne Johannes 8, 37-47*," in W. H. Eckert (*et al.*, eds.), *Antisemitismus im Neuen Testament?*, pp. 157–170.

[174] While Apoc. 2:9 and 3:9 are certainly understood generally of a Judaism

inimical to Christians, H. Kraft, in his *Die Offenbarung des Johannes*, Tübingen 1974, pp. 60f., 80f., interprets the texts in reference to Jewish Christians who have turned away again from the Church.

[175] It is difficult to write off John 4:22 as a redactional interpolation, as so many writers do, and with them, W. Bauer, *Das Johannesevangelium*, 3rd ed., Tübingen 1933, p. 70; R. Bultmann, *Das Evangelium des Johannes*, 19th ed., Göttingen 1968, p. 139; S. Schulz, *Das Evangelium nach Johannes*, 12th ed., Göttingen 1972, p. 76.

[176] G. Bertram and K. L. Schmidt, Art. ἔθνος, in *Theol. Dict. N. T.*, Vol. 2, 1964, pp. 364–372. H. Windisch, Art. Ἕλλην, *ibid.*, pp. 504–516. H. Strathmann and R. Meyer, Art. λαός, *ibid.*, Vol. 4, 1967, pp. 29–57. K. G. Kuhn, Art. προσήλυτος, *ibid.*, Vol. 6, 1968, pp. 727–744. C. Bussmann, *Themen der paulinischen Missionspredigt auf dem Hintergrund der spätjüdisch-hellenistischen Missionsliteratur*, Bern and Frankfurt 1971. J. Amstutz, *Kirche und Völker: Skizze einer Theorie der Mission*, Freiburg 1972. P. Dalbert, *Die Theologie der hellenistisch-jüdischen Missionsliteratur unter Ausschluss von Philo und Josephus*, Hamburg 1954. D. Georgi, *Die Gegner des Paulus im 2. Korintherbrief*, Neukirchen-Vluyn 1964 (pp. 83–218, "Mission in neutestamentlicher Zeit"). F. Hahn, *Das Verständnis der Mission im Neuen Testament*, Neukirchen-Vluyn 1963 [trans. F. Clarke, *Mission in the New Testament*, Naperville, Ill., 1965]. M. Hengel, "Die Ursprünge der christlichen Mission," in *New Testament Studies*, Vol. 18 (1971/72), pp. 15–38. H. Kasting, *Die Anfänge der urchristlichen Mission*, Munich 1969. G. Schille, "Anfänge der christlichen Mission," in *Kerygma und Dogma*, Vol. 15 (1969), pp. 320–339. H. Schlier, "Die Entscheidung für die Heidenmission in der Urchristenheit," in *Die Zeit der Kirche*, 4th ed., Freiburg 1966, pp. 90–107.

[177] O. Bächli, *Israel und die Völker*, dissertation, Basel 1962. J. Hempel, "Die Wurzeln des Missionswillens im Alten Testament," in *Zeitschrift für die alttestamentliche Wissenschaft*, Vol. 66 (1954), pp. 244–272. F. Huber, *Jahwe, Juda und die anderen Völker beim Propheten Jesaja*, Berlin 1975. R. Martin-Archard, *Israël et les nations*, Neuchâtel 1959. H. Schmidt, *Israel, Zion und die Völker*, dissertation, Zürich 1966.

[178] In the salvation-history vantage point of the New Testament, mankind is divided into two categories: Jews and non-Jews. This opposition is most evident with the concepts of ὁ λαός Ἰσραὴλ and τὰ ἔθνη. Is ἔθνη to be translated as "nations / Gentiles" or by "pagans / heathen"? The term ἔθνη is often found in the New Testament's quotations of the Old; hence, the linguistic usage of the term is likewise determined by the Old Testament. In contrast to the one "people (nation) of peculiar possession" (Ezek. 19:5; Deut. 7:6f.), there is the plurality of the nations (peoples) of the earth. They too have their origin in God's creation (Gen. 10). Nor are they excluded from God's salvation and plan of salvation. Yahweh is the King of all nations (Jer. 10:7). Henceforth, and probably in increasing measure, a decided note of disparagement attaches to the concept

of "nations"; that the "nations" or "Gentiles" are forfeit to idolatry and immorality, and are therefore unclean "pagans" or "heathen." The New Testament knows that the Gentiles too experience God's solicitude (Acts 14:15f.; 17:22-31). In the missionary command, the "nations" are recipients of salvation (Matthew 28:19). At the end of time the many nations will become one people of God (Rom. 11:32, 36; 15:9-13). Therefore it may be accepted as a principle that in the New Testament the term ἔθνη is generally to be translated by the neutral terms "nations" or "Gentiles", rather than by the judgmental terms "pagans" or "heathen."

Paul distinguishes peoples also as "Greeks and barbarians" (Rom. 1:4) or as "Jews and Greeks" (Rom. 2:16; 1 Cor. 1:22, *et passim*). In this respect Paul is employing the cultural-historical concepts of his own times.

[179] This is a not infrequently encountered rabbinic expression; see H. L. Strack and P. Billerbeck, *Kommentar zum Neuen Testament*, Vol. 2, 1924, p. 191.

[180] The commentaries recall that ancient Oriental prayers and Greco-Roman worship alike (e.g., the litany of Isis in the Oxyrhynchus Papyrus 1380; magic papyri) multiply the names and predicates of the gods in order, by force of magic, to gain their assistance. Elias makes a joke of this in 1 Kings 18:26-29, telling the pagan priests to call louder, for their god is perhaps sleeping; and Sir. 7:14 admonishes, "In praying, repeat not a word."

[181] D. Bosch, *Die Heidenmission in der Zukunftsschau Jesu*, Zürich 1959. J. Jeremias, *Jesu Verheissung für die Völker*, 2nd ed., Stuttgart 1968. P. D. Meyer, "The Gentile Mission in Q," in the *Journal of Biblical Literature*, Vol. 89 (1970), pp. 404–417. H. Stoevesandt, *Jesus und die Heidenmission*, typed dissertation, Göttingen 1943.

[182] The centurion is designated in John 4:46 as a "royal" or "of the king." "Royals" indicates troops in royal pay (Josephus, *Jewish War* 1, 1, 45; 2, 3, 52), and so also the troops of Herod the Great (Josephus, *Jewish Antiquities* 15, 8, 289; 17, 10, 266 and 270). They had often enough to go out against Jews, and were mostly non-Jews, belonging to the neighboring pagan tribes. As boundary of the territory of Herod Antipas, Capernaum too had a contingent of "royals," whose captain (probably Syrian) was a pagan.

[183] S. Schulz, *Q, Die Spruchquelle der Evangelisten*, Zürich 1972, pp. 323–330. D. Zeller, "*Das Logion Mt 8,11f. / Lk 13,28f. und das Motive der Völkerwallfahrt*," in *Biblische Zeitschrift*, new series, Vol. 15 (1971), pp. 222–237; 16 (1972), pp. 84–93.

[184] Is the genitive of Mathew 15:24's "the lost sheep of the House of Israel" a *genitivus partitivus* (= the part of Israel that is lost) or a *genitivus explicativus* (= the whole of Israel, all of which is lost)?

[185] J. Jeremias, *Die Gleichnisse Jesu*, 7th ed., Göttingen 1965, pp. 73f. [trans. by S. H. Hooke from 6th ed., *The Parables of Jesus*, pp. 77f.]. H. Räisänen, *Die Parabeltheorie im Markusevangelium*, Helsinki 1973, pp. 72–76. B. Gerhardsson, "The Parable of the Sower and its Interpretation," in *New Testament Studies*, Vol.

14 (1967/68), pp. 165–193. This last treats of the parable of the sower and of its application to Jesus.

[186] κόπος and κοπιᾶν are, in the New Testament Epistles, the usual terms for missionary labor and pastoral concern (Rom. 16:6, 12; 1 Cor. 3:8; 1 Thess. 3:5); F. Hauck, Art. κόπος, in *Theol. Dict. N. T.*, Vol. 3, 1965, pp. 827–830.

[187] W. Grimm, "*Die Preisgabe eines Menschen zur Rettung des Volkes. Priesterliche Tradition bei Johannes und Josephus,*" in O. Betz (*et al.*, eds.), *Untersuchungen zu Josephus, dem antiken Judentum und dem Neuen Testament (Festschrift O. Michel)*, Göttingen 1974, pp. 133–146.

[188] The figural saying about the grain of wheat, which dies in the earth and thereby brings forth much fruit, belongs to the broader category of Judeo-biblical literature referring, even if with precise import other than that of John's Gospel, to the resurrection, as also do such passages as 1 Cor. 15:37 and Clement of Rome, *Letter to the Corinthians* 24:4-5 (Jurgens, no. 13). See H. L. Strack and P. Billerbeck, *op. cit.*, Vol. 2, 1924, p. 551; Vol. 3, 1926, p. 475. O. Michel, Art. κόκκος, in *Theol. Dict. N. T.*, Vol. 3, 1965, pp. 810–812. A. Rasco, "*Christus, granum frumenti,*" in *Verbum Domini*, Vol. 37 (1959), pp. 12–25, 65–77.

[189] F. Bovon, *De vocatione gentium: Histoire de l'interpretation d'Act. 10,1–11,18 dans les six premiers siècles*, Tübingen 1967. J. Dupont, "*Le salut des gentils et la signification théologique du Livre des Actes,*" in *New Testament Studies*, Vol. 6 (1959/60), pp. 132–155. J. Jervell, "*Das gespaltene Israel und die Heidenvölker,*" in *Studia theologica*, Vol. 19 (1965), pp. 68–96. U. Wilckens, *Die Missionsreden der Apostelgeschichte, Form- und traditionsgeschichtliche Untersuchung*, 3rd ed., Neukirchen-Vluyn 1974.

[190] *Translator's note*: The statement assumes, of course, that the phenomenon described in Acts 2:5-13 was in fact identical to the phenomenon known as glossolalia. This assumption is given some credence by Acts 2:13; but if it solves the problem raised by that verse, it creates other problems of its own; and it does, of course, remain purely an assumption that the Pentecost phenomenon was one purely and simply of "ecstatic speech," which seems to be nothing more than a polite term for the gibberish uttered by the fanatic whose emotional state has brought him near to psychosis.

[191] R. Kempter, *Der Kampf des Römischen Staates gegen die fremden Kulte*, typed dissertation, Tübingen 1941.

[192] F. Christ, *Die römische Weltherrschaft in der antiken Dichtung*, Stuttgart 1938. K. H. Schelkle, "*Jerusalem und Rom im Neuen Testament,*" in *Wort und Schrift*, Düsseldorf 1966, pp. 126–144.

[193] A. Bertrangs, "*La vocation des gentils chez saint Paul,*" in *Ephemerides theologicae Lovanienses*, Vol. 30 (1954), pp. 391–415. W. Grundmann, "*Paulus, aus dem Volke Israel, Apostel der Völker,*" in *Novum Testamentum*, Vol. 4 (1960), pp. 267–291. O. Haas, *Paulus das Missionar*, Münsterschwarzach 1971.

[194] Ch. Maurer, "*Paulus als der Apostel der Völker,*" in *Evangelische Theologie*, Vol. 19 (1959), pp. 28–40. K. Prümm, "*Zum Vorgang der Heidenbekehrung*

nach paulinischen Sicht," in *Zeitschrift für katholische Theologie,* Vol. 84 (1962), pp. 427–470. D. Zeller, *Juden und Heiden in der Mission des Paulus,* Stuttgart 1973.

[105] The discourse placed in the mouth of Paul in Acts 17:30 represents a less severe judgment on paganism: "In times past God overlooked that ignorance."

[106] A.) ON JEWISH APOCALYPTICS: H. D. Betz, *"Zum Problem des religionsgeschichtlichen Verständnisses der Apokalyptik,"* in *Zeitschrift für Theologie und Kirche,* Vol. 63 (1966), pp. 391–409. W. Bousset and H. Gressmann, *Die Religion des Judentums im späthellenistischen Zeitalter,* ed. E. Lohse, 4th ed., Göttingen 1966 (pp. 202–301 and 501–519). W. Harnisch, *Verhängnis und Verheissung der Geschichte: Untersuchungen zum Zeit- und Geschichtsverständnis im 4. Buch Esra und in der syrischen Baruchapokalypse,* Göttingen 1969. K. Koch, *Ratlos vor der Apokalyptik,* Gütersloh 1970 [in English as *The Rediscovery of Apocalyptic,* Naperville, Illinois, n. d (1972)]. H. W. Kuhn, *Enderwartung und gegenwärtiges Heil. Untersuchungen zu den Gemeindeliedern von Qumran,* Göttingen 1966. M. Limbeck, *"Apokalyptik oder Pharisäismus? Zu einigen Neuerscheinungen,"* in *Theologische Quartalschrift,* Vol. 152 (1972), pp. 145–156. P. von der Osten-Sacken, *Die Apokalyptik in ihrem Verhältnis zu Prophetie und Weisheit,* Munich 1969. P. Riessler, *Altjüdisches Schrifttum ausserhalb der Bibel,* Augsburg 1928 (reprinted at Darmstadt 1966). D. Rössler, *Gesetz und Geschichte: Untersuchungen zur Theologie der jüdischen Apokalyptik und der pharisäischen Orthodoxie,* 2nd ed., Neukirchen 1962. J. Schreiner, *Alttestamentlich-jüdische Apokalyptik,* Munich 1969. H. L. Strack and P. Billerbeck, *Kommentar zum Neuen Testament aus Talmud und Midrasch,* 6 vols., 1st to 3rd eds., Munich 1961. P. Volz, *Die Eschatologie der jüdischen Gemeinde im neutestamentlichen Zeitalter,* 2nd ed., Tübingen 1934.

B.) ON NEW TESTAMENT ESCHATOLOGY: R. Bultmann, *Geschichte und Eschatologie,* 2nd ed., Tübingen 1964. R. H. Charles, *Eschatology. The Doctrine of a Future Life in Israel, Judaism, and Christianity,* 3rd ed. New York 1963. O. Cullmann, *"Eschatologie,"* in *Vorträge und Aufsätze,* Tübingen and Zürich 1966, pp. 303–465. G. Delling, *Zeit und Endzeit,* Stuttgart 1970. O. Knoch, *"Die eschatologische Frage, ihre Entwicklung und ihr gegenwärtiger Stand,"* in *Biblische Zeitschrift,* new series, Vol. 6 (1962), pp. 112–120; also of Knoch, *Eigenart und Bedeutung der Eschatologie im theologischen Aufriss des ersten Clemensbriefes,* Bonn 1964. P. E. Langevin, *Jésus Seigneur et l'eschatologie,* Bruges 1967. F. Laub, *Eschatologische Verkündigung und Lebensgestaltung nach Paulus,* Regensburg 1973. E. Lohse, *"Apokalyptik und Christologie,"* in *Die Einheit des Neuen Testaments,* Göttingen 1973, pp. 125–144. F. Mussner, L. Boros, *et al., Christus vor uns. Studien zur christlichen Eschatologie,* Frankfurt 1966. R. Pesch, *"Heilszukunft und Zukunft des Heils. Eschatologie und Apokalyptik in den Evangelien und Briefen,"* in J. Schreiner (ed.), *Gestalt und Anspruch des Neuen Testaments,* Würzburg 1969, pp. 313–329. H. H. Rowley, *The Relevance of Apocalyptics,* New York 1964. W. Schmithals, *Die Apokalyptik,* Göttingen 1973.

K. Schubert (ed.), *Vom Messias zum Christus. Die Fülle der Zeit in religions-geschichtlicher und theologischer Sicht*, Vienna 1964. W. Strawson, *Jesus and the Future Life*, 2nd ed., London 1970. A. Strobel, *Kerygma und Apokalyptik. Ein religionsgeschichtlicher und theologischer Beitrag zur Christusfrage*, Göttingen 1967. A. Vögtle, *Das Neue Testament und die Zukunft des Kosmos*, Düsseldorf 1970. E. Walter, *Das Kommen des Herrn*, 2 vols., Freiburg 1942 and 1947. S. Zedda, *L'escatologia biblica*, Vol. 1: *Antico testamento e vangeli sinottici*, Brescia 1972.

c.) ON DOGMATICS: P. Althaus, *Die letzten Dinge*, 10th ed., Gütersloh 1970. H. Urs von Balthasar, *"Eschatologie,"* in J. Feiner, I. Trütsch, and F. Böckle (eds.), *Fragen der Theologie heute*, 2nd ed., Einsiedeln 1958, pp. 403–421. E. Brunner, *Das Ewige als Zukunft und Gegenwart*, Munich 1965. F. Buri, J. M. Lochman, H. Ott, *Dogmatik im Dialog*, Vol. 1: *Die letzten Dinge*, Gütersloh 1973. J. Moltmann, *Theologie der Hoffnung. Untersuchungen zur Begründung zu den Konsequenzen einer christlichen Eschatologie*, 8th ed., Munich 1969 [in English under title *Theology of Hope: On the Ground and the Implications of a Christian Eschatology*, New York 1967.] P. Müller-Goldkuhle, *Die Eschatologie in der Dogmatik des 19. Jahrhunderts*, Essen 1966. H. Ott, *Eschatologie. Versuch eines dogmatischen Grundrisses*, Zürich 1958. J. Pieper, *Über das Ende der Zeit*, Munich 1950 [in English trans. by M. Bullock, *The End of Time*, New York 1954]. K. Rahner, *"Immanente und transzendente Vollendung,"* in *Schriften zur Theologie*, Vol. 8, Einsiedeln 1967, pp. 593–609; also of Rahner, *"Die Frage nach der Zukunft,"* in *ibid.*, Vol. 9, Einsiedeln 1970, pp. 519–540. Th. Rast, *"Die Eschatologie in der Theologie des 20. Jahrhunderts,"* in H. Vorgrimmler and R. Van der Gucht (eds.), *Bilanz der Theologie im 20. Jahrhundert*, Vol. 3, Freiburg 1970, pp. 294–315. G. Sauter, *Zukunft und Verheissung*, Zürich 1965.

[197] L. Coenen (ed.), Art. *Zeit, Ewigkeit*, in *Theologisches Begriffslexikon zum Neuen Testament*, Wuppertal 1971, pp. 1457–1497. G. Kittel, Art. ἔσχατος, in *Theol. N. T.*, Vol. 2, 1964, pp. 697–698. W. G. Kümmel, *"Die Eschatologie der Evangelien,"* in *Heilsgeschehen und Geschichte*, Marburg 1965, pp. 48–66.

[198] A. Oepke, Art. ἀποκαλύπτω, in *Theol. Dict. N. T.*, Vol. 3, 1965, pp. 563–592.

[199] G. von Rad and G. Delling, Art. ἡμέρα, in *Theol. Dict. N. T.*, Vol. 2, 1964, pp. 943–953. G. Delling, Art. ὥρα, *ibid.*, Vol. 9, 1974, pp. 675–681. G. von Rad, "The Origin of the Concept of the Day of Jahwe," in *Journal of Semitic Studies*, Vol. 4 (1959), pp. 91–108. M. Weiss, "The Origin of the 'Day of the Lord' Reconsidered," in *Hebrew Union College Annual*, Vol. 37 (1966), pp. 29–72.

[200] G. Delling, Art. καιρός, in *Theol. Dict. N. T.*, Vol. 3, 1965, pp. 455–462.

[201] G. Sasse, Art. αἰών, in *Theol. Dict. N. T.*, Vol. 1, 1964, pp. 197–209. H. L. Strack and P. Billerbeck, *op. cit.*, Vol. 4, 2, pp. 799–976. J. Becker, *Das Heil Gottes*, Göttingen 1964, pp. 96–103.

[202] G. Delling, Art. τέλος, in *Theol. Dict. N. T.*, Vol. 8, 1972, pp. 49–87.

[203] G. Stählin, Art. νῦν, in *Theol. Dict. N. T.*, Vol. 4, 1967, pp. 1106–1123. E. Fuchs, Art. σήμερον, *ibid.*, Vol. 7, 1971, pp. 269–275.

[204] The period between the Old and New Testaments was for a long time designated as "late Judaism"; and since the Old Testament times were called "Judaism," to term the intertestamental period as "late Judaism" seemed natural enough. More recently, however, the preferred usage is to term this intertestamental period as "early Judaism." The typical and abiding characteristics of Judaism, it is supposed, would have developed after the freezing of the Old Testament into a canon.

[205] K. Rahner, "*Theologische Prinzipien der Hermeneutik eschatologischer Aussagen*," in *Schriften zur Theologie*, Vol. 4, Einsiedeln 1960, pp. 401–428. H. Schlier, "*Das Ende der Zeit*," in his work of the same title, Freiburg 1971, pp. 67–84.

[206] H. Kleinknecht, G. von Rad, K. G. Kuhn, and K. L. Schmidt, Art. βασιλεία, in *Theol. Dict. N. T.*, Vol. 1, 1964, pp. 564–593. E. Bammel, "*Erwägungen zur Eschatologie Jesu*," in *Studia evangelica*, Vol. 3 (*Texte und Untersuchungen*, Vol. 88), Berlin 1964, pp. 3–32. Hans Urs von Balthasar, *Zuerst Gottes Reich. Zwei Skizzen zur biblischen Naherwartung*, Einsiedeln 1960. H. Flender, *Die Botschhaft Jesu von der Herrschaft Gottes*, Munich 1968. J. Héring, *Le Royaume de Dieu et sa venue*, 2nd ed., Neuchâtel-Paris 1959. A. Hertz, E. Iserloh, G. Klein, J. B. Metz, and W. Pannenberg, *Gottesreich und Menschenreich*, Regensburg 1971. E. Jüngel, *Paulus und Jesus*, 2nd ed., Tübingen 1964 (pp. 87–215: "*Jesus und die Gottesherrschaft*"). G. Klein, "*Reich Gottes als biblischer Zentralbegriff*," in *Evangelische Theologie*, Vol. 30 (1970), pp. 642–670. A. Kretzer, *Die Herrschaft der Himmel und die Söhne des Reiches*, Stuttgart and Würzburg 1971. W. Kümmel, *Verheissung und Erfüllung. Untersuchungen zur eschatologischen Verkündigung Jesu*, 3rd ed., Zürich 1956. E. Lohse, "*Die Gottesherrschaft in den Gleichnissen Jesu*," in *Die Einheit des Neuen Testaments*, Göttingen 1973, pp. 49–61. R. Schnackenburg, *Gottes Herrschaft und Reich*, 4th ed., Freiburg 1965. E. Staehelin, *Die Verkündigung des Reiches Gottes in der Kirche*, 7 vols., Basel 1951–1965. Ph. Vielhauer, "*Gottesreich und Menschensohn in der Verkündigung Jesu*," in *Aufsätze zum Neuen Testament*, Munich 1965, pp. 55–91.

[207] W. H. Schmidt, *Königtum Gottes in Ugarit und Israel*, 2nd ed., Berlin 1966.

[208] H. Preisker, Art. ἐγγύς, in *Theol. Dict. N. T.*, Vol. 2, 1964, pp. 330–332. G. Delling, Art. πληρόω, *ibid.*, Vol. 6, 1968, pp. 286–296. F. Mussner, "*Gottesherrschaft und Sendung Jesu*," in *Praesentia salutis*, Düsseldorf 1967, pp. 81–98. R. Pesch, "*Anfang des Evangeliums Jesu Christi. Eine Studie zum Prolog des Markusevangeliums (Mk 1,1-15)*," in G. Bornkamm and K. Rahner (eds.), *Die Zeit Jesu (Festschrift H. Schlier)*, Freiburg 1970, pp. 108–144.

[209] M. Künzli, *Das Naherwartungslogion Matthäus 10,23. Geschichte seiner Auslegung*, Tübingen 1970.

[210] On the problem of imminent expectation, see: E. Grässer, *Die Naherwartung Jesu*, Stuttgart 1973. W. Kümmel, *"Die Naherwartung in der Verkündigung Jesu,"* in *Heilsgeschehen und Geschichte*, Marburg 1965, pp. 457–470. W. Michaelis, *Der Herr verzieht nicht die Verheissung. Die Aussagen Jesu über die Nähe des Jüngsten Tages*, Bern 1942. H. Schürmann, *"Die Christusoffenbarung. Das hermeneutische Hauptproblem der Verkündigung Jesu,"* in *Traditionsgeschichtliche Untersuchungen zu den synoptischen Evangelien*, Düsseldorf 1968, pp. 13–35. A. Strobel, *Untersuchungen zum eschatologischen Verzögerungsproblem*, Leiden and Colongne 1961. Further literature below in note 241.

[211] The term ἄνωθεν γεννηθῆναι in John 3:3 can mean "to be born anew" or "to be born from above." Linguistically and contextually both translations are possible. The first, however, is certainly to be preferred, because the idea of rebirth was already confided to Christian tradition (1 Peter 1:3, 23; Titus 3:5).

[212] In my work entitled *Das Neue Testament. Eine Einführung*, 4th ed., Kevelaer 1970, pp. 134–137, I was still disposed to attribute the Second Epistle to the Thessalonians to Paul. I am now more inclined to regard the Epistle as post-Pauline and to date it at the end of the first century. See especially W. Trilling, *Untersuchungen zum 2. Thessalonicherbrief*, Leipzig 1972.

[213] J. Kopper, *"Die Philosophie des Selbstbewusstseins und der Gedanke des Reiches Gottes auf Erden,"* in *Philosophisches Jahrbuch*, Vol. 69 (1961/62), pp. 345–370. Ch. Walther, *Typen des Reich-Gottes-Verständnisses. Studien zur Eschatologie und Ethik im 19. Jahrhundert*, Munich 1961.

[214] A. Deissler, *"Das evolutionistische Weltbild und die biblischen Schöpfungsberichte,"* in *Evolution und Weltbild*, Karlsruhe 1966, pp. 23–31. W. D. Marsch, *Zukunft*, Stuttgart 1969. K. Rahner, *"Marxistische Utopie und christliche Zukunft des Menschen,"* in *Schriften zur Theologie*, Vol. 6, Einsiedeln 1965, pp. 77–88. G. Scherer, F. Kerstiens, F. J. Schierse, *et al., Eschatologie und geschichtliche Zukunft*, Essen 1972.

[215] A. Exeler, *Eine Frohbotschaft vom christlichen Leben. Die Eigenart der Moraltheologie Johann Baptist Hirschers*, Freiburg 1959, pp. 112–145. J. R. Geiselmann, *Die katholische Tübinger Schule*, Freiburg 1964, pp. 191–279. J. Rief, *Reich Gottes und Gesellschaft nach Johann Sebastian Drey und Johann Baptist Hirscher*, Paderborn 1965. P. Weins, *Die Reich-Gottes-Idee in der katholischen Theologie des 19. Jahrhunderts*, typed dissertation, Freiburg 1921. J. G. Ziegler, *"Die Reichgottesidee J. B. Hirschers unter dem Aspekt der Exegese und der Moraltheologie,"* in *Theologie und Glaube*, Vol. 52 (1962), pp. 30–41.

[216] J. Weiss, *Die Predigt Jesu vom Reiche Gottes*, Göttingen 1892 (3rd ed., 1964). A Schweitzer, *Geschichte der Leben-Jesu-Forschung*, Tübingen 1906 (6th ed., 1951). In his posthumously published work *Reich Gottes und Christentum*, Tübingen 1967, p. 204, Albert Schweitzer concludes, in respect to the modern situation and task of Christianity, that Christendom is "obligated to set aside its belief in the kingdom that is to come of itself, and to resign itself to one that has to be achieved. . . . In the thought of Paul, the supernatural kingdom be-

gins to become an ethical one, and thus it is transformed from something to be awaited into something to be realized. We have to take the path that is open in that direction."

[217] G. Bertram, Art. σαλεύω, in *Theol. Dict. N. T.*, Vol. 7, 1971, pp. 65–70. H. Conzelmann, Art. σκότος, *ibid.*, Vol. 7, pp. 423–445. G. Delling, Art. τέλος, *ibid.*, Vol. 8, 1972, pp. 49–87. G. R. Beasly-Murray, *A Commentary on Mark Thirteen*, London 1957. F. Busch, *Zum Verständnis der synoptischen Eschatologie. Markus 13 neu untersucht*, Gütersloh 1938. A. Feuillet, "*Le discourse de Jésus sur la ruine du temple d'après Marc XIII et Luc XXI, 5-36*," in *Revue Biblique*, Vol. 55 (1948), pp. 481–502; Vol. 56 (1949), pp. 61–92. R. Geiger, *Die lukanischen Endzeitreden. Studien zur Eschatologie des Lukasevangeliums*, Bern and Frankfurt 1973. J. Lambrecht, *Die Redaktion der Markusapocalypse*, Rome 1967. F. Mussner, *Was lehrte Jesus über das Ende der Welt? Eine Auslegung von Markus 13*, 2nd ed., Freiburg 1963. R. Pesch, *Naherwartungen. Tradition und Redaktion in Mk 13*, Düsseldorf 1968. A. Vögtle, *Das Neue Testament und die Zukunft des Kosmos*, Düsseldorf 1970. N. Walter, "*Tempelzerstörung und synoptische Apokalypse*," in *Zeitschrift für die neutestamentliche Wissenschaft*, Vol. 57 (1966), pp. 38–49. J. Zimijewski, *Die Eschatologiereden des Lukasevangeliums*, Bonn 1972.

[218] The apocalyptic discourse of Jesus in Luke 17:20-37 is interpreted as an announcement of the parousia in § 16, 3, a, below.

[219] R. Pesch (*Naherwartungen. Tradition und Redaktion in Mk 13*, Düsseldorf 1968, pp. 72f., 93–96, 104–106, 143f., and 234f.) and N. Walter (Art. "*Tempelzerstörung und synoptische Apokalypse*," in *Zeitschrift für die neutestamentliche Wissenschaft*, Vol. 57 [1966], pp. 38–49) are of a mind that some places in Mark 13 indicate that the destruction of the city of Jerusalem and of the Temple may already have taken place. The majority of exegetes, however, date Mark 13 in the period (immediately) before the finish of the Temple.

[220] H. Schüngel-Straumann, *Gottesbild und Kultkritik vorexilischer Propheten*, Stuttgart 1972.

[221] B. Gärtner, *The Temple and the Community in Qumran and the New Testament*, Cambridge 1965.

[222] In Luke 21:5 some are much impressed by "the beautiful stones of the Temple and the adornment of its offerings." Is it the joy of Luke, a Greek, in the beauty of the structure and in the precious ornamentation of a celebrated sanctuary that is speaking here? The commentaries refer to 2 Macc. 9:16, as also to Herodotus 1, 183; Pausanias 1, 5, 5; and Philo, *Embassy to Gaius* 157.

[223] H. Köster, "*Häretiker im Urchristentum als theologisches Problem*," in E. Dinkler (ed.), *Zeit und Geschichte (Festschrift R. Bultmann)*, Tübingen 1964, pp. 61–76. H. Schürmann, "*Das Testament des Paulus für die Kirche Apg 20,18-35*," in *Traditionsgeschichtliche Untersuchungen zu den synoptischen Evangelien*, Düsseldorf 1968, pp. 310–340.

[224] Mark 13:10 — "The gospel must first be proclaimed to all the nations" —

presupposes a long future of the Church and that the mission to the Gentiles has already experienced some successes. The statement was shaped, no doubt, by Mark. It appears also in Matthew 24:14; but it is lacking in Luke, perhaps because he would have attributed such a statement to the time of the Church. See D. Bosch, *Die Heidenmission in der Zukunftsschau Jesu*, Zürich 1959, pp. 153–174. F. Hahn, *Das Verständnis der Mission im Neuen Testament*, Neukirchen 1963, pp. 59–61. H. Kasting, *Die Anfänge der urchristlichen Mission*, Munich 1969, p. 108. R. Pesch, *Naherwartungen. Tradition und Redaktion in Mk 13*, Düsseldorf 1968, pp. 129–131.

[225] G. Hölscher, "*Der Ursprung der Apokalypse Mk 13*," in *Theologische Blätter*, Vol. 12 (1933), pp. 193–202. H. J. Schoeps, "*Ebionitische Apokalyptik im Neuen Testament*," in *Zeitschrift für die neutestamentliche Wissenschaft*, Vol. 51 (1960), pp. 101–111. R. Pesch, *op. cit.*, pp. 207–223.

[226] E. Schweizer, *Das Evangelium nach Markus*, 13th edition, Göttingen 1973, pp. 156f.

[227] The depiction presupposes the ancient image of the world. R. Pesch, *op. cit.*, pp. 158–166 and A. Vögtle, *op. cit.*, pp. 67–69, and other authors too, think that the Gospel does not intend to describe actual events, but that the texts are to be understood symbolically as metaphors concerning the judgment. The cosmic horrors signify the anger of God. It would be explained as a historico-theological event of the kingdom of God. It is hardly necessary, to exonerate the prophecy of declarations impossible in nature. Certainly there has been a frequent enough sensitivity to the problem. It is directly with these declarations that Origen already attempts to bring the Bible into harmony with the image of the world current in his times; see R. Wetzel, *Das 24. Kapitel des Evangelisten Matthäus in der Auslegung durch die griechischen Väter Origenes und Chrysostomus*, typed dissertation, Tübingen 1972.

[228] A. Weiser, *Die Knechtsgleichnisse der synoptischen Evanglien*, Munich 1971.

[229] O. Knoch, *Die "Testamente" des Petrus und Paulus*, Stuttgart 1973. J. Munck, "*Discours d'adieu dans le Nouveau Testament et dans la littérature biblique*," in *Aux sources de la tradition chrétienne* (Festschrift in honor of M. Goguel), Neuchâtel and Paris 1950, pp. 155–170.

[230] According to the calculations of N. Perrin in his *The Kingdom of God*, London 1963, Mark 13:5-27 employs a total of 165 words. Of these 165 words, 35 do not occur elsewhere in Mark's Gospel. This is more than 20%, a remarkably high figure. Of these 35 words, 15 occur again in the Apocalypse of John. These statistics, therefore, confirm a significant inclusion of traditional apocalyptic language.

[231] W. Harnisch, *Eschatologische Existenz*, Göttingen 1973, pp. 84–95. A. Smitmans, "*Das Gleichnis vom Dieb*," in H. Feld and J. Nolte (eds.), *Wort Gottes in der Zeit*, Düsseldorf 1973, pp. 43–48.

[232] I said otherwise in my writing, *Das Neue Testament. Eine Einführung*,

Kevelaer, 4th ed., 1970, pp. 134–137; but I am now more inclined to regard Second Thessalonians as post-Pauline. See above, note 212.

[233] Besides the usual commentaries on Second Thessalonians, First John, and the Apocalypse of John, see also J. Ernst, *Die eschatologischen Gegenspieler in den Schriften des Neuen Testaments*, Regensburg 1967; Ch. H. Giblin, *The Threat to Faith. An Exegetical and Theological Re-examination of 2 Thessalonians 2*, Rome 1967, pp. 167–242. B. Rigaux, *L'Antéchrist et l'opposition au royaume messianique dans l'Ancien et le Nouveau Testament*, Paris 1932. H. Schlier, *"Vom Antichrist,"* in *Die Zeit der Kirche*, 3rd ed., Freiburg 1962, pp. 16–29.

[234] The blasphemer is portrayed, not with historical-individual attributes, but with mythical ones. For that reason "the restraining" person or thing of 2 Thess. 2:6 probably should not be understood of contemporaneous powers or persons (among those that have been suggested are the Roman Empire, the Emperor, the Christian mission, and Paul himself). 2 Thess. 2:6f. employs ancient and widespread apocalyptic views of the particulars delaying the end, which ultimately lie in God's plan: this, at any rate, is the view of W. Trilling, *Untersuchungen zum 2. Thessalonicherbrief*, Leipzig 1972, pp. 82–86.

[235] R. Bultmann, Art. ζωή, in *Theol. Dict. N. T.*, Vol. 2, 1964, pp. 832–875; Art. θάνατος, *ibid.*, Vol. 3, 1965, pp. 7–25; also of Bultmann, Art. νεκρός, *ibid.*, Vol. 4, 1967, pp. 892–895. H. Balz, Art. ὕπνος, *ibid.*, Vol. 8, 1972, pp. 545–556. A. Dihle, E. Jacob, E. Lohse, E. Schweizer, and K. W. Tröger, Art. ψυχή, *ibid.*, Vol. 9, 1974, pp. 608–660. Jacques Choron, *Death and Western Thought*, New York 1963. P. Hoffmann, *Die Toten in Christus*, Münster 1966. E. Jüngel, *Tod*, Stuttgart 1971. J. Pieper, *Tod und Unsterblichkeit*, Munich 1968 [trans. R. and C. Winston, *Death and Immortality*, New York 1969]. K. Rahner, *Zur Theologie des Todes*, 5th ed., Freiburg 1965. Also of Rahner, *"Zu einer Theologie des Todes,"* in *Schriften zur Theologie*, Vol. 10, Zürich 1972, pp. 181–199. H. Thielicke, *Tod und Leben*, 2nd ed., Tübingen 1946. H. Volk, *Der Tod in der Sicht des christlichen Glaubens*, Münster 1958.

[236] P. Hoffmann, *Die Toten in Christus*, Münster 1966, pp. 30–37. W. Jaeger, *Die Theologie der frühen griechischen Denker*, 2nd ed., Stuttgart 1964, pp. 88–106. M. P. Nilson, *Geschichte der griechischen Religion*, Vol. 1, 2nd ed., Munich 1955, p. 702; Vol. 2, 2nd ed., Munich 1961, p. 350. G. Pfannmüller, *Tod, Jenseits und Unsterblichkeit in der Religion, Literatur und Philosophie der Griechen und Römer*, Munich 1953, pp. 9–222. E. Rhode, *Seelenkult und Unsterblichkeitsglaube der Griechen*, Vol. 2, 10th edition, Tübingen 1925, pp. 130f., 161–163, 264–287.

[237] As witness to this extravagant consciousness, a statement of J. G. Fichte may be adduced: "That which is called Death cannot interrupt my work. . . . I have snatched up eternity for myself. I hold my head up proudly . . . and declare: 'I am eternal.' . . . Let the last dusty particle of this body I call mine be rent: my will alone . . shall hold sway, proud and passionless, over the wreck-

age of the universe"; see. J. Pieper, *Tod und Unsterblichkeit*, Munich 1968, pp. 159f. (or, in the English trans. of R. and C. Winston, *Death and Immortality*, New York 1969, p. 111 — the passage above as quoted from Fichte, however, is my own translation — W. A. J.).

[238] A. Ahlbrecht, *Tod und Unsterblichkeit in der evangelischen Theologie der Gegenwart*, Paderborn 1964. O. Cullmann, *Unsterblichkeit der Seele oder Auferstehung der Toten?*, 3rd ed., Berlin 1964; H. Thielicke, *Tod und Leben*, 2nd ed., Tübingen 1964, pp. 192–199.

[239] In the New Testament it must constantly be decided whether ψυχή is to be translated "life," in accord with the basic Hebraic notion, or "soul," in accord with a Greek understanding. G. Dautzenberg, *"Sein Leben" bewahren: ψυχή in den Herrenworten der Evangelien*, Munich 1966, pp. 161–168. J. Schmid, *"Der Begriff der Seele im Neuen Testament,"* in J. Ratzinger and H. Fries (eds.), *Einsicht und Glaube (Festschrift G. Söhngen)*, 2nd ed., Freiburg 1962, pp. 128–147. See also the present work, Vol. 1, pp. 98f.

[240] K. H. Rengstorf, Art. κλαίω, in *Theol. Dict. N. T.*, Vol. 3, 1965, pp. 722–726. G. Stählin, Art. κοπετός, *ibid.*, Vol. 3, 1965, pp. 830–852.

[241] G. von Rad and G. Delling, Art. ἡμέρα, in *Theol. Dict. N. T.*, Vol. 2, 1964, pp. 943–953; A. Oepke, Art. παρουσία, *ibid.*, Vol. 5, 1967, pp. 858–871. O. Cullmann, *"Parusieverzögerung und Urchristentum,"* in *Vorträge und Aufsätze*, Tübingen and Zürich 1966, pp. 427–455. E. Grässer, *Das Problem der Parusieverzögerung in den synoptischen Evangelien*, 2nd ed., Berlin 1960. G. Klein, *"Apokalyptische Naherwartung bei Paulus,"* in H. D. Betz and L. Schottroff (eds.), *Neues Testament und christliche Existenz (Festschrift H. Braun)*, Tübingen 1973, pp. 241–262. Louvain 1962, *Recherches Bibliques*, Vol. 6: *La venue du Messie, Messianisme et eschatologie*. A. L. Moore, *The Parousia in the New Testament*, Leiden 1966. K. Rahner, *"Kirche und Parusie Christi,"* in *Schriften zur Theologie*, Vol. 6, Einsiedeln 1965, pp. 348–367. J. Sint, *"Parusie-Erwartung und Parusie-Verzögerung im paulinischen Briefcorpus,"* in K. Schubert (ed.), *Vom Messias zum Christus*, Vienna 1964, pp. 233–277. H. Wenz, *Die Ankunft unseres Herrn am Ende der Zeit*, Stuttgart 1965.

[242] It must be borne in mind that *parousia* means "arrival." The usual translation "second coming" or "re-arrival" presupposes that the incarnational coming of Christ is to be designated a *parousia*. This usage is first encountered in St. Ignatius of Antioch, *Letter to the Philadelphians*, 9, 2 (Jurgens, no. 61, with note). St. Justin the Martyr, in his *First Apology* 52, 3 (Jurgens, no. 124), speaks of Christ's first and second coming as parousias.

[243] Numerous examples in A. Deissmann, *Licht vom Osten*, 4th ed., Tübingen 1923, pp. 314–320.

[244] R. Geiger, *Die Lukanischen Endzeitreden. Studien zur Eschatologie des Lukasevangeliums*, Bern and Frankfurt 1973. B. Rigaux, *"La petite apocalypse de Luc (17,22-37),"* in *Ecclesia a Spiritu Sancto edocta* (a Festschrift in honor of G. Philips), Gembloux 1970, pp. 407–438. R. Schnackenburg, *"Der escha-*

tologische Abschnitt Lukas 17,20-37," in *Schriften zum Neuen Testament,* Munich 1971, pp. 220-243. J. Zimijewski, *Die Eschatologie des Lukasevangeliums,* Bonn 1972, pp. 326-340.

[245] J. Zimijewski (*Die Eschatologie des Lukasevangeliums,* Bonn 1972, p. 393) is of a mind that Luke is dealing with Pharisees within the Christian community, who, by pious works, were trying to force the coming of the kingdom and wanted to claim it for themselves.

[246] Besides the usual commentaries, see A. Rüstow, *"Zur Deutung von Lc 17,20-21,"* in *Zeitschrift für die neutestamentliche Wissenschaft,* Vol. 51 (1960), pp. 197-224.

[247] R. Bultmann, *Das Evangelium des Johannes,* 11th ed., Göttingen 1950, pp. 247, 444-454, and 479f.

[248] W. Harnisch, *Eschatologische Existenz. Ein exegetischer Beitrag zum Sachanliegen von 1. Thessalonicher 4,13-5,11,* Göttingen 1973. On the Epistles to the Thessalonians, see B. Rigaux, *Saint Paul, Les épitres aux Thessaloniciens,* Paris 1956.

[249] G. Friedrich, Art. σάλπιγξ, in *Theol. Dict. N. T.,* Vol. 7, 1971, pp. 71-88.

[250] A. Oepke, Art. νεφέλη, in *Theol. Dict. N. T.,* Vol. 4, 1967, pp. 902-910.

[251] J. Dupont, Σὺν Χριστῷ. *L'Union avec le Christ,* Vol. 1, Bruges 1952, pp. 64-73. E. Peterson, *"Die Einholung des Kyrios,"* in *Zeitschrift für systematische Theologie,* Vol. 7 (1929/30), pp. 682-702.

[252] K. G. Kuhn, Art. Μαραναθά, in *Theol. Dict. N. T.,* Vol. 4, 1967, pp. 466-472. Of the commentaries, see especially H. Conzelmann, *Der erste Brief an die Korinther,* Göttingen 1969, pp. 360f.

[253] This will be the significance of the term πολίτευμα: see H. Strathmann, Art. πολίτευμα, in *Theol. Dict. N. T.,* Vol. 6, 1968, p. 535.

[254] R. Bultmann and D. Lührmann, Art. ἐπιφάνεια, in *Theol. Dict. N. T.,* Vol. 9, 1974, pp. 7-10.

[255] R. Bultmann and D. Lührmann, Art. φανερόω, in *Theol. Dict. N. T.,* Vol. 9, 1974, pp. 3-6.

[256] R. Bultmann, *Die drei Johannesbriefe,* Göttingen 1967, p. 49.

[257] P. Schütz, *Was heisst "Wiederkunft Christi"?,* Freiburg 1972, p. 33.

[258] A. Oepke, Art. ἀνίστημι, in *Theol. Dict. N. T.,* Vol. 1, 1964, pp. 368-372; also of Oepke, Art. ἐγείρω, *ibid.,* Vol. 2, 1964, pp. 333-337. G. von Rad, G. Bertramm, and R. Bultmann, Art. ζωή, *ibid.,* Vol. 2, 1964, pp. 832-875. G. Greshake, *Auferstehung der Toten,* Essen 1969. P. Hoffmann, *Die Toten in Christus,* Münster 1966. K. Rahner, *"Auferstehung des Fleisches,"* in *Schriften zur Theologie,* Vol. 2, Einsiedeln 1955, pp. 211-225. B. Rigaux, *Dieu l'a resuscité,* Gembloux 1973. L. Schottroff, *Der Glaubende und die feindliche Welt,* Neukirchen 1970. G. Schunack, *Das hermeneutische Problem des Todes. Im Horizont von Römer 5 untersucht,* Tübingen 1967. U. Wilckens, *Auferstehung,* Stuttgart 1970.

[259] M. L. Henry, *Glaubenskrise und Glaubensbewahrung in den Dichtungen der Jesajaapokalypse,* Stuttgart 1967, pp. 104-115, 175-180.

[260] F. König, *Zarathustras Jenseitsvorstellungen und das Alte Testament*, Vienna 1964, pp. 121–141. A. T. Nikolainen, *Der Auferstehungsglaube in der Bibel und in ihrer Umwelt*, 2 vols., Helsinki 1944, 1946.

[261] H. L. Strack and P. Billerbeck, *op. cit.*, Vol. 4, 2, pp. 1166–1198. K. Schubert, *"Die Entwicklung der Auferstehungslehre von der nachexilischen bis zur frührabbinischen Zeit,"* in *Biblische Zeitschrift,* new series Vol. 6 (1962), pp. 177–214. G. Schunack, *Das hermeneutische Problem des Todes*, pp. 72–86. F. König, *Zarathustras Jenseitsvorstellungen und das Alte Testament*, pp. 213–253.

[262] There is a comparable rabbinic interpretation which concludes to the resurrection of the dead from Deut. 11:9 and 34:4, because in these passages God promised Abraham, Isaac, and Jacob that he would give the land *to them*: H. Strack and P. Billerbeck, *op. cit.*, Vol. 1, pp. 892–897. J. Le Moyne, *Les Sadducéens*, Paris 1972, pp. 123–129.

[263] N. Baumert, *Täglich Sterben und Auferstehen. Der Literalsinn von 2 Kor 4,12–5,10*, Munich 1973. R. Bultmann, *"Exegetische Probleme des zweiten Korintherbriefes: Zu 2 Kor 5,1-5,"* in *Exegetica*, Tübingen 1967, pp. 298–306. C. H. Hunzinger, *"Die Hoffnung angesichts des Todes im Wandel der paulinischen Aussagen,"* in *Leben angesichts des Todes (Festschrift H. Thielicke)*, Tübingen 1968, pp. 69–88. G. Klein, *"Apokalyptische Naherwartung bei Paulus,"* in H. D. Betz and L. Schottroff (eds.), *Neues Testament und christliche Existenz (Festschrift H. Braun)*, Tübingen 1973, pp. 241–262. F. G. Lang, *2. Korinther 5,1-10 in der neueren Forschung*, Tübingen 1973. F. Mussner, *" 'Schichten' in der paulinischen Theologie. Dargetan an 1 Kor 15,"* in *Praesentia salutis*, Düsseldorf 1967, pp. 178–188. H. F. Richter, *Auferstehung, und Wirklichkeit. Eine Untersuchung zu 1 Kor 15,1-11*, 2nd ed., Berlin and Augsburg 1969. H. Schwantes, *Schöpfung der Endzeit*, Stuttgart 1963. P. Siber, *Mit Christus leben. Eine Studie zur paulinischen Auferstehungshoffnung*, Zürich 1971. B. Spörlein, *Die Leugnung der Auferstehung. Eine historisch-kritische Untersuchung zu 1 Kor 15*, Regensburg 1971.

[264] J. Blank, *Krisis*, Freiburg 1964, pp. 172–182, 309. L. van Hartingsveld, *Die Eschatologie des Johannesevangelium*, Assen 1962, pp. 189–213. P. Ricca, *Die Eschatologie des Vierten Evangeliums*, Zürich 1966, pp. 130–152. J. Riedl, *Das Heilswerk Jesu nach Johannes*, Freiburg 1973, p. 224. R. Schnackenburg, *Das Johannesevangelium*, Vol. 1, Freiburg 1965, pp. 48–141; also of Schackenburg, *Die Johannesbriefe*, 2nd ed., Freiburg 1963, pp. 143 and 170.

[265] R. Bultmann, *Das Evangelium des Johannes*, 11th ed., Göttingen 1950: on John 5:28f., pp. 196f.; on John 6:39-40, 44, p. 162; also of Bultmann, *Die drei Johannesbriefe*, Göttingen 1967: on 1 John 2:28, p. 49; and again of Bultmann, *Geschichte und Eschatologie*, 2nd ed., Tübingen 1964, pp. 53–58. Current exegesis is largely dependent on Bultmann; thus with E. Lohse, *Die Entstehung des Neuen Testaments*, Göttingen 1972, p. 109; R. Schnackenburg, *Das Johannesevangelium*, Vol. 2, Freiburg 1971, pp. 73f., 144–147, 530–544; S. Schulz, *Das*

Evangelium nach Johannes, Göttingen 1972, pp. 220–223. Bultmann's explanation is not accepted by W. G. Kümmel, *Einleitung in das Neue Testament*, 17th ed., Heidelberg 1973, pp. 175f. Further criticism is referred to in note 264 immediately above.

[266] Thus M. Schmaus, in *Von den letzten Dingen*, Münster 1948, p. 256, says: "For the construction of the resurrection body, the smallest amount (molecule, atom) of the body's material suffices."

[267] A. Ahlbrecht, *Tod und Unsterblichkeit in der evangelischen Theologie der Gegenwart*, Paderborn 1964, pp. 105–112. F. Buri, J. M. Lochman, and H. Ott, *Dogmatik im Dialog*, Vol. 1, Gütersloh 1973, pp. 264–277.

[268] Notable among those who take exception to this are P. Benoit, "*Auferstehung am Ende der Zeiten oder gleich nach dem Tode?*" in *Concilium*, Vol. 6 (1970), pp. 719–724; L. Boros, *Mysterium Mortis*, 7th ed., Olten 1967, pp. 205–207; J. Feiner and L. Vischer (eds.), *Neues Glaubensbuch*, 6th ed., Freiburg and Zürich 1973, p. 542; G. Greshake, *Auferstehung der Toten*, Essen 1969, pp. 384–393.

[269] F. Büchsel and V. Herntrich, Art. κρίνω, in *Theol. Dict. N. T.*, Vol. 3, 1965, pp. 921–954. G. Stählin, Art. ὀργή, *ibid.*, Vol. 5, 1967, pp. 382–447. J. Blank, *Krisis. Untersuchungen zur johanneischen Christologie und Eschatologie*, Freiburg 1964. L. Mattern, *Das Verständnis des Gerichtes bei Paulus*, Zürich 1966.

[270] A. Erman, *Die Religion der Ägypter*, Berlin 1934, pp. 207–241. R. Grieshammer, *Das Jenseitsgericht in den Sargtexten*, Wiesbaden 1970. J. Spiegel, *Die Idee vom Totengericht in der ägyptischen Religion*, Leipzig 1935.

[271] F. König, *Zarathustras Jenseitsvorstellungen und das Alte Testament*, Vienna 1964, pp. 51–165, 265–285. E. Schweizer, "*Gegenwart des Geistes und eschatologische Hoffnung bei Zarathustra, spätjüdischen Gruppen, Gnostikern und den Zeugen des Neuen Testaments*," in *Neotestamentica*, Zürich 1963, pp. 153–179.

[272] W. Bousset and H. Gressmann, *Die Religion des Judentums im späthellenistischen Zeitalter*, 4th ed., Tübingen 1966, pp. 202–301.

[273] Besides the usual commentaries, see also H. L. Strack and P. Billerbeck, *op. cit.*, Vol. 4, 2, pp. 1199–1212 (portraits of judgment from old Jewish literature, in commenting on Matthew 25:31f.); D. Gewalt, "*Matthäus 25,31-46 im Ewartungshorizont heutiger Exegese*," in *Linguistica Biblica*, Vol. 25/26 (1973), pp. 9–21; J. C. Ingelaere, "*La 'parabole' du jugement dernier (Matthieu 25,31-46)*," in *Revue d'histoire et de philosophie religieuses*, Vol. 50 (1970), pp. 23–60.

[274] Unequivocally, πρόβατα are sheep. ἐρίφια could as easily be goats as rams. At night the shepherd separates sheep (white) from the goats (black-brown) that have been grazing together throughout the day, because at night the goats need more warmth than the sheep. The colors were symbolic; white signifies purity, blackness sin. Accordingly the separation would take place in the world judgment. Possibly, too, the traditional conception is valid, that ἐρίφια are rams.

In this distinction, the rams symbolize the strong and capriciously violent; the sheep are the docile and tractable. [Translator's note: German Bibles, at Matthew 25:33, usually speak of sheep and rams; English Bibles generally talk of sheep and goats].

[275] Qoh. 10:2 reads: "The wise man's heart turns to the right; the heart of the fool turns to the left." See also the judgment of the dead in Plato, below, § 18, 1. S. Morenz, *"Rechts und links im Totengericht,"* in *Zeitschrift für ägyptische Sprache und Altertumskunde,* Vol. 82 (1957), pp. 62–71.

[276] A. Wikenhuser, *"Die Liebeswerke in dem Gerichtsgemälde Mt 25,31-46,"* in *Biblische Zeitschrift,* Vol. 20 (1932), pp. 366–377.

[277] K. Rahner, *"Die anonymen Christen,"* in *Schriften zur Theologie,* Vol. 6, 1965, pp. 545–554; and *"Bemerkungen zum Problem des 'anonymen' Christen,"* in *Schriften zur Theologie,* Vol. 10, 1972, pp. 531–546. H. Ott, *"Existentiale Interpretation und anonyme Christlichkeit,"* in E. Dinkler (ed.), *Zeit und Geschichte (Festschrift R. Bultmann),* Tübingen 1964, pp. 367–379. K. Riesenhuber, *"Der anonyme Christ nach Karl Rahner,"* in *Zeitschrift für katholische Theologie,* Vol. 86 (1964), pp. 286–303.

[278] H. Braun, *"Die Problematik einer Theologie des Neuen Testaments,"* in *Gesammelte Studien zum Neuen Testament und seiner Umwelt,* Tübingen 1962, pp. 325–341. "Ultimate salvation is brought down from the heights of a metaphysical so-called world of God to the profane basis of his co-humanity. . . . The love of God is interpreted as a love of neighbor. The help and welfare extended or not extended to one's neighbor is extended or, as the case may be, not extended to Jesus himself (Matthew 25:31f.). For Paul, the ἀγάπη is directed to one's neighbor (1 Cor. 13). The love of God is accomplished concretely in demonstrating love of one's brother (1 John 4:20)"; also of Braun, *"Gottes Existenz und meine Geschichtlichkeit im Neuen Testament,"* in E. Dinkler (ed.), *Zeit und Geschichte (Festschrift R. Bultmann),* Tübingen 1964, pp. 399–421; and again of Braun, *Jesus,* 2nd ed., Stuttgart 1970, pp. 160f.

[279] A. Kretzer, *Die Herrschaft der Himmel und die Söhne des Reiches,* Stuttgart and Würzburg 1971, pp. 210–224.

[280] In the New Testament, the expectation of the thousand-year kingdom is evidenced only in the Apocalypse of John. 1 Cor. 15:23f. is hardly to be understood in this way. Chiliasm belongs to Jewish apocalyptics. It will not be able to be validated as a (binding) expression of the New Testament faith. Christian hope was alive, however, even in the chiliastic movements which flared up again and again in the history of the Church. See W. Bauer, article *Chiliasmus,* in *Reallexikon für Antike und Chirstentum,* Vol. 2, 1954, pp. 1073–1078. E. Lohse, Art. χιλιάς, in *Theol. Dict. N. T.,* Vol. 9, 1974, pp. 466–471. H. Bietenhard, *Das tausendjährige Reich,* 2nd ed., Zürich 1955. H. A. Wilcke, *Das Problem eines messianischen Zwischenreichs bei Paulus,* Zürich 1967.

[281] G. von Rad and H. Traub, Art. οὐρανός, in *Theol. Dict. N. T.,* Vol. 5, 1967,

pp. 497–543. H. Bietenhard, *Die himmlische Welt im Urchristentum und Spät-judentum*, Tübingen 1951. U. E. Simon, *Heaven in the Christian Tradition*, London 1959.

[282] H. Conzelmann, Art. φῶς, in *Theol. Dict. N. T.*, Vol. 9, 1974, pp. 310–358. S. Aalen, *Die Begriffe "Licht" und "Finsternis" im Alten Testament, im Spät-judentum und im Rabbinismus*, Oslo 1951.

[283] W. Michaelis, Art. ὁράω, in *Theol. Dict. N. T.*, Vol. 5, 1967, pp. 315–367. R. Bultmann, "*Niemand hat Gott je gesehen (Jo 1,18),*" in *Exegetica*, Tübingen 1967, pp. 174–197.

[284] The imaginal phrase "through a mirror enigmatically" contains Hellenistic as well as Jewish elements. See G. Kittel, Art. αἴνιγμα, in *Theol. Dict. N. T.*, Vol. 1, 1964, pp. 178–180.

[285] J. Jeremias, Art. ἄβυσσος, in *Theol. Dict. N. T.*, Vol. 1, 1964, pp. 9–10; Art. ᾅδης, *ibid.*, pp. 146–149; and also of Jeremias, Art. γέεννα, *ibid.*, pp. 657–658. F. Büchsel, Art. κατώτερος, *ibid.*, Vol. 3, 1965, pp. 640–642.

[286] Darkness and fire as punishments of hell pertain also to Babylonian and Iranian (Persian) representations of the beyond. It is possible that these representations had an influence on the Old Testament and on Judaism. See F. Lang, Art. πῦρ, in *Theol. Dict. N. T.*, Vol. 6, 1968, pp. 928–948. H. Conzelmann, Art. σκότος, *ibid.*, Vol. 7, 1971, pp. 423–445. F. König, *Zarathustras Jenseitsvorstellungen und das Alte Testament*, Vienna 1964, pp. 105–121.

[287] It may be asked whether numerous and powerful themes of Jewish apocalyptics (and beyond this, even Oriental fantasy), have found entry into the customary Christian notions of the beyond, and even into dogmatic expositions thereof. Worthy of some consideration in this regard is Th. and G. Sartory, *In der Hölle brennt kein Feuer*, Munich 1968, pp. 61–248.

[288] G. von Rad and W. Foerster, Art. διαβάλλω, in *Theol. Dict. N. T.*, Vol. 2, 1964, pp. 71–81. W. Foerster and K. Schäferdieck, Art. σατανᾶς, *ibid.*, Vol. 7, 1971, pp. 151–165. In the Old Testament Bible, and accordingly in the New, the powers of evil are personified as Sin, Death, and Devil. All appear sometimes as if they were persons granted autonomy. It is especially in the New Testament that personal names are given to evil: Beliar, Satan, Devil. The New Testament, however, has no intention of constructing a demonology; rather, it teaches the conquest and the end of demons. The controversy about the person of evil conducted now and then and more recently with consideable intensity is a relapse into demonology and mythology.

[289] J. Behm, Art. καινός, in *Theol. Dict. N. T.*, Vol. 3, 1965, pp. 447–454; also of Behm, Art. νέος, *ibid.*, Vol. 4, 1967, pp. 896–901. F. Büchsel, Art. παλιγγενεσία, *ibid.*, Vol. 1, 1964, pp. 686–689. L. Boros, "*Der neue Himmel und die neue Erde,*" in F. Mussner (*et al.*), *Studien zur christlichen Eschatologie*, Bergen-Enkheim 1966, pp. 19–27. G. Schneider, *Neuschöpfung oder Wiederkehr?*, Düsseldorf 1961; also of Schneider, "*Neuschöpfung des Menschen und der Welt,*" in

Lebendiges Zeugnis, 1971, pp. 47–61. A. Vögtle, *Das Neue Testament und die Zukunft des Kosmos*, Düsseldorf 1970, pp. 108–142.

[290] On rabbinism, see H. Strack and P. Billerbeck, *op. cit.*, Vol. 2, p. 421; Vol. 3, pp. 217, 801, 840; Vol. 4, pp. 1f., 1243.

[291] E. Sjöberg, *"Wiedergeburt und Neuschöpfung im palästinensischen Judentum,"* in *Studia Theologica*, Vol. 4 (1951), pp. 44–85.

[292] E. Käsemann, *An die Römer*, Tübingen 1973, p. 224. R. Balz, *Heilsvertrauen und Welterfahrung. Strukturen der paulinischen Eschatologie nach Röm 8,18-39*, Munich 1971.

GENERAL INDEX